Parke Godwin

Out of the Past

Parke Godwin

Out of the Past

ISBN/EAN: 9783744659192

Printed in Europe, USA, Canada, Australia, Japan

Cover: Foto ©Thomas Meinert / pixelio.de

More available books at **www.hansebooks.com**

(CRITICAL AND LITERARY PAPERS.)

BY

PARKE GODWIN.

———

NEW YORK:

G. P. PUTNAM & SONS.

1870.

Stereotyped by LITTLE, RENNIE & CO.,
645 and 647 Broadway, N. Y.

PRESS OF
THE NEW YORK PRINTING COMPANY,
81, 83, and 85 Centre St., N. Y.

PREFACE.

I GATHER these essays out of the anonymous and desultory writing of many past years—not because I suppose them to possess any particular literary value, but simply to show what little part I may have taken in various discussions.

Written in moments snatched from the labors of an exacting profession, they are more imperfect than they would have been with a larger leisure at my command. They are reprinted, however, substantially as they were first published; I have pruned away certain redundances with a pretty free hand; here and there, where the meaning seemed obscure, I have added a sentence or a paragraph to help it out; but no change has been made in any sentiment or thought. To have rendered the essays what I should now like them to be, would have been to re-write them, which was impossible.

My political and social papers I hope some time or other to collect into a volume like the present.

	PAGE
BRYANT'S POEMS	9
JEREMY BENTHAM AND LAW REFORM	22
EDWARD LIVINGSTON AND HIS CODE	56
JOURNALISM	75
JOHN JAMES AUDUBON	89
PERCY BYSSHE SHELLEY	111
THE LAST HALF-CENTURY	145
AMERICAN AUTHORSHIP	176
ALISON'S HISTORIES OF EUROPE	196
THE "WORKS" OF AMERICAN STATESMEN	221
COMTE'S PHILOSOPHY	251
STRAUSS'S LIFE OF JESUS	288
THE LATE HORACE BINNEY WALLACE	302
THACKERAY AS NOVELIST	326
GOETHE	341
RUSKIN'S WRITINGS	367
CAUSES OF THE FRENCH REVOLUTION	394
MOTLEY'S RISE OF THE DUTCH REPUBLIC	422
EMERSON ON ENGLAND	441

EARLIER WRITINGS.

BRYANT'S POEMS.[*]

E design to express our opinion of the merit of these poems. To speak what we think, plainly and freely, will only be discharging a debt of gratitude that has been accumulating for a long while.

That they should have passed through four large editions is some indication of the existence among us of a pure taste ; at least, the author has no right to complain. He has found favor enough to satisfy a vanity more inordinate than we take his to be. His verses have been read extensively, and praised as often as they were read ; quoted frequently, and always with admiration ; and republished time and again in every magazine and newspaper from the land of the Pilgrims to that of the Cherokees. The more accomplished his readers, the keener their relish of the repast which he has furnished. Nevertheless, would not some of his warmest admirers be surprised to learn his true rank as a poet? Suppose we were to compare him, not with "the ever-during few," with Spenser, Shakspeare, Milton, who hold the

---

* Poems by William Cullen Bryant. Fifth Edition. Harper & Brothers, 1839.

From the *Democratic Review*, Oct. 1839.

first place, but with those just below them, with Collins, Cowper, Wordsworth, and their like, would it betray any want of critical sagacity? We confess it is our conviction, that, estimated according to the strictest rules of art, his poetry is not inferior to their best. Without running a formal parallel, we shall endeavor to state why and in what respect we think so, by describing what we conceive to be its chief characteristics.

Sometimes we are disposed to think exquisite grace and propriety of expression his principal excellence. It seems as if his whole study had been how his thoughts might be most beautifully uttered. Not only are words not misused, which would be small praise indeed, but none occur that any process of refinement can improve. Their precision is remarkable, unaccompanied as it is by any loss of elegance or force. Warmth and richness are not sacrificed to mere dry and meagre chastity. Most writers, when they attempt neatness, become hard and cold ; flexibility is exchanged for accuracy ; and their frigid phrases, perhaps well adapted to a metaphysical treatise, are altogether out of place in verse. By laboring too exclusively after niceness, they neglect what is of far more importance in the effective use of words, juiciness. This is never the case with Bryant. With all his exactness of expression he is ever racy, warm, suggestive. Certain of his pieces it is impossible to read without gliding unconsciously into a thousand trains of associated thought. A single epithet sometimes tells many a secret. For instance, in the "Death of Schiller," how that one term, "the *peering* Chinese," brings up all the peculiarities as well of Chinese life as of Chinese features ! And, again in the Greek Boy, whom he regards as

> " A shoot of that old vine which made
> The nations *silent* in its shade,"

does not old Greece, in her glory and magnificence, and yet with somewhat of a mournful grandeur, move before us, as in a stately funeral procession?

Delicacy and refinement of language are of course incompatible with the least mark of turgidness. There is, therefore, no tumid pomp, no forced strength— none of the inflation of Thomson, nor of the unnatural and pompous splendor of Young. Then his versification is no less exquisite than his choice of language, and manifests no less the skilfulness of the accomplished artist. It combines melody and freedom with correctness. An ear the most perfectly attuned detects no false quantities nor discordant rhythms. Line follows line in liquid harmony. A certain mellowness and smooth flow beguiles the mind by a kind of fascination, as if the ancient conception of the lyric had been more than realized, and poetry become music. Yet the versification is adapted to the subject. In that grand ode " To the Past," the lines move with a slow and solemn step, befitting the theme, while in the "Song of the Stars," they dart away with the joyousness and buoyancy of youth, like "the orbs of beauty and spheres of flame" —that go dancing over the widening wastes of the sky.

Bryant possesses, however, other and higher requisites of the genuine poet. An eminent writer, himself aspiring to the highest place in the poetical literature of England, has told us what those requisites are, and they are just those which our poet has in a signal degree.* As to sensibility, no man ever lived more delicately susceptible of external influences. Not only is his eye open to the forms of nature, but every fibre of his being seems to be tremblingly alive to them: like

---

* Wordsworth. See preface to Lyrical Ballads.

the strings of an Eolian harp, which the faintest breath
of the wind can waken. His observation of the outward world has been both varied and minute. Natural
objects, with their infinite diversity of name, shape, and
hue, are the constant companions of his thoughts.
From the spire of grass to the huge mountain oak ;
from the violet, in its silent retreats, to the bright and
boundless firmament ; from the shy bird, brooding in
the deep and quiet woods, to the stars in their eternal
dances. Streams, and woods, and meadows, and skies
mingle in all his musings—form a part, indeed, of his
intellectual being. The seasons, with their thousand
alternating influences, with their smiles and tears, with
their sunshine and gloom ; day and night, with their
strange contrasts ; forests, where gush the silver fountains ; thick groves, with verdant roofs and mossy
floors ; trees in their stateliness and beauty ; lone
lakes ; the song of birds ; the soft whisper of the evening winds, and the gentle murmur of the brooks, have
been to him a delightful study.

This familiarity with nature gives freshness and truth
to his descriptions. They are not like the collections
of a naturalist, dry specimens of withered leaves and
decayed plants ; but at all times warm, picturesque,
faithful. They present nature in all her original life
and glowing beauty. Opening the book at any page
is like transporting one's self to the free air and broad
prospects of the country. Lovely sights and sweet
sounds are about us, and we gaze earnestly on green
leaves and running brooks, and listen, delighted, to the
lowing of herds.

Bryant's writings are also marked by instances of refined as well as vigorous imagination. How striking
is that passage in the " Prairies," in which, lost in the
musings prompted by the sublime solitude, we hear in

the domestic hum of the bee, "a more adventurous
colonist than man, the tramp of that advancing multitude which soon shall fill the borders !" And these few
lines taken from the "Earth,"

> " From battle-fields,
> Where heroes madly drove and dashed their hosts
> Against each other, rises up a noise,
> As if the armed multitudes of dead
> Stirred in their heavy slumber."

Indeed, the whole of this poem, and Thanatopsis,
The Past, and the Hymn to Death, are magnificent em-
bodiments of imagination. Vast as are the themes,
giving scope for the boldest and broadest flights, and
exciting the highest sense of sublimity, they are treated
with a corresponding grandeur of language and thought.
A vein of the most elevated philosophy pervades them,
deeply serious in its tone ; but of that seriousness which
is inseparable from the awful truths related to our mysterious human being. While we read them, a solemn
and impressive awe falls upon us ; we listen as we
should to the utterances of a prophet, or as though we
heard at midnight the choral symphonies of Heaven
floating down from the skies.

The healthy judgment of our author has shown itself
in all his writings. Both in the arrangement of the
lesser details of verse, and the utterance of sentiments
and thoughts, his judgment is equally evident. The
force of the language, the perfection of the style, the
appropriateness of the imagery, the simple and just fervor of his feelings, the fidelity of his descriptions, the
cheerfulness of his aspirations, and the manly moral
tone that pervades every line, prove that he possesses,
along with intense poetic sensibility, the most unquestionable good sense. We find nowhere indications of

disease, no want of justness and harmony, no straining after effect, no affected point or brilliancy, no starts and fits, no agonies of passion, no mawkish sensitiveness, no morbid misanthropy, no repulsive egotism, no unhealthy yearning for sympathy, no childish complaints of the neglect of the world, or of the cruel severities of Providence; but, on the contrary, all is pure and wholesome, the sincere production of one that regards nature and society with the mind and heart of a wise man, contented with the allotments of Heaven, and laboring through the humblest duties with right earnest and cheerful good-will.

The spirit of these writings is, therefore, no less to be admired than their outward graces and perfections. A gentleness as soft as that of woman, a tenderness mild and tearful as early love, simplicity like that of unconscious youth, are joined to the lofty philosophy of a sage. Innumerable are the passages that touch our best feelings, sinking quietly into the heart, and melting it, like a strain of music, into liquid joy and love. Whatever is peaceful, lovely, delicate, or kind, most strongly affects the writer's imagination. He walks abroad in the world, he takes in all things of earth and air, he ascends the stream of history, and is arrested only by the beautiful in nature, art, and the actions of men. He is like one loitering in groves of bloom to gather there the choicest flowers. In his view the rugged and the discordant have no charms, the struggles of despair, the ravages of stormful passion, the thousand jarring scenes of life, are seen only to suggest a deep commiseration. Even when our hearts, by some simple phrase, are made to burn with indignation at the wrong which man inflicts on man, when we are touched with the sufferings of the oppressed, and are full to bursting against the oppressor, a tone of gentleness softens our wrath, though the sense of justice grows keener, and purposes of tender and quiet beneficence become living convictions. This is the peculiar charm of his philanthropy ; it is susceptible, keen, fresh, and ever active ; it is unaccompanied by bitter or revengeful passion. Nothing to detract from its perfect purity is mingled with it, and nothing to confound it with mere animal impulse or physical sensibility. It is a love as immaculate as that of the angels, at the same time full of humanity and kindliness. Gentle desires, sweet affections, simple tastes, patient fortitude, tranquil recollections, and cheerful hope are the impulses that he moves. To these only are his lofty inspirations addressed. He speaks to them, not in frigid homilies or formal tones of instruction, but by interweaving delightful moral associations with all the objects and processes of the material world. Twilight hues lingering after the bright sun has set, recall the memory of good men gone ; the deep slumber of the woodlands is an emblem of inward peace ; the perishing flowers of Autumn are they who in their youthful beauty died ; a golden sunlight succeeding the tempest anticipates the day when the noise of war shall cease, and married nations dwell in harmony ; the unconscious flow of the rivulet, changeless amid change, reminds us of the perpetual onward course of time ; the flight of the lone bird in the illimitable air tells of the Power that, in the long way that we must tread alone, will guide our steps aright ; and the unceasing vicissitudes of all external things indicate the hand of a kind Providence, conducting the human race through successive trials to the scene of its noblest triumphs.

Surely such writings are those to which we most often and fondly recur. We come to regard them as

friends, ministering in all seasons of affliction and joy
to our spiritual wants, and turning us by their silent
eloquence to whatever is holy and good.   Unlike the
more dazzling productions of genius, which are read
this moment and forgotten that, or which, if we may so
express it, are perused by a flash of lightning, to be
closed the instant after in darkness, they make themselves our closest companions, to which we look for
instruction and solace.   We turn to them on the still
Sabbath-days, when we would recover our moral nature
from the shocks of the too engrossing world, on placid
summer evenings, when the remembrance of far-off
home and kindred is softest, in the silent watches of
the night, when, the world shut out, eternal things are
a reality, and the petty cares of life are only a dream.
And then if trial comes upon us in the stern struggles
of life, they administer a soothing strength ; if disappointment fills the heart with gall, they assuage its bitterness ; when sickness prostrates energy, they recover
the drooping spirit ; and when death creeps slowly
upon the sources of existence, they hover around us
like gentle memories, or whisper sweet hopes of a better world.   Would that all gifted men could learn that
to survive the oblivion that seems to be the destiny of
most human things, they should appeal only to that
which is imperishable in the nature of man, to his affections and his hopes.

One effect of Bryant's faithful observation, of which
we have spoken, is, that his poems are strictly American.
They are American in their subjects, imagery, and
spirit.   Scarcely any other than one born in this country can appreciate all their merit, so strongly marked
are they by the peculiarities of our natural scenery, our
social feelings, and our national convictions.   What
the author has seen, or what has been wrought in his

own mind, he has written, and no more. His skies are not brought from Italy, nor his singing birds from the tropics, nor his forests from Germany or regions beyond the pole. He is not indebted to the patient study of books so much as to a calm communion with outward things. He has levied no contributions on the masters of foreign literature, nor depended upon the locked-up treasures of ancient genius for the materials of thought and expression. He has written from the movings of his own mind; he has uttered what he has felt and known; he has described things around him in fitting terms, terms suggested by familiar contemplation, and thus his writings have become transcripts of external nature, appreciated by his countrymen with the readiness and ease with which truth is ever recognized.

"Lone lakes, savannahs, where the bison roves, .
Rocks rich with summer garlands, solemn streams,
Skies where the desert eagle wheels and screams,
Spring bloom and autumn blaze of boundless groves,"

are reflected from his pages as the surface of an unruffled lake reflects the surrounding banks. And where could he find aught more lovely and majestic, or better adapted to inspire the genius of descriptive poetry than in this land, with its endless variety of grove and water, with its deep forests brooding in eternal silence over the slumbering inland, with vast lakes, majestic in their repose, sending back the radiant hues of the sky; where the mountain ridges rise to prop the very heavens; where broad streams roll their mighty tides for thousands of miles through fertile plains; where green prairies stretch like oceans arrested in their mightiest heavings, and where a wildness and freshness pervades every scene, that dissociating it from human agency suggests the thought of a loftier indwelling power?

Nor is the tone of these poems less American than the imagery or the themes. They breathe the spirit of that new order of things in which we are cast. They are fresh, like a young people unwarped by the superstitions and prejudices of age ; free, like a nation scorning the thought of bondage ; generous, like a society whose only protection is mutual sympathy ; and bold and vigorous, like a land pressing onward to a future of glorious enlargements. The noble instincts of democracy prompt and animate every strain. An attachment to liberty stronger than the desire of life, an immovable regard for human rights, a confidence in humanity that admits of no misgivings, and a rejoicing hope of the future, full of illumination and peace, are the sentiments that they everywhere inspire. They sharpen the sense of right, they infuse a love of the true, they expand those emotions that comprehend in their plans of benevolence every form of human being.

We never have read a book without speculating more or less as to the character of its author. That is something, we admit, with which the public have nothing to do, and yet it is that about which they trouble themselves most. If we could gather the traits of this book and combine them in some way into a living person, we should fancy a man to whom the language of Wordsworth to Milton might be properly addressed, "Thy soul is like a star, and dwells apart," one for whom the grosser world had no allurements, endowed with kind and gentle virtues, modest, unassuming, mild, simple in taste, elevated in sentiment, dignified in deportment, pure in life, a worshipper of the beautiful everywhere in nature and in art, perpetually attended by noble and benevolent aspirations, familiar as a friend with the best spirits of the past, but shrinking instinctively from contact with society, unless to bear reproach in the cause of truth and duty. Whether such a portrait would be true, we shall not ask those who know him to say, for sure we are that the beauty and purity which abound in these writings could only proceed from a mind equally beautiful and pure ; nay, more so, since that man never lived who could give utterance to his whole soul.

Yet how strange is it, say some, that a mind of this sort should expend its energy in mere political discussions ! We can discover nothing in it either strange or lamentable. No doubt it would be more congenial to the man's feelings, could he devote himself to the prosecution of his glorious art. Indeed, we hope for his own sake, for the sake of the literature of the country, that he may be permitted, in his riper age, to withdraw to some quiet retreat, where, amid the calm and beautiful scenes in which his imagination delights, he may meditate and construct a work worthy of his genius and worthy of this great nation, one that shall grow in fame as his country expands in power, and that shall give instruction and delight to the multitudes destined in distant years to cover our vast inland deserts, and make noisy with active life the still shores of the Pacific.

This we wish : but we do not regret that the author's sympathy with the cause of his fellow-men has led him to mingle in the stirring warfare of politics ; that with all the sensibility of genius, he can yet discipline himself to meet the rebuffs and shocks of civil conflict ; that in being a poet he has not ceased to be a citizen. If there were in political life anything incompatible with the highest virtue, if his choice of it had at any time been attended by degrading compliances, if low motives of any sort had impelled his exertions, or left a single trace in what he has done, if aught else than lofty self-sacrificing devotion had led him to so uncongenial a vocation, there would be cause for regret ; not for regret merely—but for the loud and stern rebukes that should ever fall on the prostitution of noble powers, which are the property of mankind, to ignoble objects. But it is no descent for the best of us to be concerned about the moral and social condition of our fellow-men. One of the admirers of Goethe mentions it as a proof of his incomparable genius, that when the world was rent by the grandest dissensions, when revolutions of tremendous import were going on, when there was tempest and war on all sides, and it seemed as if a thunderbolt had been shot among all social arrangements, and men were yet in doubt whether it came downward from heaven or upward from hell, he all the while remained unaffected, penning soft madrigals or singing love ditties beneath the casement of his mistress. We see nothing in this to admire. If it were true, we should regard it rather as a piece of most despicable cowardice, or more despicable callousness. When it shall become disgraceful to feel for the millions, degraded and downtrodden, when it shall be a laudable thing to be indifferent to the moral progress of the human race, when, we shall have occasion to grow ashamed of our affections, or make a mockery of love, it will be time enough to put forth empty lamentations over men of genius who engage in political strife. But it is only exposing our own moral defects to entertain and utter such lamentations. No real man disdains what deeply interests the happiness of his fellows.

We rejoice, therefore, that Mr. Bryant should lend his high aid to what he has deemed the cause of justice and truth. When we think of the nobleness of that political creed which from earliest manhood he has warmly espoused, of the energy with which he has defended individual and equal rights, of the frequency

and fervor with which he has appealed in all his discussions to the best feelings of men, of the heroic consistency with which he has asserted truth in the day of
its obscurity, bearing up manfully against persecutions
from which less sensitive spirits would have recoiled,
repelling with dignified and honorable scorn the attacks of malignant enemies, yet, in the midst of cal-
umny and abuse, commiserating the moral debasement
from which they sprang,—we not only rejoice, but we
thank God that he has been placed just where he has
been placed, and that he has been able, like Milton,
to overcome the soft seductions of literary indolence,
to battle sternly in the rude lists of truth.   Long after
present storms shall cease to rage, many a young mind
made strong by his example and efforts shall rise up to
renew the

> " Friendless warfare, lingering long
>   Through weary days and weary years."

Toward the close of Schiller's noble poem, "The
Artist," he beautifully represents the dignity of man as
committed to the keeping of the Poet, and he exhorts
him earnestly to cherish the power of song destined to
dispel error and wrong from the earth.   In a similar
spirit we should like to remind the Poet of America,
that the silent influence of his writings, in purifying and
elevating the intellectual and moral nature of his countrymen, is his strongest inducement to a continuation
of his labors.   If he is faithful to his trust, as a quick-
sighted discerner of beauty, of goodness, and truth,
when his body shall have mouldered to nothingness in
the grave, his name will still be fresh and warm in the
memories of men.   Meanwhile, let the living cherish
the fame of one whom posterity will undoubtedly recognize as one of the most distinguished ornaments of
his country and his time.

JEREMY BENTHAM AND LAW REFORM.*

 WRITER in the Westminister Review remarks, that the two men of the present age who have most strongly influenced the minds of their countrymen, are Samuel Taylor Coleridge and Jeremy Bentham. Without questioning the accuracy of the observation, as it respects Coleridge, we think there can be little doubt of the truth of so much of it as applies to Bentham. Whatever may have been the influence of the former, whose researches were mostly in the region of abstract thought, it was of that occult and delicate nature which only a few are apt to feel. But the influence of Bentham, with his practical cast of mind, his rugged sense, his bold onsets upon cherished modes of faith, and the immediate interest attached to his inquiries, was more direct and obvious. He addressed himself to questions connected with the every-day business of men ; and if the results of his investigations had not arrested attention, it would have argued either a singular deficiency in his powers of thought, or a no less singular repulsiveness in his manner of treating his subjects.

Bentham, however, was in many respects peculiarly

---

* Theory of Legislation. By Jeremy Bentham. Boston : Weeks, Jordan & Co., 1840.

From the *Democratic Review*, Sept., 1840.

fitted for the task he undertook ; and yet, during his lifetime, his works, though not without reputation, were
hardly estimated at their real value. It was only after
they had founded a select school of thinkers, and many
accomplished and persevering disciples had forced them
upon the consideration of the British Parliament, that
he got to be acknowledged as one of the great lumina-
ries of his era. His place as a father of law reform, as
a founder of legislative science, and as a distinguished
friend of the social advancement of the human race, is
now generally conceded.

We propose briefly to consider his merits in these
several respects, accompanying our comments with such
personal notices only, as may enable the reader more
easily to comprehend the man.

First, then, a few words of Bentham himself. He
was born in London, in the year 1747, and was remarkable in childhood for the quickness of his parts
and the solidity of his judgment. At three years of age
he read for amusement Rapin's History of England ; at
eight was a skilful performer on the violin ; and at
thirteen commenced his collegiate studies in Oxford.
At this early period even, his inquiring and conscientious
turn of mind manifested itself ; for being asked to sign
the Thirty-Nine Articles of the established church, he
did so reluctantly, and the act ever afterward proved to
him an occasion of deep regret. He looked upon it
as deliberately setting his seal to what he thought to be
false, as a species of self-degradation which disturbed
the clearness of his moral convictions and broke the
integrity of his spirit. His father, an attorney of some
note, gave him the opportunity of becoming a lawyer.
Nor did he fail to prosecute his studies with immense
labor and research ; not, however, in the spirit of those
who ordinarily pursue that profession, but with the dis-

crimination of a philosopher and the zeal of a philanthropist. He was soon disgusted with the technical falsehood he found pervading every branch of the law, which, in connection with the repugnance excited by its indirectness, inconsistencies, unjust arrangements and barbarous phraseology, inspired him with the ambition of devoting his life to its reform.

The first fruits of his purpose appeared in a short essay, called a Fragment on Government, published anonymously in 1776, as a criticism of an episode in Blackstone's Commentaries. Written with singular clearness and vigor, but hypercritical in its tone, many passages of it are marked by astute observation, and reasoning at once logical and profound. The estimation in which this work was held on its first appearance, both as a literary and philosophical performance, may be inferred from the fact that it was successively ascribed to Lord Camden, Lord Mansfield, and to Mr. Dunning, all among the most accomplished lawyers of the day. It was followed by the publication, two years afterward, of a review of the " Hard Labor Bill," with observations relative to jurisprudence in general, which contained the germ of several sagacious doctrines unfolded at length in later works. Then came the " Defence of Usury," a tract of remarkable force, and one of the best specimens of the exhaustive mode of reasoning ever printed. In less than two years, the " Introduction to the Principles of Morals and Legislation" appeared, being the first extended and methodical exposition of his peculiar notions that had been given. This work gave him a place at once among thinkers. The originality of its arrangement, together with the boldness of its views and the pertinacity with which they were pressed, arrested the attention of leading minds of that period. Some few hailed the new teaching as the harbinger of more liberal and consistent methods of treating the great questions of government and moral science, but the greater number looked upon it as an extravagant reproduction of exploded theories, better adapted to excite merriment than to awaken inquiry, or to become the occasion of a radical and comprehensive reformation of the laws. Yet the book worked its way. One after another, distinguished men were compelled to admit, if not the soundness of its conclusions in detail, the general necessity of subjecting law to a thorough revision.

Meanwhile, the author himself, apparently content to allow his theories to bide the test of time, busied himself in sending forth pamphlets upon the various minor and collateral branches of the great subject to which he had given his life. Draughts of codes, essays on political tactics, on colonial emancipation, on pauper management, on parliamentary reform, on church abuses, on the art of instruction, on the liberty of the press, on codification, and a hundred other matters, followed each other in rapid succession. But a treatise on the "Rationale of Judicial Evidence" was the largest and most elaborate of the works then published. It was filled with profound thoughts and instructive suggestions, and soon became the foundation of important changes in the law of procedure. No one can read it, certainly, without acquiring a deep conviction of the strength and astuteness of the intellect from which it sprung. It detected the absurdity of the old practice with so much keenness, exposed it with so much point and vivacity, and unfolded a better scheme with so much judgment and tact, that it readily obtained for the author the reputation and rank of a master-mind.

Three of Bentham's treatises, and those not among the least important, were published in French, and

possessed a wide continental reputation before they were
generally known to his countrymen. This was occasioned by a careless habit into which, in the latter
part of his life, he suffered himself to fall. Abandoning
the clear and nervous style of his earlier works, he began to indulge himself in loose, capricious, irregular,
and unintelligible modes of expression. His thoughts
were no more written out, but dotted down, sometimes
in mere outline, and, at others, in an uncouth and
perplexing jargon. Catalogues, synoptical tables, sum-
maries, references, brief hints, interspersed with long
dissertations, composed the bulk of his manuscripts.
Fortunately for him, they happened to fall into the
hands of an ardent and accomplished disciple, in the
person of Dumont, a citizen of Geneva, for some time
an eloquent preacher at St. Petersburg, but who had
come to London at the request of the Lansdowne
family. Forming the acquaintance of Bentham, there
he entered at once with zeal and activity into all his
speculations and plans. Never was a literary friendship contracted under happier auspices. To a thorough
appreciation of Bentham's genius, Dumont united patience of labor, quickness of apprehension, indefatigable public spirit, and a felicitous style of writing.
"His manners," says Lord Brougham, "were as gentle as they were polished and refined. His conversation was a model of excellence ; it was truly delightful.
Abounding in the most agreeable and harmless wit,
fully instinct with various knowledge, diversified with
anecdotes of rare interest, enriched with all the stores
of modern literature, seasoned with an arch and racy
humor, and occasionally a spice of mimicry, or rather
of acting, but subdued, as to be palatable it must always be, and giving rather the portraiture of classes
than of individuals, marked by the purest taste, en-

livened by a gayety of disposition still unclouded, sweetened by a temper that nothing could ruffle, presenting especially perhaps the single instance of one distinguished for colloquial powers, never occupying above a few moments at a time of any one's attention, and never ceasing to speak that all his hearers did not wish him to go on, it may fairly be said that his conversation was the highest which the refined society of London and Paris afforded."

To this man was committed the task of compiling, arranging, condensing, filling out and translating several of the best of Bentham's manuscripts. The services which he rendered in this way were an invaluable assistance to his master, but not so great as has sometimes been represented. Mr. Macaulay, in one of his reviews, says that "if Mr. Dumont had never been born, Mr. Bentham would still have been a very great man. But he would have been great to himself alone. The fertility of his mind would have resembled the fertility of those vast American wildernesses in which blossoms and decays a rich but unprofitable vegetation, 'wherewith the reaper filled not his hand, neither he that bindeth up the sheaves his bosom.' It would have been with his discoveries as it had been with the 'Century of Inventions.' His speculations on law would have been of no more practical use than Lord Worcester's speculations on steam-engines." But this is an exaggeration. Much as Bentham was indebted to Dumont, it was only for a small part of his fame. To say nothing of works in which the latter had no hand, works that under any circumstances would have raised the author to eminence, it is enough to remark that Bentham was capable of the task which another accomplished for him. Dumont, besides, was at all times solicitous to decline the merit of having been the author of the works published under his editorship. "I declare," said he, "I have no share, no claim of association in the composition of these works. They belong entirely to the author, and to him alone." Again he observes: "My labor, subaltern in its kind, has been limited to details. It was necessary to make a choice among various observations on the same subject; to suppress repetitions; to throw light upon obscurities; to bring together all that appertained to the same subject; and to fill up those gaps which in the hurry of composition the author had left. I have had more to retrench than to add; more to abridge than to expand. A profusion of riches left me only the care of economy." This, while it explains the nature of Dumont's labors, acquits Bentham of the debt with which in Mr. Macaulay's essay he is charged.

The work at the head of this paper presents, in a portable form, the best summary of his doctrines that has been published. It is a translation, by Richard Hildreth, of Boston, from the French edition of Dumont, originally printed in Paris in 1802, with a supplementary essay upon "The influence of time and place on laws," which does not appear in this edition. If any person would obtain a correct general idea of Bentham's system, without wading through the ponderous and often repulsive tomes through which the details of it are scattered, he will find all that he wishes in this succinct yet comprehensive digest of Dumont.

Now, what was this system? As the fairest, as well as completest method of stating it, we shall confine ourselves, as near as may be, to the expressions of his own treatises. His fundamental principle is, that "general utility," sometimes designated as "the greatest good of the greatest number," is the only legitimate foundation of legislative science. This utility is exclusive of every other principle, and is to be faithfully applied to all cases of legislation by the most rigid processes of moral arithmetic. Nature has placed man under the dominion of two motives, and no more. His only object in life is to seek pleasure and avoid pain, even when he imagines himself most free from the empire of those sentiments. Utility, therefore, is the property or tendency of a thing to procure some pleasure or prevent some pain. Everything, therefore, is conformable to the utility or the interest of a community, which tends to augment the sum of the happiness of the individuals of which it is composed. Virtue is to be esteemed by the disciple of the principle of utility as a good, only because of the pleasure that it produces ; and vice is to be regarded as an evil, only on account of the pains which result from it. If one finds, in the ordinary lists of virtue, an action from which there follows more pain than pleasure, it is to be instantly classified among the number of vices ; and so, on the other hand, if there is found in the common lists of offences some indifferent action, some innocent pleasure, you must not hesitate to transport this pretended offence into the class of lawful actions.

But to arrive at a correct notion of utility, in any given case, it is necessary to have a full and accurate knowledge of the different kinds of pleasures and pains. The variety of sensations which we momentarily experience must be minutely analyzed, dividing the simple from the complex, and arranging the whole in catalogues, which will assist the memory while it renders the judgment more precise. Not only the number, but the value or power of pleasures and pains, both as they relate to individuals and as they relate to communities, must be learned ; and this value we shall find to depend upon their intensity, their duration, their certainty, their proximity, their productiveness, their purity, and their extent. Inasmuch, however, as all causes of pleasure do not give the same pleasure to all persons, nor all causes of pain produce the same pain, that difference in human sensibility from which that difference of pleasure and pain proceeds must also be investigated. This difference of sensibility is either in degree or kind : in degree, when the impression of a given cause upon many individuals is uniform but unequal ; in kind, when the same cause produces opposite sensations in different individuals ; and in both cases turns primarily upon temperament, health, strength, corporeal · imperfections, knowledge, intellectual faculties, firmness of soul, perseverance, the bent of inclination, notions of honor, notions of religion, sentiments of sympathy, antipathies, disorder of mind, and pecuniary circumstances.

Possessed of a knowledge of the true nature of the various kinds of pleasures and pains, we may then take up the analysis or political good and evil, and of the manner in which they are diffused through society. It is with government as with medicine, that its main business is a choice of evils. Law, being an infraction of liberty, is an evil ; and hence the legislator, in devising any scheme, is to consider, first, whether the acts which he .undertakes to prevent are really evils ; and secondly, whether, if evils, they are greater evils than the means he employs to suppress them would be. In other language, is the evil of the disease or the evil of the remedy the greater ? He is to remember that evil seldom comes alone, but takes different forms, and spreads on every side as from a centre. It first affects the persons immediately concerned in it, and then, by arousing the idea of danger and alarm, affects the whole community. For the protection and welfare of society, therefore, certain acts are to be erected into offences, by which is meant that they deserve punishment. But some evil acts are not of this sort, and had better be left to the punishments attached to them by the natural or social sanctions, than included in the number of those which are touched by the political sanctions. In making the discrimination, between those which belong to the domain of politics and those which belong to morals exclusively, resort must be had to the same great doctrine of utility, which accompanies the whole inquiry.

This is the sum in brief of Bentham's theory. The first thing that it occurs to us to say of it is, that Bentham does not seem to have had a very deep penetration into the metaphysics of that part of it relating to morals. He appears to have taken his moral doctrine for granted, without investigating the grounds of it, and without giving due weight to the researches of other philosophers. More of a thinker than a reader, he fell into a contemptuous mode of treating the inquiries of older speculators. Indeed, he regards the results of their speculations (those, we mean, which respect a moral sense, and the grounds of moral obligation) as the mere expressions of their individual prejudices and sentiments. They were excuses for dogmatizing, indirect modes of asserting peculiar biases, or adroit contrivances to avoid the appeal to anything like an external standard of right and wrong. He represented them as quite unintelligible, or intelligible only so far as they inclined toward his own favorite doctrine. In no instance does he make a full and candid statement of what they are, or assign in detail the reasons why they are rejected. He simply enumerates them under one name or another, and then, by a fell stroke of the pen, sweeps them all from the board, as unworthy of further notice. Nor is he any more explicit in establishing the theory which he sets up in their place. He asserts it boldly, frequently, without compromise, but he never demonstrates it, scarcely indeed makes an attempt to demonstrate it, and his readers must receive it on his dictum, or seek elsewhere for an exposition.

This logic, summary as it is, might be retorted upon Bentham. If his own doctrine were dismissed without examination, neither he nor his disciples could justly complain of discourtesy. But the moral question, lying as it does at the foundation of the whole subject, is too important to be passed over so cavalierly. It must be looked into with no loose nor divided attention, if we would avoid the worst errors into which Bentham himself fell—to wit, a confusion of several palpable and necessary distinctions, a disregard of some of the most important facts of the human constitution, and a too rigid and sometimes fantastic application of the main principle.

The truth is, that Bentham was in many respects qualified as we have said, but in others disqualified, for the career he had chosen. He was fitted for it, by the peculiar practical structure of his intellect, by his questioning spirit, by his subtilty of scent, if we may call it so, and by his independence of judgment. Law involved details which only the most patient and practical mind could endure to investigate : it was surrounded by so many dear and venerable associations, that no one who deferred to ancient wisdom would dare to attack its outworks, much less the citadel ; the spirit of injustice lurking through it, and covered by innumerable subtile and plausible pretexts, could only be detected by one possessing the quickest sense of wrong ; and so thoroughly had it been interwoven with the habits and notions of society, that to make an onslaught upon its

weaknesses was to sever the assailant almost from all
the sympathies of his fellows. Bentham was adapted to
meet these difficulties at every point. He was inquisi-
tive, persevering, and fearless. He had the sagacity to
perceive defects, the boldness to suggest remedies, and
the fortitude to expose the one and defend the other, in
spite of opposition. But, on the other hand, these very
excellencies led him into an opposite excess. His readiness to question degenerated into skepticism, his ability
to reconstruct begat a vain desire of superfluous and
fantastic theorizing, and his firmness and self-reliance
betrayed itself into a contemptuous disregard of all former opinions. This last disposition in fact grew into a
besetting sin. From doubting the conclusion of others,
he soon came to despise their capacities. He took
nothing for granted : he proved by formal demonstra-
tions the simplest truisms ; and he addressed his readers as a pedagogue would his pupils, as so many abece-
darians.

Bentham's moral theory involves two questions, at
least, that are quite distinct : first, are pleasure and pain
the sole governing motives of men ?—and secondly, is
the tendency of an act to produce the greatest amount
of happiness the only reason why it is binding upon the
conscience ?

We take issue with him on each of these points.
His first proposition, that pleasure and pain are the sole
motives of men, revives the old bone of metaphysics,
as to the disinterestedness of human virtue. The doctrine of many philosophers, and, we believe, of most
men of the world, is, that whatever a man does has relation to his own good : if he is virtuous, it is because it
is more agreeable for him to be so than otherwise ; and
if he is vicious, it is because he finds his greatest pleasure
in vice. All human conduct is only a balancing of in-

terest, either immediate or remote ; and benevolence itself, or what is sometimes called a generous sacrifice, is
a mere prudential calculation as to the pleasure and
pain involved in the act.   When a missionary, for example, leaves the comforts of a civilized home for the
miseries of a savage wilderness, he pursues his pleasure merely ; he is driven by his fear of remorse and of
hell on one side, to brave the perils of want and death
on the other, and in this way selects simply the more
agreeable alternative.   In his view, there is a higher
pleasure in preaching to the savages, than in sharing the
luxuries of refined society.   In preferring the former,
he acts upon the same principle of self-love as the
chimney-sweeper would in giving up his sooty rags for
the purple and fine linen of a prince.   He adds to the
number of his agreeable experiences, and on that account, and on that account alone, he changes one
condition for another.

Now, in reply to such reasoning, we shall begin by
admitting that a lofty pleasure attends the exercise of
any form of benevolence ; but is that pleasure—and
here is the point—is that pleasure the immediate *object*
of the benevolence?   Bishop Butler,* the profoundest
and acutest of the English metaphysicians, set this
matter at rest, we think, when he first urged this distinction, viz., that the direct object of any human
affection is altogether distinct from the pleasure which
may accompany its exercise.   Though virtue is pleasant
and vice painful, the object of the mind in pursuing a
virtuous or vicious course, is not the pleasure or pain
that attends it, but something entirely different, such
as the conferring a benefit or inflicting an injury.   The
motive, therefore, may be separated from all consider-

---

* See his celebrated Sermons on Human Nature, etc.

ations of a self-regarding nature, although the result
of the act when performed, or the performance of it
in itself, yields the highest degree of satisfaction. A
mother, who devotes herself during long and sleepless
nights to the care of a suffering child, has a certain
sort of pleasure in the midst of all her painful vigils : it
is more agreeable to discharge the anxious duty than it
would be to leave it undone, or to abandon the child to
alien cares. Her affections, in the one case, are gratified and her conscience set at rest ; while in the other
case her affections would be wrung and her conscience
made to bite. But is her own satisfaction the motive of
her conduct, and not the good of her offspring, considered apart from her own satisfaction? Is she interested mainly in her own state of body or mind, or in
that of the child? Is she seeking her own relief, or
another's? Does she so much as think of her own
state, present or prospective? If the former, then
Bentham is right ; but if the latter, then he is wrong.
He is wrong, because we see clearly that there may be
actions which are not self-regarding, which are disinterested, which contemplate ends outside of ourselves,
and which cannot therefore be reduced to a calculation
of our own pleasure or pain.

Pleasure or pain, we repeat, may be the accompani-
ment or the result of an action without being the object
for which that action is performed. It gives a hungry
man pleasure to relieve his hunger, and yet his motive
in eating may be, not the pleasure, but the support of
his animal powers. It gives a good man pleasure to
succor the distressed, but it is the relief he gives others,
not the pleasure reflected back upon himself, by which
he is moved. Moreover, if that pleasure were consciously or confessedly his object, the act would lose
its merit as a virtuous act. It is virtuous to tell the

truth, but to tell the truth, not because it is truth, but
because it will bring us some advantage, is not virtuous. It is virtuous not to steal, if we refrain from
stealing out of respect to the rights of others ; but it is
not virtuous to be honest from a fear of detection and
the consequent exposure. That would be but a piece
of prudent selfishness, such as any dog might exhibit
who had been once whipped for taking the wrong bone.
So a woman who is chaste, because she calculates that
it is more reputable to be so than to be otherwise—
whose chastity is not a deep inward preference for a
pure life, but a calculation—may be irreproachable, but
she is certainly not admirable. Or, if John Howard
had avowed that his predominant aim, in his protracted
labors to reform the prisons of Europe, was to procure
himself a subtle and exquisite kind of satisfaction,
would he have won the fame he has as a philanthropist?

Or, the question, raised by the selfish school may be
put in another shape, which is this : whether a man
can propose to himself any other end of action than
his own enjoyment? and that is, in reality, to ask
whether a man is a man or only an animal. Animal
or sentient life does depend upon the balance of pain
and pleasure. No sentient being could exist except on
the condition of an equilibration of pain and pleasure ;
for if either of them were in excess, it would perish.
If the relation between the medium in which we exist
and our sensitive nerves were such that pain alone re-
sulted, life would no longer be life, but torture ; we
should speedily die of it, as happens often in cases of
excessive nervous depression. On the other hand, if
our sensations were pleasurable only (besides having
no motives for action), we should die of ecstasy or intoxication, as fishes do in the air, or insects in a jar of

oxygen, or men who inhale too much ether or nitrous oxyde gas. It is, then, on the balance of pain and pleasure, or on an equal liability to each, that the operations of the animal functions become at all possible. But human or moral life is different, and it is conditional, not upon the balance of pain and pleasure, but upon the balance of good and evil,—that is, upon the freedom of the human being to choose the one or the other, and to impose that choice upon his Will, as a principle of conduct. The animal is the subject of his nature, and *must* act according to his inclinations or aversions—*i. e.*, according to his pleasure or pain ; but man is the master of his nature, and *may* act according to the perceptions of his Reason and the dictates of his Conscience, toward an end which transcends his inclinations or aversions. Not being simply animal, but spiritual, he is lifted out of the animal sphere of pleasure and pain into the moral sphere of good and evil—*i. e.*, into a sphere in which he deliberates, or legislates for himself according to general maxims, and not individual ends. Now, it is the "flesh" and the "spirit," as the Scriptures say—the "old man" and the "new man," the "members," and the "law written on the heart," coming into play and antagonism,—while the antagonism is not exclusive of either element, neither of good nor of evil,—which together constitute the field of human morality. If man were all evil, he might be tiger or fiend—if he were all good, he might be dove or angel ; but not man, which he is, solely because both good and evil.

This again brings us to the second point in Bentham's assumption, which is, that an act is obligatory, morally, on the sole ground of its tendency to produce the happiness either of the agent himself or of other similar agents. Is that true ? and if so, how do we know it? Firstly, is there such a stated antecedence and sequence in human actions, that the idea of producing happiness is invariably followed by the sense of obligation? We venture to answer that not a soul in the world is conscious of this alleged connection. When the production of happiness is proposed to us, it strikes us always as something desirable, but it does not always strike us as something obligatory. Parents, teachers, orators, writers, when they want to awaken moral conviction, appeal directly to the mind without a preliminary descant upon the production of happiness. And the great practical moralists, the Confutses, the Moseses, the Christs, speak invariably in an imperative, not a calculating mood,—"Do as you would be done by," "Thou shalt not steal," "Thou shalt not bear false witness," "Do not commit adultery," "Love the Lord thy God with all thy heart, and thy fellow as thyself,"— all which commands imply in man a capacity to conceive duty immediately, without going through a process of arithmetic : like this for instance, so much pleasure on one side, so 'much pain on the other ; *ergo*, so much obligation on one side, and none on the other.

Or, secondly, Bentham's assumption may mean that the idea of right and wrong, and the idea of producing happiness, are coextensive with each other—*i. e.*, interchangeable ; in which case, he is bound to tell us which is the cause and which the effect. Does virtue produce happiness, or happiness virtue? He has nowhere vouchsafed the answer. The general impression, the instinctive judgment, is, that they are not identical ; we have a distinct idea of each, and, in all practical cases, assume a difference. It is agreeable and useful to me to wash my body daily in cold water, but it is not obligatory on me to do so ; I teach my children to ride, skate, and swim, because these are pleasant and healthful exercises; but I teach them to be honest and truthful for quite other reasons. I throw open my orchards certain days in summer to all the neighboring poor to eat their fill of fruit, because I take delight in their delight ; but I urge them to be upright, and sober, and chaste on other grounds than either my pleasure or theirs. As therefore actions, in fact, produce happiness, which have no moral character, any more than the relief administered by a bootjack or the gambols of a kitten.

Or, again, thirdly, Bentham's assumption means that utility, or the production of happiness is the test, measure, criterion, standard, of right and wrong (which we have no doubt is his real understanding of the subject). But here again we cannot go with him, for a threefold reason. First, that all the consequences of an act cannot be reached, *i. e.*, adequately known, unless we suppose ourselves capable of following them out, as they go sounding on through all the realms of being, through infinite spaces and infinite times, to the last syllable of recorded experience. Secondly, that if we limit our view to the mere tendency of acts to produce consequences, the standard becomes too fluctuating. Men's opinions differ in nothing more than in their estimates of what is expedient, as they happen to study immediate or remoter tendencies, such as affect this or that interest, this or that intellectual taste, this or that moral affection, this or that social institution or convention, this or that religious doctrine, natural or revealed. What, indeed, are all the debates of Parliaments, the wranglings of newspapers, the conflicts of private opinion, but efforts to determine the very "utility" which is offered us as a standard of rectitude and judgment? But, thirdly, we say that this alleged standard confounds mere error or mistake with crime. Consequences of the most deleterious kind are produced by momentary infirmities of temper, or hastiness of decision, as well as by deliberate wickedness. A general may sacrifice his army at a critical moment, when the very liberties of his country depend upon a battle about to be fought, through impetuosity or procrastination, or the miscarriage of a despatch, or the lie of a scout; or, he may sacrifice it through overindulgence in wine, through secret complicity with the enemy; and in both cases the consequences will be the same: but how different our estimate of his guilt! We should denounce him as an imbecile in one case, but as a criminal in the other; we should degrade him in one, but shoot him in the other: but why the distinction estimated by the results? A mother of a family, by a constant peevishness and irritability will produce more unhappiness to herself, her children, and her friends, than she would by an occasional secret infidelity; and yet the one fault we merely regret, while the other we brand as infamous. Why so, on the calculation of consequences? Because something more than "consequences" enters into our judgment of the act, which is what the utilitarians precisely leave out, the moral disposition, or the state of the Will.

This fatal defect of the utilitarian standard the religous moralists have seen : they have seen that there could be, for a moral being responsible for his acts, no standard outside of the human consciousness; and they have erected intention into a measure of merit and demerit. But intention can relate only to the individual's estimate of his own end, and it fails of the universality which is implied in any common standard of action. A criterion ought to be valid for all judgments. Besides, this doctrine of intention is apt to degenerate into a mere casuistry, such as prevailed in the Jesuitical schools, that Pascal castigated with ·immortal wit and severity. The end is soon lugged in to justify the means, and then no abomination so gross or so subtle that it may not walk abroad in a shining panoply of good purposes. What is wanted is, some principle of universal application, which the Reason may at once discern and impose as an imperative law upon the Will.

The following circumstances, we think, will be admitted to be facts : 1st. That all rational beings stand in various relations to each other, such as the relation of parent to child, of man to woman, of brother to brother, of man to man, etc. 2d. That as soon as these relations are apprehended by the mind, there springs up in it spontaneously a conviction that certain dispositions are proper, *i. e.*, ought to be manifested toward the beings to whom we are thus related. A man, for instance, who is a free rational Person, recognizing in another being the same freedom and rationality, perceives intuitively that he too is a Person, who is to be treated as a person,—*i. e.*, always as an end, and never as a means. Reciprocally, they owe to each other respect ; and that respect generalized, forms the sentiment of universal human justice, which is the basis of all morals.

This conviction, then, having a real existence, is capable of becoming a motive, and a motive acting independently of all notions of pain or pleasure. Whoever has experienced how often it sets itself in opposition to his most cherished notions of pleasure, will testify to the power of its workings. It acts as the great antagonist of the inferior forces of the soul. An intense and anxious struggle is incessantly waged between it and the swarms of our selfish appetites. If it be allowed to be overcome, it is turned into an avenging monitor, shooting arrows of keen remorse ; but when it conquers, it is the angel of peace, shedding its soft influences over and irradiating by its genial smiles the depths of the inmost soul. There are now, and there have been in all ages of the world, men in whom the sentiment of benevolence, the love of friends, devotion to country, in other words, of fidelity to humanity, have been never-failing springs of action, invincible by all the motives of self-interest which could be brought to bear against them ; men who in the accomplishment of a lofty purpose would pass days and nights of pain and labor, who would sacrifice without regret the most cherished gratifications, to bring aid to the needy, or balm to the distressed ; men who would recoil from the thought of meanness or wrong with as much quickness as the instinct of a pure woman shrinks from the approach of contamination ; men who in a contest for principle would spurn the suggestions of policy with an instant scorn, and who would relinquish property, comforts, rank, children, and friends with joyful alacrity, before they would surrender one jot of their faith or compromise in a single point the integrity of their aims. There are now, and there have been in all ages of the world and in every nation, men who have kept loyal to their sense of duty in the midst of the frightfulest tortures which human ingenuity, whetted by malice, could inflict ; men who, when nailed to the stake, when the fagots have crackled in the flames, when the devouring jaws of wild beasts have been opened for their destruction, when their limbs, by a cruel variety of infernal mechanism, have been torn piecemeal one from the other, have preferred the serenity of rectitude to an escape from these most terrible sufferings, crowned with the plaudits of a surrounding world. They have willingly confronted death rather than lose honor, or tarnish their innocent consciousness by the indelible stains of injustice or untruth.

Here, then, is a radical defect of Bentham's moral teachings. He takes no account of this deep-seated sense of right, so wide and irresistible in its influences over the volitions of human will. That all good acts have a beneficent tendency—that temperance, fortitude, generosity, justice, truth, produce the happiest consequences both to the agent and to society—that whatever we feel to be virtuous would be beneficial if performed by all men under the same conditions—that the disposition to confer happiness is accompanied by a feeling of moral complacency—in short, that the production of the greatest amount of good is an inseparable consequence of virtue—we admit to be among the established facts of moral science. But that this ulterior happiness is to be the motive with which virtuous acts are to be performed, and not the virtues in themselves, or because they are virtues, we cannot admit. It strips virtue of its very character as virtue, and sinks it from an end into a means. No man who is bold because it is more dangerous to be cowardly, is a brave man. No man is benevolent who distributes pleasure, not because it is generous, but because it is reputable. No man is just who acts impartially, not because it is right, but because it is safe or commanded by the laws. Virtue is an imperious goddess exacting a willing service, a service for her own sake, and not permitting it when performed for any extrinsic objects. The moment the motive is divided, the worship is no longer acceptable, and, innocent as it may apparently be, is in her sight impure.

We object, then, to the theory of utility on the very ground of utility. Whenever any other motive of virtue than virtue's self is substituted for it, the moral character loses something of its tension as well as of its dignity. We diminish by it that intrinsic pleasure which always attends the performance of a virtuous act. It weakens

the force of those habitual feelings which are the best
promoters of rectitude and probity. It supplants a
strong present motive by a more distant, and consequently weaker, inducement. It renders moral judgments uncertain, fluctuating, and difficult. It opens
the heart to the more easy approaches of self-
delusion. It shifts the attention from the interior impulse to the bare outward act. It enables the selfish
and unamiable passions to mingle themselves with less
probability of detection among nobler impulses—tends
to justify wrong actions under the disguise of expedi-
ency—allows too broad a discretion in the application
of moral rules—and admits too readily of the passage
from the consideration of general, to that of particular
and specific, consequences. No man who makes
pleasure his chief aim can give a full development to
his character, or form an adequate notion of the great
purposes of human existence, or of the destinies of society.

But these objections do not apply in all their force to
the principle of utility as it operates in the province of
the legislator. It is true, the legislator, like the moralist, must place himself under the guidance of the immutable principles of Justice. He must obey the instinctive dictates of that moral conviction in which is
laid the foundation of all righteous law. Justice, eternal
and unchangeable Justice, is to be his supreme aim in
establishing the fundamental or constitutional relations
of the State. But within this primary limit he legislates,
not for himself, but for a community, and a community which presupposes, in the very meaning of the
term, a collection of conflicting interests and of equal
claims. He adjudicates between a host of widely-vari-
ous pretensions ; is to neglect none, and favor none ;
yet is to distribute the advantages of law over a wide

space, and among a multitude of competitors. How can he discharge his duties impartially? How is he to ascertain what is best in all circumstances? Here the necessity for some general rule of legislation intervenes, some guide to direct him in his perplexities, and to preserve him from shifting, uncertain, and confused decisions. Now we know of no better rule in such cases than that which insists upon producing the highest good to the greatest number of people.

While we do not subscribe, therefore, to Bentham's moral theories, we confess to a high degree of admiration for his labors in the reformation of jurisprudence. All his services it would be impossible, in this brief review, to enumerate, but the more essential parts may be recapitulated in a few sentences.

1. The attempt at a thorough reform of legal science was in itself no small service. He found the English law what blind usage, occasionally altered by hasty legislation, and from time to time corrected by fettered judicial decisions, with such improvements as professional writers added, had made it. It had come to be what it was piecemeal, irregularly, without order or system. Founded originally on the feudal relation, it retained the feudal spirit long after society had outgrown its barbarisms. One stage of civilization had succeeded another, but the law had not kept pace with the change. A warlike people had become an industrious and commercial people, but there was no introduction of laws fitted to their new modes of existence. Whatever alterations took place, were made by forced applications of old rules, or by new rules brought to square with the old, through a process of violent adjustment. As opinion and social customs advanced, its structure became constantly more heterogeneous and confused. Here a part would fall into

disuse, and make a huge hiatus in its theory.   There a portion would be knocked off, in the struggles of society to enlarge itself, and the place supplied by some strange and uncongenial substitute.   The courts would strain a point one day, to adapt themselves to the growing wants of a more active and refined state of human intercourse, and the legislature would strain another point another day, either to rebuke or justify the courts. Thus, construction was heaped upon construction, evasion followed evasion, one fantastic fiction became the excuse of a fiction still more fantastic, until the whole mass seemed like a vast pile of rubbish, or rather like some of those ancient structures which are seen in Italy, with here a broken column, there a shattered portico, in the third place a crumbling roof, but the whole grotesquely stuck together with plaster and wood, to make a modern habitation.

In the entire course of its existence, there had been no attempt to remodel it, or bring its parts into more perfect symmetry and shape.   Of the thousands that in every age devoted their lives to the study of it, no one cared to investigate its corruptions or undertake the labor of improvement.*   Those who read it, read it to learn what it was, and not to inquire what it ought to be.   Those who wrote about it, wrote as expositors and not as critics.   All the publications put forth concerning it aspired to no higher character than that of digests, abridgments, commentaries, synopses, or didactic essays.   Not that its defects were unperceived, nor that its cumbrous and illogical reasonings had not forced themselves into notice, nor that its injustice had not often been felt; for there had been many and various complaints uttered from time to time on all

---

* The attempts of Bacon and Hale are no exceptions.

these points. Sometimes a judge in the course of a decision would diffidently suggest an improvement, and sometimes a general writer would speak in harsh terms of certain of its details. But generally the system was revered in proportion as it was absurd. Elegant dissertations, like those of Blackstone, had persuaded men that it was "the perfection of reason;" and as few were disposed to question with any earnestness the dicta of profound and skilful lawyers, there was an almost unbroken acquiescence where there should have been as unbroken an opposition.

It was in this state that Bentham found it, when he ventured upon the opinion that it was all wrong. It was in this state he found it, when he began to ridicule its pretensions, and lash its absurdities. It was in this state he found it, when he began an investigation, with a view to root up its very foundations, and build the entire structure anew. He was not satisfied with the examination of a single title, nor an isolated branch, but he applied an unsparing analysis to each and every part, picking to pieces, demolishing, tearing down, and building up, until scarcely a particle of the original fabric was left, and a fairer proportioned edifice rose on its ruins. Even if his efforts had been less successful, the attempt would not have been without its uses. It would have broken, at least, the charm which had been thrown around the subject, it would have attracted attention from thinking minds, and it would have prepared the way for subsequent exertions more pertinent and beneficial than his own.

2. A more essential service rendered by Bentham was the manner in which he discharged his task. He began, not in a hap-hazard way, destroying wantonly whatever seemed to him unworthy, but in obedience to a regular and consistent design. His method was not

novel in itself, although it was original in its application.   It was essentially the same method which for
more than a century had been the glory of physical
science.   It was in another form the observation and
induction of Bacon, the method which rejected authority, which dissected sophism, which labored for
precision, which investigated facts, which put questions, in Bacon's own expressive phrase, to the object.
He settled in the outset his guiding principle, and then
made use of it unflinchingly in the treatment of the
minutest parts of his inquiry.   One of his profoundest
chapters was that in which he expounds the false methods
of reasoning used in legislation.   He showed that there
could be but one right reason, and that the various
and conflicting principles on which jurists commonly
relied could not be that reason.   He showed that antiquity, though it might create a prejudice in favor of a
law, was not a reason for it ; that the sanctions of religion, such as those cited from the Old Testament in
the famous work of Algernon Sidney, were not reasons ;
that an arbitrary definition, such, for instance, as that
with which Montesquieu opened his great treatise, was
not a reason ; that metaphors, like that of the English
jurists as to a man's house being his castle—that a fiction, such as that certain offences work a corruption of
blood—that a fancy, such as Cocceiji's, as to the right
of a father over his children, because they were a part
of his body—that antipathies and sympathies arising in
the breast of the legislator—and that imaginary laws,
such as the thousand-and-one laws of nature that were
spoken of—were not reasons, but mere pretences put
forth to escape the obligation of deciding upon solid,
consistent, and tenable principles.   In rejecting the
pretexts by which the law, as well the good portions of
it as the bad, were defended, and vigorously enforcing

the strict rules he had prescribed, it became necessary for him to take the whole body of the law apart, to dissect its vessels, articulations, and muscles ; to penetrate the mysticism which had all along enveloped its logic ; to examine its generalities in detail ; to inspect the maxims which had grown gray in its service ; to probe the fictions interwoven through its entire texture ; to compare piece with piece ; and to prove the whole by reducing it without mercy to the test of his impartial standard.   He found it encumbered with useless forms, fettered by arbitrary precedents, abounding in flagrant absurdities, and pervaded by an unwise and pernicious spirit.

3. But not content with pulling down so conglomerous a mass, he set to work with no less indomitable energy on the task of putting up something in its stead. In this process, too, he taught mankind several invaluable truths.   He demonstrated that the framing of laws was a matter of practical business, to be conducted with the same good sense which plain men use in their ordinary affairs.   He took the law from the number of those objects of human study which have their roots and defences in authority, and attempted to give it a place among real sciences—by the side of mathematics, chemistry, and general physics.   He did more ; he brought discredit upon all mere technical systems, by setting before us, in great beauty of arrangement and considerable completeness of detail, a system founded upon a natural characteristic of those actions which are the subjects of law.   He practically exhibited the advantages of that system, showing how it was equally applicable in all nations and at all times ; how it detected bad laws by the mere force of its arrangement, giving them no place in its nomenclature ; how it effectually excluded all barely technical offences ;

how it closed the door upon technical reasonings, which only the lawyer can understand ; and how it simplified and illustrated the institutions and combinations of institutions that compose the matter of legal science.

4. Had he done no more than demonstrate the possibility of LEGAL CODES, Bentham would have accomplished a great good. His views in this respect are peculiarly original and just. He has shown how it was practicable to make a code which should reduce all the laws of a country into a body of written enactments, coming directly from the legislator, and adapted to the immediate guidance of the judge in the decision of all the various cases falling under his cognizance. This, of course, embraced much more than had been included in the codes suggested by the eminent jurists of either ancient or modern times. The code of Justinian, admirable as it proved as a digest, was nothing more than an attempt to bring into a more manageable shape the existing laws of the empire. Tribonian, and those who were engaged with him, merely undertook to make a more compendious arrangement of what was found in the Rescripta Principium, the Edicta Prætorum, the Leges et Plebiscita, which they regarded as the established rules of the State. Nor did the code of Frederic, designed for the Prussian monarchy, nor even that of Napoleon, aspire to a much higher character. The latter, which is the most perfect of all, and a vast improvement upon the old French law, fails, in leaving its meaning in too many instances to be determined by the decisions of the judges, which in time accumulate precedents, and make the study of the science a matter of as immense labor as that of the common law of England. It did not contain within itself a definition of its own terms, nor an accurate and appropriate classi-

fication of its parts. Bentham's idea went farther than this. A code in the true sense, he thought, should be one comprehending whatever was necessary to enable the judge to put in force, without extraneous or adventitious aid, the will of the legislator; which should possess, if we may so term it, the power of self-interpretation; and which should make provision for its own improvement and correction. In his plans for the codes of Russia and the United States, he endeavored to realize this general theory, by showing of what parts a code should consist, and the relation of the parts. But the nearest actual approach to his own notion is effected in the Penal Code, prepared by the Law Commissioners of Great Britain for the government of India, published in 1837. Whoever will consult it, will discover, if not a thoroughly unexceptionable code, one that proves the practicability of codification, and the beauty of an orderly and systematic arrangement. How it has operated practically we are not informed, but we have no doubt of its success, from the fact that it combines, as the framers of it state, the advantages of a statute book and of a collection of decided cases. It is, at any rate, an approximation to something better than the miserable jumble of rules called law, to be found in most nations of the civilized world.

5. Be the opinion, however, what it may in respect to the practicability of codification—and we know that many, even among law reformers, are dubious—it must be conceded that Bentham, by the enthusiasm with which he prosecuted his task, if not by any actual success, kindled a spirit of active inquiry on this subject, which is working in the bosom of society with more and more power to this day. Beginning with the private student and the philosopher, it has gradually stolen its way into houses of legislation. At first Dumont, then

Mill, then Romilly, then Brougham, and then less conspicuous men, caught the impulse, and by a series of
persevering exertions, in the midst of strong opposition,
directed public attention to the serious evils which he
had unveiled. The progress of opinion, it is true,
has been slow, but when we contemplate the obstacles
it has met, in the general worship of authority, in the
pride and indifference of the legal profession, and in the
stubborn habits of society, we are surprised that so
much has been already accomplished. We were struck,
in reading a late English work,* at the number of
changes that had been already imperceptibly effected.
Of these may be enumerated alterations materially improving the relation of debtor and creditor, diminishing
the number of oaths, softening the penalties and ame-
liorating the spirit of criminal law, simplifying the
proceedings and forms of pleading at common law,
defining more distinctly the rights, duties, and revenues
of ecclesiastical persons, consolidating statutes, and
harmonizing and modernizing the barbarous provisions
of the law of real property. All these we attribute in-
directly to Bentham, because his was the seminal mind
from which the movement sprang.

6. Nor should it be forgotten, in an enumeration of
the services of the same great mind, what ought to have
been insisted on before, that wrong as he was in his
general theory of politics, yet he has done much theo-
retically toward establishing the true functions of government. He has stated with more clearness than any
preceding writer the real objects of civil law, and the
best methods of attaining them. If he has not carried
his ideas to the extent to which American statesmen
are disposed to push their theories of government, he

---

* Miller on the Unsettled Condition of the Law.

has made a near approximation to it. Indeed, the most radical of American statesmen can find much instruction in what he has uttered on this head. Law of any kind he regards as a retrenchment of liberty, and is never to be imposed without a sufficient and specific reason. For there is always a reason against every coercive law in the fact that it is a restraint upon the liberty of the citizen. Unless, therefore, he who proposes a law can prove that there is not only a specific reason in favor of it, but a reason stronger than the general reason against it, he transcends his province and invades the rights of the individual. Again, assuming that the single aim of the legislator should be to promote the greatest possible happiness of the community, and that as the care of his enjoyments ought to be left entirely to the individual, he argues that it becomes the principal duty of the government to guard against pains. If it protects the rights of personal security, if it defends property, if it watches over the general safety, it accomplishes its main purposes. Government approaches perfection in proportion as the sacrifice of liberty on the part of the subject is diminished, and his acquisition of rights is increased. Can the most rigid democrat carry his own theory much farther? Is it not, indeed, precisely the thing for which we, who are the advocates of equal justice, contend? Adopt these principles in legislation, and would they not simplify government until it became what it ought to be, a mere instrument for the protection of person and property? Would they not abolish all partial legislation, root out exclusive privileges, destroy monopolies, prevent the granting of acts of special incorporation, do away with unequal laws, and leave society to its own energies and resources, in the conduct of its business and the prosecution of its enterprises? And this is all for which the great democratic party, the party of impartial Justice, is striving. It seeks to direct government to its true ends, to restore its action from the partial direction that has been given it, and urge it on to the accomplishment of those general objects, for which alone it was instituted, and which alone are compatible with the rights, the interests, and the improvement of man. Bentham himself, it must be admitted, has sometimes departed from these objects, but only when he violated unconsciously his own logic.

We have dwelt longer upon these topics than it was our intention when we began, and longer, we fear, than the patience of the reader will excuse. We have done so, because, enamored of the theme, we have endeavored to kindle the interest of others. If we have quickened the purposes of any to engage in the great study of law reform, the time has not been lost. It is a great subject, connected with the best interests of society, and worthy of the patient labor of the noblest minds. We know of no way in which the intellect could be more profitably tasked, or the purest sympathies more suitably indulged, or the firmest moral purpose more honorably tried, or greater good conferred on men, or a richer harvest of reputation reaped, than in prosecuting the inquiries which Bentham so auspiciously commenced. The law is yet a fallow field, covered with stubble, thorns, and weeds. There are many briers to be rooted out, and many vigorous and wholesome shoots to be planted in their place. What obscurities perplex its theory, what inconsistencies confuse its details, what vexations attend its practice! How numberless the absurdities that disfigure the statute-books! How expensive, wearisome, and ambiguous the greater part of its proceedings! Would any one confer a blessing on the poor, let him shorten its delays and diminish its costs. Would any one spread peace among

men, let him simplify its rules and make certain its decisions. A worthier name could not be achieved than
by taking part in the effort to correct its abuses, and to
conform it to the image of immutable Justice. There
may be more lucrative, but there are certainly no more
honorable or useful spheres of exertion, than in the department of LAW REFORM.

EDWARD LIVINGSTON AND HIS CODE.*

E endeavored in a late number of this Review to make our readers better acquainted with one of the great intellects of England, and we now turn to a kindred genius of our own country, who in many respects reduced to practice what Bentham had only suggested ; who, taking up the subject of law reform where the master had left it, pursued it to a complete consummation. Edward Livingston, in the code known as the Code of Louisiana, raised himself to the first rank among jurists as well as among public benefactors ; and he conferred a distinction upon his chosen State more glorious and lasting than ever warrior gave to the land his blood had defended.

Livingston was born in the colony of New York, in the year 1764. His family, descended from one of the most powerful and illustrious clans in Scotland, driven

---

* Eloge Historique de M. Livingston, par M. Mignet, Secrétaire Perpétuel de l'Académie des Sciences, Morales, et Politiques. Lu à la Séance Publique, du 30 juin, 1838. Paris, 1838.

A System of Penal Law for the State of Louisiana, prepared under the authority of a law of said State. By Edward Livingston. To which are prefixed a Preliminary Report on the plan of a Penal Code, and introductory reports to the several codes embraced in the system of Penal Law. Philadelphia, 1833.

From the *Democratic Review*, July and Sept., 1841.

away by religious persecution, had been among the earliest settlers of America. Its members brought with them to the place of their exile, along with lofty tastes and generous manners, an indestructible love of liberty. When the infant colonies, oppressed by the mother country, began to stir with the aspirations of independence, their sentiments and principles had already prepared them to take part with those who struck for freedom. Edward Livingston, the youngest of eleven children, was a witness of many of the exciting scenes of the revolutionary war. His brother Robert, a member of that magnanimous Congress which, for seven years during the vicissitudes of a bloody contest did not despair of its country, shared with Jefferson, Franklin, Adams, and Sherman the honor of drawing up that Declaration of Independence which became the "birth-act" of a nation. His brother-in-law, the chivalrous Montgomery, in the young vigor of his hopes and faculties, perished gloriously in the assault upon Quebec. And his hearth was ever the hospitable home of La Fayette, and those other noble auxiliaries who so gallantly battled for the rights of humanity, in sustaining the feeble but spirited arms of the small band of American patriots.

Under the influence of such associations the basis of his character was laid ; and when he afterward came to act for himself, a long life of public usefulness and unspotted purity testified that early impressions had been durable. He never forgot the love of justice, nor the disinterested patriotism that had always marked the characters of his ancestors and friends.

He devoted himself to the profession of the law. In his preparatory studies, which were alike thorough and discursive, he made himself familiar with the doctrines of the common law, adopted from the mother-country, and with the principles of the civil law, as they were found in the old writers, and illustrated on the continent of Europe. His practice in the courts was followed by all the success that a distinguished and wealthy connection could give a young man of extraordinary industry and talent. He rose rapidly into fame ; and in 1794 was chosen a representative of New York in Congress.

It was an important epoch. The American people, just emerged from a fierce and protracted struggle for independence, had formed a government before then unknown to the legislation of the world. Washington had been selected as the first to administer it ; and around him were gathered those who, either in the council or the field, had assisted him in the mighty work of revolution. A new constitution, binding free and sovereign States in an indissoluble league, was about to be tried. Its strength and its weaknesses, its tendencies, whether for good or for evil, were soon to develop themselves in practical operation. Parties, taking their color from their proclivities toward a stronger government or a stronger people, were already formed. At the head of one division stood Thomas Jefferson, the ardent friend of liberty—sanguine, far-sighted, sagacious—and from his youth a champion of the French humanitarian philosophy. At the head of the other was Alexander Hamilton—accomplished, ambitious, and eloquent—a friend of liberty, but distrustful of the people, and inclined to the politics of England. Livingston lost no time in ranging himself among the former. He entered with enthusiasm into the defence of the popular measures of his day. He opposed the British treaty of 1794 ; he fought resolutely against the sedition law ; and to this day, in many of the log huts of the western frontiers, his able speech against the alien acts hangs upon the walls. Then, too, he formed the acquaintance of a delegate from the distant and obscure territory of Tennessee, with whom he was afterward destined to perform so conspicuous a part, both in war and peace—Andrew Jackson.

Livingston continued in Congress till the end of Adams's term. Selected by his fellow-citizens then to discharge the duties of chief municipal magistrate of New York, he had occasion to manifest other traits of character than those which had given him political prominence. Soon after his election the yellow fever broke out with unusual violence. Livingston gave himself up entirely to the care of the sick ; and, by personal visitation, the gratuitous distribution of his fortune, and a wise direction of the city charities, contributed greatly to the restoration of health. When seized himself with the disease, just as it began to abate, the spontaneous gratitude of the whole population, shown by anxious inquiries, by expressions of sympathy, and by gifts, told how deeply his noble generosity had fastened him to the affections of all classes.

But that freedom from selfish feeling which had saved others, sacrificed himself; and, in the fortieth year of his age, when he had fondly thought that leisure would be afforded him to resume those elevated studies that were the charm of his life, he found himself stripped of wealth, and compelled a second time to begin his professional career.* To a man of less energy this would have been no ordinary trial ; to Livingston it was only an occasion for the display of his lofty virtues. He speedily arranged his affairs, and a few months saw him

---

* We should dwell more minutely upon these incidents of Mr. Livingston's life, had not the elegant pen of an admiring friend, Mr. August Davezac, already anticipated us. See Democratic Review, First Series, Vol. viii., No. xxxiv.

an emigrant to the new territory of Louisiana, recently purchased by the United States from the French. It was then a new and uncultivated country, but beautifully placed by Providence in one of the largest and richest valleys of the world, watered by the grandest of rivers, and at the head of a magnificent gulf, communicating with the main ocean. The great stream of population, so long hemmed in by the ranges of the Alleghanies, had burst its barriers, and was already spreading over the almost boundless prairies of the West. In a few years the forests had disappeared, and fertile plantations and growing towns covered their sites ; a fine city at the mouth of the Mississippi served as an outlet to its productions ; and wealth, order, and civilization rewarded the toils of the enterprising settlers.

Livingston engaged once more in the practice of the law, and fortune followed his exertions. Not satisfied, however, with the mere accumulation of property, he suggested, and accomplished in connection with others, important reforms of his favorite science. The various fortunes of Louisiana, as a dependency, first of Spain and then of France, next under a territorial government, and, finally, as an independent State, had introduced a world of confusion into its law. It was a vast hodge-podge of Spanish customs, French decrees, English precedents, and conflicting legislative enactments. In its forms of procedure, particularly, it was as defective as it was inconsistent. Livingston set about correcting its evils. Rejecting alike the interminable proceedings of French, and the absurd fictions of English practice, he formed a short and simple code which combined the advantages of the various systems that prevailed, while it was free from their defects. He digested and methodized also the more ancient civil laws that were still recognized as authoritative. Nor was it the least of the benefits flowing from these preparatory labors, that his mind was directed to that grand and comprehensive scheme of law-reform which he subsequently carried into effect, with such honor to himself and to the legislature that had had the wisdom to engage his talents.

The war of 1812 interrupted his plans. Ready as he was to do good to his country with his pen, he was no less ready to take up the sword in her defence. During the siege of New Orleans, he seconded the efforts of the patriotic Jackson ; he shared in the danger and glory of the battle ; and when the strife had ceased, he was employed in the benevolent task of negotiating an exchange of prisoners.

With the return of peace, the great purpose of his life was renewed. Legal studies again absorbed his thoughts ; he completed a plan of penal reform ; and getting himself elected to the Legislature of the State, he there unfolded his enterprise. In February, 1820, he was appointed to prepare a report, at length, of all that he proposed to accomplish. Livingston undertook the task with avidity, making himself acquainted with whatever had been done in his own country and abroad in relation to the subject, corresponding with distinguished jurisconsults of all nations, comparing the principles of every theory—and before the end of four years had the satisfaction to see his plan approved.

It is of that plan we design to give some account, but we shall advert beforehand to what had been done for a reformation of penal law at the time Livingston began his labors.

In the earlier stages of modern civilization, those who made the laws for the trial and punishment of criminals seem to have been moved solely by a spirit of blind and unmitigated ferocity. Society, in departing from many of the barbarous usages of the feudal age, retained much of its savageness of manners and disposition. The discipline of force under which it had been educated, continued long after to exert an influence upon the habits and opinions of the people. The increasing intercourse among States and men, a consequence of the growth of commerce, while it liberalized the pursuits and refined the courtesies of life, did not efface the traces of former selfishness and brutality, or remove from existing institutions those fierce and vindictive provisions which a ruder condition had originated. Mistaking severity for justice, supposing vengeance to be the single object of public, as it had been of private punishment, criminals (unless protected by rank or interest), were treated by the law as outcasts ; they were arrested without cause, condemned without trial, and punished with the most excruciating tortures and the most infamous deaths. Denied the right of being heard in their own defence, they were subjected to insult and caprice, and often compelled, by the rack or flame, to confess crimes of which they had never been guilty, or to purchase immunity by the grossest and most degrading falsehoods. Secret tribunals, inquisitions, lettres-de-cachet, mutilations, and indiscriminate butchery were the instruments with which it often executed its purposes, alike upon offenders of every age and sex and of every degree of guilt.

Even in England, distinguished from other nations by the institution of the trial by jury, by the habeas-corpus act, and by the sturdy and independent spirit of the people, these harsher features of criminal jurisprudence were relieved, but not obliterated. "Prisoners were deprived the assistance of counsel ; men were executed because they could not read ; those who refused to answer were compelled to die under the most cruel torture. Executions for some crimes were attended with butchery that would have disgusted a savage. The life and honor of the accused were made to depend on the uncertain issue of a judicial combat. A wretched sophistry introduced the doctrine of corrupted blood. Heretics and witches were committed to the flames. No proportion was preserved between crimes and punishments. The cutting of a twig and the assassination of a parent ; breaking a fish-pond and poisoning a whole family or murdering them in their sleep, all incurred the same penalties ; and between two and three hundred different actions, many not deserving the name of offences, were punishable by death."

Society was particularly inert in emancipating itself from this capricious despotism. Nothing is changed with more difficulty than practices that have received the sanction of antiquity and habit. Even political evils, falling upon large classes of the community, and thus arraying against them a combined opposition, are long permitted to develop their effects before the masses are aroused to demand a change. How much greater the delay in regard to laws which inflict their curses only at intervals and upon single and friendless persons! Criminal legislation, more than all other kinds of legislation, was thus marked by the slowness of its progress. Now and then, when the public sense of justice was offended by some extraordinary instance of severity, slight modifications were made in the existing arrangements ; but the great body of them were suffered to remain in all their original deformity. The bench and the bar, apparently infatuated by a system which had neither beauty nor truth, nor any charms save the equivocal charms of age to recommend it, applied themselves diligently to its study, but did not give a thought to its improvement. The meliorating influ-

ences of a growing civilization, that seem to have touched
with a quicker life every other sort of human activity,
did not reach the secluded precincts of the courts.
Had it not been for the liberal spirit of popular writers,
penal law would have continued what barbarism had
made it. But Montesquieu, by the spirit of justice that
pervaded his great work, Beccaria, by his solemn protests against the punishment of death, Filangieri, by
his wise and noble sentiments, prepared the way for the
great English luminary, Bentham, who shed such a
flood of light upon every department of legal reform.

It would be hard to put together a more heterogeneous and, but for the importance of the subject, a more
amusing mass than was formed by the criminal laws of
Louisiana, when Mr. Livingston began his task. The
province having been successively under the government of Spain, France, and the United States, had received from each its peculiar traditions, customs, and
statutes. These had been variously modified in the
several stages of transformation, by local enactments
which the changes rendered necessary. But the most
glaring defects arose from a combined recognition of
the authority of the English common law and of the
equally old institutions of Spain. The common law
of England, much as it has been extolled, is, at the
best, a rude, uncertain, inconsistent, and dangerous
jumble of precedents and usages. It is confessedly
founded upon general and local customs, the origin of
many of which is lost in antiquity. It is unwritten,
and liable to be determined by the variable and arbitrary decisions of the courts. Twenty years of laborious study are insufficient to acquire a knowledge of
what it declares; and, when it is once learned, it
abounds in the absurdest fictions, and the most capricious technicalities. It is an unseemly piece of patch-

work, a residuum of the conceit and insolence of uncultivated centuries, a depository of all the *débris* of society, crumbled off under the influence of advancing intelligence and refinement. It was, however, outdone in absurdities by the relics of the ancient Spanish laws, in which the most ludicrous and the most horrid provisions were conjoined. The legislation of the fifteenth century was considered law for the people of the nineteenth ; and offences that only could be committed in the days of witchcraft and judicial astrology, were ranged side by side with invasions of property or attacks on the person. Infamous punishments could be inflicted at the option of any choleric magistrate. Political disabilities were attached to the most innocent acts ; gamblers, buffoons, usurers, recreant knights, promise-breakers, comedians, and procurers, were classed together as persons equally dishonorable ; a child born out of wedlock could never serve as a witness ; a lawyer who should cite the law falsely was indictable ; and the use of incantations, love-powders, and wax images, was specially punished. Divination was a capital offence, except when done by astronomy, "one of the seven liberal arts, taken from the books of Ptolemy and the other sages." Sorcerers, fortune-tellers of every description, and enchanters who raised the spirits of the dead, "except it was done to exorcise the devil, or to preserve the crops from hail, lightning, and insects," were threatened with death. Blaspheming the Virgin Mary, heresy against the Catholic church; crucifying young children at Jewish festivals, were all enumerated misdemeanors ; and for a thousand frivolous things, as well as for more important matters, a man was liable to lose his head or his limbs. It was doubtful, indeed, whether the torture, in its most excruciating application, could not be legitimately used at the discretion of the judges. Surely, vagaries of this kind were as disgraceful as they were dangerous to the. people by whom they were endured. Laws so absurd, so conflicting, so pernicious, called for a reform ; and yet the task of accomplishing it was no easy labor.

Mr. Livingston, aware of the high responsibility he assumed, gave to the discharge of his duty his best faculties and most profound study. While he determined that no dread of mere innovation should restrain him from proposing the most radical changes, he was yet fully conscious of the importance of consulting the habits and feelings of the people. A simple repeal of laws that had become offensive would not be enough ; the modification and arrangement of existing statutes would in a short time have led to the same evils that were then deplored ; and the introduction of a body of laws before unknown, might be viewed with prejudice and alarm. He resolved, therefore, upon the construction of a code, at once simple and congruous, which should retain whatever of the old laws might be pertinent, but conform at the same time to principles deduced from just and enlightened reason. In this, he evinces his sagacity and wisdom. A code is the best·form in which the supreme rules of the State can be presented, particularly in relation to criminal matters. It embodies, in a brief compass, accurately defined, methodically classified, complete as a whole and in its parts, all that it concerns the public to know of their legal rights and duties. ·The judge it enables, in a moment, to ascertain his own powers, to detect what is an offence, to discover how it is to be proved, to administer the punishment ; the citizen is informed, with no less ease, when his rights have been infringed or how his interests are to be protected ; and the legislature, without legal acquirement or experience, is made competent to re-

peal, supply, or amend any incongruity or defect developed in the course of its practical working. By its
brevity, its order, its accuracy, and its comprehensiveness, a code must ever be superior to every other form
of instituting and publishing the supreme will of the
State. Let it contain within itself a provision for self-
rectification, and the acts of subsequent legislatures,
which have now the effect of multiplying and confusing
laws, would bring them at each step nearer to perfection.

Four codes (comprised in one general code) were
matured by Mr. Livingston's sole and unassisted labors. They were : (1) the code of Crimes and Punishments ; (2) the code of Procedure ; (3) the code of
Evidence ; and (4) the code of Reform and Prison
Discipline : to each of which was prefixed a preliminary
title, declaring its fundamental principles, followed by
a book of definitions.

[Here followed a long analysis of these several codes,
which is now omitted.]

This analysis will enable the reader to form an idea
of the extent of Mr. Livingston's labors, and of the
wisdom shown in their execution. No man could have
been better qualified than he for the work he undertook. A combination of dissimilar and almost conflicting qualities conferred upon him a peculiar fitness
for the task. He was a lawyer equally skilled in the
technicalities of practice and in the subtleties of principle. Yet he had not become so enamored of the
profession as to close his eyes to its defects. He saw
at once its excellence and its weakness, and was as
willing to acknowledge the one as he was to extol the
other. A profound and patient thinker, he still saved
himself from the abstraction and impracticableness of
the mere student by practical habits of business which
had trained him to bold and decided action. Daily

intercourse with men had had the double effect of creating tact and sympathy—tact to discover the laws best adapted to the actual relations of society, and sympathy to infuse into them the sentiment of a broad benevolence. If he investigated as a philosopher, he recommended as a man of the world ; if he felt as a philanthropist, he acted as the practician. Thus he was prepared for every kind of opposition, as well from the criticisms of the learned as from the assaults of the ignorant and interested. Superior knowledge availed him in answering the first, and logic, eloquence, and enthusiasm, in discomfiting the second. Fearless but prudent, theoretical and yet practical, indefatigable in vindication as well as in pursuit, there was no hostility he did not encounter, none, we believe, that he did not overcome.

We are aware that many competent people object to the principle of codification, but we do not estimate their objections very highly. They proceed either from a misunderstanding of the subject or a groundless fear. All new things are received with caution and prejudice, and often the only objection to that which is new, is the simple fact that it is new, independently of its merit, and without regard to the necessity that may exist for its adoption. But such as these objections are, we propose to answer them briefly before closing this discussion.

1. First, then, of the objection, that a code of laws is new. If it be meant by this, that everything which is new is mischievous, it applies equally to every change in the existing order of things. It takes for granted that the human intellect has exhausted its own stores of thought, and that nothing that may hereafter be struck out is worthy of a wise man's consideration. It supposes that society has already reached a state of ultimate perfection, and that no modification of it for the better is possible. It

proceeds upon the ground that the human race came into the world in the maturity of its vigor and beauty, so that nothing in its condition is susceptible of improvement. For, if we admit the progress made by the human mind to be imperfect ; if we admit the existence of social evils at all ; if we do not impute to our forerunners the possession of the highest wisdom and the most consummate power, we must also admit that many things are capable of being reformed. Now, the truth is, in regard to all new measures, that the only real question is, not how long they may have been known, but what they promise to accomplish, and the means they possess of effecting the end. If they be found reasonable, let them be adopted ; but if they be found unreasonable, attack them on the ground of that defect. That an untried plan is an innovation is often, indeed, the best reason why it should be regarded with favor. Christianity was once an innovation, and because the moral state of mankind was such as to entitle it to that name, the more imperative the necessity for its advent. The history of democracy is the history of a series of innovations. All the beneficent changes that we know of were at first esteemed by the timid and time-serving as so many innovations. All the loftiest hopes and aspirations of man are, in fact, connected with the success of these "innovations." They are the pioneers of all that is great and grand in human action, and the pledges of a glorious advancement for the future.

2. But written codes, it is said, may be very well in theory and very bad in practice. Another of those commonplace utterances which rest upon a confusion of terms as well as a confusion of ideas. What is meant by saying that a thing may be very good in theory ? If it means anything, it is that the measure is both rational

in its objects and in its means ; otherwise it is not good in theory, and the question of its practicability may be left out of the discussion. Now, in this matter of law reform, it is evident that if it be good in theory it must be good in practice. If it be adapted to the end pro-posed—that is, if the principles it asserts are wise, just, and pertinent, suited to the people and the times for which they are intended, then it cannot fail to be good in practice. But if it does not possess these charac-teristics, then it is bad in theory, and is to be con-demned on that ground. The fact of being bad in practice, is sufficient of itself to prove it bad in theory,—is indeed the very quality which makes it bad in theory.

If, however, the objectors mean, that written codes invariably are found to work badly, the question be-comes one of fact. Viewing it as such, then, we as-sert, that whenever written codes have been used, and to the extent they have been used, their practical work-ing has shown their superiority to every other form of law. It is true, our instances are few, but yet suffi-ciently numerous to furnish a basis for argument. The Louisiana Code of Procedure were alone adequate to establish the point. "An experiment in the occult sciences," says Livingston, "is said to be most success-fully made, when the desired effects have been pro-duced under the most unfavorable circumstances. It is the same in legislation, and we may consider the favorable result as completely ascertained ; for an ex-periment has been thus made. It has succeeded in the most difficult branch ; succeeded under every disad-vantage of imperfect execution, and in opposition to professional and national prejudices ; succeeded, too, so completely as to silence every objection to the meas-ure itself, and leaving none but to some of the details which more mature revision may remove." Or will any one be hardy enough to allege, that the Code of Napoleon, the code to which more than thirty millions of people have not looked for justice altogether in vain for nearly half a century, is impracticable or inefficient? That code is badly constructed in several respects; yet in spite of its defects, it fulfils the functions of a supreme law much more simply, and quite as effectually, as the vaunted Common Law of England. Suitors acquire and maintain their rights, and the demands of public justice are satisfied; and whatever vexations and delays grow up under it are to be ascribed to those features in which it has departed from the strict idea of a code and introduced the practices of the more ancient law.

But not to multiply citations, there is one fact we hold to be a complete answer to the charge we are combating. It is this—that all modern attempts to improve the existing laws are only so many approaches to the formation of a code. The revised statutes, the abridgments, the digests, and the indices that constitute so respectable a part of a legal library, are endeavors to give scattered and conflicting statutes, rules, and decisions the precision, the conciseness, and the method of a written code. They are efforts to appropriate its form, if not its spirit, and need merely to be carried a little further to realize all that is contained in the great idea of codification. Thus, those who are loudest in their objection to written and organized bodies of law, are among the first to avail themselves, in a partial and inadequate degree, of their advantages. In practice, they measurably confess a principle, which, in argument, they repugn.

3. If it be rejoined, that these are attempts to methodize laws that are already known and interwoven with the habits of society, while the introduction of a new sys-

tem would be attended by great inconvenience and expense, we are ready to meet the argument on that issue. The inconvenience alluded to, we suppose, means the inconvenience of learning what the new laws are, and the expense of reducing them to practice. We acknowledge both the trouble and the cost ; but we reply that the trouble and cost will be much less than is now involved in the labor, time, and money expended under the present system. We ask, in the first place, are the present laws known—known to the people, known even to the judges? From the multiplicity of recorded decisions, can the most skilful jurisconsult always extract the truth? Does one man in a thousand know what are his legal rights, the means of ascertaining them, or the modes of prosecuting their violation? Are the millions who are perpetually rising up to assume the responsibility of social life, informed as to their duties, and can they be informed without mature study, or without feeing counsel? "It may safely be asserted," says an eminent authority, "that less time will be required to obtain a perfect knowledge of any law that is reduced to writing, and framed with a tolerable attention to clearness and method, than would be necessary to learn that part of those which now govern us, which is unknown even to its professors. But should it be conceded that this supposition is unfounded, and that greater trouble would be required than is supposed to master the differences between an old and new system, for those who have studied the former, yet this can apply only to ourselves, to those who are now on the stage of public life. But those who are just about to take their places there—the countless succession of legislators, judges, advocates, magistrates, and officers, who are to replace them!—the multitude even in the present day, who have not yet studied the present laws, but who are bound to obey them !—the millions who are to follow them in the lapse of those ages which every good citizen must wish his country and its institutions to endure !—is the curse of bad laws, and the odious and painful task of learning them, to be entailed on these forever, to save ourselves the task of a few days or weeks mental application?"

4. A more considerable objection to the code, however, is urged by those who represent, that if a new system were established, judicial decisions would still be required to settle the meaning of terms, and to declare the application of principles, which in a few years would accumulate a vast mass of legal learning. Reference is made, in proof of the assertion, to the codes of Justinian and Napoleon, under each of which the commentaries, glosses, and decrees have grown to an immeasurable magnitude.

True : but it is to be observed that the various bodies of law prepared by Justinian were the merest approximation to what is now comprehended in the idea of a code. His Code was only a collection of the imperial statutes from Hadrian to his own time, that were thought worth preserving ; the Institutes were compends—admirable, it is true, but still compends, of the more ancient laws ; the Pandects were voluminous abridgments of the decisions of prætors and the opinions of legal sages, without precision and logical arrangement, abounding in contradictory doctrines, and full of the very uncertainty which was their object to avoid ; while all were vitiated by the fatal defect of admitting a recourse to an authority out of themselves—the authority of the Emperor. An analogous fault is to be remarked in the Code of Napoleon. Explicit as it is in many of its definitions, and felicitous as it is in arrangement, it recognizes the doctrine of usage, and

4

thus opens an avenue for the advent of the whole jurisprudence of precedent and decrees.

Now a true code would altogether avoid sources of
error like these. The great evil we have found in the
English law is, ·that it tolerates this reference to the
decrees of judges. Nearly all the uncertainty with
which it is chargeable, has its origin in this single defect.
In recognizing the determination of its ministers as an
authority equal to itself, its worst features originate.
Law loses the character given it by the definition of
Blackstone, as "a rule of action prescribed by the
supreme power of the State," and becomes an unknown
and variable jumble of *dicta*. It is no longer "a rule
of action," since it sleeps in silence in the heart of the
judge, until some case shall arise to call it into existence ;
it is not "prescribed," inasmuch as it is not known
before it is applied, thus, in many instances assuming
an *ex post facto* operation ; and "the supreme power
of the State" has nothing to do with this jurisprudence
of construction and decrees, which is confined exclusively to the courts, that in theory are supposed to be
the mere interpreters of the law. A true code would
find a remedy for this, in that it is a something entire in
itself ; in its parts, and as a whole, it is complete ; or
should the experience of its practical working discover
points in which it could be improved, it provides regularly for its own systematic amendment till it shall reach
the highest possible perfection. Not the wanton caprice
or prejudices of the judge—not his sinister motives or
base subjection to prevailing influences—no prevari-
cating and self-constituted tribunal—but the legitimate
agents of the community, the only proper law-devising
and law-establishing power, are made the arbiters of
rules in which the properties, happiness, and lives of
the people are involved.

JOURNALISM.*

GREAT is Journalism," exclaims Mr. Carlyle, in his rhapsodical but striking way, "Great is Journalism. Is not every able editor a ruler of the world, being a persuader of it : though self-elected, yet sanctioned by the sale of his numbers? whom indeed the world has the readiest method of deposing, should need be—that of merely doing *nothing* to him ; which ends in starvation." Again, says the same original writer : "There is no church, sayest thou? The voice of prophecy has gone dumb ! This is even what I dispute ; but in any case, hast thou not still preaching enough? A preaching friar settles himself in every village ; and builds a pulpit, which he calls newspaper. Therefrom he preaches what most momentous doctrine is in him, for man's salvation ; and dost not thou listen and believe ?"

We cite these passages, because they recognize the fact that Journalism is a distinct profession, exerting an influence over society like that of the king over his subjects, or of the preacher over his hearers. Much as has been said of the power of the press, it is a power that has never yet been measured. Let us, then, detain the reader with a remark or two upon the functions of editorship, and the place it holds among the moral agencies of the world.

* From the *Democratic Review*, Jan., 1842.

No man requires a larger range of intellect, more varied acquirements, or greater strength of character, than the conductor of a public journal. Of course, we allude to one who acts with a full sense of the dignity and worth of his calling, and a conscientious desire to discharge its duties. Neither statesman, lawyer, nor divine moves in a broader sphere, or has more occasion for the use of the noblest faculties both of mind and heart. The journalist stands in immediate contact with the public mind ; he gives a tone to public sentiment ; he is the guardian and guide of public morals. Thousands of men, each morning and evening, listen to his voice, are moved by his persuasions, are chastised by his rebukes, or corrupted by his license. He may elevate the bad, or degrade the good—he can stimulate the worst or the best passions.

His influence again differs from that of others not only in its directness but its persistency. While theirs is confined to particular and distant occasions, his acts incessantly. The orator agitates only while he is speaking ; the preacher is hemmed in by the walls of his church and the limits of a Sabbath-day ; the statesman seldom steps out of his bureau ; the man of science is fixed among his retorts and crucibles ; and the teacher's sway is confined to his school-room. But the editor is universally as well as perpetually at work. As the mails carry his speculations from one city to another, his action spreads like the waves of a pool, and before the last ripple has subsided, the waters at the centre are again disturbed. Even while he sleeps, his thoughts are awake, entering other minds, and moulding them to good or evil.

> " They rest not—stay not,--on, still on they wing
> Their flight,"—

and whether benign or pestiferous, produce their inevitable impressions. Says the adage, "Give me the making of the songs of a people, and I will make their characters ;" with greater propriety one might say, "Give me the making of the newspapers of a nation, and I will make its minds." The newspaper is everywhere,—in the counting-house and in the parlor, in the bar-room and in the bedroom, on board the steamboat and in the student's chamber. All subjects are discussed in it ; all classes of men read it ; and all men, to an extent, are affected by what it contains. "He," says one of the class,* "should have a head cool, clear, and sagacious ; a heart warm and benevolent ; a nice sense of justice ; honesty that no temptation could corrupt ; intrepidity that no danger could intimidate ; and independence superior to every consideration of mere interest, enmity, or friendship. He should possess the power of diligent application, and be capable of enduring great fatigue. He should have a temperament so happily mingled, that while he easily kindled at public error or injustice his indignation should never transgress the bounds of judgment, but, in its strongest expression, show that smoothness and amenity which the language of choler always lacks. He should, in short, be such a man as a contemporary writer described that sturdy democrat, old Andrew Fletcher of Saltoun— 'a gentleman, steady in his principles ; of nice honor ; abundance of learning ; brave as the sword he wears, and bold as a lion ; a sure friend and irreconcilable enemy ; who would lose his life readily to serve his country, and would not do a base thing to save it.' This is the *beau ideal* of a conductor of a public newspaper."

---

* William Leggett.

But it is an ideal that, like most of the ideals of men of ardent temperament, has been seldom if ever realized. In casting our eyes over the history of newspaper literature, we scarcely recall a man who has fulfilled the high character that pertains to the profession. There have been divines to whom Cowper's beautiful description of St. Paul might well be applied—Fletchers, Halls, Brainards, and Channings; there have been Mansfields, Romillys, and Marshalls, in law; Garricks, Siddonses, Kembles, and Talmas, as actors; there have been Boerhaaves, Jenners, Goods, and Bells, in physics; there have been Boyles, Newtons, and Bacons, in science; and Cæsars, Bonapartes, and Washingtons, in war; in short, in all departments of intellectual exertion there have been crowds of notable men; but nowhere on the lists of great or distinguished persons do we find the name of one whose celebrity has been acquired in the walk of the Journalist. Carrel has produced an impression in France, Fonblanque in England, and Leggett in the United States, but it has been an impression as fleeting as that of fallen leaves; neither of them can be said to have made a permanent reputation.

How are we to account for this extraordinary fact? Why is it that a means so intimately connected with human happiness as the press, so powerful over social issues and human destinies, has so seldom been used by men of the loftiest endowments?

It is not because the sphere of the Journalist is too contracted for a noble ambition; for it is a sphere as wide as the universe of intelligence, and as durable as language. As a means of swaying the minds of men, which is the essence of power, as an instrument for elevating society, which is the object of goodness, as a vehicle for the expression and enforcement of thought, the press is without an equal among all the constituted agencies of human utterance. No voice reaches so far as the voice of the press; no book arrests a wider attention or penetrates a deeper retirement.

It is not because the subjects with which newspaper writing is mostly occupied, are temporary and incidental. That species of composition is not confined to chronicling events, or to fighting the battles of transient parties. Higher objects often engage it. The instruction of society in the nature of government, the inculcation of great principles, the application of judicious criticism, the development and control of social tendencies, the direction of public opinion, the exposition of public characters, the prosecution of grand moral reforms, and the correction of prevailing iniquities and frauds, are among its principal functions. The editor is stationed, as a sentinel upon the watch-towers of society, to warn it of the approach of dangers; to summon it to battle, and to cheer it on to success.

Nor is it because there is anything in the condition of the press to cripple its activity and arrest its influence. No better condition could be required for it than obtains in this country. It is founded on a basis of perfect freedom. Liberty of action, which it is the aim of the democratic doctrine to introduce into all kinds of business, it has enjoyed from the beginning, Government has never dared to impose a restraint upon it; it has been exposed to the stimulus of competition; it has received favor from all political parties. Whoever may have fancied that he possessed talent enough to undertake a public journal, has been at liberty to do so, and he has had the opportunity of displaying all the enthusiasm and talent that he could bring to the task.

We must look elsewhere, then, for the causes of the singular fact to which we refer. We must look, not so much to journalists themselves, as to the community in which they live. It is because so low a standard has been established in regard to journalism, that so few men of the strongest intellect and character have taken it up ; they have sought distinction in other spheres less influential, but supposed to be more honorable. Because society has not required more, more has not been done. Journalists are what society has made them ; if they fall short of the lofty dignity of their vocation, it is because society falls short in its demands. Johnson, in his prologue, says that "they who live to please, must please to live," which is especially true of the press. It has been regarded as a mere agent for pleasing society, and therefore it has aspired to no higher function. It has failed to perceive its real value ; it has failed in asserting its claims ; it has failed in discharging its duties as an instructor ; it has failed in asserting the moral power of which it is capable.

But its conductors, we repeat, are not so much to blame for this result, as its patrons, as they are called— the public. True, it has been courted by some, and feared by others—courted by the ambitious and feared by the timid : yet, while courted and feared, it has been neglected and despised. Very little discrimination has marked the public judgment of its character. So long as it could be made to minister to prevailing prejudices, so long as it could be turned to the purposes of party, so long as it lent itself to the cause of demagogues, so long and no longer has it met with favor. Discerning, genuine, and hearty approbation for independence, integrity, and talent, it has seldom or never received.

A sort of double and inconsistent conduct has been expected of editors. While they have been solicited to furnish aid to all kinds of partial schemes, they have yet been blamed for a want of fidelity to principle ;

while the whole strength of great parties is brought to bear upon them to secure their aid or crush their opposition, they have yet been derided for suppleness of purpose and pliancy of doctrine ; while every man who has an object to accomplish, besets them with seductions and promises of reward, they have yet been scorned for venality and time-serving. A high unvarying moral test has never been applied to them. When a man of lofty faith and stern virtue has arisen among them, when he has shown a disposition to discuss questions in the light of great principles, when he has refused to listen to the whispers or move at the beck of cliques and factions, when he has regarded politics as the most important branch of morals, and sought to acquit himself of the duties of his calling, with a nice regard to truth and conscience, how has he been received by the community ? As a worthy, noble, fearless man ? As a patriot who deserved well of his fellows ? As a Christian filled with a strong sense of the responsibilities of human existence ? Far otherwise. Hostility and contempt, rather, have been his rewards. His professed friends have dropped away from him ; his enemies have redoubled and sharpened their abuse, until a strong public opinion was aroused against him, and he was compelled in the end, from sheer want of support, to relinquish his pursuit, and seek in some other employment the means of subsistence.

Can we forget the career of the lamented Leggett ? There was a man who, during one of the most exciting and critical periods of our political experience, pursued a line of determined and intrepid honesty. A course of corrupt legislation, openly defended by one party, and connived at by a large portion of the other, had fastened upon the people a system of finance and banking which was fast undermining their liberties and morals. The firm old soldier-statesman, who was then President, more sagacious than many of his supporters, more honest than any of his opponents, had given the first blow to the insidious evil. After a long and desperate contest, he succeeded ; and yet it was only by a partial success. Mr. Leggett, who had stood side by side with him in the most trying positions of the fight, saw, even in the moment of victory, that the triumph was not completely achieved. The enemy, overcome by the energies of the General Government, was still acting in full strength under the protection of the individual States. That enemy, he conceived, was to be attacked in his strongholds there ; instant to his convictions of duty, he began a vigorous assault ; neither persuasion on one hand, nor persecution on the other, could induce him to soften his ponderous blows ; and day after day he aroused the public mind with discussions full of strong thought and eloquent invective. What was the result? Desertion and poverty for the time—to be followed, but not till he was cold in his grave, with monumental honors and eulogy.

The fault, we cannot too often repeat, is with the community. What they ask for, they receive. If their praise and money are showered upon those who pander to a depraved taste, they must expect depraved and worthless writers. But if they will recognize the claims of a better order of men, such an order will immediately arise. There cannot be a demand in this branch of political economy without a supply.

1. The community should require its editors to be intellectual men. By this we mean, men who should possess both power of thought and facility of expression. The first is needed because it is incumbent upon them to grapple with difficult questions ; the second, because they are to make those questions plain to

minds of every cast. All that interests men as members of a social and political body—the measures of parties, the relations of States, the merits of laws, the pretensions of artists, the schemes of projectors, the movements of reformers, the characters of politicians—all are, in turn, themes of newspaper controversy and remark. Politics, international and municipal law, political economy, moral and social science, and the art of reading individual character, must be understood by the editor—and not only understood, but explained. He must have that clear insight into general principles, and that familiarity with details, which will enable him to speak with clearness, originality, and decision.

Topics, moreover, are often sprung upon him with the suddenness of surprise—topics in which are involved the happiness of immense numbers of people, who look to him for information and guidance. His faculties, fully prepared and rightly disciplined, must be at his command. He must stand ready, with argument, with illustration, with eloquence, to awaken the dull, to convince the doubting, to move the inert, and to instruct and interest the more enlightened. But, to do this effectually, he must be at once a patient thinker, a profound scholar, and a practised writer. He must have accomplished his mind by the observation of mankind, by the reading of books, and by habits of quick and appropriate expression. He must, above all, be penetrated by that deep Christian philosophy which estimates all questions in their bearing upon the most exalted and permanent interests of human nature.

2. The community should require of its editors that they be firm and independent men. Force of will is no less necessary to them than greatness of thought. Few men have more temptations to an expedient and vacillating course. Regarded by many, and often re-

garding themselves, as the mere hacks of party, or mere instruments of gratification to prevailing passions, they are not expected to exhibit a fervent zeal in the prosecution of great ends. Like advocates paid by a client to carry a particular point, they are supposed to have fulfilled their obligations when they have made the worse appear the better reason. In many instances, if they have succeeded in embarrassing an adversary, if they have covered an opponent with ridicule, if they have given a plausible aspect to falsehood, if they have assisted a schemer in imposing upon credulous or ignorant people, if they have been faithful to the interests of their employers, they are clapped upon the shoulders as serviceable fellows, and rewarded with a double allowance of governmental or mercantile patronage. The notion that the press has a worthier destiny, seems hardly to cross their minds. That it should become a fountain of truth and moral influence; that it should take its stand upon some high and good principle, to assert it boldly, in the face of all opposition; that it should strive to carry it out with the earnestness of a missionary, with the self-denial of a martyr, despising as well the bribes of those who would seduce it, as the threats of those who would terrify it, acknowledging no allegiance to any power but justice—in a word, be willing to face danger and death in the discharge of duty—is an intrepidity which, we fear, to most of the managers of public journals would seem to the last degree chimerical. Yet it is an end for which they should strive. No less than this should society require of them; nothing less than this can render them worthy of the trust which is committed to their keeping.

3. Journalists, again, must be required to imbue themselves with a just and Christian spirit. Few things are more to be deplored than the low tone, the unkind

feeling which characterizes their intercourse with each other. We do not speak merely of those flagrant violations of decency which degrade the lower class of journals. We speak of the puerility, the violence, and the want of justice, which even the most respectable journals exhibit; we speak of their proneness to distort and to exaggerate, of their recklessness of fair-dealing, of their want of candor, and of their base subservience to particular classes. Indeed, so frequent have been their offences, in these respects, that their dishonesty has almost passed into a proverb. "I only," said Jefferson, "believe the advertisements of a newspaper;" to which another distinguished man added, "and he ought not to have believed them." "He lies like a newspaper," would not be a far-fetched comparison. We are aware that it is urged in extenuation of these faults, that they are to be ascribed to the circumstances of haste and confusion in which daily editors write; we know it is alleged that in other pursuits, law and commerce, for instance, the average honesty, of those who follow them is not greater than that of journalists: but, with all these palliations, with every wish to deal charitably, we must say that a large amount of moral aberration remains against them which admits of no excuse. What! shall we be told, because a man writes in haste, that he must therefore write falsely?—that because lawyers and merchants fall below the standard of virtue, therefore editors should be allowed to do the same,— editors, whose influence is so much more extensive, whose duties are so much more important? It is a shallow defence. Better relinquish their profession forever, than sacrifice to it their integrity. Better drop the pen, and take up the axe or the hammer, than wield the former only to sap and extinguish public morals! No! we demand a more exalted morality at their hands.

When a man assumes to direct the opinions and form the characters of his contemporaries, when he voluntarily places himself in the attitude of a leader of the general mind, he should be compelled, by the force of public sentiment, to cherish habits of the strictest accuracy and honor. We require of the preacher of the pulpit, that he should not degrade his office by inconsistencies of conduct; can we require less of the preacher of the press? Should a Channing, or a Hawkes, or a Dewey, or a Hughes, act in a manner derogatory to their sacred calling, would society overlook it? If a magistrate on the bench pollutes the ermine he wears, do we admit of any apology for his venality or corruption? Should a Tancy, or a Story, or a Baldwin, or the meanest functionary of a county court, accept bribes from the parties to a suit, or be intimidated by popular clamor, or swayed in his decisions by personal feeling, could he avert disgrace? Could any circumstance of his position—press of business, want of time, haste—be pleaded in defence of his crime? Why, then, should we excuse similar defections in those who occupy higher places, and whose truth, consistency, and justice are even more necessary than theirs to the good order, virtue, and happiness of society?

We have spoken freely of the present condition of the press: we have spoken with equal freedom of what it might become. It is in no censorious spirit that we have pointed to its failings: it is with a spirit of benevolence and hope that we have indicated its duty. We are sorry that our strictures are deserved, but we are glad to know that instances exist in which they are inapplicable. It gives us pleasure to acknowledge that within the last few years the character of the American press has greatly improved. Were it not invidious, we could point to editors who, to the best of their ability,

have striven to realize the ideal which we have depicted.
We could refer to a Bryant, foregoing the applause that
the world would willingly render to his great poetic
talent and individual character, to become an example
of the true, accomplished, unyielding editor;—to a
Brownson, who prefers the fame of a candid, fearless
writer, to the seductions of clerical supremacy;—and
to several others, still young and obscure, to whom the
emoluments and honors of professional and political
distinction have no blandishments, in comparison with
those of becoming, as journalists, upright advocates of
all that is good. But our object is not personal. We
wish only to rescue Journalism from its infidelity to
itself, and from the indifference and contempt of the
public. We wish only to assert its claims, to vindicate
its dignity, to exhort it to do its duty.

It is among the cheering signs of the times that
young men of education and talent, who have been
accustomed to crowd the professions of law, medicine,
and theology, are many of them now directing their
energies to the business of editorship and popular instruction. The growing demand for newspapers, for
cheap books, for literary and scientific lectures, is a
proof that the love of knowledge is spreading through
all classes ; that the treasures of philosophy and poetry
are no longer to be shut up in rare caskets, as the possession of the few ; that the general mind, too long
satisfied with low and sensual delights, is seeking
for higher aliment. The mass of men are availing
themselves of the means of improvement which a condition of freedom furnishes, and call for an increased
number of instructors and guides. Many who are
competent to the task are answering the call. Already
they constitute a considerable body. They are marching forward to scatter the seeds of good or evil. It is

important that their movement should take a right direction, for, if they are animated by the right spirit, no one is able to calculate the good that will be accomplished. Let them be true to the cause of liberty, justice, refinement, and progress, and they will give an incalculable impulse to the upward and onward march of society. But let them fail in this, let them be false to their high trusts, and we know of no class of men whose guilt would be more deservedly deep and damning.

JOHN JAMES AUDUBON.*

"That cheerful one, who knoweth all
The songs of all the winged choristers,
And in one sequence of melodious sound
Pours all their music."—*Southey's Madoc in Aztlan.*

 FEW years ago, there arrived at the hotel, erected near Niagara Falls, an odd-looking man, whose appearance and deportment were quite in contrast to those of the crowds of well-dressed and polished figures which adorned that celebrated resort. He seemed just to have come out of the woods. His dress of leather stood dreadfully in need of repair, apparently not having felt the touch of laundress or needlewoman for many a long month. A worn-out blanket, that might have served for a bed, was buckled to his shoulders; a large knife hung on one side, balanced by a long rusty tin box on the other; and his beard, uncropped, tangled, and coarse, fell down upon his bosom, as if to counterpoise the weight of thick, black hair that curled about his shoulders. This strange being, to the spectators seemingly half-civilized, half-savage, had a quick glancing eye, an elastic firm step, and a sharp face that promised to cut its way through the cane-brakes, both of society and the wilderness.

He pushed into the sitting-room, unstrapped his little

---

* From the *Democratic Review*, May, 1842.

burden, looked round for the landlord, and then modestly asked for breakfast. The host at first drew back with an evident repugnance from the apparition which thus proposed to intrude its uncouth form among the genteeler visitors ; but a word whispered in his ear speedily removed his doubts. The stranger took his place among the company, some staring, some shrugging, and some even laughing outright. Yet, there was more in that single man than in all the rest of the throng. An American Woodsman, as he called himself—a true, genuine son of nature, he had been entertained with distinction at the tables of princes ; learned societies, to which Cuvier and his like belonged, had bowed to welcome his entrance ; kings had been complimented when he spoke to them ; in short, he was one whose fame will be growing brighter, when the fashionables who laughed at him, and many even much greater than they, shall have perished. From every hill-top, and every deep shady grove, the birds will sing his name. The little wren will pipe it with her matin hymn about our houses ; the oriole carol it from the slender grasses of the meadows ; the turtle-dove roll it through the secret forests ; the many-voiced mocking-bird pour it along the evening air ; and the imperial eagle, as he sits in his craggy home, far up the blue mountains, will scream it to the tempests and the stars. He was John James Audubon, the Ornithologist.

Mr. Carlyle, in his book about Heroes, has given us the heroic manifestation of human nature in a variety of aspects. He has told us of the Hero as divinity ; of the Hero as prophet ; of the Hero as poet ; of the Hero as priest ; of the Hero as man of letters ; and of the Hero as king. But one species of hero was entirely omitted? He did not recognize the Hero of science ; he did not know that, at the time he was writing, there travelled alone, somewhere in the vast primeval forests of America, a simple naturalist, and yet a character full of manhood and heroic nobleness—possessed of every quality of energy and endurance to be found in the most illustrious of his Great Men? If he did not know it, let us inform him. Let us show him—not after any manner of our own, but from those indubitable evidences, the works of the man himself—that there are heroes of the best sort, even in these dull days. "Heroism," says Mr. Carlyle's fast friend, Emerson, "is contempt for safety and ease,"—"it is a self-trust which slights the restraints of prudence in the plenitude of its energy and power,"—"a mind of such a balance that no disturbance can shake its will, but pleasantly, and as it were, merrily advances to its own music,"—"the extreme of individual nature,"—"obedience to the secret impulses of an individual character,"—"is of an undaunted boldness, and of a fortitude not to be wearied out." If this be a good definition, then our hero is one of the truest of the world's heroes, worthy to be ranked and recorded on the same page with the greatest.

We do not propose to write the biography of Mr. Audubon. There will be time enough for that when his work here shall have been finished.* We wish only to present some phases of his singular and estimable character, as nearly as we can in his own words. Fortunately, he is of a communicative disposition, and we shall not be compelled to wander far for our materials. Those delightful interludes of description and

---

* He has prepared an autobiography, which will be published after his death. What a treat for the readers of that day—that *distant* day, we hope it may be! [This has been published by Putnam & Co. within the past year.]

adventure, that are woven into the woof of his equally delightful sketches of birds, are full of suggestions for us. Would only that our space were equal to the abundance of our means of interest! Would that the dimensions of this publication were consistent with a full display of the simplicity, single-heartedness, enthusiasm, and perseverance of the subject of our brief talk; of that genius, as Wilson has it, "self-nursed, self-refined, and self-tutored, among the inexhaustible treasures of the forest, on which, in one soul-engrossing pursuit, it had lavished its dearest and divinest passion."

Mr. Audubon was born about 1782, in the State of Louisiana, not Pennsylvania, as has been many times stated. His parents, who were French, were of that happy nature which disposed them to encourage the first indications of talent in the minds of their children. They early perceived in the subject of these remarks that love of the woods and fields which has since made him so conspicuous as a naturalist. "When I had hardly learned to walk," says he, in the preface to the first volume of his Ornithology, "and to articulate those first words always so endearing to parents, the productions of nature that lay spread all around were constantly pointed out to me. They soon became my playmates; and before my ideas were sufficiently formed to enable me to estimate the difference between the azure tints of the sky and the emerald hue of the bright foliage, I felt that an intimacy with them, not consisting of friendship merely, but bordering on frenzy, must accompany my steps through life; and now, more than ever, am I persuaded of the power of those early impressions. They laid such a hold of me, that when removed from the woods, the prairies, and

the brooks, or shut up from the view of the wide Atlantic, I experienced none of those pleasures most congenial to my mind. None but aerial companions
suited my fancy. No roof seemed so secure to me as
that formed of the dense foliage under which the
feathered tribe were seen to resort, or the caves and
fissures of the massy rocks to which the dark-winged
cormorant and the curlew retired to rest, or to protect
themselves from the fury of the tempest. My father
generally accompanied my steps; procured birds. and
flowers for me with great eagerness; pointed out the
elegant movements of the former—the beauty and softness of their plumage—the manifestations of their pleasure or their sense of danger—and the always perfect
forms and splendid attire of the latter. My valued
preceptor would then speak of the departure and return of birds with the seasons; would describe their
haunts, and, more wonderful than all, their change of
livery; thus exciting me to study them, and to raise
my mind toward their great Creator. A vivid pleasure shone upon those days of my early youth, attended
with a calmness of feeling that seldom failed to rivet
my attention for hours, while I gazed in ecstasy upon
the pearly and shining eggs, as they lay embedded in
the softest down, or among dried leaves and twigs, or
were exposed upon the burning sand or weather-beaten
rock of our Atlantic shore. I was taught to look upon
them as flowers yet in the bud. I watched their opening, to see how nature had provided each different species with eyes, either opened at birth or closed for
some time after; to trace the slow progress of the
young birds toward perfection, or admire the celerity
with which some of them, while yet unfledged, removed
themselves from danger to security."

Nor did the tastes thus early implanted in the mind of the young enthusiast desert him in maturer years. As Wordsworth chants,

> ———"The sounding cataract
> Haunted him, like a passion ; the tall rock,
> The mountain, and the deep and gloomy wood,
> Their colors and their forms, were then to him
> An appetite ; a feeling and a love
> That had no need of a remoter charm,
> By thought supplied, or any interest
> Unborrowed from the eye."

"I grew up," he continues, "and my wishes grew with my form. These wishes were for the entire possession of all that I saw. I was fervently desirous of becoming acquainted with nature. For many years, however, I was sadly disappointed, and forever, doubtless, must I have desires that cannot be gratified. The moment a bird was dead, no matter how beautiful it had been when in life, the pleasure arising from the possession of it became blunted ; and although the greatest care was bestowed in endeavors to preserve the appearance of nature, I looked upon its vesture as more than sullied, as requiring constant attentions and repeated mendings, while, after all, it could no longer be said to be fresh from the hands of its Maker. I wished to possess all the productions of nature, but I wished life with them. This was impossible. Then, what was to be done ? I turned to my father, and made known to him my disappointment and anxiety. He produced a book of *Illustrations*. A new life ran in my veins. I turned over the leaves with avidity, and although what I saw was not what I longed for, it gave me a desire to copy nature. To nature I went, and tried to imitate her, as in the days of my childhood I

had tried to raise myself from the ground and stand
erect, before time had imparted the vigor necessary for
the success of such an undertaking. How sorely disappointed did I feel for many years, when I saw that
my productions were worse than those which I ventured
(perhaps in silence) to regard as bad in the book given
me by my father! My pencil gave birth to a family of
cripples. So maimed were most of them, that they
resembled the mangled corpses on a field of battle,
compared with the integrity of living men. These difficulties and disappointments irritated me, but never
for a moment destroyed the desire of obtaining perfect
representations of nature. The worse my drawings
were, the more beautiful. did I see the originals. To
have been torn from the study, would have been as
death to me. My time was entirely occupied with it.
I produced hundreds of these rude sketches annually ;
and, for a long time, at my request, they made bonfires
on the anniversary of my birthday."

In his sixteenth year, that is, about 1798, he went to
France to pursue his education. He received lessons
in drawing from the celebrated David. But the "eyes
and noses of giants, and the heads of horses represented
in ancient sculpture," were not the themes he would be
at ; and, although he prosecuted his studies sedulously,
his heart still panted for the sparkling streams and interminable forests of his "native land of groves." He
returned home the following year, with a rekindled
ardor for the woods, and commenced a collection of
designs, destined shortly to swell into that magnificent
series of volumes which the world has applauded as the
" Birds of America." They were begun on a beautiful
plantation which his father had given him, situated on
the banks of the Schuylkill, and near a creek known
as the Perkioming. There, amid its fine woodlands, its

extensive fields, its hills crowned with evergreens, he meditated his simple and agreeable objects, and pursued his rambles, from the first faint streaks of day until late in the evening, when wet with dew, and laden with feathered captives, he returned to the quiet enjoyment of the fireside.

Yet the passion for birds did not seem to seal his heart to the influences of a still more tender and exalted passion. He married, and was fortunate in marrying a lady who in vicissitude has animated his courage, and in prosperity appreciated the grounds and measure of his success. "But who cares," says he, speaking of the event, "to listen to the love-tales of a naturalist, whose feelings may be supposed to be as light as the feathers of the birds he delineates?"

For many years the necessities of life drove him into commercial enterprises, which in the end involved him in a series of losses. His mind, in fact, was so filled with Nature, that all his traffickings proved unprofitable. From observation and study only could he derive gratification. He was compelled to struggle against the wishes of all his friends, who, excepting his wife and children,—to their lasting honor be it said,—strove to wean him from pursuits that, in the world's eye, are so barren and unproductive. These importunities had an effect directly the contrary of what was intended. They only kindled instead of dampening his ardor. He undertook long and tedious journeys; he ransacked the woods, the lakes, the prairies, and the shores of the Atlantic; he spent years away from his family. "Yet, will you believe it," says he, "I had no other object in view than simply to enjoy the sight of nature. Never for a moment did I conceive the hope of becoming, in any degree, useful to my kind, until I accidentally formed acquaintance with the Prince of Musignano (Lucien

Bonaparte), at Philadelphia, whither I had gone with a view of proceeding eastward along the coast." This was the 5th of April, 1824.

Of his public labors we shall speak a word in the sequel ; but for the present, let us follow him in his solitary wanderings. Having lived on his beautiful plantation for ten years, he was induced to remove to the West. With a mattress, a few prepared viands, and two negroes to assist him in the toils of emigration, he departed, accompanied by his wife and child, for a residence which had been procured for him in the village of Henderson, Kentucky. The method of travelling at that day, which he has faithfully described, furnishes a striking contrast to the more easy and expeditious modes of modern conveyance. It was in the month of October that the small party set out. The autumnal tints, he says, already decorated the shores of that queen of rivers, the Ohio, along which they rowed their feeble skiff. Every tree was hung with long and flowing festoons of different species of vines, many loaded with clustered fruits of varied brilliancy, their rich carmine mingling beautifully with the yellow foliage, which yet predominated over the green leaves, reflecting more lively tints from the clear stream than ever landscape painter portrayed or poet imagined. The days were still warm. The sun had assumed the rich and glowing hue which at that season produces the Indian summer. They glided down the river, meeting no other ripple of the water than that formed by the propulsion of the boat. Now and then a large catfish rose to the surface, in pursuit of a shoal of fry, which starting simultaneously from the liquid element, like so many silvery arrows, scattered a shower of light, while the pursuer, with open jaws, seized the stragglers, and with a splash of his tail disappeared from view. At night, the tinkling of bells along the shore told them that cattle were gently roving from valley to valley in search of food, or returning to their distant homes. The hooting of the great owl, or the muffled noise of its wings as it sailed smoothly over the stream, were matters of interest to them ; and so was the sound of the boatman's horn, as it came winding more and more softly from afar. When daylight returned, many songsters burst forth with echoing notes, more and more mellow to the listening ear. Here and there the lonely cabin of a squatter struck the eye, giving note of commencing civilization. The crossing of the stream by a deer foretold how soon the hills would be covered with snow. Sluggish flat-boats were overtaken and passed ; some laden with produce from the different head-waters of the small rivers, that pour their tributary streams into the Ohio ; others, of less dimensions, crowded with emigrants from distant points, in search of "a new home." The margins of the rivers were amply supplied with game. A wild turkey, a grouse, or a blue-winged teal, could be procured in a few moments ; and the voyagers fared well, for, whenever they pleased, they landed, struck up a fire, and, provided as they were with the necessary utensils, easily dressed a good repast.

After jogging on for many days at this rate, they at last reached their habitation in the wilderness. "When I think of these times," continues Mr. Audubon, at the close of his narrative, "and call back to mind the grandeur and beauty of those almost uninhabited shores ; when I picture to myself the dense and lofty summits of the forests, that everywhere spread along the hills, and overhang the margins of the streams, unmolested by the axe of the settler ; when I know how dearly purchased the safe navigation of that river has

been by the blood of many worthy Virginians ; when I
see that no longer any aborigines are to. be found there,
and that the vast herds of elks, deers, and buffaloes,
which once pastured on those hills and in these valleys,
making to themselves great roads to the several salt
springs, have ceased to exist ; when I reflect that all
this grand portion of our Union, instead of being in a
state of nature, is now covered with villages, farms, and
towns, where the din of hammers and machinery is
constantly heard ; that the woods are fast disappearing
under the axe by day and the fire by night ; that hundreds of steamboats are gliding to and fro over the
whole length of the majestic river, forcing commerce to
take root and to prosper at every spot ; when I see the
surplus population of Europe coming to assist in the
destruction of the forest, and transplanting civilization
into its darkest recesses ; when I remember that these
extraordinary changes have all taken place in the short
period of twenty years, I pause—wonder—and, although I know all to be fact, can scarcely believe its
reality."

His new domicil at Henderson gave him ample opportunities for the prosecution of his ornithological inquiries. He was accustomed to make long excursions
through all the neighboring country, scouring the fields
and the woods, and fording the lakes and rivers. He
describes himself as setting out early in the morning,
with no companion but his dog and gun ; the faithful
tin box, containing his pencils and colors, slung to his
side ; now popping down the unconscious warbler that
makes the air vocal from some neighboring tree ; now
hastening to the broad shelter of a venerable oak, to
draw the form and paint the variegated plumage of his
victim ; now crouching for hours underneath some
withered trunk, to observe the habits of some shy and

timid bird ; now climbing the jagged side of a rocky
precipice, to find the nest-eggs of the eagle that screams
and flutters upon the dry top of the storm-blasted beech
still higher up ; now treading upon the head of the
serpent that hisses and wreathes among the thick leaves
of the copse ; now starting the bear and cougar from
their secret lairs in the fastnesses ; now cleaving with
lusty sinew, his gun and apparatus fastened above his
head, the troubled waters of a swollen stream ; now
wandering for days through the illimitable and pathless
thickets of the cane-brake, at night sleeping upon the
hard ground, or across the branches of trees, and by
day almost perishing with thirst ; and now hailing .
with pleasure, at sunset, the distant but cheerful glim-
mer of the lonely log-cabin fire.

The incidents, it may be imagined, of expeditions of
this sort are many and striking : exposed to danger on
every side, by floods, by tempests, by fires, by wild
beasts, and by the hands of man, his life was a perpetual scene of vicissitudes and adventures.   At one
time, in the month of November, he tells us, travelling
through the barrens of Kentucky, he remarked a sudden and strange darkness issuing from the western horizon.   At first he supposed it might be a coming storm
of thunder and rain.   He had proceeded about a mile,
when he heard what he imagined to be the distant
rumbling of a violent tornado.   He spurred his horse,
with the view of galloping to a place of shelter, but the
animal, apparently more sagacious than the rider,
nearly stopped, or rather moved forward slowly, placing
one foot before the other with as much precaution as
if walking on a smooth sheet of ice.   He dismounted
to ascertain what was the matter, when the steed fell to
groaning piteously, hung his head, spread out his fore-
legs, as if to save himself from falling, and stood stock-

still. At that instant, all the shrubs and trees began to move from their very roots, and the ground rose and fell in successive furrows, like the ruffled waters of a sea. It was an earthquake. "Who can tell of the sensations I experienced," he says, "when rocking on my horse, and moved to and fro like a child in his cradle, with the most imminent danger around, and expecting the ground every moment to open, and present to my eyes such an abyss as might ingulf myself and all around me? The fearful convulsion, however, lasted only a few minutes, and the heavens again brightened as quickly as they had become obscured ; my horse brought his feet to their natural position, raised his head, and galloped off as if loose and frolicking without a rider."

At another time, he had just forded Highland Creek, and was entering the tract of bottom land between that and Canoe Creek, when he discovered a hazy thickness in the atmosphere, and apprehended another earthquake ; but his horse did not stop, as before, nor exhibit any propensity to prepare for such an occurrence. He dismounted near a brook to quench his thirst. As his lips were about to touch the water, he heard a most extraordinary murmuring sound in the distance. He drank, however, and as he arose, looked toward the southwest, where he observed a yellowish oval spot, quite new to him in appearance. At the next moment, a light breeze began to agitate the taller trees ; it gradually increased, until branches and twigs were seen falling slantingly to the ground ; and two minutes had scarcely elapsed, when the whole forest was in fearful motion. The noblest trees, unable to stand against the blast, were breaking in pieces. Before he could take measures for his safety, a hurricane was passing opposite the place where he stood. "Never can I forget," says he, "the scene which that moment presented itself. Some of the largest trees were bending and writhing under the gale; others suddenly snapped across; and many, after a momentary resistance, fell up-rooted to the earth. The mass of branches, twigs, foliage, and dust, that moved through the air, was whirled onward like a cloud of feathers, and, on passing, disclosed a wide space filled with fallen trees, naked stumps, and heaps of shapeless ruins, which marked the path of the tempest. The horrible noise resembled that of the great cataracts of Niagara, and as it howled along in the track of the desolating tempest, produced a feeling in my mind which it is impossible to describe."

Nor to the fury of the elements alone was our intrepid man of science exposed. Once—and, singular to say, only once, in wandering for twenty years—was he threatened with death by the hand of man. This was, when returning from the Upper Mississippi, he was forced to cross one of the wide prairies of that region. It was toward the dusk of the evening, when wearied with an interminable jaunt, he approached a light that feebly shone from the window of a log hut. He reached the spot, and presenting himself at the door, asked a woman of tall figure whether he might take shelter under her roof. Her voice was gruff, and her dress carelessly thrown about her person. Answering his question in the affirmative, he walked in, took a wooden stool, and quietly seated himself by the fire. A finely formed young Indian, his head resting between his hands, with his elbows on his knees, was seated in the centre of the cabin. A long bow stood against the wall, while a quantity of arrows and two or three black raccoon-skins lay at his feet. He moved not: he apparently breathed not. Being addressed in French, he raised his head, pointed to one of his eyes with his finger, and gave a

significant glance with the other. His face was covered
with blood. It appeared, that an hour before, in the
act of discharging an arrow at a raccoon, the arrow split
upon the cord, and sprang back with such violence into
his right eye, as to destroy it forever. "Feeling
hungry," Mr. Audubon continues, "I inquired what
sort of fare I might expect. Such a thing as a bed was
not to be seen, but many large untanned bear and buffalo hides lay piled up in a corner. I drew a fine time-
piece from my vest, and told the woman that it was late,
and that I was fatigued. She had espied my watch, the
richness of which seemed to operate upon her feelings
with electric quickness. She told me that there was
plenty of venison and jerked buffalo meat, and that on
removing the ashes I should find a cake. But my watch
had struck her fancy, and her curiosity had to be gratified with a sight of it. I took off the gold chain that
secured it from around my neck, and presented it to her.
She was all ecstasy, spoke of its beauty, asked me its
value, put the chain around her brawny neck, saying
how happy the possession of such a chain would make
her. Thoughtless, and, as I fancied myself in so retired
a spot, secure, I paid little attention to her talk or her
movements. I helped my dog to a good supper of
venison, and was not long in satisfying the demands of
my own appetite. The Indian rose from his seat as if
in extreme suffering. He passed and repassed me
several times, and once pinched me on the side so vio-
lently, that the pain nearly brought forth an exclamation
of anger. I looked at him. His eye met mine; but
his look was so forbidding that it struck a chill into the
more nervous part of my system. He again seated
himself, drew a butcher-knife from its greasy scabbard,
examined its edge, as I would do that of a razor I
suspected to be dull, replaced it, and again taking his

tomahawk from his back, filled the pipe of it with to-
bacco, and sent me expressive glances whenever our
hostess chanced to have her back toward us. Never till
that moment had my senses been awakened to the
danger which I now suspected to be about me. I returned glance for glance with my companion, and rested
well assured that, whatever enemies I might have, he
was not of the number."

In the mean time, he retired to rest upon the skins,
when two athletic youths, the sons of the woman, made
their entrance. She whispered with them a little while,
when they fell to eating and drinking, to a state bordering on intoxication. "Judge my astonishment," he
says, "when I saw this incarnate fiend take a large
carving-knife, and go to the grindstone to whet its edge !
I saw her pour the water on the turning-machine, and
watched her working away with the dangerous instrument, until the sweat covered every part of my body, in
spite of my determination to defend myself to the last.
Her task finished, she walked to her reeling sons, and
said : 'There, that'll soon settle him ! Boys, kill yon
——, and then for the watch !' I turned, cocked my
gun-locks silently, and lay ready to start up and shoot
the first who might attempt my life." Fortunately, two
strangers entering at the moment, the purpose of the
woman was disclosed, and she and her drunken sons
were secured.

But no earthquakes, nor hurricanes, nor carving-
knives of the wild denizens of the desert, afflicted him
half so much as what he once suffered in consequence
of an attack by a wild and ferocious animal—neither
more nor less than—a rat. It was a calamity, the like
of which is seldom recorded in literary history. Edward
Livingston, it is said, having completed his great code
of Louisianian law, beheld the labor of three persevering

years perish in an instant in the flames; Thomas Carlyle, too, when he had finished the first volume of his French Revolution, had every scrap of it burned through the carelessness of a friend ; and so Mr. Audubon, having wandered and toiled for years, to get accurate representations of American birds, found that two Norway rats had in a night destroyed two hundred of his original drawings, containing the forms of more than a thousand inhabitants of the air. All were gone, except a few bits of gnawed paper, upon which the marauding rascals had reared a family of their young. "The burning heat," says the noble-hearted sufferer, "which instantly rushed through my brain, was too great to be endured, without affecting the whole of my nervous system. I slept not for several nights, and the days passed like days of oblivion—until the animal powers being recalled into action through the strength of my constitution, I took up my gun, my note-book, and my pencils, and went forth to the woods as gayly as if nothing had happened." Ay, go forth to the woods, lover of divine nature, with thy serenest hopeful heart ! there is joy there still for thee !—for the whole earth is laughing in its brightness and glory, and the forests re-echo the carols of innumerable sweet voices that call thee to the duty of love.

" There are notes of joy from the hang-bird and wren,
    And the gossip of swallows through all the sky ;
The ground-squirrel gayly chirps by his den,
    And the wilding bee hums merrily by.

" There's a dance of leaves in that aspen bower,
    There's a titter of winds in that beechen tree,
There's a smile on the fruit, and a smile on the flower,
    And a laugh from the brook that runs to the sea."*

---

* Bryant.

He went forth, and in less than three years had his portfolio again filled.

It was in 1824, we remarked, that Lucien Bonaparte suggested to him the idea of collecting and making public the treasures which had been amassed in his wild journeyings. For some time, in the depths of the solitudes, his mind brooded over the thought. At length he resolved upon a visit to Europe, and with that instant action which has been the secret of his success, he prepared for his departure. He sailed—but maturer reflection taught him to approach the shores of England with despondency and doubt. There was not a friend in all the nation to whom he could apply. When he had landed, his situation appeared to him precarious in the extreme. He imagined, he says, in the simplicity of his heart, that every individual he was about to meet might be possessed of talents superior to any on our side of the Atlantic. Traversing the streets of Liverpool for two whole days, he had looked in vain for a single glance of sympathy.

But how soon did the aspect of things around him change ! There are kind, generous hearts everywhere ; men of noble faculties to discern the beautiful and true, and women of warm gushing affections. In a little while, he was the admired of all admirers. Men of genius, the Wilsons, the Roscoes, the Swainsons, frankly recognized his claims ; learned societies extended to him the warm and willing hand of fellowship ; the houses of the nobility were opened to him ; and, wherever he went, the solitary, unfriended American backwoodsman was a conspicuous object of remark and admiration. Under such auspices, in 1831, at Edinburgh, he put forth his first volume of Ornithological Biography. Its striking and original merit procured him subscribers to the remaining volumes, from all parts of the kingdom. At once, he took rank as the most worthy ornithologist of the age,—able as an observer and describer to wear the mantle of the gifted Wilson, and, as a painter of animals, to take his place by the side of the most famous artists.

From England, Mr. Audubon proceeded to France, where he received the homage of the most distinguished men of science of that learned nation ; among the rest, of that gigantic but graceful genius, Cuvier, the glance of whose eye into the great valley of death has infused life into the dry bones of a thousand years.

When he returned to his native land, it was only to renew with a more burning ardor his labors in the woods. His first expedition was to the coast of Florida, where, amid flocks of snowy pelicans and cormorants, tortoises and flying-fish, he laid up treasures for his forthcoming volumes. Having examined every part of the coast, and of the different keys, passing even to the Tortugas Islands, he returned to Charleston, S. C., anxious to bend his course to the northeast, that he might keep pace with the birds during their migrations. Illness detained him for the greater part of the summer at Boston, but having recovered about the middle of August, he left his Boston friends on his way eastward. He explored the whole of the State of Maine, the British province of New Brunswick, a portion of the Canadas, and when there were no more prizes in those districts to carry away, he made his way to the shores of ice-bound Labrador. His researches into the habits of the birds, beasts, and men of this hyperborean region were successful, and he returned, rich with materials, to the abode of his family and friends. Of the industry with which he pushed his inquiries, and of the startling and touching adventures to which his various excursions gave rise, his volumes are full of entertaining and instruct-

ive proof. Our plan does not allow us, as we should
wish, to introduce them here. Let us add, however,
that his Ornithological Biography has expanded into
five large books ; that his "Birds of America" are
finished in glorious style, and that his magnificent
"Illustrations," being those birds drawn to the size of
life, have, for some time, been the astonishment and
delight of the cultivated world. Yet his wanderings
continue, and he labors in the cause of his favorite
science as sedulously as ever.*

What a life has that been of which we have here
given a faint outline ! What a character is that of
which we have made only a rough sketch ! Is not John
James Audubon, as we said in the outset, an admirable
specimen of the Hero as a man of science ? For forty
years or more he has followed, with more than religious
devotion, a beautiful and elevated pursuit, enlarging its
boundaries by his discoveries, and illustrating its objects
by his art. In all climates and in all weathers ;
scorched by burning suns, drenched by piercing rains,
frozen by the fiercest colds ; now diving fearlessly into
the densest forest, now wandering alone over the most
savage regions ; in perils, in difficulties, and in doubts ;
with no companion to cheer his way ; far from the smiles
and applause of society ; listening only to the sweet
music of birds, or to the sweeter music of his own
thoughts, he has faithfully kept his path. The records
of man's life contain few nobler examples of strength

---

* During the last winter, which he spent in this city (New York),
he has worked on an average fourteen hours a day, preparing a work
on the Quadrupeds of America, similar to his work on the Birds.
The drawings, already finished, of the size of life, are masterpieces in
their way, surpassing, if that be possible, in fidelity and brilliancy, all
that he has done before. Early in the summer, he will depart to continue his labors in the woods.

of purpose and indefatigable energy. Led on solely by his pure, lofty, kindling enthusiasm, no thirst for wealth, no desire of distinction, no restless ambition for eccentric character, could have induced him to undergo so many sacrifices, or sustained him under so many trials. Higher principles and worthier motives alone have enabled him to meet such discouragements, and accomplish such miracles of achievement. He has enlarged and enriched the domains of a pleasing and useful science ; he has revealed to us the existence of many species of birds before unknown ; he has given us more accurate information of the forms and habits of those that were known ; he has corrected the blunders of his predecessors ; and he has imparted to the study of natural history the grace and fascination of romance.

By his pencil and by his pen, he has made the world eternally his debtor. Exquisite delineations of the visible and vocal ornaments of the air, drawn with so much nicety, colored with so much brilliancy, as they are seen in their own favorite haunts, who can adequately describe ? We remember well the effect wrought on our mind, when we first saw the whole of his wonderful collection of paintings, as they were exhibited a few years since in New York. It produced an overpowering sense of wonder and admiration. As John Wilson has said of the same scene, shown at Edinburgh, the spectator instantly imagined himself in the forest. The birds were all there, —" all were of the size of life, from the wren and the humming-bird to the wild turkey and the bird of Washington. But what signified the mere size ? The colors were all of life too, bright as when borne in beaming beauty through the woods. There, too, were their attitudes and postures, infinite as they are assumed by the restless creatures, in motion or rest, in their glee and their gambols, their loves and their wars, singing, or caressing, or brooding, or preying, or tearing one another to pieces. The trees on which they sat or sported, all true to nature, in bole, branch, spray, and leaf, the flowery shrubs and the ground-flowers, the weeds and the very grass, all American—as were the atmosphere and the skies. It was a wild and poetical vision of the heart of the New World, inhabited as yet almost wholly by the lovely or noble creatures that "own not man's dominion." It was, indeed, a rich and magnificent sight, such as we would not for a diadem have lost.

A peculiar ease, simplicity, and elegance mark Mr. Audubon's written style. His description of birds in their various moods are not the dull and dry details of a naturalist, but the warm, lively picturesque paintings of a poet. To open at any page of his volumes is to step at once into a region of agreeable forms and enrapturing sounds. He seems to enter into the very spirits of birds themselves, sings when they sing, and rises upon the wing when they fly. And his whole life, like theirs, seems to have been a perpetual and cheerful ascription of praise, to that

> "Power whose care
> Teaches their way along the pathless coast,
> The desert and illimitable air—
> Long wandering, but not lost."

[Parts of this hurried sketch were afterward used in an article I contributed to Putnam's "Homes of American Authors."]

PERCY BYSSHE SHELLEY.*

"A pard-like Spirit, beautiful and swift,
A Love in desolation masked; a Power,
Girt round with weakness; it can scarce uplift
The weight of the superincumbent hour;
It is a dying lamp, a falling shower,
A breaking billow—even while we speak
Is it not broken?"—ADONAIS.

E design to make this work the occasion of
some remarks upon Shelley as a poet and a
man. We think that justice has never yet
been done him. His countrymen are not in a mood
either to apprehend or to confess his value. The gall
of prejudice has not yet passed from their eyes; their
judgments are still warped by old remembrances; and
it is left to posterity and other lands to form a proper
estimate of what he was. No time or place more
fitting for the formation of such an estimate, than this
age of progress and this land of freedom!

Shelley was born at Field Place, in the county of
Sussex, on the 4th of August, 1792. His father was
Sir Timothy Shelley, a gentleman of property and high

---

* The Poetical Works of Percy Bysshe Shelley. By Mrs. Shelley:
4 vols., morocco. London, 1839.
From the *Democratic Review*, December, 1843.

family distinction, who traced his remote ancestry to
the chivalrous and poetical Sir Philip Sidney. As a
child, Shelley appears to have been delicate and sensitive to a painful extreme, ardent in his affections, and
tenderly alive to the influences of nature. The residence of his friends, amid the stillness and beauty of
rural scenes, early impressed him with a love for tranquil and domestic enjoyments. He has himself, in the
Revolt of Islam, touchingly described those aspects of
mankind and nature, which were the first to mould his
young imagination.

> " The star-light smile of children, the sweet looks,
>   Of women, the fair breast from which I fed,
> The murmur of the unreposing brooks,   .
>   And the green light, which shifting overhead,
> Some tangled bower of vine around me shed,
>   The shells on the sea-sand and the wild-flowers,
> The lamp-light through the rafters cheerly spread,
>   And on the twining flax—in life's young hours,
> These sights and sounds did nurse my spirit-folded
>   powers."

These—the friends of his youth, his mother, the
home circle, and the green and sunny looks of outward
nature—were his earliest teachers. He was, under
their mild discipline, gentle, studious, warm-hearted,
and contemplative. The stream of his life flowed on,
like the brooks near which he wandered and dreamed,
in silent and cheerful harmony.

But the placidity of the current was destined soon to
be ruffled by rough winds. His avidity for knowledge,
and the premature growth of his mind, fitted him, at
a greener age than usual, for the preparatory studies of
Eton. When he was sent thither, the trials of his
life began. His career in that seat of learning was a

series of disappointments. Burning with a zeal for truth, and expecting to find companions willing, like himself, to devote days and nights to the pursuit of it, he was mortified to discover that the votaries of learning could be filled with a spirit of worldliness and false ambition. This was the first revulsion which his feelings received ; and the intensity of it was increased when he was made the victim of that disgraceful custom called *fagging*, which compels a certain class of the students to wait as servants upon the others ! Shelley had too much pride and independence to submit to such a degradation. He refused to "fag," and he was consequently treated with arrogance, and even despotism. His spirit, sensitive as it was, was no less firm. Neither the cruel jibes of his fellows, nor menaces of punishment on the part of his superiors, could bend a will whose single law was the self-imposed law of truth. He rejected an obedience which could only be performed at the expense of self-respect. It was not long, therefore, before he was removed from Eton school. He was afterward sent to Oxford College, which he soon found as uncongenial as the school had been. His appearance there must have been like that of a stray beam of light amid the dust and darkness of an old, cloistered hall. Slight and fragile of figure, youthful even among those who were all young, retired and thoughtful, yet enthusiastic, pursuing with eagerness all branches of science, and exploring, with the impetuosity of first impressions, whatever struck his fancy as novel or useful, he found the college only a continuation, on a larger scale, of the school. The selfishness, tyranny, and falsehood which had shocked him at the one, he also found at the other. Was it not natural that he should contract an aversion to the society of his fellows ? Taking no pleasure in the gross and boisterous enjoyments of those about him, he retired to the fellowship of books and his own thoughts. He became enamored of solitary reading, solitary rambles, solitary experiments. Even the necessary usages of discipline grew to be irksome to him. He could not endure the servitude of regular hours and established forms. An overfine notion of freedom brought him in conflict with masters and laws. He was corrected ; but instead of being corrected by gentle methods, he was used with severity and imperiousness. His impatience was not subdued, but aggravated, by this unnecessary rigor, and he passed on to other, and still more offensive acts of independence.

At the same time, his restless desire of knowledge had brought him acquainted with the bold speculations of the French philosophers. As might have been expected in a youth consumed with zeal for freedom and justice, he was convinced by their reasonings and captivated by their promises. He rejected the more commonly received opinions in politics and religion ; but too honest and fearless to hold his new faith stealthily, he openly declared his convictions, and sought to make proselytes to his creed. He was seized with an "ambition to reform the world." He threw down the gauntlet of defiance at the feet of his teachers, and challenged them to an encounter of reason, on such normal questions as the truth of Christianity and the being of a God. A student who thus formally set himself up as a teacher of atheism, which he hurled in proud scorn at the heads of his professors, could not, of course, be tolerated in a secluded academical community. He was again made the subject of discipline, and deliberately expelled from a society whose prejudices he had assaulted, and whose authorities he had wantonly contemned.

This event exasperated and embittered his mind to an extreme of almost madness. He was only. confirmed in his false but sincere convictions by what he esteemed the despotism of his enemies. He came to regard himself as a victim of oppression. He ceased to respect and love those whose main arguments had been force, whose only replies to his appeals were execrations and reproaches, who shut him out from their sympathies, and branded him as a reprobate and a criminal. There was, undoubtedly, much morbid exaggeration in all this—yet it had its effect in driving him further from the religion to which most erroneously it was intended to bring him back. Religion to him no longer wore an aspect of loveliness and charity, but was associated in his mind with falsehood, intolerance, and hatred.

Entertaining such feelings, Shelley was not the man to shrink from giving them definite form and shape. Filled, at the same time, with a sentimental compassion for his fellow-men, he mourned over the injustice, wrong, and misery of human society. He fancied that he everywhere saw the wicked triumphing and the righteous ground to the earth. The whole history of mankind, indeed, struck his fevered sensibilities as one continuous chronicle of woe, want, wretchedness, on one hand,. and of blood-stained tyranny on the other.

> "He heard, as all have heard, life's various story,
>   And in no careless heart transcribed the tale,
> But, from the sneers of men who had grown hoary,
>   In shame and scorn, from groans of crowds made pale
> By famine, from a mother's desolate wail
>   For her polluted child, from innocent blood
> Poured on the earth, and brows anxious and pale
>   With the heart's warfare ; did he gather food
> To feed his many thoughts." *   *   *

In this spirit he composed his first poem, Queen Mab., Although it was not published until several years afterward, and then surreptitiously, it suits our plan to speak a word of it here.

Queen Mab must be regarded as one of the most extraordinary productions of youthful intellect. The author was but seventeen when he wrote it, yet in boldness of thought, vigor of imagination, and intensity of language, it displays the maturest power. Resembling Southey's Thalaba in metre and general form, it is superior to that poem in wild grandeur and pathos. The versification, though often strained and elaborate, is, for the most part, melodious. Its narrative portions are well sustained, while the descriptions are, if we may so express it, hideously faithful. It is easy to perceive, throughout, however, that the writer's ungovernable sensibilities ran away with his other faculties. In the fragmentary state, indeed, in which it is given to us in the later editions, there are long passages which are merely rhapsodical. Yet it has one broad, deep, pervading moral object—a shout of defiance sent up by an unaided stripling against the powers and principalities of a world of wrong. Every page is a fiery protest against the frauds and despotisms of priest and king. Like the outburst of a mass of flame from a covered and pent up crater, it may be regarded as a struggle of nature amid the fiercest wails to escape from oppression. Its irregular convulsive movements, its lurid and dreadful pictures, alternating with passages of mild beauty and soft splendor, seem like the protracted battle of Life with Death, of Giant Hope with Giant Despair. The blasphemy and atheism of it are the tempestuous writhings of a pure and noble spirit, torn and tossed between the contending winds and waves of a heart full of Love and a head full of Doubt.

It was never the intention of Shelley to publish this indiscreet and immature effort of his genius. But the unfortunate notoriety which certain events in his domestic life had procured him, induced a piratical bookseller to give it to the world. When it did appear, he wrote a note to the London Examiner, disclaiming much of what it contained.

The domestic events to which we refer, were his marriage and separation from his first wife. We speak of them only so far as the knowledge of them is necessary to the right understanding of his poetry and character. In very early life—some of his friends say, impelled by interested advisers—he married a young woman, whose tastes he soon found altogether unsuitable to his own, and from whom, after the birth of two children, he separated. A few years subsequent to this voluntary divorce the wife committed suicide ; not, however, before Shelley had united himself to another woman. This woman was one of illustrious birth, being the daughter of Mary Wollstoncraft and William Godwin, and inheriting in some measure the splendid abilities of both parents ; but great as she was in herself, and glorious as were the associations that radiated around her history, there was no defence for their conduct while his first wife lived.

But the most melancholy part of this tragedy was the catastrophe enacted in the court of chancery, under the presidency of Lord Eldon. The children of Shelley's first marriage, to whom he was devotedly attached, were taken from him, on the ground that his opinions rendered him incompetent to provide for their education. This wicked act of tyranny, this shameless violation of the most sacred ties of the heart, filled the cup of Shelley's woe. He never forgave the injustice, but to the hour of his death felt the keen and cruel pangs of the blow.

Shelley, before these events, had been living with his second wife on the Continent. He had already angered his family, and been exiled from their protection and sympathy. It is just, however, to say that this abandonment did not take place without attempts on their part to reclaim him from his errors. One of them made him the offer of an immense fortune if he would enter the House of Commons, to sustain the cause of the Whigs. But he despised alike the money and the motive, preferring the life of an outcast, true to his convictions, to that of the idol of a party, false to his own soul. The spirit which seems to have actuated him on this occasion, was the spirit of his whole life. He held no half-faced fellowship with God and Mammon. What he believed he acted out, leaving to the developments of time the issues of his conduct.

Shelley's first acknowledged poem, Alastor, or the Spirit of Solitude, written in 1815, exhibits his mind in a more subdued state than that in which he must have composed Queen Mab. He was then residing at Bishopgate Heath, near Windsor Forest, made immortal in the early lays of Pope. There, in the enjoyment of the companionship of cultivated friends, reading the poets of the day, and visiting the magnificent woodland and forest scenery to be met with in a voyage to the source of the Thames, several months of health and tranquil happiness glided away. The more boisterous excitability of earlier years gave place to habits of calm meditation and self-communion, while the vicissitudes and disappointments which had already checkered his young life, tempered, no doubt, his exalted hopes and restrained the impetuosity of his zeal.

In Alastor, accordingly, we find the traces of more

mature and deeper inward reflection. It contains none
of those intense and irrepressible bursts of mingled
rage and love, which are at once the merit and defect of
Queen Mab ; but is a quiet and beautiful picture of the
progressive condition of the mind of a poet. It represents, to borrow the language of his preface of 1835,
"a youth of uncorrupted feelings and adventurous
genius, led forth by an imagination inflamed and purified through familiarity with all that is excellent and
majestic, to the contemplation of the universe. He
drinks deep of the fountains of knowledge, and is still
insatiate. The magnificence and beauty of the eternal
world sink profoundly into the frame of his conceptions,
and afford to their modifications a variety not to be exhausted. So long as it is possible for his desires to
point toward objects thus infinite and unmeasured, he
is joyous and self-possessed. But the period arises when
those objects cease to suffice. His mind is at length
suddenly awakened, and thirsts for an intercourse with
an intelligence similar to itself; he images to himself the
being he loves, and the vision unites all of wonderful,
wise, and beautiful, which the poet, the philosopher, or
the lover could depicture." He, however, wanders in
vain over the populous and desolated portions of the
earth, in search for the prototype of his conceptions..
Neither earth, nor air, nor yet the pale realms of
dreams can accord him the being of his ideal love.
Weary at last of the present, and blasted by disappointment, he seeks the retreat of a solitary recess and yields
his spirit to death.

Such is the story of a poem, which, as much, if not
more than any of his works, is characteristic of the
author. It is tranquil, thoughtful, and solemn, mingling the exultation caused by the sunny and beautiful
aspects of Nature, with the deep, religious feeling that

arises from the contemplation of her more stern and majestic moods, and with the brooding thoughts and sad or stormful passion of a heart seeking through the earth for objects to satisfy the restlessness of its infinite desires. Full of a touching and mournful eloquence, the impression it leaves is that of a soft and chastened melancholy.

In the summer of this year Shelley paid another visit to the Continent, where he met Lord Byron, with whom —an "uncongenial spirit"—he spent the greater part of the time on the shores of the Lake of Geneva. He seems to have written little this year, besides a few shorter pieces, among which are the Hymn to Intellectual Beauty, and the Mount Blanc. But the following year he returned to England, and though heart-harrowing events, referred to above, awaited him there, though his sufferings from illness grew more frequent and severe, his mental activity revived. The very weakness that depressed his physical powers, appeared to enliven and incite his brain. Pain, which kept his mind awake and restless, quickened his sympathies with the afflictions of others.

He was established at Marlow, near London, a sequestered abode on the banks of the Thames. He led a meditative and studious life, but his meditations and studies were of a nature unlike those of most secluded scholars, for the claims of his fellow-men were not forgotten. Floating quietly down the stream of the river, under the rich beech-groves of Bisham, or along the exuberant and picturesque meadows of Marlow, his head was filled with the gathering visions, and his heart expanded with the noble affections that were destined to give immortality to the Revolt of Islam. It was finished in little more than six months, and given to mankind.

The "Revolt of Islam," though by no means

Shelley's greatest work, if his largest, is the one which
will endear him most strongly to sympathetic minds. It
is written in twelve cantos of the Spenserian stanza,
and in his first design was to be entitled "Laon and
Cythna, or the Revolution of the Golden City," thereby
implying that it was intended to be a story of passion,
and not a picture of more mighty and broadly interesting events. As he advanced in his work, however, as
the heavy woes of mankind pressed and absorbed his
heart, the mere individual figures, around which the
narrative gathers, dwindled in importance, and he poured
out the strength of his soul in the description of scenes
and incidents involving the fates of multitudes and
races. The poem may have lost in interest as a narrative by the change, but it has gained much as a poem.
It is now a gallery of glowing and spirit-stirring pictures,
painting—sometimes in dim and silvery outline, and
sometimes in broad masses of black and white—"the
most interesting conditions of a great people in the passage from slavery to freedom."

The first canto, like the introduction to an overture,
runs over, in brief but graceful and airy strains, the
grand harmonies that are to compose the burden of the
music. After illustrating with great beauty the growth
of a young mind in its aspirations after liberty, and how
the impulses of a single spirit may spread the impatience
of oppression until it takes captive and influences every
soul, the poet proceeds at once to his topic—the awakening of a whole nation from degradation to dignity ; the
dethronement of its tyrants ; the exposure of the religious frauds and political quackeries by which kings and
hirelings delude the multitude into quiet subjection ;
the tranquil happiness, moral elevation, and mutual
love of a people made free by their own patriotic endeavors ; the treachery and barbarism of hired soldiers ;

6

the banding together of despots without to sustain the
cause of tyrants at home ; the desperate onset of the
armies of the allied dynasties ; the cruel murder and
expulsion of the patriots, and the instauration of despotism, with its train of war, pestilence, and famine. It
then closes with prophecies for the sure and final reign
of freedom and virtue, which may be called the choral
hymn of struggling nations.

In this *argument*, to use the phrase of the older
poets, Shelley had a high moral aim. We refer not
merely to what he himself describes as an attempt "to
enlist the harmony of metrical language, etherial combinations of fancy, and refined and sudden transitions
of passion in the cause of liberality, or to kindle in the
bosom of his readers a virtuous enthusiasm for those
doctrines of liberty and justice, that faith and hope in
something good, which neither violence, nor misrepre-
sentation, nor prejudice can ever totally extinguish ;"
but to that fixed purpose with which he has avoided the
obvious conclusion that an ordinary mind would have
given to the poem. It ends, as we said, with the triumphs of despotism. What Shelley wished to teach
by this, was the lesson, so necessary in that age, when
the hopes of mankind had been crushed by the disastrous events of the French Revolution, that every revolt against the oppression of tyranny, that every struggle for the rights of man, though for the time it might
be unsuccessful, though it might fail in its resistance of
arbitrary power, was, in the end, worth the effort. It
destroyed the sanctity that surrounded and shielded the
dogmas of the past ; it broke the leaden weight of authority ; it kindled fear in the breast of the oppressors,
by awakening among the people a knowledge of their
power ; and it strengthened the confidence of men in
each other, while it filled them with visions and hopes

of the speedy prevalence of a more universal justice and love.

No lesson could then have been more needed by the world. The excesses and apparent failure of the French people had frightened even the warmest lovers of freedom from their early faith. They had scarcely foreseen, in the outset, that the weight of long centuries of oppression could not be thrown off without terrific efforts. At the first demonstration, therefore, that the populace were really in earnest, the flush fled from their faces and they gazed upon the scene aghast and trembling. They were seized with a panic of dread. They deprecated what they had before abetted. To the wild exultation which hailed the opening of the outbreak, there succeeded a feeling of despondency and gloom. The people were no longer the objects of sympathy and hope, but the victims of misgiving and distrust. Men who had once espoused their cause, now doubted their capacity of self-government. An uneasy suspicion was diffused that the principles of liberty and justice, having so signally failed in one instance, were never to be tried in a second.

But in the number of these Shelley was not included. To him, the French Revolution was not a failure. Its atrocities and crimes, so far from diminishing his attachment to free principles, cemented and strengthened it. He saw in every frantic outrage, in every unnatural vice, in the mummeries, the violences, and the excesses, only additional arguments for a milder and more benevolent government. "If the Revolution," says he, "had been prosperous, then misrule and superstition would lose half their claims to our abhorrence, as fetters which the captive can unlock with the slightest motion of his fingers, and which do not eat with poisonous rust into his soul." The evils of that frightful upturning of so-

ciety seemed to him, as they now seem to every observant mind, transient, while the good was durabla.

Under such convictions he prepared his poem. Bold
as it is, in many of the sentiments, it is a noble monument to the loftiness of his aims, the brilliancy of his
imagination, the wealth of love in his heart, and the
breadth and power of his intellect. It is an armory
from which the young enthusiasts of many generations
to come may draw their weapons, in the assurance that
they are of tried temper and exquisite polish. We have
never read it without feeling our soul stirred as with the
sound of a trumpet—it has enlarged our thoughts, expanded and warmed our affections, quickened our purposes of good, and filled us with an unquenchable
flame of philanthropy and love.

In 1818, Shelley left England, never to return.
That divine region, "the paradise of exiles," Italy, became his chosen residence.   Under the influence of its
beautiful climate, and the inspiration of its scenery, his
poetical life seemed to have received a new impulse.
Three subjects presented themselves to his mind as the
ground-works of lyrical dramas : the first, the•touching
story of Tasso ; the second, the woes and endurance of
Job ; and the third, the Prometheus Unbound.   With
the instinct of genius, or led by his growing delight in
the Greek dramatists, he selected the last of the three
as the one best suited to his purpose.   In the very
choice of the subject, he betrays the tendencies of his
nature.   There is not in the whole round of thought
any real or imaginary personage so well fitted to dramatic or epic representation as Prometheus.   The mythology of his existence is the grandest fable that the
human mind ever conceived.   In the Lear of Shakspeare
we behold a grand conception ;—we have a man,—a
noble, towering man—yet passionate and weak,—bat-

tling, heedless of the war of the elements around him, with the wilder storm of emotion in his own breast. Again ; in the Satan of Milton we see the demigod, fierce, defiant, unconquerable, wage a proud strife with the Omnipotent ; but while we pity his fancied wrongs and sympathize with his ambition, the nature of the combat forbids us to applaud his courage, and the exhibition of his envy, falsehood, and revenge destroys our admiration. But in the Prometheus of the ancient fabulists, we behold an Innocent One exposed to the oppressions of evil, for the good which he had conferred upon others ; bearing for ages, without complaint, the tortures of tyranny ; a spirit full of godlike fortitude and hope, warring with the gods ; a calm sufferer, exempt from bitterness or hatred, though sustaining the foulest wrongs that Infinite Power can inflict ; an immortal nature triumphing over mortal pangs ; a moral will rising superior to the agonies of physical torment ; embodied goodness and beauty, recovering from the struggle of centuries of darkness into the clear light of Heaven, and diffusing universal joy through the realms of space.

In the treatment of the ancient fable Shelley has seen fit to alter it so as to adapt it to his more exalted conceptions of the character of its hero. Prometheus, as we gather his story from the ancient writers, was chained to the rock by Jupiter, for having bequeathed to mankind the gift of knowledge. But there was in the possession of the Titan the secret of a prophecy which it much concerned the perpetuity of Jupiter's kingdom that he should know. On condition that this should be revealed to him, he offered the sufferer a full pardon for his primitive crime. The Titan resists, and in the sternness and stubborn power of this resistance, the moral sublimity of the myth consists ; but after enduring the inflictions of the god for ages, he purchases freedom from torture by communicating the secret. This latter part of the fable Shelley rejects. His Prometheus is true to himself to the last, since, to have made him "unsay his high language, and quail before his successful and perfidious adversary," would have been reconciling the champion of mankind with its oppresser. He had a nobler aim—

> " To suffer woe, which Hope thinks infinite ;
> To forgive wrongs, darker than death or night;
> To defy Power, which seems omnipotent ; ·
> To love and bear; to hope till Hope creates
> From its own wreck the thing it contemplates ;
> Neither to change, nor falter, nor repent:
> This was thy glory, Titan ! 'tis to be,
> Good, great, and joyous, beautiful and free,
> This is alone Life, Joy, Empire and Victory !"

It was the lost drama of Æschylus which suggested this poem to Shelley. In the earlier portions of it, where he describes the trials of the Titan, he has imitated the lofty grandeur and solemn majesty of the Grecian master. But to avoid the charge of mere imitation, he has varied the story, and enlarged the groundwork of plot and incident. It would be an exaggeration to say that he had rivalled the sublimity of the Father of the Dramatists ; but it is no exaggeration to assert the moral superiority of his conceptions. He has not the force, the strength, and the awful and imposing sternness of his robust and rugged model—but he has, we think, more delicacy, softness, and elegance. Indeed, the lyrical parts of the drama are only surpassed in graceful ease and harmony by Sophocles. They rise upon the ear like strains of sweet melody, ravishing it with delight, and leaving, after they have passed away, the sense of a keen but dreamy ecstasy. For delicacy and beauty, nothing in the range of verse is finer than the description of the flight of the Hours— not even the imagery in which Ione and Panthea dis- course to each other while listening to the music of the rolling worlds. The whole leaves the impression of a noble oratorio, expressive of the Life of Humanity in its passage from early darkness through pain and strife, through weariness and anguish, to the overflowing joy and sunshine of its maturer development.

During the following year, the tragedy of the Cenci appeared. It has since attained so wide a popularity, and been so often criticised, both in England and among the Germans, that we shall have little to say of it in this place. It has more of direct human interest in it than any other of the author's poems, but, like all the rest, it serves to display his character. His keen insight into the workings of the human heart—his dread of evil—his hatred of oppression—and above all, his quick sympathy with the delicate and graceful emo- tions of the female nature, are exhibited in language of unsurpassed fidelity and force. Through all the developments of the terrible story there appears a lofty, moral aim, not taught, as is the case with Euripides, in formal declamations, but as Shakspeare teaches—by the unfolding of an actual life—as if a curtain were lifted suddenly from before an actual scene, to reveal all the actors in their living and breathing reality. As in the Prometheus, he had shown what Will could ac- complish under the dominion of Love ; so in the Cenci he showed what that same Will could do when under the adverse guidance of subversive passions. The elder Cenci is the personification of unbridled Will. Rich enough to indulge every desire, and yet purchase im- punity for every crime, the old human father, opposing his own will, in bursts of tremendous and fearful rage, to the will of the Almighty Father, becomes thereby an incarnation of all that is inhuman.   What a dreadful contrast is drawn between his demoniacal spirit and that of his angelic daughter, Beatrice, the lovely, sincere, high-minded woman, formed to adorn and grace the most exalted position, but bearing about a load of remediless griefs, of unparalleled sorrows !   She is purity enveloped in a cloud of falsehood and strange vice.   Herself sportive and serene, yet the victim of unnatural crimes and endless woes.   "Around her are the curtains of dread fate—no lark-resounding Heaven is above her—no sunny fields before her—no passion throbs in her breast"—but

> " The beautiful blue Heaven is flecked with blood.
>   The sunshine on the floor is black !   The air
>   Is changed to vapors such as the dead breathe
>   In charnel houses ;"

and the wronged though beautiful maid is cut off from life and light in youth's sweet prime.

We must here close our remarks upon Shelley's separate poems, and proceed to give our opinion of his general character as a poet.   Let it suffice to say of what he has written at a date subsequent to that of the poems to which we have referred, that he everywhere manifests the same general powers, enriched by experience and use.   We should like to have spoken in detail of the "Rosalind and Helen," that touching tale of the sufferings of woman ; of the " Hellas," in which he celebrates the revival of the ancient spirit of Grecian freedom, with much of the spirit of the old Greek lyrical poets ; of the "Adonais," so full of pensive beauty ; of the spiritual " Prince Athanase ;" of the wild " Triumph of Life ;" of the " Ode written in dejection at Naples,"

most pathetic of the lyrics of melancholy; of the
" Hymn to Intellectual Beauty," so high and grand in
its invocations ; of the "Skylark," in the profusion and
melody of which the author rivals the bird he sings ;
and, no less, of those translations from the Greek,
German, and Spanish, which are among the best specimens of that kind of composition in the English language ; but our space will not suffer us to engage in
this agreeable task.

What, then, are the claims of Shelley as a poet ?
This is a hard question to answer in the case of any
poet, and particularly hard in that of Shelley. His
poetry, like his life, is set round by so many prejudices,
that it is with difficulty the critic preserves his mind
from the influence of common opinion on one side, or
the exaggeration of a reactive sympathy on the other.
Shelley's faults, too, are so nearly allied to his excellences, springing as they do, for the most part, from the
very excess of his intellectual energy, that the task of
discrimination is felt to be an embarrassing one. Aside
from these considerations, besides, there were some
notable and obvious defects in the very structure of his
mind. These are shown partly in his use of a peculiar
language and diction, but chiefly in the excessive subtlety of his thought. Words were often used by him,
not in their common or obvious meaning, but in a
sense derived from remote and complicated relations.
He indulges in such phrases, for instance, as the
" wingless-boat," meaning thereby, not a boat without
wings, which would be commonplace enough, but a boat
propelled by some mysterious power beyond the speed
of flight. Again, because of this over-refinement and
too great delicacy of perception, his descriptions are often
strangely unreal. They seem to be enveloped in a hazy
wavering atmosphere, as if they were not actual scenes,

but the combinations of a remembered dream. One does not look upon them, as he looks upon living nature, when he stands face to face with her beauty; but they are seen through a gauzy medium of memory, like places which may have impressed the mind in the earliest period of its consciousness. They strike us, in the same way as those views which come suddenly upon us, when travelling in strange lands, as something which we have seen before, but of which we know neither the time nor place. It may be objected further, that his imagery possesses too much of dazzling glare and splendor. It is seldom sufficiently subdued for the nature of the subject. This fault, however, is the common fault of young artists. Their pictures are all in warm colors. We believe it was Sir Thomas Lawrence who was accustomed to say to his pupils, put out the lights. Some such monitor should have stood over the writing-desk of Shelley. His many-colored fancy needed frequent chastisement. Arrayed in gold and fire, the objects of it were made to flame, like the forest which lies between our eyes and the horizon, when both trunks and leaves are lit up by the evening sun.

But a greater fault of Shelley's poetry is the obscurity of which so many readers complain. His more enthusiastic admirers, we are aware, answer, that as much of this obscurity may lie in the minds of the readers as in the mind of the poet ; and they answer with no little truth. Yet we think that Shelley is chargeable on this score, and chargeable because the fault springs from a misuse of some of his highest powers. It takes its origin from two peculiarities—from the exceeding subjectivity of his mind, of which we have just spoken, and the exquisite delicacy of his imagination. What we mean by his subjectivity is the disposition to dwell upon the forms and processes of inward thought and emotion, rather than upon those of the external world. Shelley no doubt loved the external world ; he was ever living in the broad, open air, under the wide skies ; and was keenly alive to the picturesque and harmonious in Nature. But his emotional power dominated his intellectual power. He was thus ever proceeding from the centre of his own mind, outward to the visible universe. He was ever transferring the operations of his feelings to the operations of Nature. Of this tendency he was not himself unaware. " The imagery which I have employed," he says in the preface to Prometheus, "will be found, in many instances, to have been drawn from the operations of the human mind, or those external actions by which they are expressed." An appropriate instance of this we have in the same poem, where the avalanche is compared to the thought, not the thought to the avalanche, reversing the usual process of comparison. There is a class to whom this kind of comparison may appear natural, but to the larger number of men, and those even intellectual men, it is, to use a vulgar adage, putting the cart before the horse ; it is illustrating the known by the less known ; it is an attempt to make an object clear and intelligible, by comparing it with that which is not clear and intelligible.

This is one cause of Shelley's obscurity ; but a more frequent cause is the excessive subtlety and refinement of his imagination. So keen was his intellectual vision, that he saw shapes where others saw none, and shades and distinctions of shade where, to others, it was blank vacuity or darkness. He possessed, in an eminent degree, that faculty which peoples the universe with tenuous and gossamer existences, which sees a faëry world in drops of dew, which sports with the creatures of the elements, which is of finer insight and more spiritual texture than the brains of ordinary mortals.

If Shelley has erred in the excessive use of this faculty, we are also indebted to it for some of the most beautiful conceptions that ever adorned the pages of poetry.

But we pass from the faults of Shelley to a rapid consideration of his excellences. One of the first things to be observed in entering upon the topic, is the elevated conception which he had formed, and always strove to carry with him, of the true function and destiny of the Poet. The vocation of the bard impressed him as the highest of all vocations. " Poetry," says he, in a glowing passage of an exquisite prose composition, " poetry is, indeed, something divine. It is at once the centre and circumference of knowledge : it is that which comprehends all science, and that to which all science must be referred. It is at the same time the root and blossom of all other systems of thought; it is that from which all spring and that which adorns all ; and that which, if blighted, denies the fruit and the seed, and withholds from the barren world the nourishment and the succession of the scions of the tree of life. It is the perfect and consummate surface and bloom of all things ; it is as the odor and color of the rose to the texture of the elements which compose it, as the form and splendor of unfaded beauty to the secrets of anatomy and corruption." Again he says : " Poetry is the record of the best and happiest moments of the happiest and best minds"—" Poetry turns all things to loveliness. It exalts the beauty of that which is most beautiful, and it adds beauty to that which is most deformed ; it marries exultation and horror, grief and pleasure, eternity and change ; it subdues to union, under its light yoke, all irreconcilable things. It transmutes all that it touches, and every form moving within the radiance of its presence is changed by wondrous sympathy to an incarnation of the spirit which it

breathes : its secret alchemy turns to potable gold the
poisonous waters which flow from death through life ;
it strips the veil of familiarity from the world and lays
bare the naked and sleeping beauty, which is the spirit
of its forms."

In this spirit Shelley composed his own poems. It
would be absurd to rank him among the highest of the
great English poets as an artist, although it would not
be absurd to put him among the highest in other respects. We do not mean that he was altogether deficient as an artist, but we do mean that the qualities of
the artist were not those which predominated in him.
The opening chorus of Hellas alone, not to refer to
other instances, would prove that he possessed great
artistic capabilities ; yet the same poem, not to mention others, would also prove that these capabilities
were smothered beneath his exuberance of thought and
imagery. So, the skilfulness with which he has used,
in Prince Athanase, the *terza rima* of the Italians, and
in the Witch of Atlas, the stanza of Pulci, show how far
he could have been successful in the region of mere
art, but he would not submit his chainless impulses to
the laborious discipline of Art. When the leisure and
humor for such discipline allowed, his minor lyrics betray no want of the most dexterous and versatile power
to perfect ; but in general, he impetuously tramples
upon the finer laws of creative effort. Like an improvi-
satore, he gives the rein to his fancy, and dashes wildly
onward wherever the bewildering trains of thick-coming
associations may lead. He was mastered by his genius,
rather than master of it, as Homer, Dante, Shakspeare,
and all the greater poets were masters.

Shelley's fertility of imagination, however, was no
less a part of his strength than it was of his weakness.
As Mr. Macaulay, in his beautiful essay on John Bun-

yan, finely says : "Out of the most indefinite terms of a hard, dark, cold, metaphysical system, he made a gorgeous Pantheon, full of beautiful, majestic, and life-like forms. He turned atheism itself into a mythology, rich with visions as glorious as the gods that live in the marble of Phidias, or the virgin saints that smile on us from the canvas of Murillo. The Spirit of Beauty, the Principle of Good, the Principle of Evil, when he treated of them, ceased to be abstractions. They took shape and color. They were no longer mere words ; but 'intelligible forms,' 'fair humanities,' objects of love, of adoration, or of fear. Some of the metaphysical and ethical theories of Shelley were certainly absurd and pernicious. But we doubt whether any modern poet has possessed in an equal degree the highest qualities of the great ancient masters. The words bard and inspiration, which seem so cold and affected when applied to other modern writers, have a perfect propriety when applied to him. He was not an author, but a bard. His poetry seems not to have been an art, but an inspiration."

It was chiefly in the glow and intensity of his sentiments that the vast fusing powers of his imagination were manifest. His heart, burning with the purest fires of love, seemed to melt all nature into a liquid mass of goodness. Over the wildest and darkest wastes of human experience he cast the refulgence of his own benignant nature, as the many-colored rainbow glorifies the dark bosom of the thunder-cloud. Out of the rankest poisons he extracted the most refreshing of sweets.

> ———— "Medea's wondrous alchemy,
> Which, wherever it fell, made the earth gleam
> With bright flowers, and the wintry boughs exhale
> From vernal blossoms fresh fragrance,"

was his ; and from the exceeding fulness of himself he poured out into the mighty heart of the world a perpetual stream of life. No poet that has come after him, and few that were gone before him, had equal power of stirring within the soul of humanity such noble aspirations—such fervent love of freedom—such high resolves in the cause of virtue and intelligence—and such strong prophetic yearnings for the Better Future.

In the earlier part of his career, as we have seen, he had been touched by the spirit of skepticism and despair, which was the malady of those times. He sent up to heaven, from a heart full of anguish, a keen and infinite wail—as the wail of a vast inarticulate multitude without God and without Hope in the world. But through the rifted clouds of the night he saw, more clearly than any contemporary, the dawnings of the day. With jubilating voice he prophesied its glories. While the capacious genius of Scott was exhausting its energies in rummaging the magazines of a forgotten past, to amuse the fancy, or beguile the languor of children, both great and small ; while Byron, like a lubberly boy, was whining and scolding over his self-inflicted and petty miseries—Shelley, with dauntless heart and kindling eye, wrestled in the wild, frightful conflict of incoherence and discord, struggling upward, till he stood upon the mountain-tops of the century in which he lived, watching the dying agonies of the decrepid Old Order and hailing the swift approaches of the New.

As a man, Shelley seems to us to have been worthy of both admiration and love. He exhibited a rare combination of all that was tender with all that was noble and daring. Like his own Alastor, he was "brave, gentle, and generous." The delicacy and refinement we are accustomed to ascribe to the female nature were

united in him to the impetuous boldness of the masculine.   A life of early suffering,—of intense and protracted illness,—had trained his spirit to those passive
virtues of endurance and gentleness which often best
illustrate the greatness of the human soul.   Except in
wisdom and knowledge, he never ceased to be a child.
He carried into manhood the same guileless simplicity,
the same ardent enthusiasm, the playful innocence, the
meekness, the modesty, and the truth, which were the
characteristics of his boyhood.   Time did not blunt the
sharpness, nor the delusions of the world corrupt the
purity, of his keen and lively sensibilities.   No seductions nor wrongs could warp his judgment from the
perfect law which seems to have been impressed upon
his inmost nature.   He was ever the same unspotted,
mild, genial, sensitive, yet lion-hearted being.   All
who approached him loved him, and all whom he approached he loved.

> " 'Mid the passions wild of human kind,
> He stood like a spirit calming them."

Not only did he bear himself manfully amid the rude
shocks and pitiless struggles in which he was destined
to walk, but his heart melted with pity and love for the
world that hated him, and his purse was ever the open
response to his sympathy.   As deep as were his personal
griefs, he did not forget the deeper grief of his race.
He was the ready friend of the friendless, the instant
helper of the distressed, the companion, no less than
the benefactor of the poor.   In the halls of the rich
and gay he singled out the despised and deserted, and
wherever he went he identified himself with the multitude.

This singular kindliness appeared in the minutest as
well as the greatest actions of his life.   It was the grace of

his manner no less than the virtue of his heart. Lord
Byron once said that Shelley was the completest gentleman he ever knew. He was regardful of the happiness of others, not always showing it in the vulgar way,
by relieving their distresses, but by consulting all their
shades of feeling. At the same time he was not un-
mindful of the larger and broader manifestations of
good-will. A never-ceasing course of active effort
showed that his benevolence was not a sentiment but a
principle. It was both good-wishing and good-doing.
He who could walk the wards of a hospital, filled with
dangerous diseases, that he might qualify himself to
minister to the maladies of the poor, must have possessed, not the sickly sentimentalism of Rousseau, but
the philanthropy of a Howard. He who could·give
the half of his whole income to a single work of charity
(the building a dyke to prevent inundations upon the
huts of a poor settlement), must have possessed a genuine sympathy. He who, when his funds where exhausted, could pawn his books, or favorite instruments
of science, to help a needy scholar, to cover a naked
child, or give warmth and plenty to the hearth of a
destitute widow, and be more careful to conceal his
deeds from the world than others are to publish them,
was actuated by no theatrical love of display, but by a
sincere and heartfelt fellow-feeling with his race.

It was a consequence of this exalted benevolence
and conscientiousness that the political principles of
Shelley were intensely democratic. It does not appear
that he had digested those principles into a system, or
that he had matured his notions into practical measures,
but every act and sentiment of his life shows him
friendly to every reform by which freedom is to be
extended or the condition of the multitude of men improved. In all the efforts of the masses, particularly to

shake the tyranny of the aristocratic classes, he felt the strongest sympathy.   When the oppressed workingmen of England manifested a determination to throw off the despotism of their laws, he was their fast friend ; when the Italian republics seemed about to make a stand against their despoilers, he was raised to a pitch of enthusiasm in their behalf ; and when the Greeks appealed to his mind by the double attraction of their glorious literature and history, and their equally glorious resistance to the murder-breathing Moslem, he shared the dreams of their heroes, and made their struggle immortal by his pen.   The noblest fires of his spirit were kindled by every cry of the oppressed against the oppressor.

Nor did he confine his love of freedom to its external and grosser forms.   The peculiar splendor of his career as a democrat was, that he fought the battles of intellectual freedom.   He was the vigilant enemy of spiritual slavery and degradation.   Others were content to resist the encroachments of power, only when it invaded plain and palpable rights—when it robbed men of property, or trampled upon their persons.   But Shelley pursued it with hatred—in its most secret lurking places, as well as in the open air, in the recesses of the soul, as well as in the despotisms of the State.   He dreaded tyranny of any kind less because it produced social unhappiness than because it crushed the human mind.   It was there that he hated it most, and it was there that he most resolutely resisted its approaches.

Shelley was, furthermore, a democrat because of his hopeful nature.   It was the habit of his mind to look forward to the future with bright and expanding anticipations.   In casting his eye over the arrangements of society, he saw what prodigious advances it was capable of making in all the dispositions of trade and social intercourse, and in all the departments of knowledge, and he saw no reason why these advancements should not be made. He believed that they would be made. He believed that a glorious development awaited humanity, when it should cast off its ancient superstitions. So, in every attempt of the people to break through the thick night of ignorance that enveloped them, in every throe of the nations to snap the chains by which they were bound, his fancy discerned the beginnings of this more than millennial glory. His soul leaped with joy at the faintest flash of the coming light. An iris of hope was ever stretched across his horizon.

Yet Shelley's, it must be confessed, was far from being a perfect character. His judgment was always too much overborne by his excitabilities. His mind wanted that repose which is the emblem of the highest power. His efforts were consequently too convulsive— more like the throes of a hampered giant than the calm and sustained efforts of a Hercules. It is evident that he never had settled, to the satisfaction of his mind, the theories of the Universe, Man and God, which perplex and disturb all thoughtful persons. He was still struggling doubtfully when he died, with the great problem of existence. He questioned earth and heaven, to relieve the weary doubts of his soul, but they made him no response. At length he appealed to the soul itself for a reply. Then, over the mists of the dark conflict, rose the rainbow of Hope in the form and aspect of Love. This, he cried in the agony of his distress, shall be my God ; Love is the soul of the universe ; Love explains all mysteries ; Love comprehends all beauty ; Love is the splendor of truth ; Love is the consummation and flower of all things. Love is the highest power—Love is God.

Shelley was not a Christian in the technical sense, but

he was essentially a religious man, not an atheist, but rather, like Spinoza, "intoxicated with God." From the gross form of materialism in which he—like all other students of the English universities of that day—was educated, his etherial nature had led him into the idealism of Berkeley. His latter works are all, more or less, tinged by the subtle and delicate colors of the spiritual theory. It penetrated and modified all his conceptions. His Supreme Being was not, like the venerated object of the grosser superstitions, a person of human foibles and passions—the mean and miserable worshipper projected out of himself and magnified— but a pure, self-existent, intellectual, and moral Spirit, a spirit of infinite Truth and Love. The world apparent to our senses, was but an inconsiderable unit in the measureless creation of which this Spirit was the substance and centre. All human spirits were but separable portions of a stupendous whole, bound to each other by myriad sympathies and infinite desires, and passing, in the successive stages of existence, to higher forms of thought, and keener and nobler emotions. Death, in this view, was not destruction, but the passage or rather melting away into a better Life. The forms and organs which reveal us to each other, he thought, drop away at death—our bodies fade from our vision—but the spirit remains in a congenial world, intelligent, impassive, and unshackled. All things that it loved are still around it, but it is no more the victim of space and time. It has joined the company, and lives in the presence of the Immortals, dwelling in that spiritual world which enwraps the more material and visible sphere of our present being.

But there was a cause still more powerful, though more remote, in determining the mind of Shelley to Infidelity, as it is called. It was the prevailing Christian philosophy of the era. The disciples of Locke had long held possession of the schools. Their dogmas were generally received for the truth. Locke himself was a Christian in theory and practice, but the intellectual system of Locke was not Christian. His firm faith in the Scriptures, his experimental knowledge of their truth, prevented him from carrying his doctrines out to their ultimate conclusion. He lived, therefore, and died a Christian. But not so many of his immediate followers. They received the seed he had sown in no Christian hearts. There were no obstacles to prevent them from pushing, indeed it was inevitable that they should push, his doctrines to their more ultimate principles. Condillac, in France, when he propounded his system of sensualism, borrowed it directly from Locke. Hume, of England, more consecutive and more acute than the rest of Locke's disciples, only developed, although it may have been unconsciously, the principles of their common master. The long controversy, which took place in England in the time of Shaftesbury, respecting the truth of the Christian Religion, was a controversy that grew out of the system of Locke. The champions of Christianity fought under a disadvantage. Their philosophy and their religion were at variance. To go into the fight against infidelity, with weapons drawn from the magazine of Locke's philosophy, was to fight with a broken reed and a battered sword. The infidels had the best of the battle, until some superior minds, perceiving the folly of their philosophy, cut loose from its untenable grounds, fought for Christianity on its own merits, and turned the tide of victory. It is the misfortune of Locke's system, as Cousin has shown, that its three great theories, of Freedom, of the Soul, and of God, lead, by inevitable consequence, to Fatalism, Materialism, and Atheism. Now,

Shelley, though he had logical power enough to follow
the system of Locke to its inferences, like the other
men of that day, did not have sagacity enough to
detect the falsehood of its premises. ˙ He was .only
more fearless than other thinkers in giving a public
expression to his opinions.   Too pure in heart to compromise with fraud and wrong in any shape, and too
noble to harbor even the wish to conceal his sentiments, he at once proclaimed his opposition to Christianity.

   Yet, be it borne in mind, it was the Christianity of
tradition and the Old Church that incurred his hatred.
The misfortune of our beneficent religion is, to have had
its glory obscured in all ages by the absurd and repulsive dogmas of its teachers, and by the follies and vices
of its friends.   At no single period of its existence, since
its heaven-commissioned founder was nailed to the awful
tree, have its external aspects conformed to its inward
spirit ; at no period have the lives of its votaries corre-
sponded to the high, divine, and eternal ideal which it
was intended to reveal.   Its history has been a record
of selfish pretentions, absurd creeds, and pernicious
practices.   From the close of the first˙ century down to
the present time, how often has the Church been the
theatre of disgraceful broils and wicked persecutions !
Under the dynasty of the earlier Romanists, indeed, the
Church became the nursing-mother of fraud and tyranny.
She crushed the human soul,—she aspired to make good
her aspiration to universal despotism by fagot and
flame.   And when her high claims, in this respect, were
contested—when the giant-monk of Erhfurt brought in
the solemn protest of the enslaved soul, the new sects
that sprung up upon her ruins were filled with much
of her intolerant and persecuting spirit.

It is true, there was much at all times to redeem the character of Christianity, in spite of its abuses and corruptions. But this, unfortunately, consisted in those virtuous influences which escape the eye of the world, which do not force themselves upon the public observation, and whose presence, indeed, is never recognized until after they have wrought their effects. While Christianity, in its external aspects, presented features of dread and repugnance, it was silently regenerating the world. Even when its professed teachers and friends were most unfaithful to it, it was the great centre of moral and civil elevation. It was working, with the might of God, in secret places and among obscure men, the overthrow of oppression. But the Free Thinkers were blind to this aspect of its history. It was their misfortune to have identified religion with the external Church. Their sensibilities were arrested by the mockeries and wickedness of the latter, without being touched by the pure and beautiful benignity of the former. Most gross and fatal mistake !

But we must tear ourselves from the subject : our space, already exhausted, warns us that we can make only the briefest allusion to the circumstances of Shelley's death. He perished during a storm on the Gulf of Lerici, in the 29th year of his age. It was a death in singular correspondence with his life ; and in the closing stanza of his Adonais, suggested by the untimely death of Keats, a friend and brother-spirit, he seems to have had prophetic glimpses of his fate. He says :

> "———— my spirit's bark is driven
> Far from the shore, far from the trembling throng,
> Whose sails were never to the tempest given ;
> The massy earth and sphered skies are riven !

I am borne darkly, fearfully afar;
Whilst burning through the inmost veil of Heaven,
The soul of Adonais, like a star,
Beacons from the abode where the Eternal are."

His remains rest beneath the mouldering walls of
Rome—the sepulchre of his ashes and the shrine of
our sincerest sympathy.

THE LAST HALF-CENTURY.*

HE half-century which has just closed has been one of prodigious movement and significance. Seldom, if ever, has the world seen a fifty years of equal moment. Every day of it almost has teemed with great events—with events not of transient or local, but of deep and world-wide interest. Those years have been fertile also in great men, and not in any single walk of human exertion, but in all departments, —in literature, philosophy, war, statesmanship, and practical enterprise.

Doubtless, in the eyes of Providence, to which a thousand years are as one day, all periods of human history are alike,—of equal weight or equal nothingness. But to Man, who is controlled by the events in which he lives, all periods of history are not alike. Each age has its distinct character, is adverse or propitious to him, pushes on or retards his civilization, his refinement, his progress in knowledge and art, and his practical conquests in the realms of space and time. For this reason history is divided into epochs or eras, of which we speak as good or bad, as ages of light or of darkness,—as ages when our race seems to have been kept back in its course or impelled onward and upward.

The last half-century, therefore, we call an age of

---

* From the New York *Evening Post*, Jan. 1st, 1851.

great moment and significance—because it has been a
time of grand events—a destructive, and yet a prolific
period—in which so many things have gone out and
so many other things come in, so many horrible errors
and prejudices been killed, and so many new and
beautiful truths born—that mankind, we believe, to the
end of their days, will rejoice in this period. They
will turn to it in after ages, as we now turn to the age
of the Greek dramatists, to the Apostolic age, to the
age of Shakspeare, to the Reformation, to the scientific years of the sixteenth century, etc., as to a great
fructifying season of the race—when humanity was more
than ordinarily genial, and shot up into new growths and
blossomed into a more luxuriant bloom. Its mighty
political changes, its varied and novel discoveries in
science, its stupendous applications of art, the richness
and universality of its literature, the spread and ramifications of its trade, and the lofty moral enterprises it
has begun, are the characteristics of its eminence—the
tokens and titles of its glory.

I. POLITICAL CHANGES.

The year 1800 opened with Napoleon Bonaparte, first
Consul of France.   Beginning his career as a subaltern
officer in the armies of the republic, that extraordinary
man had risen, by one brilliant achievement after another, to the highest posts of command.   He had given
a finishing stroke to the tumults of the old revolution ;
he had conducted a campaign against the Austrians in
Italy, in which he imparted new terrors and new glories
to war, and by triumphant victories at Montenotte, Mil-
lissimo, Castiglione, Dego, Arcola, and Rivoli, by the
unprecedented passage of the bridge of Lodi, and by
the masterly siege of Mantua, established his position

as the greatest military genius of all time. Elevated by intrigue and stratagem to consular power, with colleagues that were merely his tools, and an authority that was almost despotic, he professed at first to exercise his functions with moderation and justice. He made overtures of peace to England, with which France had been so long at war ; but the ministry of Pitt, distrustful of his sincerity, and elated by the recent triumphs of Nelson, on the Nile, repelled his advances, and prepared for a general European conflict.

Then followed those movements of armies more tremendous than Europe had before known, in which the forces of Russia, Prussia, Austria, and England, combined for the overthrow of a single man, were successively repulsed. Millions of men were precipitated upon the field of battle, and a series of brilliant exploits, at Marengo, at Austerlitz, at Wagram, at Jena, at Eylau, gave the military chieftain almost universal dominion. He reconstructed society abroad, and remodelled the laws at home ; he subdued dynasties that had been founded for centuries ; he dethroned monarchs by edict ; he seated his brothers upon the most ancient thrones, and caused the whole world to tremble at his nod.

But with his unexampled successes came also unprecedented disaster. The foolish expedition into Egypt, the offensive war on the peninsula, where Wellington worsted his best Marshals, the gigantic but insane invasion of Russia, which ended in the conflagration of Moscow, the awful retreat from the burning city, where every step was marked by the bones of thousands who perished of cold and famine, the final overthrow at Waterloo, and the lonely imprisonment at St. Helena, were the leading incidents in a drama of stupendous grandeur and catastrophe.

The effect of these immense adventures, of these signal triumphs and woeful calamities, was to derange the despotic system that had prevailed, to break down the prestige of kings, to emancipate the smaller States from the oppressive weight of the larger, to accustom the people to the exercise of their forces, and to establish new relations among the powers of Christendom. Europe was prepared for new organizations; the leading sovereigns, no longer able to manage the affairs of their respective kingdoms, entered into a Holy Alliance for mutual protection and general tranquillity. They parcelled out countries, they partitioned nations, they divided races, with as much arbitrary exercise of command as was ever shown in the regulations of a camp, and in complete disregard of tradition, nationality, and popular feeling. The consequence was, a perpetual uneasiness on the part of the people, and a perpetual struggle on the part of power, to retain its position and to enforce its rule. The thirty years that followed the Congress of Vienna, though nominally years of peace, have been at no time exempt from war. The disorders in Spain, the insurrections of Piedmont and Naples, the revolt of Belgium, the dethronement of Charles X. in France, with the revolutionary agitations that grew out of it, and finally, in 1848, the overthrow of French monarchy, the establishment of a republic, and the general uprising of the whole continent, when kings fled and the Pope abdicated, and the entire aristocratic system began to totter and reel like a vessel struck by opposing winds, were the direct outgrowths of the false and tyrannic constitution adopted in the treaties of 1815.

In the midst of these grander perturbations two new powers, that had before exercised but little influence on the politics of Christendom, were silently rising—Russia and the United States. The former, at the opening of the present century, was only regarded as an immense unknown tract of country, inhabited chiefly by boors and savages. It is true, that the fame of Peter the Great and of Catherine had spread through Europe; that the vigorous wars kept up for years along the shores of the Baltic, in which Sweden was conquered, and an obstinate series of skirmishes with the Ottomans and Turks, had demonstrated great military resources; but, until the attempt to subjugate Poland, and the war against Napoleon, Russia was estimated rather as an Asiatic than a European power. Now, she is the predominant influence among the absolute governments. Her territory, embracing one-seventh of the globe, is possessed by fifty-four millions of people, with inexhaustible resources of wealth, a disciplined army of one million soldiers, extensive manufactures and commerce, a rapidly increasing civilization, and the most ambitious hopes.

The other nascent power to which we refer, also just beginning to be known in 1800—the United States—is now second to none. The five millions of people of that time have grown to twenty-five millions; the fifteen States of the Union are now thirty-one; a superficial area of territory, then measuring one million of square miles, is now nearly four millions; and a commerce which was then small, precarious, and timid, now reaches every sea and every extreme river and lake of the globe. We had then no possessions on the Gulf of Mexico, and none beyond the Mississippi, but our landmarks now are the two oceans. The developments of agricultural industry have been enormous; a single seed alone, that of cotton, has come to control the trade of the world; three successful wars and a skilful diplomacy have given us fame abroad; those great political questions which have deluged the old world for centuries in blood, are here practically determined ; an experiment of the most unlimited popular freedom is triumphantly sustained ; while the progress of intelligence, industry, peace, and general good-will sets at naught all the previous experiences of the race.

Coeval with the immense changes in the political state of Europe, and with the rise of Russia and the United States, there have been great results effected elsewhere. The South American republics, though still unsettled, have by successive throes cast off colonial bondage, and redeemed a continent from foreign dominion. Modern civilization has penetrated into Egypt, Algiers, and other parts of Africa ; Persia feels the pressure of Christian intelligence and liberal art ; and while England, through the ramifications of her trade, has built up an empire of one hundred and fifty millions of souls in the East, who are subjected to her laws and her civilization, she has discovered and peopled a fifth division of the globe, in Australia. Battering down the barbarian walls of China, she has carried trade, refinement, law, and religion to more than one-half the race. The wild tribes of the desert, the furious savages of the south seas, the wandering herdsmen and hunters of India, as well as the stolid denizens of the Flowery Land, have been breathed upon by the influences of a higher life ; they are arrested and brought face to face with a nobler social order ; vanquished by its strength or reduced by its skill, they are made to feel its superiority ; and thus, in various ways, ignorance, brutality, prejudice, horrid faiths, and oppressive castes are giving way before the gradual advances of knowledge, art, and social discipline.

II. LEGISLATIVE REFORMS.

The spirit of progress manifested on the continent of Europe in violent overturnings and changes, has shown itself among the freer people of England, in a grand reform of laws and institutions. This movement was begun at the close of the last century, in those trials for constructive treason, in which Tooke, Thelwall, Hardy, and others figured, when the eloquence of Erskine exploded the absurd maxims of constructive guilt, and established the right of Britons to free speech, against the combined influence of king, ministry, and judges. The discussions that grew out of those trials gave a new meaning to the law of libel and sedition, to the rights of juries, and to the liberties of the subject. The total abolition of the slave-trade, not long after, was another great gain to the cause of humanity. It brought into the ascendant, in the first nation of the earth, such men as Sharpe, Clarkson, Wilberforce, Fox, Stephen, Macaulay (father of the essayist), and Brougham, whose humaner sentiments and progressive tendencies have been infused into general opinion. Their efforts again prepared the way for those legal reforms in which Bentham, Romilly, Macintosh, and Brougham won an undying renown. The common laws of England, but especially the penal codes, with all their good features, were yet atrociously severe, bloody, and unjust. Hundreds of the most trivial minor offences could be punished with death ; stealing a fish, marrying a couple out of church, maiming cattle, transporting wool, pulling down turnpike-gates, etc., were placed in the same category with murder, arson, and rape ; counsel were not allowed to prisoners, even in cases of high treason ; while the penalties prescribed were barbarous, and the poor wretch condemned in any capital case, might be dragged to the place of execution at the heels of horses, might be quartered, might be embowelled, might be slit in the nose, or have his skeleton left hanging on the gallows to rot. But, thanks to the wonderful sagacity and courage of Bentham, to the indefatigable parliamentary labors of Romilly, to the stately eloquence of Macintosh, and the sledge-hammer logic of Henry (not then *Lord*) Brougham, the crueller features of these provisions were mitigated or removed. At the same time, the fearful abuses of Chancery were purged, the perfidies of the courts exposed, useless forms retrenched, old and oppressive processes superseded, the statutes consolidated, and a considerable number of titles codified. It was in reference to these ameliorations that Brougham said, citing the boast of Augustus, that he found Rome brick and left it marble,—"How much nobler the sovereign's boast, when he shall have it to say, that he found Law dear and left it cheap, found it a sealed book and left it a living letter, found it the patrimony of the rich, left it the inheritance of the poor, found it the two-edged sword of craft and oppression, and left it the staff of honesty and the shield of innocence !"

The struggle between Right and Prescription, thus begun in the sphere of criminal law, was extended even within the domain of religious prerogative. The bishop's mitre, like the monarch's crown—the gown of the churchman, as well as that of the lawyer and judge—were subjected to the same rigid scrutinies of reason and justice. Those venerable strongholds of bigotry, the Corporation and Test Acts, were the first of the "bulwarks erected to secure the Established Church," as Blackstone described them, which fell before the modern assault. That no person could be legally elected to certain offices without having previously taken the sacrament of the Lord's Supper in the forms of the

Establishment, or that all military and civil functionaries should have declared against the doctrine of transubstantiation, were adjudged to be political tests so unreasonable, so intolerant, and in their practical working so pernicious—levelled, as they were, equally at Protestant dissenters and Catholic recusants—that, after a series of stormy and protracted debates, they were blotted forever from the records.

III. LITERARY ASPECTS.

How many and what brilliant names pass before us when we recall the literary history of the period of time under review? As we hurriedly travel down the vista, it seems as if our eyes swept the heavens when the night is glorious with stars. Each object is in itself a world, radiating from its single centre beams of many-colored light, while the whole, gathered into constellations, or poured along the skies in galaxies, floods the air with its illumination. Scott, and Wordsworth, and Byron, and Shelley, and Keats, and Southey, and Coleridge—and what multitudes of others, of scarcely inferior genius: Goethe, the Schlegels, Tieck, Heine, Hoffman, Freiligrath, Tegner, Chateaubriand, De Staël, De Genlis, Hugo, Lamartine, Sand, Guizot, Thierry, Michelet, Sismondi, Manzoni, Carlyle, Macaulay, Dickens, Thackeray, Hood, Emerson, Irving, Bryant, Hawthorne, and a host of lesser lights, many of them gone out, but the most of them still active in their various spheres of influence ! Who shall compute their numbers ; who estimate the amount and variety of the intellectual wealth they have contributed to the common treasury of the world ; or who describe the extent and intensity of the delight they have spread ?

Modern literature, while it has degenerated in but a single branch, falling short in its dramatic efforts, of the splendid execution of the Greek dramatists and of the noble vigor and pathos of the age of Shakspeare, has yet made the most rapid advances in almost every other.   In the art of writing history, Niebuhr, Guizot, Arnold, and Macaulay have little to learn from Herodotus, Thucydides, and Tacitus.   Esthetics, or artistic criticism, has reached a depth of insight, and a breadth of critical principle which show an immeasurable superiority ; while the century may be said to have originated the style of periodical writing, and the infinite fecundity of prose fiction.   It is true, there had been Guardians, Spectators, Gentlemen's Magazines, and Critical Reviews, before the establishment of the Edinburgh Review (1802), but they were mere penny whistles of thought and criticism compared with the trumpet blasts of our recent quarterlies.   It is true, also, that Cervantes, Rabelais, Le Sage, Boccaccio, Bunyan, Defoe, Swift, and Fielding had written stories before the mighty Wizard of the North began to pour out of his inexhaustible fount, that series of tales in which he almost rivals Shakspeare in the creation of character, and surpasses Lope De Vega in fertility of invention.   But the peculiar distinction of our time is, that while those immortal narrators illustrated at distant intervals, and each by himself, the age in which he lived, the fruitful effort of Scott was but the beginning of an activity that has gone on widening and extending its influences, until novels have become an article of daily production and daily luxury.   Every well-educated man or woman is a reader of them ; and almost every well-educated man or woman a writer.   Expatiating over every subject—illuminating history, science, government, and religion, as well as the manners and customs of all classes of the people—invading all realms of earth and air, and, at times, even the bottomless abysses, they have opened new worlds of thought and sentiment, and purveyed to millions of minds an infinite diversity of nourishment and pleasure.

But, in addition to this rapid and multifarious development of certain kinds of writings, our age has witnessed the creation of an almost entire national literature. Germany, which in literary productiveness and vigor is now the foremost nation, was scarcely known to the rest of Europe at the beginning of this century. Saving Luther, and a few other reformers, her writers were mostly of a jejune and imitative class, who withered under an emasculate dependence on Roman and French models. But with the advent of Wieland, Lessing, Herder, and especially of Goethe and Schiller—nearly all of whose efforts date since the French revolution— her literature has expanded until it has finally become the most fruitful source of modern culture. In any one year now, it produces more sound learning, more useful science, more genuine criticism, and more beautiful fiction than it was usual to produce in whole centuries before.

Another striking peculiarity in the literary history of the time is, that literary men of different nations are becoming more and more acquainted with all that is grand or beautiful in their respective productions. The barriers of ignorance which formerly separated them are thrown down, and they begin to regard themselves, for the first time, as a real Republic of Letters, consecrated to the loftiest purposes, and laying up for all mankind an indestructible inheritance of Beauty and Truth. No Père Bowhours, as Carlyle says, now inquires whether a German can possibly "possess a soul;" no Voltaire ridicules Shakspeare as a huge *Gilles de*

Foires, or drunken savage ; no English critic describes Goethe or Schiller as mere master-workers in a great stagnant pool of indecency and dulness. The once ex- clusive treasures of the nations are thrown open to com- mon possession, and the mind of each people, confessing the characteristic worth of all the others, finds everywhere traits of excellence and nobleness. It finds that we all live by one human heart, and are advancing in differ- ent ways to the same great goal of human elevation.

Yet the tendencies of modern literature are shown quite as strongly by another fact, which is, that it aims to become universal, both in the subjects it han- dles and in the persons to whom it is addressed. It seeks for its materials, as its recipients, on every side ; no longer confined to a narrow list of time- consecrated themes, it expands itself to broader and more general interests. It has learned the inestimable secret, that no object in the universe is unworthy of note, that nothing which concerns the human heart is either low or trivial or commonplace. It sees that every sprig which falls to the ground is connected with that won- derful Tree of Life, whose roots, ramifying through the earth, make the solid foundation of the globe, while its branches, growing year by year, reach up to the top- most Heaven. It sees that every emotion in the mean- est human soul is the emotion of an infinite spirit, sus- ceptible of an infinite happiness or infinite fall. It rev- erences the whole of Nature ; but, above all, it sympa- thizes with the whole of Man. It strives to reveal the beauty and the grandeur there is in all existence ; and to show how rich in delight and nobleness are the lowly and the habitual, even more than the lofty and distant. Behind the realities of daily routine and toil, we are made to see an exhaustless ideal world, glorious in en- chantments and fertile with every joy. Our homes and poorest social duties are filled with dignity, and our mother earth, trodden and trailed in the dust as she has been, raised to her proper place among the planets of the skies.

Consider, again, the unexampled rapidity with which literature has been diffused ! Consider that the nineteenth century has been the teeming age of the printing-press—the age of cheap books and cheaper newspapers —the age when infant, and Sunday, and ragged, and free, and classical schools, have taught multitudes of all classes to read. In Germany alone any year's book fair would exhibit more new publications than was contained in many an ancient world-famous library. One leading publisher now will often have upon his shelves a larger variety of books than would have supplied the reading of the world a century ago. Every day the groaning press pours out its thousands of volumes. Not light, trashy, or worthless works ; on the contrary, the best specimens of the best literatures of all ages. The choicest treasures of ancient art—the ample tomes of the learned eras—the sacred classics of England's ripest period—books of science, of research, of antiquities, of criticism, of philosophical inquiry and theological disquisition—mingled with an overwhelming profusion of travels, biographies, essays, poems, novels, pamphlets, and tracts—are issued and reissued till one wonders how the world contains them all. What books fail to hold, overflows into the periodical and the newspaper. A single print now will circulate among its fifty thousand subscribers, and be read daily by twice that number of persons ; yet there are hundreds of these penny prints. A single religious society will send the words of Paul or John to a greater number of minds in seven days than Paul or John could have preached to had they preached incessantly for seven times seven years.   All the pulpits in the city do not address, once a week, a congregation as large as that daily addressed by half a dozen editors.   So swift and prolific, in short, are the multiplying energies of the press, that it alone would have placed the people of the Nineteenth Century in possession of a power more tremendous than was ever before wielded by our race.   .

IV. SCIENTIFIC DISCOVERIES.

It is in the sphere of physical science that this activity of the modern mind has been most conspicuously displayed.   The achievements here have been signal and resplendent indeed, surpassing those of all previous time, and conducting our race to the verge of discoveries still more comprehensive and wonderful.   We are already so accustomed to acknowledge the truth of its vast deductions—we have come to receive their general principles as so unquestionable, that it seems to most of us they must have been always known.   We can hardly believe that it is within the memory of men still young that the most important doctrines of Astronomy, of Geology, of Optics, of Mineralogy, of Chemistry, of Zoology, of Comparative and Fossil Anatomy, of Paleontology, of Magnetism, of Electricity, of Galvanism, of Actinism, etc., have been first published.   That the world should have been ignorant of so much, and got along with its ignorance, is surprising ; and it is still more surprising that such an accumulation of facts as now compose the body of the sciences, should have been gathered within so short a period of time.   But so it is. Nearly all that we know of the natural sciences, as contradistinguished from the mathematical and moral sciences, has come to us from the explorations, experiments, and reasonings of the last fifty years.   Some of them have originated entirely within that time ; others have been so extensively developed, as to be regarded as almost new ; while others, in which the direct progress has been less, have reached a precision and exactitude in their details, that have placed them, for the first time, on a fixed and certain basis.

The leading principles of astronomy, for instance, were ascertained by Copernicus, Kepler, Newton, Huygens, and others, centuries since ; immense tables of observation had been constructed by the old astronomers, the size and distance of several planets measured, a consistent theory of the stellar universe attained, and knowledge of the heavens almost indefinitely enlarged. Yet a philosopher of their days—were it Newton himself—would scarcely comprehend the latest treatise on the subject, without preliminary study. For hundreds of acute and patient minds, in the constant investigation of the movements of the heavenly bodies, have added fact after fact to the knowledge then reached, until the whole aspect of astronomical science has changed. Eleven new planets, and three new satellites have been added to our system, their dimensions and orbits calculated, and their relations to other bodies explained. The distance of the fixed stars, which was once thought to be an impossible problem, has been measured, and some of those stars, inconceivably remote as they are, weighed. A new system of binary and trinary stars, with their positions, their motions, their periodical brightness, have been discovered, and the law of gravitation shown to prevail among them, linking them to our own simpler system. A large number of comets, with their precise paths ; immense circles of meteoric bodies, with their periodical changes ; and Kirkwood's recent law, which binds the entire system in harmony, have been added to our knowledge.

Kepler predicted that between the orbits of Mars and Jupiter, a large planet ought to be found, and, strange to say, the very opening of the present century was illustrated by the discovery of four small planets, Ceres, Pallas, Juno, and Vesta, occupying the very place anticipated. Ceres, the first of these, was discovered by Piazzi, at Palermo, in 1801 ; Pallas, the second of them, by Dr. Olbers, of Bremen, in 1802 ; Juno, the third, by Mr. Harding, in 1804 ; and Vesta, the fourth, by Dr. Olbers, in 1807. After the discovery of the third, Dr. Olbers suggested the idea that they were the fragments of a planet that had been burst in pieces ; and, considering that they must all have diverged from one point in the original orbit, and ought to return to the opposite point, he examined these parts of the heavens, and thus discovered the planet Vesta. But though this principle was in the possession of astronomers, nearly forty years elapsed before any other planetary fragment was discovered. At last, in 1845, Mr. Encke, of Driessen, in Prussia, discovered the fragment called Astræa, and in 1847 another, called Hebe. In the same year, Mr. Hind discovered other two, Iris and Flora. In 1848, Mr. Graham, an Irish astronomer, discovered a ninth fragment, called Metis. In 1849, Mr. Gasparis, of Naples, discovered another, which he calls Hygeia ; and, within the last three months, the same astronomer has discovered the eleventh fragment, to which he has given the name of Parthenope. "But human genius has been permitted to triumph over greater difficulties. The planet Neptune was discovered before a ray of its light had entered the human eye. By a law of the solar system just disclosed, we can determine the original magnitude of the broken planet long after it has been shattered into fragments, and we might have determined it even after a single fragment had proved its existence.

This law we owe to Daniel Kirkwood, of Pottsville, a humble American, who, like the illustrious Kepler, struggled to find something new among the arithmetical relations of the planetary elements."

"In passing from our solar system to the frontier of the sidereal universe around us," says Sir David Brewster, "we traverse a gulf of inconceivable extent. If we represent the radius of the solar system, or of Neptune's orbit (which is 2,900 millions of miles), by a line two miles long, the interval between our system, or the orbit of Neptune, and the nearest fixed star, will be greater than the whole circumference of our globe—or equal to a length of 27,600 miles. The parallax of the nearest fixed star being supposed to be one second, its distance from the sun will be nearly 412,370 times the radius of the Earth's orbit ; or 13,746 times that of Neptune, which is thirty times as far from the Sun as the Earth. And yet to that distant zone has the genius of man traced the Creator's arm working the wonders of his power, and diffusing the gifts of his love—the heat and the light of suns—the necessary elements of physical and intellectual life. It is by means of the gigantic telescope of Lord Rosse, that we have become acquainted with the form and character of those great assemblages of stars which compose the sidereal universe."

In these instances we speak of a science which began many centuries ago, and which was supposed at the end of the last century to be almost perfect. How much more striking the advances of the mind in sciences which were then unknown ! Geology, but barely heard of in the fanciful conjectures of Buffon, Hutton, Whiston, etc., has since been erected into a distinct department of knowledge. It embraces millions of well-observed and carefully recorded facts ; it has arrived at the most impressive and startling generalizations; and it has laid bare the history of the globe for thousands of years. All continents, islands, seas, coal-pits, and oceans have been explored by its devotees, and it is rapidly advancing to a confirmation of a beautiful theory of the material universe. Public encouragement has been conjoined with private enterprise in the prosecution of its objects; the leading governments of Europe, and most of the States of the Union, have sent out expeditions to facilitate its researches; and there is no considerable portion of the globe, except at inaccessible heights or depths, or among barbarous nations, where the geologist has not been at work with his hammer and spade.

Half a century ago huge bones were dug out of the alluvion; the forms of reptiles, fishes, and shells were embedded in the solid rocks; gigantic ferns and other tropical plants were found among the coal strata, but they attracted little notice and had no name. Now the classification of the fossil world is well-nigh as complete and exact as that of existing life. The fossil species, animal and vegetable, discovered and classed, amount to nearly ten thousand; and the additions continually made to this number, not merely tend to complete the series of these remains of former conditions of the earth, but often even fill up the *lacunæ* or gaps in the forms of animal life around us. The Memoir of Owen on British Fossil Marine Reptiles is a striking example of what has been done in a single subdivision of the subject. The results obtained by this eminent naturalist from microscopic examination of the internal structure of teeth, are further curiously illustrative of that strictness and minuteness of research which have been extended to every part of comparative anatomy, as well of fossils as of existing animal life. And yet more remarkable in this light are the discoveries of Ehrenberg among the fossil Infusoria, showing conditions and changes of animal life before unknown ; and the production, from the silicious or calcareous coverings of those microscopic beings, of aggregate masses of some of the hardest rocks forming the crust of the globe.

The same may be said of all departments of mineralogy and Natural History, whose students have spread like a net-work of observers over the whole face of the earth, diligently laboring without cessation in the collection of materials or in the description of nations, and transmitting to great central depositories the results of their labor, which, when they are once got together, are arranged and classified into an instructive and beautiful order. The gigantic labors of Cuvier, St. Hilaire, Edwards, Kirby, Spence, and ten thousand others, have mainly fallen within the present century.

In respect to Natural History, it is stated, that owing to increased zeal and enterprise of naturalists—favored, indeed, by facilities of travel before unknown—the number of distinct species collected and classified within the last twenty years, has been nearly doubled in every class. We might particularize the ratio of increase of each, but will merely state as instances, that the Mammalia, numbered in 1828, by Cuvier and Desmarest, at seven hundred, now reach nearly one thousand two hundred ; the Fishes, estimated somewhat earlier, by Lacépède, at two thousand, are now increased to about eight thousand ; while the Insects, calculated by Humboldt, in 1821, at forty-four thousand, have at this time reached the amount of more than one hundred thousand collected species ! A profuse variety in the forms of animal life, scarcely less confounding to the imagination than are the numbers by which we measure the heavens, or record the velocity and vibrations of light. We might draw from the progress of Botany instances not less remarkable, did our limits allow of such detail.

The foundations of chemistry were laid by Black, Fourcroy, and Lavoisier, during the latter part of the last century; but its most substantial acquisitions and most rapid advances are owing to the law of definite proportions, revealed by Dalton, in the year 1803, and extended and conformed by Berzelius, Wollaston, Gay-Lussac, and their successors. This has given a mathematical basis to chemical affinities, and enabled experimenters to get deeper into the secrets of nature than they ever before penetrated. That all bodies, in their interior structure, had a fixed and invariable composition, that they would combine and replace each other in determinate proportions, of weight or volume, that these proportions could be expressed in numbers, whose ratios could be arranged in certain simple series of multiples so as to yield numerical formulæ instead of vague tables of names—these were the pregnant truths which presented the key to nature, and unlocked the storehouses of a vast knowledge. It showed that one great law, capable of numerical statement, lay at the base of all material phenomena, determining the relations of the invisible atoms of matter, and the largest visible globes, and subjecting the minutest as well as the grandest portions of creation—the mote in the sunbeam as well as the sun itself—to the most precise and unchanging expression. That compound bodies should unite together in multiples of their combining proportions, as well as in single equivalents, was an almost inevitable inference from the same law. But when our knowledge in that direction was further extended by the discovery of Isomerism, which showed that the same elements combine in exactly the same proportions, yet produce compounds of different chemical properties,—and by Isomorphism, or the fact that the chemical elements of certain bodies may be arranged in groups so related together, that when similar combinations are formed from elements belonging to two, three, or more of them, such combination will crystallize in the same geometric forms,—new floods of light were thrown into the darker recesses of Nature.

To enumerate the results of these doctrines would be to write a complete history of chemical science—to describe all its important decompositions of gases, earths, and alkalies—to expound its manifold combinations, whereby it has produced so many new substances, unknown in nature, and giving to it an almost creative dignity—to unfold its reductions of various gases into the liquid or solid form, to explain the phenomena of catalysis and of compound radicals, and to expatiate over the endless field of organic chemistry, which the daring and brilliant Liebig has cultivated with such fruitful results. It is enough to say, that every part of the material world has been subjected to the crucible or the retort, and made to give up its secrets, while the mysterious streams of life itself, in the animal economy, are ascended almost to their source.

In electricity, the relation of which to lightning was disclosed in the well-known experiment of Franklin toward the close of the last century, the first grand impulse was given by Volta, in the year 1804, and was followed by Oersted's experiments in magnetism, and the identification of the electric and magnetic forces as one element. The further determination by Faraday of the identity of voltaic and animal electricity, and his recent researches on electric induction, electrotyles, and the measurement of electric power, have opened new and fertile questions, and carried the sciences forward to the most brilliant practical applications, and the verge of astounding developments.

"In optical science, the discoveries of Young, Fresnel, Malus, Brewster, and others scarcely less eminent, as to the diffraction and interference of light—double refraction and polarization in its several forms and incidents—the phenomena connected with the optical axes of crystals, and other properties of this great element—gave a sudden impulse and new directions to the inquiry which the genius of Newton had originated. The undulatory theory of light, fortified by these discoveries, became the means of carrying them yet further ; affording anticipations of unattained results—as in the case of the conversion of the plane polarization of light into the circular—which it was the province of the most refined experiment to justify and realize. And when Arago found it possible, through certain phenomena of polarized light, to determine by a mere fragment of Iceland crystal, whether the light of comets is their own or not, and whether that of the sun is from its solid body, or a gaseous envelope around it, it was evident that we were entering into the midst of principles and relations of the highest order. About the same period the several phenomena of the solar spectrum, ascertained by the elder Herschel, Wollaston, and Frauenhofer, laid a foundation for those more extended and delicate researches which have rendered the investigation of the solar beam, in its whole complex constitution, but particularly in its chemical relations and application to photography and thermography, one of the most interesting problems in physical science, the complete solution of which is yet reserved as a triumph for future inquiry."*

---

* See an article in the *Edinburgh Review,* on the " Present State of the Physical Sciences" (from which we have merely condensed these facts and illustrations), for a more extended history of scientific discovery.

Let us take Meteorology as another example—a part of our knowledge still very imperfect, from the number of elements conjointly concerned, and the complexity of all the phenomena, yet how entirely altered from its state forty years ago! With instruments far more perfect, and at innumerable stations over the face of the globe, the most minute and authentic registers are now kept of the weight, temperature, and humidity of the atmosphere—of its electrical and magnetic conditions—of the direction, velocity, and duration of winds—of the quantity of rain falling—and of the meteoric phenomena which more irregularly affect our planet, either from causes proper to itself, or from external agents in its orbital passage through space.

Physical Geography, too, even in the early part of this century, was not an object of systematic study. It is now pursued with all the ardor that characterizes scientific research; has attained the most beautiful and comprehensive results; and fairly illuminates our earth, and with it the whole social history of man, by the splendor of its various generalizations. The magnificent Physical Atlas of Johnson, recently published, is an admirable evidence of the indefatigable activity with which it has been prosecuted.

We might further speak of the various discoveries regarding Heat, as it comes to us in the solar ray—as it exists in planetary space—as it is present in the interior of the earth—and as it acts, or is acted upon by the various forms of matter, in reflexion, absorption, radiation, conduction, polarization, etc.;—researches begun by Black and Leslie; extended under high mathematical formulæ by Fourier; and by the elaborate experiments of Dulong, Melloni, and others, carried forward to new and unexpected results. We might yet further allude to the physiology of animal and vegetable life,

where the attainments have been equally remarkable;
bringing all sciences to bear upon vital phenomena—
better defining the types of form and structural development—substituting cellular for vascular action in em-
bryology and the formation of tissues—applying chemistry to objects, and through methods, heretofore untried,
classifying anew the structure and functions of the
nervous system, and from every side approaching nearer
to the mysterious springs of life.

We might also refer to the series of observations—
not yet science—made by the followers of Gall and
Spurzheim on the anatomy and functions of the brain ;
to those wonderful manifestations of Animal Magnetism, which are too well authenticated as facts to be denied, though not yet referred to any satisfactory laws ;
to the gradual amelioration and improvement of medical science, and the diffusion everywhere of better notions as to life and health ; but that we have scarcely
space to indicate the existence of what are deemed certain sciences, and cannot, therefore, refer to those which
are yet unacknowledged by the majority of the established authorities in such matters.

Many branches of science, it is true, are yet in their
infancy; they are only employed in the collection of facts,
and in the preparation ·of individual isolated results.
But this is the necessary course of all sound induction :
it begins with observation ; it concludes with principles.
All sciences at the outset are mere accumulations of details.   But in the course of time, the efforts of scientific
explorers take another direction.   They see that their
work is not separated from that of others ; that all the
objects of their study are more or less directly connected ;
that one can scarcely advance without the other ; that
discovery in any one throws light upon the path of the
others ; and that each new relation detected in any depart-

ment becomes an additional bond of union for the whole. Heat and light, and electricity and magnetism, are melting into one single science ; this, again, is more and more involved in general physics ; and even the three kingdoms of animal, vegetable, and mineral nature, once thought insuperably distinct, have lost their boundaries, and are blending into one physiology. An identity of composition and structure is exhibited in all parts of the vegetable world, which is but an integral manifestation of all the possible forms of vegetable life. So the whole animal kingdom is but a single collective animal, each class of which manifests one of the epochs of its development.

Nor among the physical sciences alone are these ties of a close affinity maintained. Between the world of mind and the world of matter, identical processes and analogous phenomena are every day unfolded. The development of humanity proves to be but the development, on a larger scale, of the individual man. Cosmology and noology proceed in parallel lines, while the perfect accord of religion, philosophy, and science is hourly receiving new proofs. Nature, amid the prodigious variety and shock of her forces, is ever the same,—a magnificent and glorious universality, evolved by a few simple laws from an eternal and pervading unity ; and modern science, lately threatened to be engulfed in the deluge of its own materials, finds its chief glory in exploring the wonderful analogies of creation.

V. MECHANICAL IMPROVEMENTS, ETC.

The applications of science to the useful arts and mechanical improvement, present results more likely to impress the general mind than any of its successes, however glorious, in the sphere of abstract principle.

The former are tangible and visible results, which produce tremendous changes in practical life, so that while
they are on a level with everybody's observation, they
more or less affect everybody's interest. The various
phenomena of heat are merely curious to the great
majority of men, so long as they are confined to the
region of law or general fact, but when they are made
to bear on the best and cheapest means of providing
fuel, or on the powers of steam as a propelling agent,
they become of absorbing importance to all of us.

Among the most remarkable contributions that
science has lately made to the arts, are the innumerable
methods of gliding the coarser metals with those which
are more rare and valuable, which are imparting so
much elegance and grace to many kinds of useful art ;
gun-cotton, an explosive material, much cheaper, and
quite as effective for many purposes, as gunpowder ;
sulphuric ether and chloroform, those compounds
which have the singular property of suspending the
sensibility of the nerves to pain ; and, most curious of
all, the various photographic processes, made known
by Daguerre, Niepce, Talbot, and others, wherein the
sun becomes the painter of pictures, and the thousand-
fold objects of nature are delicately preserved on
imperishable tablets. The machines for economizing
time and expense, and for facilitating the different
processes, in agriculture and manufacture, are numberless. Patents issued from the office at Washington
alone, amount, since A. D. 1800, to over fifteen thousand—the greater part of which, it is supposed, have
gone into successful operation, and in one way or
another, abridged the labor of human hands.—Every
year increases, by an accelerating ratio, the number of
these contrivances and inventions. In fact, mere mechanical implements promise to dispense altogether with

the fatiguing and wearing kinds of human agency. What are to be the consequences to society, not only in cheapening products, but in relieving laborers from oppressive and degrading toils?

These results are, no doubt, threatening enough to the temporary welfare of the artisan and the laborer, but it has been proved that in the end they are a vast benefit, not merely to society itself, but to those who, in the outset, are molested and almost destroyed by their success. By cheapening products, and creating demands for industry in new directions, they aid the progress of society, and extend the means of human well-being.

But the grandest triumphs of inventive genius, during the last half-century, have been achieved within the province of Commerce. The plank-road, the canal, the steamboat, and the railroad, are all the products of the last few years. At the close of the European wars of the last century, with the exception of a few military roads inherited from the Romans, and the roads of the same class constructed by Napoleon, the means of communication between distant parts was almost confined to inland seas and the larger rivers. It is for this reason that the maritime cities and provinces attained such disproportioned wealth. The want of modes of transit imposed insuperable obstacles to internal commerce; such roads as they had were impracticable, and the constant recurrence of desolating wars diverted the minds of both princes and the people from this most important element of civilization.

The time formerly consumed by common carriers over such routes is, now-a-days, incredible. The postman from Selkirk to Edinburgh, a distance of less than forty miles, was always a fortnight in going and returning. For years, after the beginning of the present century, the mail time between this city and Albany was eight days. Emigrants to the Genesee Valley, only twenty years ago, were sometimes twenty days in reaching their new purchases. There is a book still extant, written by a lady, within the memory of middle-aged persons, to describe a perilous journey she made from Boston to New York. Even as late as 1835, there were only seven coaches that ran daily from the capital of England to that of Scotland, and until several years within the present century, the internal transport of nearly all the trade of Great Britain was performed by wagons, at the slowest rates and an enormous expense. The charge for carriage averaged about fifteen pence, or thirty cents, a ton, per mile. Of course, all bulky articles were excluded from exchange. These articles are now carried over the same ground, the same distance, at the rate of a penny, or two cents, per ton. The speed of the wagons, then, did not exceed twenty-four miles a day ; steam-cars now run thirty miles the hour.

Canals were known to the ancients, and have been used, in a small way, by all civilized nations, but especially in Holland, for many years. But the world did not fully awake to their importance, until it was aroused by the vehement enthusiasm with which the State of New York, in 1817, entered upon the project of the Erie Canal. Since then, thousands upon thousands of miles of canal have been made by England, France, Russia, Sweden, and Belgium, as well as by our own country.

The invention of steamboats for river navigation, and of locomotives for railroads, has superseded canals, and invested them with an air of antiquity. It was only in 1807, that Fulton put his first vessel on the Hudson, and now our rivers, our lakes, our vast inland seas, and

the ocean itself, are covered with steamers, while the
entire surface of Europe and North America is reticu-
lated with net-works of iron, in which iron-ribbed and
flame-breathing monsters whirl enormous loads of
freight and multitudes of passengers with the rapidity
of the bird's flight. Add to this, the nineteen hundred
steamboats in America—the one thousand in England, and the several thousands of other nations,
and we shall get some idea of the incalculable, yet
silent revolutions that have sprung from a simple
series of inventions, which almost any child can comprehend !

Yet more astonishing than the railway is the Magnetic
Telegraph, the exploits of which are literally miraculous, annihilating space and anticipating time. The
extremities of the globe are brought into immediate
contact ; the merchant, the friend, or the lover con-
verses with whom he wishes, though thousands of miles
away, as if they occupied the same parlor ; and the
speech uttered in Washington to-day, may be read at
St. Louis an hour *before* it was delivered. Could the
wires be extended around the globe, we should be able
to hear the news one day before it occurred. Surely, in
view of such results, the gas discoveries of Mr. Paine,
or the aerial machines of Mr. Wise, seem not only
possible but certain.

It is well, therefore, on this opening year of a new half-
century, and as the crowning glory of modern industry,
that it should receive the tribute of a World's Fair, in
which men and women, led on by princes and emperors,
shall come from the uttermost parts of the earth to do
it homage ; when its gorgeous and delicate products
shall be enshrined in a crystal palace hitherto known
only to fairy lore ; and all the wealth, the intellect, the
beauty, the skill, and the power of mankind, combine

to assist in its apotheosis.   Never before has there been
called together such an assemblage for such a purpose.
May we not say that it portends an era of national good-
will and universal peace? and, that the mechanical
improvements that have removed the material barriers
of nations, will be followed by those spiritual advances
which shall melt all hearts into one?

CONCLUSION.

Had this progress of mankind taken place in the
scientific or material sphere alone, it would have been
a doubtful question whether the fact should be regarded
as a cause of rejoicing or sorrow.   But, fortunately, the
Moral and Religious advancement of our race, ulti-
mating in improved social conditions, has been no less
marked and encouraging than any of its other characteristics.   The world has been as active in doing good,
as it has in increasing comforts—are they not, after all,
much the same?—and in the comprehensiveness of its
benevolent undertakings, rivals the zeal of science and
the enterprise of trade.   The eyes of Philanthropy,
with a sedulous and tearful care, have sought out the
lurking-place of indigence and misery, and ministered
to their wants,—comprehending in their providence,
the health and habitations of the poor, as well as the
deeper needs of the vicious, and striving to elevate all,
with an impartial hand, in their physical, intellectual,
and moral condition!   How numerous and well-
managed the charitable organizations of the day!   How
extensive the agencies, and how indefatigable the zeal
of those great religious societies, which propose to
themselves nothing less than the Christianization of the
world!   Above all, what thorough and penetrating
significance in the problems raised by what, many in

fear and others in contempt, designate as Socialism, but which, in reality, despite the occasional folly of its disciples, looks to the adjustment of all political and social relations on a basis of perfect equity and truth? The very thought of such a consummation fills the generous mind with the most ardent wishes for its success. Was a nobler scheme ever conceived,—one more benevolent, more pacific, more promising of good in every way, than that of the Organization of Labor? Oh ! how the heart kindles with hope and sympathy when it thinks of the vast forces of human society,— hitherto too often turned to mere human destruction,— combined in a unitary effort to develop, mature, and elevate every individual member of our race !

AMERICAN AUTHORSHIP.*

LI BABA, when he entered the cave of the Forty Thieves, could scarcely have been more amazed by the wealth of its contents, than some people will be by the contents of this book. Its very title flies in the face of two very sacred traditions. It implies, firstly, that the ambiguous class of men called authors, may be in the possession of *Homes,*—consequently of wealth, social position, and respectability ; and, secondly, that among the three thousand American writers who pretend to the name, there are some at least who are really authors ; by which is meant, literary creators or men of genius. Are not both of these, assumptions which the general mind will regard as extremely bold.

The records of literary adventure have produced the impression the world over, that authors are a peculiar and exceptional class,—shiftless, seedy, and improvident, who, unable to live by any of the recognized methods of society, have betaken themselves to the expedient of living by their wits. It is understood that they reside, when they reside anywhere, in some vacant corner of a garret ; that they pass their days in lurking out of the way of bailiffs and landladies ; and that, after leading

---

* The Homes of American Authors, etc., etc. G. P. Putnam & Co. New York, 1853.

From *Putnam's Monthly*, January, 1853.

lives of vicissitude, poverty, neglect, and sorrow, when they come to die, they revenge their long quarrel with mankind by bequeathing to it certain inestimable treasures of poetry, wit, or thought, over which it will gloat and glow forever.

Who cannot recall a multitude of disquisitions written on the hapless lot of the poet who "learned by suffering what he taught in song ?" How often have literary men themselves bewailed the cruel injustice of society to their order! What sighs have we not exhaled, what tears not wept, over the pitiful stories of misconceived and unrewarded genius! The sad experiences of Savage, the miserable death of Otway, the more miserable death of Chatterton, "the sleepless boy who perished in his pride," the miscarriages of Burns, the indigence of Coleridge, the protracted struggles of Hook and Hood, the suicide of Blanchard, and a thousand other mournful histories, are still fresh in all our memories. Have not "the calamities of authors," indeed, furnished the indefatigable Disraeli with the materials for a volume? Or is there any possibility of our forgetting those lines of Moore, how

> Bailiffs will seize his last blanket to-day,
> Whose pall shall be held up by nobles to-morrow?

Schiller, in a pretty fable, represents Jupiter as dividing all the wealth of the world among the different classes of his creatures. To the kings he gives taxes and tolls, to the farmers lands, to the merchants trade, and to the abbots and monks most excellent wine ; but after having disposed of all his worldly possessions, he espies a poet wandering away from the rest, destitute, shabby, and forlorn. "What ho ! my good fellow," exclaims the father of men, " where wert thou when the general distribution

was going forward?" The bard modestly replied,
"Mine eyes were drunk with the glory of thy coming,
and mine ears filled with the harmonies of thy heaven!"
When the monarch of the gods, apparently no less
open to delicate flattery than any mortal, rejoined:
"Well, it's a sad case, my boy! I have nothing left on
the earth to give you; but, as a compensation, you shall
have, after death, the topmost step of my throne in the
skies." The poet was doubtless pleased, and went
away; and ever since, it is said that this has been the
principal inheritance of his tribe.

Incidents and memories such as these have given rise
to a most unfavorable estimate of authorship as a profession. In the minds of many, the writing of sonnets
is equivalent to going shirtless; and the perpetration of a
romance, the next thing, in its social consequences, to
the perpetration of crime. And although the distinguished successes of a few individuals—the facts, for instance, that Scott could build a baronial castle, and Dickens live like a lord, and Disraeli achieve the chancellor-
ship, and Bancroft get to be a foreign ambassador, etc.,
have partially corrected the opinion, there is reason to
believe that a majority of the world still looks upon literature as no better than a miserable and desperate *dernier
ressort.* Only the other day, Mr. William Jerdan, himself pretending to be one of the leading critics of Great
Britain, wrote a book which is one long wail over the unhappy conditions and prospects of writers as a class, and
an earnest appeal to young men to avoid the professional
pursuit of letters as they would avoid any temptation of
the devil. "Let no man," he says, "be bred to literature, for, as it has been less truly said of another occupation, it will not be bread to him. Fallacious hopes,
bitter disappointments, uncertain rewards, vile imposi-
tions, and censure and slander from the oppressors, are

his lot as soon as he puts pen to paper for publication, or risks his peace of mind on the black, black sea of printers' ink."

This is the old story, but we think there is a great deal of misconception in it ; at least we ought not, from Mr. Jerdan's failure, which is to be ascribed to his own want of capacity and prudence, to infer the inevitable fate of the whole circle of authors. Literature is as lucrative and promising as any other profession, to men who are really qualified to discharge its exacting and lofty functions. It records the disastrous rout of many of its followers, because so many rush into it without the requisite capacities ; and when they fail, their defeats are chronicled for all the world to read. Hardly a shiftless Corydon fails in walks of art that demand the finest endowments of the mind, that he or his friends do not parade him as another example of melancholy shipwreck, as if he deserved or could fairly have anticipated any other end. Now, if the same note were taken of the miscarriages in law, medicine, and divinity—if every briefless barrister, every physician without a patient, every clergyman without a cure, could make his griefs the talk of the town, as authors manage to make theirs, the disadvantages of their vocations would be no less apparent than those of letters, and literature would no longer stand solitary in its aggravations.

For, it is not true that literature is a peculiarly unkind and unnatural mother. Her favors to those children that are worthy of her, if not exuberant, are yet not stinted. Writing is not so productive of money as cotton spinning or merchandise, because, as a late Westminster Review argues, the conditions of literary and of ordinary commercial labor are very different. The latter supplies a constant want : the former ministers only to an intellectual luxury, or to wants that do not wear out the

supply with such rapidity as to keep up a high and incessant demand.   Both must he regulated, to some extent, by the vulgar law of supply and demand ; and their
profits, by the same law, cannot be forced beyond the
natural level of cost and competition.   "The latter
combines the joint action of capital and labor ; it feels
a continual competition ; it is not dependent upon the
humor or the accidents of the time ; no prosaic transition of the public taste converts its productions, like
poetry, into a drug ; however people may become indifferent to books, they are never likely to dispense with
shirts, or to decline the advantage of the steam-engine ;
and although the writer to whose merits the age is in-
sensible, or whose merits are of no utility to the age,
may be left to starve, the manufacturer will thrive.   Is
it reasonable to protest against a state of things which
has been inevitable from the beginning of the world,
and which will continue to be inevitable, so long as the
material wants of the world must be served, let its intellectual wants shift as they may ?   The aims of the two
classes are essentially different, and each has its own
reward.   The literary man has a glory which is denied
to the manufacturer, nor could he envy the latter his
wealth, if he knew how to appreciate his own position
at its true value.   He has fame, if he deserves it,—
honor, if he merits it : nor need he doubt of achieving
the highest social distinctions, if he asserts his right to
them as he ought, and maintains them with integrity
and self-respect ; while the other may be left to the un-
envied possession of wealth and obscurity."

   This is well put ; but it should also be admitted, in
behalf of literary men, to explain and excuse, if not to
justify their complaints, that with most of them, the difficulty is not so much the insufficiency of their incomes,
as the liberality of their outgoes.   A thousand peculiar

temptations, springing partly from those mental suscep-
tibilities which difference them from others, and partly
from their social aptitudes, beset them to spend more
than they make. The very qualities which form their
greatest glory, are those often which lead them into the
deepest humiliations. If they were as hard, as unim-
aginative, as careful of the main chance, as the cotton
spinner or the merchant, they would grow rich like the
cotton spinner or the merchant; but they are not so
constructed. The delicacy of organization out of which
literature comes, renders them keenly sensitive also to
the pressures and discomforts of existence,—to the
sands which grit between the shell of their outward
condition and the fleshy fibres. Yearning then to
bring their surroundings into a better correspondence
with their tastes, their perpetual tendency is to gather
costly appliances and comforts about them, and to
shut out actual existence by one of ideal refinement.
Again, with superior powers to entertain, or an elevated
fame to render their acquaintance a distinction, authors
are more sought for than others by general society,
where, whether they contract nice or dissipated habits,
they equally expose themselves to expense. It is impossible to keep up a varied and generous intercourse,
without falling into more or less extravagance; and
genius with its irritable fancies and impetuous impulses,
is least of all likely to resist the allurements of luxurious living, or to temper the seductions of taste with the
cold discipline of judgment. Not that genius is ever
destitute of judgment,—for subtle, strong, unerring
judgment is its very essence,—but then its judgment is
the theoretic judgment, which is displayed in the creation
and providence of a great drama or poem, and not the
practical judgment which controls every-day affairs. It
is not the judgment that keeps one from running into

prodigality, or, for want of an appropriate and ample nourishment, from resort to questionable indulgences. Ah ! then the clouds darken about it : the present grows comfortless and the future minatory ; and poor genius, losing its freshness and glow, is genius no more. It utters its wail into the uncaring universe, like one who falls at midnight from some on-rushing steamship, and hearing no reply but the splash of his own sinking, goes down into the unyielding depths ! But is the world to blame for such miscarriages ? Is the literary profession, as a practical pursuit, to blame ? Is such a lot worse, in its external liabilities, than that of other men ; and would not the chimney-sweep or the lawyer, who should forget the actual conditions of social existence, to indulge in dreams and idealizations, fail as signally as the author ?

Let us not be understood, however, to maintain that want of success in authorship is evidence either of want of merit or of want of prudence. We mean no such thing : on the contrary, we know that works of the most unquestionable excellence have often to wait a long while for appreciators—that genius, as a general thing, must create its own audience ; but this is as true of other professions as it is of literature. It is true in art ; true in science ; true in respect to mechanical inventions ; and sometimes true in practical enterprise. All that we design to urge is simply that authorship is no exception to other pursuits. If competent men engage in it with industry, patience, and consistent purpose, conducting their affairs with average foresight, they will reap at the least the average pecuniary rewards. The depreciatory view that prevails is both unjust and injurious ;—unjust, because it exaggerates the disparagements of a true and worthy literary life ; and injurious, because in the world's estimate, the respectability of a pursuit mainly depends upon what the Californians call the "prospecting," or the chance of turning up some ravishing deposit of sunny ore.

Nowhere has the literary profession been supposed to be more hopeless than in the United States ; and yet, we are persuaded that here as elsewhere, in spite of all drawbacks, adventitious or necessary, a career of honor and profit is open to all who engage in it with the proper qualifications, and pursue it with fidelity and self-control. We do not say that the pecuniary rewards of it are as generous as they ought to be, or probably will be hereafter ; we do not say that it will become in the present state of society as fertile as trade, or even as the learned professions ; but we do say that besides its peculiar harvests in the way of reputation and of influence on the great contemporary and prospective movements of thought, it holds out the guerdon of a reasonable pecuniary success, and of social compensations that ought to satisfy reasonable desires.

In proof of this, we appeal to the experience of those writers among us who have shown by their works a proper fitness for their vocation. They are nearly all in comfortable positions, and many of them are affluent. Mr. Putnam's book contains an account of some twenty of them (announcing others that are to follow)— and scarcely one of the number can be said to be poor. Prescott enjoys a princely income,—a part of it inherited, it is true, but the other part derived from his books ; the old age of Irving is made glad by more than competence, worthily won by his pen ; Cooper's novels enabled him to live generously during his whole life ; Bancroft is indebted for his political and social success to his merits as an historian ; Bryant, though not altogether by his poetry, yet by the exercise of his literary abilities, for the newspaper is a branch of literature, has

been placed at his ease ; while among those not included in this volume, Willis, Melville, Mitchell, Taylor,
Stephens, Curtis, and others, have reaped large rewards
from their publications. On the other hand, if Hawthorne
and a few others are not yet at the summits of fortune,
they have at least caught a glimpse of the golden heights.

These results are the more remarkable, because in
this country literary success is rendered doubly difficult
by the artificial obstructions thrown in its way. The
American author has to contend against two rivalries,
both formidable—first, that of his native, and second,
that of the foreign competitor. Nay, he enters the lists
against the latter, indeed, under this further disadvantage, that while his own works must be paid for by the
publisher, those of the foreigner are furnished, like the
showman's wonders, "free, gratis, and for nothing."
No sooner is a literary venture of Bulwer, Thackeray,
or Dickens afloat, than a whole baracoon of "book-
aneers," as Hood called them, rushes forth to seize it ;
and so long as they are able to do this, they will not
spend money—not much of it certainly—in any more
regular trade. Who will buy domestic goods when he
can import foreign goods without price? Our manufacturing friends of the protectionist school declaim
dolorously against the policy of government which exposes their arts to the cheap competition of Europe ;
but what a clamor would they raise if the exotic productions, that come into market against their own,
were admitted, not merely duty free, but without having
been subjected to an original cost ! Yet this is precisely the sorrow of the American author ! At great
expense himself, he works against an antagonism which
costs nothing ; for the slight *percentage* allowed to
foreign writers by our American publishers, for the
privilege of a first copy, is hardly to be taken into the

account. His case, therefore, is even worse than that of the broomseller of the old anecdote, who, stealing his raw materials, wondered how his rival could undersell him ; until he was told that the cunning rogue stole his brooms ready-made. Our publishers get their commodities ready-made, and flood the market with them, while the poor American producer hawks and sings his articles about the streets in vain !

But these considerations take for granted the second assumption of Mr. Putnam's book, to which we alluded in the outset, viz., that we have genuine American authors. Is it so ? We know that a different opinion obtains, and that foreign writers declare, with some degree of emphasis, that, as yet, we are mere imitators,—unfledged provincials,—repeating the copies set us in the Old World, and quite destitute of originality, independence, or native force. It is not three months since a callow Scotch critic, speaking *ex cathedra*, in the *North British Review*, conceded to us only three poets, and those, as he dogmatically alleged, mere servile echoes of Wordsworth and Tennyson. Other writers before him have repeatedly and triumphantly asked for our dramatists, novelists, essayists, and wits ; and Monsieur Philarete Chasles, in his late self-complacent French summary of American literary achievement, finds it difficult to drum up more than half-a-dozen authors on whom he is even willing to bestow a passing approval. There is, therefore, considerable unanimity in the judgment against us ; and, though the *London Times*, in its recent notice of the "Blithedale Romance," relaxes a little of its accustomed severity, and warns contemporary British writers to bestir their pens, it must be confessed that there still exists abroad a general incredulity, if not a lurking contempt, in respect to our literary pretensions.

We shall not gainsay the partial justice of this sentence, nor endeavor to hide the rags and tatters of our poverty. We are poor ; we are feeble ; we have little to show, compared with the older nations ; but is the comparison implied in all this altogether fair? Ought as much to be expected of us,—in our national teens as yet,—as of others, with two thousand years of Past behind them? What was Greece, during the early centuries ; what Rome in A. U. C. 70 ; what England, up to Elizabeth's day ; or what France, till the Grand Monarque? The issue never having been accurately stated, the discussion of it has shot wide of the mark. The real questions are, whether we possess a native literature at all,—whether that literature, if it exists, is equal to what might be justly asked of us under the peculiar circumstances of our career,—and whether, such as it is, it furnishes any adequate and generous ground of hope for the future?

It would be absurd to expect of us, in this the seventieth year of an independent national existence, as full and rich a literary growth as that of the older nations,—absurd, for the reason that we have had no time to produce it in, while our intellectual energies have been absorbed in other ways. A man who has his fields to clear, his house to build, his shoes and clothing to make, his ways of access to his neighbors to open, and above all, his government and social order to invent and institute,—in short, who has to provide by dint of the severest toil for the most immediate and pressing wants of his existence, is not the man who constructs epics, or amuses his fancy with the invention of dramas or tales. His epics, and dramas, and romances he finds in his work. The giants of the woods are the giants most formidable to him, and whose conquest is more important than any imagination might conjure from the dim twilight of mythology. He is battling face to face with the frost, and hail, and mud jotüns that Carlyle speaks of; and while the battle lasts, he has as little relish as he has opportunity for idle songs about them. Let him be deeply engaged the while in a novel and somewhat momentous political experiment, working out into practical and victorious solution a problem in which the destinies of half a world are involved, and the stern and trying task laid upon him will scarcely permit of his turning aside to the gentle and capricious arts. If, therefore, the whole of his earlier life should exhibit an absolute want of literary result, the fact would not argue against his capacity for that kind of production, but simply that his powers had been diverted into other channels. But this consideration is so obvious that we need not press it further.

Again, if in the progress of wealth and leisure, with the growth of intellectual wants and refinements, we should find him prone to imitate the artistic efforts of those who had gone before, it would merely show a very common trait of youth. Nothing is more natural than for juniors to copy their seniors. Even men and nations, endowed with indisputable genius, are apt, in their first crude endeavors, to pursue the paths and ape the manners of their predecessors, whose successes they admire, and for whose qualities they feel a kindred sympathy, but the secrets of whose self-dependence they have not yet learned. Fearful at first of the strength of their untried wings, though full of impulse for flight, like young birds they watch the motions of their elders, until in due time they may themselves launch forth into the air. Indeed, we remember years ago to have read the work of some unrecognized western philosopher, who maintained,—with an abundance of instances to confirm his theory,—that early imitation is a characteristic mark of genius, and that the greatest of men have begun their careers by a more or less conscious adoption of some much-loved model. Be that as it may, we know, in respect to nations, how much of the earlier art and science of Greece was derived from the opulent store-houses of the East, though Greece became the mistress of the intellectual world ; we know how dependent the Romans were upon Greece, though Rome subsequently enriched mankind from her native sources ; and we know, too, what infusion of the Latin there has been into French and English speech. May we not infer from these examples, then, that if America, as she is tauntingly charged, has sucked too much of her infantile instruction and culture from the breasts of her noble mother, it does not prove that she is now unable to go alone ; but simply that she was once young. Speaking the language of England, was it not inevitable that we should read the literature of England, and draw thence much of our intellectual nurture ? The whole of the earlier literature of England was, in one sense, just as much ours as it is the modern Englishman's. Up to the time of our revolutionary separation, it was the common possession of the English race ; and the mere change in our political relations worked no defeat of our claim. We have a birthright of appeal to Chaucer, Spenser, Shakspeare, Milton, &c., as to our ancestors in the direct line, just as the younger members of a family call the common progenitor father, though they may not have inherited the title and the estates. They may have quarrelled with the elder brother even, and quit the paternal roof, and begun new life-methods for themselves in some distant region of the globe, but their lineage remains as clear and indisputable as that of the first-born sons.

Now, all this being admitted, the question of American originality narrows itself down to this—whether the stock has degenerated by crossing the ocean, or in being exposed to the different influences of new natural and social conditions? Do such of us as have devoted our energies to literature give evidence of deterioration and decay ; or is the old vigor still in our loins?

We think that no fair mind can hesitate as to the answer. We believe that our authors have at least not retrograded. On the other hand, we believe that they are worthy scions of the old stock ; and more than that, that under the inspiration of a new order of things, such as exists in this country, they have laid the foundations of a peculiar literature,—not yet copious, not yet comparable for richness, depth, variety, or grace with either of the ancient or modern literatures, but still full of native freshness and promise. Like a noble youth rounding into manhood, we are wild, extravagant, and impulsive, betraying the faults of want of discipline and culture, but strong in the consciousness of mighty powers, and bounding forward to a future of glorious developments.

No! we may not point to bright galaxies like those which shed lustre from other heavens ; we have no thickly-studded constellations and luminous groups scattered all above us ; but we do claim single stars that shine with an unborrowed and unfading brilliancy. Few will be disposed to deny that in metaphysics and moral reasoning Jonathan Edwards is of the same order of men with Locke and Butler; that in experimental philosophy, Franklin, and in the science of navigation, Bowditch, are names consecrated by history ; that Hamilton, Jefferson, and Madison rank with the statesmen of any age ; that the historians Bancroft and Prescott take their places by the side of the best modern historians, whether we regard the ac-

curacy of their research or the perspicuity and finish
of their style ; that Cooper, as a novelist, is only inferior
to Scott, to whom all others are inferior ; that the
pleasant essays of Irving fear no comparison with those
of Addison and Goldsmith ; and that poems of Bryant
will be read with delight as long as Gray's Elegy, or
Coleridge's Genevieve, or Milton's Lycidas, or Burns'
songs, because, like those immortal productions, they
are perfect in their kind.   When, moreover, we name
the only eloquence in our language which approaches
the comprehensive and masterly speeches of Burke, we
recall that of Webster ; the artist of modern artists who
approaches nearest to Titian is Allston ; the liveliest
magazinist of the day, not excepting Jules Janin, is Willis ; the woman, who has written a book which has had
a wider instant circulation than the book of any other
woman, is Mrs. Stowe.   Well, this is not much : it is
not Shakspeare, Milton, or Bacon—it is not Swift,
Fielding, Thackeray, but it is some proof of what we
contend for—that the old Saxon blood has not turned
to water in our veins, nor the old fire of the heart
become a putrid phosphor.

It is a piece of unworthy prejudice to pretend that
our leading writers are only second editions of European
celebrities.   Cooper is no more an imitator of Scott
than is Bulwer or Dickens : his materials and his
methods of presenting them are his own ; and no man
not born in America, in the shadow of her primeval
woods, under the inspirations of her unsettled pio-
neer, could have written any of the best of his works.
Bryant is wholly American, or if he resembles Wordsworth or Cowper, it is because he writes English with
the deep meditative wisdom of the one, and the pensive
grace of the other ; but neither Wordsworth nor Cowper
have written more true, beautiful, or indestructible

poems than the Waterfowl or the Prairies. Whom does Emerson imitate? Carlyle! Why, with scarcely a quality in common with Carlyle, he is just as much the superior of Carlyle, in clearness and depth of insight, as he is in simplicity and melody of style. Has Mr. Dana a prototype, has Channing, has Audubon, has Webster, has Hawthorne, has Melville, has Uncle Tom?

There always must be more or less of structural uniformity in the literature of nations which speak the same language. Out of the same deep heart of the national life, from which language comes, literature also is born; and those mysterious indwelling causes, and hardly less mysterious external influences, which mould and modify the one, must give form and color to the other. It is impossible to separate ourselves wholly from the features or the predominant traits of our parents. Had the earlier settlers of this country been French or German, as they were English, our subsequent growth would probably have partaken of a French or German bias. What literature we might have created would have borne a family likeness to Voltarie or Goethe, to Victor Hugo or Freligrath, instead of to Milton and Sir Walter Scott, to Addison and Pope; and we should in that event have had to struggle ourselves clear of German mysticism and French elegance, as we now have to make our way out of the heavy and melancholy gravity of John Bull.

But this resemblance between our own literature and that of England, springing from an identity of race and tongue,—made especially apparent during the formative and transitional stages of our growth,—will not prevent a new self-prompted development in the maturer future. Already we have cut ourselves loose from the leading-strings which were inevitable to our childhood,—not in

our political system only, but in our manners, morals,
and arts ; and, under the various influences pouring in
upon us from the vast accessions to our population
from the Old World, our whole literary and social character is undergoing change.   This is not the place to
speak of the social indications, but, as it regards the
literary, we allege that our younger writers abound in the
unmistakable evidences of a new and vigorous direction
given to their habits of feeling and thought.   They are not
only less English than their predecessors were ; they are
not only more universal in their affinities and tastes, the
consequence of wider sympathies, and the infusion of
the European element ; but they are more entirely independent, and self-sustained.   They have a more decided
character of their own.   A certain ready, open impres-
sibility, which takes in all the wonders of nature and all
the excellences of art, and has a quick feeling for every
variety of human character,—is the mark of most of
them, accompanied by a fresh, buoyant, genial enthusiasm.   Without losing the earnestness of their northern
origin, they have had superinduced upon it the volatile
and graceful vivacity of the south ; they are more
external, sensuous, impassioned, but none the less
intense and thoughtful.   The Saxon and the Celtic
bloods unite in their veins, giving brilliancy and facility
to a foundation of endurance and power.

It is scarcely time for these new combinations to show
themselves in full force—except in practical enterprise,
where our achievements both in grandeur of conception and force of execution surpass all that is recorded
in modern annals ; but in that branch of literature,
which comes nearest to enterprise—in narratives of
travel, there are many signs of departure from the
old types.   Stephens in Central America, Melville in
the South Seas, Curtis in Egypt and Syria, have

marked out styles of their .own, each differing from the other, and each differing from any travellers that have gone before them. They are full of freshness and broad sensuous life,—not like the worn-out debauchees of Europe who travel to get rid of themselves or to find a new sensation, but like marvellously wise children, capable of surprises, but accepting all novelties with good-humor ; indeed, with a certain rollicking fun in them, and yet estimating things at their true value with unerring practical sagacity.

Among our nascent poets, too—such as Lowell, Boker, Read, Taylor, and Stoddard—we discern the earnest of a departure from old methods, and an entrance upon a new and original career. They are more free, frank, and expansive than the modern British poets, and superadd to the concentrated force and strength of their insular models a more affluent, ·richly colored, and catholic view of life. A luxuriance, as of some deep virgin soil shooting up into weedy extravagance at times, betrays the inspiration of our prolific nature, and reminds us of broad rivers and lakes, flowery prairies, and interminable leafy woods. Their faults, mainly, are faults of excess and not of deficiency. They want discipline, but they do not want sensibility nor native vigor. They have the hale, ruddy-complexioned look of health, and above all, a sincere fearless spirit, which betokens the capacity for lusty human growth. Let them be true to the promises of their youth, and their manhood will ripen into luscious and fragrant fulfilments.

But we cannot pursue these topics ; we have already dwelt so long upon them, that we have left ourselves little space to speak of the work by which they have been suggested. It is confessedly the book of the year. In the elegance of its embellishments no less than in the interest of its contents, we know of no holiday book that can compare with it,—none at least issued on this side the ocean. Still, we have some faults to find with it : the plates are, here and there, hastily executed ; and the letter-press of a few of the contributions is not so sprightly, anecdotal, personal as we should liked to have found. It is a prevailing vice of our writers to be too didactic and sedate ; and in such a book, of all others, heavy writing is out of place. But this criticism does not apply to the whole volume, in which there is much admirable and vivacious writing ; while the entertainment which it furnishes could not well be better. It introduces us, by pencil and by pen, to the haunts of novelists and poets, who are dear to the hearts of some, and will live long in the imaginations of others. We visit Audubon in his snug retreat on the Hudson, while his favorite deer are stalking about us on the grass, and his favorite birds sing to us from the trees ; we wander with Bryant through his island woods, where his heart has learned its lessons of severe simplicity, and his imagination caught the glow of its bright autumnal foliage ; we loll in the sumptuous study of Longfellow, where the old panels suggest the memory of Washington, while the poet sings us golden legends of the Old and the New Worlds ; we hold high discourse with Emerson, in the shadows of his Concordian Mecca, while the weird Hawthorne, himself a shade, flits through the umbrage of the Old Manse ; the opulent library of Everett is opened to us ; Lowell, fresh from his European harvest, conducts us about the nooks of his paternal mansion ; Miss Sedgwick roams with us amid the glorious hills of Berkshire ; Simms chaperons us among the wild bays and pines of the Carolina plantation ; Kennedy welcomes us to the hospitality of the warm South ; the generous

Cooper throws open his lordly Northern hall; Irving tells quaint stories of the Western hunters, or of Spanish Dons, or of old English cheer, as we sit beneath the fantastic gables of Wolfert's Roost; and Dana strolls silently by our side, along the shores of the far-resounding sea, where we listen to the beat of its mighty pulses, till some image of its boundlessness and glory passes into our souls. But there is one Home, near that same sea, in which we loiter with pleasure no more; for the presiding genius has departed from it, and we tread the vacant lawns, and walk through the deserted halls of Marshfield, full of sad and thoughtful memories of Webster.

ALISON'S HISTORIES OF EUROPE.*

DR. JOHNSON, in one of his ursine growls, is reported to have expressed a very contemptuous opinion of the writers of History; for, if they narrate what is false, said he, they are not historians, but liars; and if they narrate what is true, they have no field for the display of ability, because, as truth is necessarily one, it must be told by everybody alike.

But this dilemma of the Leviathan is a superficial one, or rather no dilemma at all, for the reason that the historian does not deal with absolute truth, with naked or abstract propositions of logic, nor yet with mere individual and disconnected facts, but with phenomena that may be variously interpreted, with complicated and warring movements, that spring from violent passions in the actors concerned in them, and that excite similar passions in the beholders of them; and with institutions and usages which represent vast and irreconcilable differences of political and social faith. His art, there-

---

* The History of Europe, from the commencement of the French Revolution, in 1789, to the Battle of Waterloo. By Sir Archibald Alison, Bart.: 8 vols., 1843.

The history of Europe, from the fall of Napoleon, in 1815, to the accession of Louis Napoleon, in 1852. By Sir Archibald Alison, Bart.: Vol. 1, 1852.

From *Putnam's Monthly*, May, 1853.

fore, like that of any other artist, consists in the selection of his topics, and in his method of treatment. He must have his color and form, his foreground and background, his light and shade, and his variety as well as unity of composition. An ample scope is thus afforded him for the display of any ability that he may possess, for the nicest judgment, the most profound and active imagination and consummate skill ; and, so far from finding him either a liar on one side, or the utterer of bald truisms on the other, we shall see that his function is allied no less by the powers of the mind which it demands, than by the dignity of its objects, to the loftiest forms of intellectual effort. The art of the historian, indeed, is of so high a kind, and demands such rare and various powers, such an almost impossible combination of great faculties, that examples of really successful writers in this department are very few. We find more great architects, great sculptors, great painters, great musicians, great poets, great dramatists, great novelists, great essayists, than we do of great historians. To be a great historian requires some share in the endowments of nearly all the others—some knowledge of their specialties, some sympathy in all their aims, besides many aptitudes peculiar to his own walk. A historian, certainly, ought to be familiar with the origin and influence of the plastic arts, which are so important in the development of society. He should be able to feel and conceive with the poet, to discern and distribute character with the play-wright, and to tell a story consecutively and interestingly with the novelist. Again, the historian, besides his descriptions of the scenes and characters of the drama of life, in which, like the artist, he strives to produce the best general effects—effects infinitely more true than the most microscopic minuteness of detail would be without this artistic management—is required to refer these scenes and characters to great general principles, and to evolve comprehensive and permanent laws of development out of the kaleidoscope of ever-shifting and variable appearances. He is, therefore, the philosopher as well as the artist, and needs the penetration and insight of the clearest reason, in addition to the finer qualities of the rhetorician and the poet.

We have thought it well to premise thus much, in order to show that it is with no low or narrow conceptions of the province of the historian that we approach a survey of the labors of Mr. Alison. He holds a prominent place among the historians of his day. He is a leading writer in the leading journals of the British Empire; he has put forth voluminous books, widely accepted as authorities; he traverses periods of time which are among the most important in the annals of our race; he utters positive judgments on important men and important things; and, in short, he aspires to the highest character in the department of literature to which he is devoted. His position and pretensions, then, entitle him to be judged according to the most elevated standards of criticism. In an inferior walk of art, with a more humble aim, or a less ambitious style of execution, we might dismiss him in few words, to find his level as he could among the multitude of authors.

The period which Mr. Alison has chosen for the subject of his researches extends from the time of the first French Revolution to the accession of Napoleon the Third, if we must call that adventurer by a dynastic name. It covers a space of about sixty years—perhaps the most busy, brilliant, and pregnant years that the world has ever known—full of grand events and crowded by great characters—and, in many respects, an era decisive of the destinies of mankind for a long time to come. Indeed, we do not suppose that any six decades that have fallen upon man, scarcely excepting the most glorious age of Greece, the epoch of the advent of Christianity, or that of the Reformation in the sixteenth century, have been more prolific of great men, more agitated by great thoughts, more splendid in great discoveries, or more marked by signal and tremendous changes in the condition of society, than the sixty years embraced in the design of Mr. Alison's volumes.

The period begins, as we have said, with the first French Revolution, which, strictly speaking, was the end of the previous, rather than the beginning of the present age ; or, more strictly still, it was the transition between the two, " the Phenix birth and fire consummation," in which an old economy passed away and a new one sprang from its ashes. It was confessedly one of the most stupendous events in the history of our race. Huge, astounding, uproarious, memorable to all men, and to the end of time, alike in the causes which led to it, in the unparalleled scenes that attended its progress, and in its far-reaching consequences, no event in the annals of mankind is fuller of an absorbing interest. Covering in its duration only a few rapid years, confined for the most part to a single city and its adjacent provinces, costing, amid all its terrors, less bloodshed than often marks a single pitched battle—it still stands apart, from all other occurrences, as one of the grandest and fearfulest products of any age.

Timid and unreflecting minds are accustomed to consider the French Revolution as a mere wanton explosion and whirlwind of frantic passions, and to stigmatize the chief actors in it as fiends ;—a holiday of malignant merriment to which all the devils of the earth rushed as the witches rushed to the mad midnight revels of the Blochsberg. Other minds, which strive to pierce deeper into things, which believe that no effect exists without a cause, and a justifying cause, which cannot suppose that God ever abandons a whole people to sheer imbecility and madness, or that he has no deeper design in allowing the errors and crimes of men than that they may serve as a bugaboo, or death's-head and cross-bones for conservative moralists—find in the excesses and riots of this wonderful event another significance, however terrible. They discern a law of Providence amid its sad dislocations and irregularities, a rhythmic order in its wild Bacchic dances, a spark of genuine fire through its meteor lights, a noble and great thought in even its most monstrous utterances. It is this thought, and not alone the carnage, which has been greatly exaggerated, nor the ferocity which is more or less incident to all civil wars, nor the sudden overthrow of a dynasty, of which we before have had many examples, that fastens our attention to the external events as it was never before fastened.

For the first time in the history of man had the conviction of the divine rights of men, as opposed to the pretensions of governments, institutions, and society itself, taken possession of the hearts of a whole people, to be proclaimed as a vital and inextinguishable fact. Revolutions there had been before, but none so deep, thorough, and radical as this—none which penetrated so directly into the very core of the relations of the individual to the State. The contests in England, during the reign of James the First, and the earlier years of that of his successor, were parliamentary contests, carried on mainly by learned lawyers, and ending only in a change of reign. The Revolution of 1688, conducted by the appointed organs of the corporations, the landed aristocracy, the town magistrates, and borough proprietors, scarcely touched the frame of the government, and did not ask, as it had no need, of popular interference. Again, the American Revolution was at first but a strife between revolted colonies and an imperious mother country, and only in the minds of its more exalted spirits looked to that final and broad assertion of the supremacy of the people which it afterward uttered. It was, even in the end, a conflict of State with State. But the French Revolution, prepared from afar by the whole course of European thought and experience, was a solemn and unqualified proclamation of the rights of man as man ; the protest of the individual against every form of domination, whether it pretended to be human or divine.

It was a matter of course, that an assertion so extreme, provoking every conservative resentment, and arousing every aspiring passion, should issue in actions equally extreme. The mean and petty squabbles of cabinets, the windy debates of politicians and quidnuncs, were no longer in place. The questions which had come to be debated involved the very foundations of government, the very basis of Society. How could they be debated with the cold and formal logic of the schools? The people, stung to an intense sense of wrong, by the injustice and licentiousness with which for ages they had been governed, had rushed together, not to listen and deliberate, but to act. Twenty-four millions of them, courageously casting off the trammels of centuries, dislodging temporal and spiritual tyranny from its strongholds, elevating the multitudes from servile and superstitious submission, and assuming the control of their own destiny, presented a spectacle, which, in the midst of its bloodshed and atrocity, is too original and magnificent not to be admired, even while we tremble. We may condemn and denounce those millions as we please ; but they struck a blow with which humanity still vibrates, and the echoes of their wild screams will go down as jubilant harmonies to the end of time.

Yet great as the opening incident of the age we are considering was, it scarcely surpasses in interest the national convulsions by which it was followed. The waves of the tumult had not subsided, when a majestic figure appears, emerging from the ooze and slime of the deluge, like Milton's postdiluvian lion,

> " pawing to get free
> His hinder parts; then springs as broke from bonds,
> And rampant shakes his brinded mane."

The year 1799—the last of the last century—saw Napoleon Bonaparte First Consul of France.

[Here followed an outline of the events of the 19th century, which, as it has been anticipated substantially by the foregoing essay on " The Last Half-Century," is omitted.]

These, then, are the characteristics of the period of which Mr. Alison has made himself the historian—a period, as we see even in the hasty sketch we have given of it, of tremendous activity and expansiveness, marked by great events on every side, not only in politics and war, but in literature, science, social improvement, and in practical as well as moral enterprise.   In what manner has he treated the rich materials placed in his hand?

Hegel, one of the profoundest and acutest, as well as most brilliant of the Germans, has divided history—by which he means history as an art, and not the course of events—into primitive, systematic, and philosophical. By primitive history he means a simple narrative or chronicle of events, as it might be given by an actual witness of them, of which sort we have specimens in Herodotus, Thucydides, and Cæsar. Systematic history aspires to a slightly higher character, and records the life of a nation, or of nations, according to some general scheme of thought in the author's mind, not founded, however, upon any profound view of the logical order of events, so much as upon external relations of time and place, or the rhetorical requirements of the subject; it is exemplified in Gibbon, Hume, Robertson, Macaulay, and Prescott. But philosophical history takes a more connected and deeper, as well as wider view; it looks upon human actions and their developments as illustrations of some principle, or at least of some universal tendency, which is the work of the Supreme Reason, realizing its purposes toward humanity. In this style Vico, Herder, Guizot, Thierry, Louis Blanc, and, to some extent, our own Bancroft, are examples. For a higher order of history still, the scientific order, which would blend perfect accuracy of narrative with a deduction of absolute scientific principles, the time has not come, for the reason that the science of history is not yet known, and cannot be known except as the crown and summit of every other science.

Mr. Alison modulates variously through all the different styles, but has attained a brilliant success in none, and only a mediocre success in either; and, in any large view of the historical function, must be content to take a very humble place.

As a narrator of events, he has the two important merits—of patient and laborious industry, and of considerable animation and vigor of description. He shrinks from no effort of research in collecting his materials, and he puts them together with a ponderous diligence. His works, as repositories of certain selected facts, will save the inquirer a deal of pains that he would otherwise be at, in reading newspapers, debates, bulletins, memoirs, and letters. He depicts occasional scenes, too, especially the movements of battle, in strong and vivid colors. But the ordinary current of his narrative betrays constantly the want of every quality necessary to a skilful or an interesting story-teller. His vocabulary, in the first place, is remarkably deficient; he cannot handle words, the elementary tools of his art, with any facility or power; and his diction, in the second place, is equally poverty-stricken. His sentences are often heavy, confused, straggling, and ill-joined; he commits blunders in grammar that a child would be punished for at school; and being utterly destitute of fancy and imagination, his metaphors are the stereotyped phrases of literary commerce or the commonplaces of the street. We are reminded of the "Alexander and Clytus" illustration of Coleridge's school friends in almost every page of Alison, by the recurrence, *usque ad nauseam*, of the same similes and comparisons. What is worse, his figures, hackneyed as they are, seldom run upon all-fours; they are both halt and blind, and, like the monsters in Horace's Art of Poetry, have joined a horse's neck to a human head, or spread the plumage of birds over the limbs of beasts.

As proofs of these defects we refer to expressions such as these : "the *vast* and *varied* inhabitants" of the French empire, as if Frenchmen were vaster than any other people; "an acquisition which speedily *recoiled upon the heads* of those who acquired them;" "Murat, who made 1800 of their wearied *columns* prisoners," which would have been more prisoners than the whole Austrian army contained of men. We are told of a narrative "tinged with undue bias;" and of a historical

work "closing with a ray of glory." Of a certain event
it is said, "*il could hardly have been* anticipated that it
would have been attended by effects," etc., with innumerable other similar carelessnesses. In respect to sentences, take this : "In 1789, Goethe, profound and
imaginative, was reflecting on the destiny of man on
earth, *like a cloud which turns up its silver lining to the
moon ;*" or this astronomical glorification of the age of
George III., " Bright as were the *stars* of its morning-
light, more brilliant still was the *constellation* which
shone forth at its meridian splendor, or cast a glow
over the twilight of its evening shades," which is neither
poetry nor science. Again, he says, speaking of modern enterprise and emigration, which he capriciously
calls the second dispersion of mankind : "No such
powerful causes, producing the dispersion of the species,
have come into operation since mankind were originally
separated on the Assyrian plains ; and it took place"—
what took place ?—"from an attempt springing from
the pride and ambition of man, as vain as the building
of the tower of Babel." The first three sentences of
the Preface to his New Series read thus : " During a
period of peace, the eras of history cannot be so clearly
perceived, on a first and superficial glance, as when
they are marked by the *decisive* events of war ; but they
are not on that account the less obvious when their respective limits have been once ascertained. The triumphs of parties in the Senate-house or Forum are
not, in general, followed by the same immediate and
decisive results as those of armies in the field ; * * *
but they are equally real and *decisive.*" The triple duty
imposed upon *decisive* in these three sentences is one
that Mr. Alison very often exacts of his sorry and jaded
vocables.

Because these secondary defects are so habitual with

him, marring his most studied and elaborate passages, we speak of them at length ; but they should not be allowed to detain us from the consideration of those more grievous faults which mark his works as a systematic historian, or one who writes according to an avowed scheme.   Mr. Alison's arrangement comprehends the history of Europe from 1789 to 1852 : the first part, already published, closed in 1815 ; and the second part, of which the first volume only is issued, is intended to carry on the narrative to our own day. Now, what will be the surprise of the reader to learn that, in the proposed systematic view of Europe, there is scarcely more than a reference to those great movements of thought, to those grand discoveries in science, to those magnificent moral enterprises, of which we have spoken in the outset of this article, as so characteristic of the period ?   The whole ten volumes of his first series are exclusively occupied with the French Revolution and the wars that grew out of it, while "the literature, the manners, the arts, and the social changes," which he admits are far more permanently interesting and important than the doings of statesmen in general, are quite omitted !

A critic has well objected to Niebuhr's great History of Rome, that he exhausts his efforts in clearing up and rendering intelligible the merely civic life of the Roman people, while he tells us little or nothing of the people themselves, of their ideas and feelings, of their religion, morality, and domestic relations, of their women as well as their men, of their children and their education, and of their slaves and the treatment of slaves. "The central idea of the Roman religion and polity," he says, "the family, scarcely shows itself in his voluminous works, except in connection with the classification of the citizens ; nor are we made to perceive in what the beliefs and modes of conduct of the Romans, respecting things in general, agreed, and in what disagreed, with those of the rest of the ancient world. Yet the mysteries of the Romans and their fortunes must be there." But with how much more pertinence and force may we apply similar objections to the oversights of Alison, who speaks of wars, and battles, and intrigues, as if Europe, for the last half-century, had done nothing but fight. Were all Europeans ministers, or generals, or diplomats, or monarchs, that no other characters are permitted to figure on the scene? Were there no other movements but those of armies, no words uttered but those of protocols, no letters written but the cipher of secret agents, or the despatches of commissaries? Had not those thirty millions of Frenchmen, and those other millions of Germans, Spaniards, Italians, Russians, English, etc., like Shylock, "eyes, organs, senses, affections, passions?" or had they only hands to handle swords, and bodies to be riddled by balls? Left to Mr. Alison's accounts alone for our sources of information, we should be compelled to give a most abhorrent answer to these questions, and to suppose that Christendom, for a quarter of a century, had been surrendered to Milton's apostate angels, who "only in destruction took delight." His pages remind us of the *Salon des Batailles,* at Versailles, where every picture is some grand state ceremonial, or a battle-piece, covered with charging troops, and the carcases of the slain, with noisy trumpeters in the foreground, and vast masses of lurid smoke blotting out the green earth and the skies. We are not unaware, as we trust we have shown, of the surpassing greatness of the external events of which his history is composed, nor do we complain of the minute and laborious zeal with which he has gathered every particular concerning them, ransacking archives and measuring fields of slaughter; but we do complain that he has allowed the tumult and dust of these vast contests to stop his ears and blind his eyes to every object but themselves.

Mr. Alison acknowledges this serious deficiency in the Preface to his Second Series, and attempts to supply it by a promise to present "subjects of study more generally interesting than the weightier matters of social and political change," and he gives a chapter of the literary history of England in the body of the work, by way of specimen. The reparation comes too late; for we cannot see with what propriety he begins in 1815 an exposition that ought to have commenced in 1789, or how he can be so weak as to suppose that desultory sketches of certain prominent writers and discoverers is a history of Arts, Manners, Literature, and Society. These have as much a connected life, interdependent relations, and an order of development, as the "weightier matters of social and political change," and, in any consistent historical survey, ought to be treated with the same abounding completeness and accuracy. A few scraps of commonplace criticism,—such as one reads in the book-notices of Ladies' Magazines, or in the essays of young collegians, scraps loosely strung together by mere contemporaneousness or sequence of time, and as if their subjects had no relation, either to the spirit of the age or to the condition and movements of society,—cannot be called history, even in the lowest sense of the term; much less can they be called systematic history. Yet it is precisely such scraps that he has set before us in the chapter entitled "The Progress of Literature, Science, the Arts and Manners, in Great Britain after the Peace,"—a chapter designed to shadow forth his intentions as to the future treatment of the Literature, Art, etc., of the rest of Europe.

After a brief reference to the rapid growth of steam navigation and of cotton manufactures, and to the impulse given to intellectual activity by great wars, he sketches the literary or artistic characters of Scott, Byron, Rogers, Southey, Wordsworth, Coleridge, Paley, Malthus, Herschel, and others, down to Miss O'Neil and Helen Faucett. We say he sketches them, and yet a meagre term like that can hardly be applied to the wretched chalk-and-water outlines he parades as pictures. Not to remark upon the singular anachronism which permits him to speak of many of his personages, such as Paley, Sir Thomas Lawrence, Scott, Crabbe, Dugald Stewart, Davy, Kemble, Herschel, etc., as attaining their chief celebrity "after the Peace" instead of before it; nor upon the still more singular oversight, of omitting Shelley and Keats from his list of poets, Faraday from that of philosophers, Godwin from the novelists, De Quincey and Leigh Hunt from the critics, and Sheridan Knowles from the dramatists; we must say that his characterizations of the men he names are the most puerile, vague, and unsatisfactory that we ever read in a book of any pretention. As to any distinct or discriminating description of the peculiarities of these worthies, there is none whatever; "charming," "delightful," "fine," "brilliant," "graphic," "interesting," are the epithets that exhaust his thesaurus of praise; and these are applied equally to all, with a slight change of posture, in each case, but without a particle of insight in either. Take Tennyson, whose merits and defects as a poet are alike obvious, as an example of Mr. Alison's method of estimating literary character. "Tennyson," he says, "has opened a new vein in English poetry, and shown that real genius, even in the most advanced stages of society, can strike a fresh chord, and, departing from the hack-

neyed way of imitation, charm the world by the conceptions of original thought. His imagination, wide
and discursive as the dreams of fancy (*sic*), wanders at
will, not over the real so much as the ideal world. The
grottoes of the sea, the caves of the mermaid, the realms
of heaven, are alternately the scenes of his song. His
versification, wild as the song of the elfin king, is
broken and irregular, but often inexpressibly charming.
Sometimes, however, this tendency (what tendency?)
leads him into conceit ; in the endeavor to be original,
he becomes fantastic ; there is a freshness and originality, however, about his conceptions, which contrast
strangely with the practical and interested views which
influenced the age in which he lived, and contributed
not a little to their deserved success. They were felt to
be the more charming, because they were so much at
variance with the prevailing ideas around him, and re-
opened those fountains of romance which nature had
planted in every bosom, but which are so often closed
by the cares, the anxieties, and the rivalry of the
world."

Now this mass of stuff, this feebleness, nonsense, and
mixed metaphor, might have been written, if any one
but Mr. Alison could have written it, about any poet
that has flourished since Pope, and would have given a
reader ignorant of him just as clear an idea of his qualities as it does of those of Mr. Tennyson. That is, it
would have given him just no idea at all. Tennyson's
subtle insight, intellectual intensity, refined spiritual
fancy, elaborate sculptural art, and pervading melody,
or any other traits that separate him from the rest of his
tribe, are *terra incognita* to the "great historian," who
seems, also, quite as impartially innocent of any real
knowledge of the other two or three score of personages
whom he attempts to delineate.

In this literary patchwork, Mr. Alison revels in his fondness for repetitions. We read, not without amusement, of Scott's "wide-spread reputation," Byron's "most wide-spread reputation in the world," the "wide-spread interest of Moore's lines," Campbell's "wide-spread fame," Dickens's "wide-spread reputation,"—phrases that recur on every second page—on the very page, indeed, in which we are reminded, truly enough, that "repetition and monotony are the bane of literature and imagination." We are informed besides, on one page, that Moore is "the greatest lyric poet in the English language;" on the next, that Campbell is "the greatest lyric poet of England," and in a third, that Gray "has made the most popular poem in the English language." Again, Joanna Baillie's dramas are said to be written "in sonorous Alexandrine verses," which is a new measure for dramas, and Mrs. Hemans is called "a rival to Coleridge, if not in depth of thought, in tenderness of feeling and beauty of expression." "Lalla Rookh" is made to "*clothe* oriental images and adventures with the genius and refinement of the Western world;" and Alison, who wrote the most jejune of books on Taste, is said to have been "inspired by a genuine taste for the sublime and beautiful." Macaulay is spoken of as one whose "imagination often snatches the reins from his reason," whose "ardor dims his equanimity," whose "views, always ingenious, are not uniformly just," whose "powers as a rhetorician make him forget his duties as a judge," who is "splendid rather than impartial;" while in the same passage we are told that "his fascinating volumes" cause us "to regret that the first pleader at the bar of posterity has not yet been raised to the bench." Fine qualities those for a judge!

Nor are we less amused in hearing that Wilson, the

truculent editor of *Blackwood*, "wields his aerial flights through the heavens, without alighting, or caring for the concerns of the lower world"—*i. e.*, Wilson of the *Noctes ;* and whose criticisms, "if they have any imperfections, it is that they are too indulgent"—*i. e.*, Wilson of the Chaldee MS. Mitford's dull and bigoted history of Greece, as we learn, "combines the interest of the romance of Quintius Curtius, with the authenticity and accuracy of Arrian." Thackeray, the greatest satirist of England, since the days of Swift, is dismissed as a writer of Mr. Dickens's school—*i. e.*, the school which "aimed at the representation of the manners, customs, ideas, and habits of middle and low life,"—"distinguished by great talents and graphic powers," but not "destined to be durable," because "imagination is a winged deity, whose flight, to be commanding, must ever be upward ;" and because, further, "ridicule is valued only by those who know the *persons* ridiculed." We might fill a volume with such crude and preposterous judgments, if we had space to waste in copying them—judgments formed without principles, and expressed in the loose language of the newspapers.

Of criticism as an art—an art which treats the great products of literature and science, as the vital outgrowth of genius, having their deep inward laws of being, and related to the age in which they were produced, by the profoundest ties and influences—Mr. Alison appears to have no more conception than a common house-painter has of *chiaro oscuro*. When he has given the title of a writer's principal works, adduced a few facts of his external life, pronounced him charming, widely celebrated, and enduringly known, or a man of sane moral convictions, he fancies that he has written the history of that writer. Of his individuality, as distinguished from other writers, from what stand-point he looked on life and nature, and interpreted their lessons, or of his relations to great contemporaneous developments in his own sphere, as well as in other spheres, we are taught literally nothing. Sir Walter Scott, as a novelist, for instance, was an altogether peculiar and significant phenomenon, making its appearance in the midst of English literature, to revive the images of feudal life, at a time when the whole current of the world was agitated, and rushing on to an unknown future. What did he express, what were his uses, what his value to the age? Can a thoughtful mind consider him, without asking questions such as these? Has he any real interest to us, as a fact of history, except in his relations to the general course of literature, and to the general life of society? Yet Mr. Alison is satisfied with a few personal details, and a very vague talk about his "brilliancy of fancy," his "poetic conceptions," his "great and varied powers," and that poetic temperament which "threw over the pictures of memory the radiance of the imagination ;" adding, as a proof, both of Scott's morality and immortality, in true Alisonian style, that "nothing ever permanently floated down the stream of time but what was buoyant from its elevating tendency !"

Coleridge was no less than Scott a notable man, not in himself merely, but in the important influence which he exercised upon the poetic taste of his generation, and the new era which he may be said to have created in the speculative tendencies of the English mind. More than any man of his age, therefore, he deserves at the hands of the historian a rigid analysis of his splendid powers, and a careful estimate of his bearing upon contemporary thought. At the least, he should have been described as something more than a considerable poet, and an excellent translator, "with a strongly metaphysical turn of mind," less "abstract and philosophical," though "more pictorial and dramatic" than Wordsworth, and not destined to "lasting celebrity," because his "ideas and images are too abstract." How is it possible that any one could have lived in Coleridge's own time, and perhaps read his masterly essays, and yet describe him in this asinine way ?

Our readers may, perhaps, object that it is too much to expect of Alison any philosophical view, either of men or things ; and we should admit the force of the objection if he were not constantly thrusting reflections, meant to be philosophical, into the course of his narrative. Not content with his verbose details of incidents, and his attempted portraitures of character, he deals sweeping judgments "round the land," uttering them with the most positive confidence, and claiming for them at times the authority of Heaven. One feels bound, consequently, to look a little into his right to assume this lofty judicial attitude, and to ask on what principles he arrives at these elaborate philosophical deductions.

It is difficult, we confess, to ascertain distinctly what his philosophical views are ; but as near as we can gather them from the maxims and theories he is fond of sporting, they amount to this : that man is universally corrupt, destitute alike of the goodness which should lead him into the right path, and of the intellect that enables him to discern it ; and as an inevitable result, running perpetually into errors, from which he is alone saved by an inscrutable Providence. Thus, when a French Revolution comes, in a sudden access of frenzy, to spread its Jacobinical wickedness over the continent, a sober and constitutional England is raised up to stay the deluge ; when a wicked Mr. Peel contracts the currency or establishes free trade, to the infinite damage of the landed aristocracy, Providence opens the way to California, to supply the precious metals and give an impulse to emigration ; and so on every occasion when the iniquity and short-sightedness of mortals get them into hopeless straits, Providence stands ready with a method of relief! We have as much faith in Providence as Mr. Alison has, but we believe that it works through human agency and according to a fixed and intelligible order, which is no further inscrutable than we are ignorant, and which proceeds in every respect rationally, because it is itself the Supreme Reason. We cannot so degrade it as to regard it as a mere Jack-at-a-pinch. There was once a class of talewrights and dramatists in German literature, which somebody called the Need-and-Help School, because it was their habit to allow their characters to fall into all manner of dangers and difficulties, in order at the critical moment to come to their aid, either by providing some unexpected rescue, or killing them all off in a heap. They very well illustrate the kind of Providence to which Mr. Alison seems to commit the universe—a Providence which creates a certain number of ninnies and villains, places them in the midst of the scenes in which they are to move, sets them at work until they are all at loggerheads and begin to throttle the life out of each other, and then, at last, interposes to make a display of its own adroitness and superiority.

We say this *seems* to be his theory of the course of providential guidance, but he is not always consistent in his expositions of it. He accounts for the French Revolution, in one place, for example, by alleging that it was a part of "the universal frenzy which at times seizes mankind from causes inscrutable to human wisdom;" and yet, in another place, he assigns a dozen natural causes, such as the oppressions of the previous reigns, for all its sanguinary violence. At one time he insists on the radical depravity of man, and his inevitable tendency to all sorts of self-destruction, while at another time he tries to make out that there is, after all, a steady progress and general improvement of the race. Now, it is evident that both these views cannot be true ; for if there is progress, there must be a law of progress, and consequently, no incessant proclivity to evil ; or if there be that uniform proclivity to evil, then there can be no general progress, only a capricious, occasional, and useless fluctuation from bad to worse. We must do Mr. Alison the justice, however, to confess that for the most part he adopts the obscurant theory, or that view of human affairs which, when it cannot confirm its own prejudices by the actual facts, refers the whole to inscrutable wisdom.

As a matter of course, Mr. Alison distrusts all popular movements, even to the extent of doubting whether popular education does any good. He regards representative government everywhere as a failure, but detests the United States especially, because it is an illustrious example of its success. He imagines England on the verge of bankruptcy and dissolution, because free trade has been carried there, and the popular element of the constitution is coming into the ascendant ; and he vaticinates like another Jeremiah over the entire future. We do not, in fact, know a philosopher on the face of the earth, who, if his own philosophic essays on man and nature be correct, ought to feel more uncomfortable than he, in the present advancing condition and brightening prospects of mankind. It were scarcely worth while, however, to quarrel with him for his inveterate and silly toryism ; nor take him to task, as we might, for those reiterated misrepresentations

in which he chooses to indulge in respect to the character and progress of Democracy, particularly as it has
developed itself in this country. We shall merely
proffer him our sincerest compassion for the difficulties
of his position. A man who writes the history of the
nineteenth century, under a serious conviction that its
experiences are a solemn warning against liberalism, is
one of the saddest spectacles that can be presented to
our eyes. The labor of Sisyphus was nothing to his :
the fruitless experiments of the Danaides, nothing : and
only the swimming pig of Southey's Devil's Walk can
be his parallel. Every stroke that he makes helps to
cut his own throat—every fact that he records upsets his
theory. His painful task is to read the riddle of things
backward. Nor ought we to be surprised that Mr. Alison
should give such sterile and incomplete accounts of the
great movements in literature, science, and practical
art, which have distinguished the years of which he
writes ; for if he had done otherwise, in good sooth
he would have been compelled to abandon his obscu-
rantism, and to adopt a view of the progress of human
affairs quite damaging to his pet notion of the extreme
naughtiness and littleness of God's noblest creature,
Man.

Gervinus, one of the most accomplished and profound of German historians, lately sentenced to prison
at Baden for the publication of his opinions, taking up
the doctrine of Aristotle, that the law of human development was from the participation of the few to that of
the many in government, demonstrates and confirms it
by the subsequent experiences of two thousand years.
·It is not a fancy, he says, nor a declamatory phrase, nor
a hypothetical judgment, but the absolute, scientific
order, as certain as the courses of the stars, or the
process of growth in the individual being. But what

Gervinus proves, mainly in the political sphere, made still more manifest by the entire course and consequence of the development of literature and science, is particularly striking in the wonderful achievements of the last half-century. In the death-blows which it has given to the old feudal and aristocratic maxims and practices, in the ameliorations it has wrought in the spirit of laws, in the growing political power, moral elevation, and intellectual enlightenment of the masses of the people, in the almost universal diffusion of letters, as well as in their humanitarian tone, in the greater cheapness of all the appliances of every-day life, whereby the luxuries of the past age have become the daily comforts of this, in the prodigious movements imparted to trade, by the discovery of new outlets for population, new fields for labor, new rewards for enterprise; in short, in the indescribably numerous and inexhaustible sources of enjoyment and wealth, bestowed upon all communities by the revelations of science and their practical application, we find the condition of mankind advanced beyond the dreams of the most sanguine enthusiasts of former generations, and we see in them, also, a pledge of the more rapid and surprising conquests of the future. But Mr. Alison finds in them, and sees in them, no such things; he finds in their past effects only a disturbance of his cherished notions of law and order, and he sees in their future promises only another "dispersion of mankind," like that on the plains of Shinar,—produced, too, by the same unholy pride and ambition which raised the vain tower of Babel!

Now, it is because he does not find and see these things, or, in other words, because he does not comprehend the spirit of the age he undertakes to describe, but stands in a relation of antagonism to it, that we pronounce him wholly incapable of his task. No actual specimens of his unskilfulness are necessary to convince us of his unfitness. He may string facts together with never so much industry, describe isolated scenes with the animation of a Napier, analyze individual character with the eye of a Scott; but so long as the characters and events he portrays are no more than so many shadows dancing upon the wall, he cannot become their historian. A Sandwich islander, suddenly placed before the footlights at Niblo's, when Sontag or Alboni is electrifying the intelligent spectators with splendid visions of beauty, might as well hope to write a competent criticism of the performance for the next day's *Tribune,* as a historian of Mr. Alison's sympathies to depict the Nineteenth Century. Granting that he sees the incidents and events with as comprehensive and minute an eye as any other man, he can yet see only the outside of them, like the Otaheitan at the play; it is impossible that he should see the motives of the performers, and much less the scope of the drama. The principle which explains all—the struggle for human freedom—that contest of man for the mastery of nature, of society, of himself, which is the open secret of all history, he winks out of sight, and he puts in its place some marrowless and conservative ignorantism.

For it is no less true of history in general, than it is of the history of the last half-century, that without this guiding principle of freedom, it becomes a vast and innavigable ocean, clouded with mists and darkness. The historian who puts his little bark forth into it, moves forward without compass or chart. Innumerable counter currents baffle him on all sides; huge sandbanks arrest his course; coral reefs and the wrecks of stranded systems scrape his keel, the storms and winds of fierce war harry the skies, so that he is driven he knows not whither, and makes the shore, when he arrives at all, by merest chance. But had he carried with him the chart and compass of freedom, which is the great law of all the evolutions of history, he might have defied the tempests and mastered the stormy seas, beholding beyond the chaos of the elements a beautiful sunshine and the green world of peace.

THE "WORKS" OF AMERICAN STATESMEN.*

E TOCQUEVILLE, who has written the most appreciative book on the United States that has been published, yet falls into many errors, among which we are disposed to class what he says of our want of permanent national records. His words are these : " The public administration (of the United States) is oral and traditionary. But little is committed to writing, and that little is wafted away, like the leaves of the Sibyl, by the smallest breeze. The only historical remains are the newspapers ; but, if a number be want-ing, the chain of time is broken, and the Present is severed from the Past. I am convinced, that in fifty years it will be more difficult to collect authentic docu-ments concerning the social condition of the Americans at the present day, than it is to find the remains of the administration of France during the middle ages ; and, if the United States were ever invaded by barbarians, it would be necessary to have recourse to the history of other nations in order to learn anything of the people who now inhabit them."

It is a curious comment on this speculation, that we have, perhaps, more materials for the minute and faith-ful history of our political and social life, and for il-lustrating the characters of our great men, than any

---

* From *Putnam's Monthly*, June, 1853.

other nation.   Our habit of preserving memorials, even insignificant ones, of public occurrences, as well as of men who have made any conspicuous figure, is almost a vice.   The voluminous correspondence of the Revolutionary worthies, from Washington and Franklin down to the obscurer personages of their time ; the private memoirs, that the families, or friends, of the Adamses, Morris, Livingston, Jay, Story, Randolph, Jefferson, and Hamilton, have so carefully compiled : the labored collections of the Historical Societies of the several States, extending to tracts, pamphlets, maps, state papers, and books ; the records of local celebrations and festivities preserved in the archives of towns and cities ; and, finally, the newspapers, of which, in their multiplicity, there is no fear, as De Tocqueville somewhat ludicrously intimates, that the issue of a single day will be lost, to break the chain of events—are so many hostages given to Time to secure us against his fatal inroads.

We are reminded also of another disproof of the remark we have quoted, by this series of the "Works" of some of our eminent later statesmen, put forth by themselves or their admirers, to give extension and permanence to whatever they may have said or done worthy of notice.   There is now lying before us a score of volumes, issued within the last few months, which contain the speeches and writings of Levi Woodbury, William H. Seward, Henry Clay, John C. Calhoun, and Daniel Webster, together with attempts, more or less elaborate, in the form of biographies and notes, to convey "to other nations and to future times" some knowledge of their deeds and characters.   Mr. Woodbury's "Works" are in three volumes, consisting mainly of his speeches as Senator, his reports as Secretary of the Treasury, and his occasional addresses ; Mr. Seward

appears similarly in three large tomes; Mr. Clay in
two, chiefly of speeches; Mr. Calhoun, in one, containing his dissertations on Government and on the
Constitution, to be followed by four other volumes of
reports and speeches; and Mr. Webster in six, embracing his orations, diplomatic papers, forensic arguments, and debates. There is, consequently, great
sameness in the subject-matter of these publications;
but that fact rather heightens than impairs their utility,
at least in a historical sense, because it furnishes us
with the views of several different minds, in respect to
the same great questions and events.

Embracing as they do, moreover, discussions of
nearly all the more important issues that have arisen
since the origin of our democratic government and
under the peculiar structure of our mixed societies,—
questions of agriculture, industry, education, and religion, as well as of State and Federal politics,—by men
who moved in the midst of the agitations they caused,
and applied the best energies of mind and heart to the
peaceful solution of each as it arose, these volumes not
only secure us, so far as they go, from the reproach of
De Tocqueville, but are valuable contributions to letters, as well as to history.

For it should be remembered that the literature of a
nation is not confined to magazines, books, journals, and
poems, or to those other forms in which the intellectual
life of a people is ordinarily expressed. All sincere
and vigorous utterances of national feeling and thought,
become, when recorded, a part of that literature. Political debates, especially in a nation where the powers
and attainments of men are almost universally devoted
to active pursuits, as they are with us, are likely to
be a most original and vital part of it; and springing
warm from the brains of foremost men, under the im-

pulse of great exigences, when their minds are taxed to the highest extent to overcome opposition and to bring about worthy and noble ends, they are likely to possess an earnestness, freedom, and depth of purpose, which we do not always find in the colder essays of the professed man of letters. At least they will be truer to the form and pressure of the time, though, perhaps, less marked by scholastic perfections.

The editors of these books then have, in our opinion, rightly called them "Works;" for the men from whom they came were not only legislators, orators, magistrates, but authors as well. They did not aim at literary reputation, yet their efforts have the characteristics of literary performances. They are an expression of our national peculiarities ; they abound in pleasant narratives of facts, skilful dialectics, comprehensive and close argument, impassioned eloquence and sarcastic retort ; and so they have a value beyond the occasion in which they originated.

Mr. Woodbury, the first on our list, was not a man who widely influenced his day and generation, and we may dismiss him in few words. As a Senator of the United States, in which capacity he served for some years ; as Secretary of the Treasury during the administration of Mr. Van Buren, and latterly as a District Judge, he attained to a respectable position : he served his party with diligence, and was evidently a man of solid judgment and sincere faith in his opinions ; but he was scarcely a leader out of the small State of New Hampshire, in which he lived, and he never rose to such eminence as to become the representative of any distinctive or vital policy. He wrote with vigor, but yet without grace ; his sentences are cumbrous ; what he saw clearly even, he did not always state clearly ; and when he seeks to illustrate a position, he rather overloads it with commonplace ornament, than simplifies it by apt and lucid figures. A politician and a jurist, the habit of his mind was reserved and cautious. His propositions come to us with so many qualifying phrases,—with so many *ifs*, *buts*, and *provideds*, that they are shorn of their strength, and are often more of a puzzle than an impulse to the intellect. At the same time, Justice Woodbury had strong popular sympathies, cherished an enlightened and liberal political philosophy, was an enthusiast, almost, in his hopes of human progress, and only needed to have surrendered himself more entirely to the inspirations of this side of his nature, to have become an eloquent writer and a great man.

Mr. Seward, we think, a higher order of mind, not because he is more comprehensive or profound, but because he has a finer fibre of brain, and rises more easily into the region of general principles. He is a yet living statesman, surrounded by prepossessions and hostilities, and we are therefore aware that our estimate of him may be influenced by current prejudices ; but we have read his writings attentively, and are prepared to give an honest judgment as to their merits.

Most men, engaged in the actual contests of politics, are liable to be overrated by their friends, and underrated by their enemies ; but the peculiarity of Mr. Seward's case has been, that he has reversed the process, and, if not underrated by his friends, is at least overrated by his enemies. In other words, the peculiar kind of opposition that he has encountered, has given him a prestige beyond the influence he is entitled to by his real abilities. The masses of the people, hearing him decried so vehemently as a most dangerous fellow, the contriver of every nefarious plot, and the secret agent of every disorganizing movement, are apt to take his opponents at their word, and to believe that one who is so fertile in expedients and so hard to baffle, must be a prodigious force, destined sooner or later to the most commanding sway. Men admire success, and even the reputation of it, and have a secret liking for those who are roundly abused. This was proved in another case lately, that of Martin Van Buren, who was more indebted to the magical influence his foes ascribed to him, than to the attachment of his friends or any native sagacity. Give a man a name for rare shrewdness and management, and you give him a host of admirers ; in fact, open his way, without efforts of his own, to almost any advancement.

The characteristics of Mr. Seward's mind are clearness, activity, and cunning, to use the last term in its best sense. He grasps his subjects sharply, manages them with subtle and quick dexterity, and being of a sanguine temperament, never wearies of the labor of elucidation and display. His logic, however, is not of the close and compact sort which may be compared to mailed armor, impregnable to all assaults. It is rather demonstrative than convincing, and consists more in the adroit linking together of facts, than in the rigid deduction of principles. But he has great facility of expression, both as a writer and speaker ; is always perspicuous, generally pleasing, and sometimes eloquent ; he has read considerably, and understandingly ; and his style, without being idiomatic or classical, is not offensively incorrect. He avoids, for the most part, that excessive ornament, that turgid floridity so common to our orators ; although there is a tendency to diffuseness, and a swelling, and consequently, languid wordiness in his hastier efforts which greatly impair their strength. He expatiates too much, is too long in covering his ground, and is apt to be tedious when he ought to be touching. Had he compressed what he has published into one-third the space, he might have said everything that he has now said, and much better. Nor is it any excuse for this carelessness of composition, to say that his addresses and letters were prepared in the midst of active occupations, on the spur of the moment, and without time for that *limæ labor* which gives finish to language. This might have been an excuse for them, as originally uttered, but not for them as deliberately collected and edited. Besides, it is not impossible to acquire a compact, precise, and simple style, even in extemporaneous effusions—to make compression the habit of the mind—and when we consider what a lasting charm it lends to speech, the neglect of it, especially by men who desire to be read widely, and in after-times, seems a strange imprudence.

There is another defect of his compositions, arising partly in the same causes which produce diffuseness, and partly in a limited range of cultivation, which is, the use of worn and current metaphors, or commonplace turns of expression. Not remarkably original in his views, he is less so in his language. We miss that nice choice of words, those racy, idiomatic phrases, those graceful and happy allusions, those pregnant epithets, which condense a whole argument into a word, and those novel and picturesque suggestions, which relieve the weight of argument, to be found in the masters of art. Yet Mr. Seward goes far toward supplying the place of these finer strokes of genius by his amiable and conciliating manner, his temper singularly free from gall, his vivacious readiness, and his elastic, almost exuberant vitality, answering the purpose of a genuine enthusiasm. If he does not produce deep and vivid impressions, he carries his readers with him by the lucidity of his statement, the intrepid and manly spirit in which he meets difficulties and announces principles, and his obvious command of his position.   Never impassioned, even in his most declamatory passages, he is yet always animated and fresh, full of hope, and thoroughly American.

It is no part of our duty, as reviewers, to question the sincerity of Mr. Seward's convictions as a politician ; the less so, as we find his opinions cohering in an intelligent and consistent scheme of political doctrine. Nor do his volumes furnish us any occasion for doubting the perfectly unaffected nature of his popular tendencies.   He everywhere expresses his opinions frankly, even in the face of a known hostile sentiment.   We do not detect him in any of the meaner arts of the demagogue, cannot lay our hands upon any single act of political trimming, but, on the contrary, note an unusual persistence of purpose, and a manly assertion often of generous though unaccepted truths ; and yet we fear the while that his virtue is not of "the incorrigible and losing" sort.

Perhaps our utter disagreement with the school of statesmen to which Mr. Seward belongs, may account for this uneasy feeling.   The school we allude to is that which tends to aggrandize the action of government at the expense of the spontaneous action of the people. It makes the State a sort of omnipotent and omnipresent, and consequently omnivorous power in society—a Jack-of-all-trades, a supreme moralist, a universal pedagogue, a high Justice Rotulorum, a beneficent Providence.   It comprises, within the sphere of government, every function almost of society and of individuals, causing it to build railroads and canals, regulate commerce, encourage trade, equip steamships, promote agriculture, educate children, and support the poor—all in addition to its ordinary and more legitimate duties of protecting, on terms of perfect equality, the persons and property of its citizens! Now, is it not obvious at a glance, that this theory of the objects of legislation, whatever advantages it may have in other respects, opens the way to enormous abuses, inviting the assaults of schemers and profligates, and inflaming while it debases the contests of parties? Wherever it is adopted a State must be looked upon, not as the arbiter of an absolute justice between man and man, but as the dispenser of corrupt and mercenary favors ; and those statesmen who make themselves conspicuous in bending legislation from its lofty, important, and true ends, to the advancement of local and individual privileges, must inevitably excite against themselves the suspicion of sinister and unworthy motives. Of course that suspicion is often misplaced, but the general prevalence of it cannot be denied. Only a man of Washington's continence, or of Hampden's integrity, could escape the taint of imputation ; and Mr. Seward, therefore, who has long been active in pushing projects of one-sided benefit, should not complain if the public, in spite of his nobler and more disinterested performances, should confound his motives with those of his sordid clients. The whole system of special legislation and patronage, is deplorably wrong, and those who dabble in it can hardly avoid defilement.

We think this idea of the sphere of government is deplorably wrong, and yet we are not prepared to state with any precision where the limit of State action properly begins or ends. How much should be left to the individual, and how much the State may legitimately do, is the great unadjusted question of political science. If we adopt the extreme democratic theory, which confines the State to the simple protection of person and property, or to those objects which are common to every member of society, we deprive ourselves of an important means of advancing individual and social welfare, which could not be so well advanced in any other way; whilst, on the other hand, if we assume the unlimited authority of government to interpose in every subject of public concern, we cannot stop short either of gross despotism or gross corruption. The liberty of the citizen to achieve his own fortune in his own way, provided he does not infringe on the same right in others, ought to be sacred under all circumstances; yet, who will deny that there are objects of vast general utility, "enterprises of pith and moment," which cannot or will not be accomplished, if abandoned to the voluntary efforts of individuals? Take a case in point, of immense interest just now—the railroad to the Pacific! Ought it to be undertaken by the Government or by individuals? If you say by individuals, the reply is, that it would require an outlay of labor and capital to which no private company could be competent, even were such a prodigious company itself not a dangerous thing to create. Again, if you say by the Government, you must see that it would inevitably lead to a most pernicious concentration of patronage, to a wholesale jobbing in the Legislature, and to acts of aggravated injustice in respect to different localities. Who will draw the line, therefore, between what the State ought to do, and what it ought not? Who will tell us how far individuals ought to surrender to society, or where its interference is an encroachment, or where a right? Everybody admits that society ought to punish crime, for without such discipline the continued existence of society would be impossible—but ought it not then, for a stronger reason, to institute means for the prevention of crime—to guarantee the poor against anxiety and dependence, the most prolific causes of crime; to educate the ignorant;

to remove the means of temptation, and to encourage virtue in every way? You answer yes! Then why not establish a religion which experience has proved is a most efficient agent of social regeneration? But by establishing a religion you are a long way on toward despotism. Or to reverse the process of the argument, we may say, that if you leave religion to the voluntary action of the people, why not the whole subject of education; why not the support of the insane and poor; why not the organization of the police; why not the line of coast defences; in short, why have any government at all, why not surrender the care of every interest of society to voluntary action? But this would be anarchy, and thus on either hypothesis we fluctuate from one extreme to the other, until our faith in the existence of any stable political science is quite lost.*

Henry Clay, whose works are the next on our list, was, by general consent, the most finished and splendid orator of a nation prolific of orators. Versatile, adroit, bold, profound, pathetic, and imperious—an able tactician, a far-sighted statesman, a born leader of men,— his eloquence was of that masterly order which "wielded at will the fierce democratie," but commanded no less the selecter applause of senates. But great as was its influence on his contemporaries, and intense and fervent the admiration which it excited, it will be perpetuated, we suspect, rather as a remembrance and a tradition, than as a still living power. The volumes in which it is recorded convey some idea of its combined fervor, grace, and force, but a most inadequate one. They are not as bad as the skeletons of Whitfield's

---

[* I allow this passage to stand, although since it was written I have been led to adopt the democratic theory in all its length and breadth.]

sermons, which cause us to wonder how the man could have left such a reputation—mere *simulacra* of a departed reality; for they contain his arguments, his facts, his illustrations, his appeals; in short, some indications of the large make and movement of the man ; but the charm and the spirit are spent.   The flashing eye, the rich melodious voice, the commanding form, "the snowy front, curled with golden hair," which gave them their original life, are gone ; and, as we read them, we feel like one who walks through the cavern of some mighty dead magician—the tools and instruments of his spells are about us, his gems, his treasures, his magic rings, his weird circles and diagrams—in fine, all the evidences of his art—but the fire smoulders in his furnace, and he himself hath vanished into thin air.

> Both roof and floor, and walls, are all of gold,
> But overgrown with dust and old decay.

This is the proverbial disadvantage of the orator, compared with the writer, that the best part of his performance escapes with the occasion ; and if he be an active politician, he has no time to compensate, by the labors of the study, for the haste and immaturity of his extemporaneous efforts.   His words are given loosely to the wind, and the wind carries them on its swift wings to the distant interlunar caves, to be returned to him no more forever.   On the other hand, the writer, ripened by nutritious culture, and purified from taint by the refining processes of his art, commits his treasures to the imperishable amber of print.   So, being dead, he yet speaks, and, in addition to the effects he wrought and the honors he enjoyed while living, diffusion and perpetuity are given to his fame when he is dead.

Mr. Clay, perhaps, less than most other orators,

requires to be embalmed in type, because his services
as a statesman, though not always successful, were so
active and comprehensive, as to have connected his
name with the history of his country, and left an enduring
mark upon its legislation. Nevertheless, we cannot
but think that the world has been a loser by the liberal
share of time and talent which he allowed the cares
of office, and the details of party management, to
absorb. His endowments were so generous, that he
needed only to have nurtured and husbanded them, to
have raised himself to the loftiest niche of greatness.
The love and admiration, which are now confined to
his countrymen and his friends, would, in that case,
have been expanded into the love and admiration of
mankind ; and no position, in the universal respect,
that it was possible for penetration, sagacity, vigorous
powers of reason, affluent imagination, quick sympathies,
and high aspirations to attain, could have been too
exalted or permanent for his reach.

Mr. Clay, in genius and character, was not unlike
Hamilton, whose work he may be said to have taken
up where it was left, and to have carried on with the
same indomitable purpose, and a no less brilliant display
of power. Cherishing the same tendencies toward
a strong and splendid government, gifted with the same
courteous and seductive personal qualities, dividing
opposition by the assiduity of their address, and rallying
support by their exultant confidence in success ;
alike bold, ambitious, and patriotic,—they identified
their names with every great question of the day, both
of domestic administration and of foreign policy; they
infused their own spirit into a vast and powerful party,
while they held its opponents in check ; and after the
glory of having founded our institutions, they share the
next honor of having modified and controlled their

character and development. It was the superior fortune of Mr. Clay, however, to have lived to the mellow fruitfulness of his autumn : envious Death did not snatch him away untimely, while the glow of his young hopes was yet fresh on his cheeks ; but, full of honors, full of years, the little enmities of partisan warfare softened by his venerable age, as the fierce heats of the sun are cooled by the coming night—

> " Life's blessings all enjoyed, life's labor done,
> Serenely to his final rest he passed."

Mr. Calhoun, in respect to the preparation and finish of his works, enjoyed no inconsiderable advantage over Mr. Clay. Engaged, like him, for the greater part of his life, in the arduous labors of leadership and office, the peculiar habits of his mind yet enabled him to preserve more pure and compact, and consequently more lasting qualities of style. The dissipations of debate never prevailed over his stern intellectual integrity. He read little, but reflected much, and when he spoke, which was not often, considering his multiplied opportunities, he spoke from a full mind, with extreme precision and directness, and always in view of some single and important end. His speeches, therefore, are models of severe and cogent reasoning, and no less complete as compositions than they are crowded as storehouses of thought. The intense will that pervades them, carrying the reader along with impetuous force, as if he were in the hands of a giant, stamps them with an individual and peculiar life. Besides this, Mr. Calhoun was permitted, in his latter days, to embody the maturer results of his lifelong studies in the permanent form of a treatise on Government. Those original views of politics, which are scattered through his reports and addresses, in incomplete expositions, were thus condensed into an elaborate system, perfect in its parts and finished as a whole. We see in it the mother-thoughts of all his political action ; explaining whatever may have been supposed to be inconsistent in it ; and exhibiting him as an acute and profound metaphysical philosopher as well as an orator and statesman.

The characteristics uniformly conceded to Mr. Calhoun, by men of all shades of opinion, were, a powerful and subtle analytic intellect, a subdued and chastened but intense enthusiasm, fearless reliance upon the conclusions of his own mind, chivalric honor, and a stainless purity of personal character. Another impression, however, was no less universal in regard to him, namely, that he carried his logical processes to an impracticable degree of refinement, allowing mere abstract speculation to override his more practical conclusions ; while the earnestness of his convictions, hurrying him into hasty judgments, narrowed his sympathies, and blinded him to the broader interests of humanity. His Book both confirms and relieves this estimate. It deepens our sense of his abilities, and also of the dangers they were exposed to from his metaphysics ; but at the same time it raises his extreme Southernism, from the suspicion of a mere sectional bias, into a systematic principle. We see that a singular unity pervaded his opinions because they were legitimate outgrowths of his fundamental ideas, and in no sense transient or temporary feelings. He was the fanatic—using the words in no offensive sense—of his reason, and wherever that led him, he pursued it, regardless of the consequences.

Two curious inconsistencies strike us in the intellectual constitution of Mr. Calhoun. Born in a region where the tropical sun is apt to ripen human passion into the rank luxuriance which it imparts to physical nature, he was yet the severest dialectician and the least ornamental writer among all our distinguished men. His style, though intense, was rigidly intellectual, — plain, direct, cogent, sinewy, and unyielding. No flowers of fancy ever bloomed along its path ; it never wandered into rich meads or leafy woods ; but, arid and hot, like a way across the desert, it bore along its burdens of thought, without furnishing us a single cooling oasis or one refreshing shade. The voluptuous life, the magnificence and pomp, the exuberant fulness and deep-toned harmonies of the Southern zones, seem not to have moved the springs of his being, — never made his brain delirious or kindled his heart into poetry. As well might he have been born in Nova Zembla, or anywhere above the line of perpetual snow, as in the South, for any effect that climate produced upon his imagination and fancy. On the contrary, the sobriquet given to him, of "the cast-iron man," would show rather that he came out of the bowels of our rugged northern mountains ; like iron, he was capable of intense heat and a slight glow, but of no brilliancy or sparkle. Stern, dignified, upright, he was at all times neither more nor less than the great Senator. A witticism, proceeding from his mouth, would have seemed a sort of *felo de se ;* and a capricious, fantastic, or grotesque conceit, the beginning of mental aberration. It is said that in the bosom of his family, among his friends, neighbors, and servants, he relaxed into some lambent play of the affections, but we who saw him only wrapped in his senatorial robes, like a stern old Roman, must regard the report as a myth.

The second peculiarity of Mr. Calhoun consisted in this :—that he, the only one of our statesmen who defended the social anomaly of slavery, not as a political expedient or a necessity of circumstance, but as an intrinsic and actual good, yet passed his life in the elaboration of a scheme of government for giving the amplest security to individual freedom. A republican by conviction, as well as a democrat by party affinity, he was so dissatisfied with that democracy which allows the majority of the people to rule, that he contrived an ingenious system of checks and negatives for protecting minorities against its oppressive domination. His posthumous treatise on Government has for its principal object a demonstration of the despotism of the many, and the absolute need of a constitution of society in which every interest, and as near as possible every man, shall be represented. All the acumen of his analysis, all the craft and vigor of his logic, all his experience of affairs, and the untaxed energy of his imperious will, were turned to the elucidation and enforcement of these views, in the hope of restraining power and enlarging liberty. No man ever inveighed more vehemently than he against the encroachments of the State upon the rights of the citizen, except that when he depicted the blessings of slavery, he was equally vehement. He thus exhibited to the world the spectacle of a democrat who resisted the organized expression of the will of the majority, and a republican who consecrated his days to the support and extension of a state of society founded on the subjugation of one race by another. Nor is it less worthy of note, that his countrymen, convinced of his thorough simplicity and truthfulness, forgot the inconsistency of his opinions in their admiration of his character.

Mr. Calhoun's theory of government was simply this : That as society is the natural state of man, and man prefers his own interests to the well-being of others, government is necessary to balance the selfish by the social propensities. But then, as the exercise of its powers must be lodged in the hands of individuals who are prone to prefer their own interests to the general good, a constitution is necessary to restrain the government. How, then, is that constitution to be framed? We see that it can only be administered by men ; and we see, too, that those men will be tempted by the universal tendency of their natures, to become unfaithful to their trusts. By what contrivance shall the public be secured against the abuse of their power, against extortion, oppression, and wrong? *Quis custodes ipsos custodiat?* If you say, by universal suffrage, you only substitute a dominant majority for your former authority, and which would have the same tendency to the misuse of its powers as any other irresponsible ruler. Nor would a free press be any restraint, because, firstly, it cannot change that principle of human nature in which the necessity of governments originates ; and secondly, because the press always leans to the heavier side of the scale, to the strongest interest or combination of interests, so that it exasperates rather than cures or alleviates the evil.

The only solution of the difficulty Mr. Calhoun finds in his doctrine of "concurrent majorities," as opposed to numerical majorities, whereby he gives to separate parts or interests of society a negative upon the action of the other parts or interests. Thus, in the Roman republic, the power of the patricians, which would have been otherwise exorbitant, was restrained by the unqualified veto of the tribunes, who represented the plebeian orders ; thus, in the Polish diet, each member had a *liberum veto*, an absolute negative upon the passage of offensive laws ; thus, too, in the Iroquois confederacy or league of the Six Nations, in our own history, each tribe possessed a power to resist its decisions ; and thus, in the United States, he would have given a power of nullification to each of the separate States, in all cases of fancied grievance or outrage.

This original and ingenious system, to which we only allude, not pretending to furnish more than the meagerest outline of it, Mr. Calhoun develops with amazing energy of argument.* His incidental remarks, especially on the tyranny of majorities, and the odious practice known in this country as "the division of the spoils," are replete with the profoundest wisdom. But his system, as a whole, is, in our opinion, unsound in its premises, and impracticable in its applications. In the first place, we do not believe that government originates in this supposed conflict between the selfish and social propensities of mankind, but that it is as much an original impulse of nature as society itself. In other words, we think that the tendency of man to some form of unitary organization is an instinct of his being, prior to all reflection, and as strong as his inmost soul. History has given us no instance of society, even in its most savage state, without government, nor can we conceive of society as possible, without some kind of central authority and direction. Society, to be a society at all—*i. e.*, to act as a corporate existence in any sense—must also be a government, and that, too, whether we suppose its members to be the devils in hell or angels in heaven. In the second place, admitting Mr. Calhoun's notion of the predominance of the selfish propensities, it seems to us that he does not allow sufficiently for those other tendencies which concur in mitigating and modifying their practical action, such as the affections which bind families and neighborhoods together, and even the governors to the gov-

---

* We have considered it at length in another Essay

erned—such as the natural sense of justice, which re-
strains all men more or less—and the common interest
which all men have in order, peace, and security.   He
takes his single principle, of the all-pervading force of
individual selfishness, and pushes it to its conclusion
without regard to opposing principles or moderating
circumstances.

Again, in his provision of remedies for the abuses of
power, he runs into an impracticable conclusion, because his scheme, if carried out, could only result in
anarchy.   If you give to every interest in society a constitutional ability to arrest the action of the government,
whenever it might please to withhold its concurrence
from a law, we do not see how there could be any
government at all.   Some one or other of the parts
would be forever in conflict with the whole; for though
Mr. Calhoun alleges that the effect of his arrangement
would only be to cause the different interests, portions,
or orders to desist from attempting to adopt any measure calculated to promote the prosperity of one or more
by sacrificing that of the others, and then to force them
to unite in such measures as would promote the prosperity of all—we are quite sure, from the almost universal experience of our race in schemes of concerted
action, that the practical operation would be no action
at all.   The case of a jury which he cites, as to the
practicability of unanimous decisions, is not in point,
for the reason that a jury is chosen expressly on the
ground that it has no interest in the verdict; but if we
suppose that each of the twelve men who compose it
had a separate personal interest to be determined, what
would become of, not the unanimity only, but the concurrence?   A compromise, founded on the majority of
their interests, is the nearest approach that they would
be likely to make to any just decision.

But while we are disinclined to adopt the theory of Mr. Calhoun, we are eager to remark that he seems to us to have been aiming at a most important principle in the sphere of political and social organization. It is this : The necessity of restricting the powers of our general governments, and of referring society back more and more to its local and individual elements. The leading peculiarity of our political system has been said to be the recognition of the township ; and we see no reason why the township itself should not be organized, with its separate industrial interests, so as to give a larger scope to individual freedom, and at the same time provide for an affiliated or combined action. This, however, is not the place nor time for advancing new theories, and we return to our task.

What Mr. Calhoun is supposed by many to have wanted, Mr. Webster had in perfection—robust, broad, practical understanding. He was the personification of the Understanding, as distinguished from the intuitive Reason and the creative Imagination. Our reading does not enable us to recall many men, of any epoch, more largely endowed with what is best expressed by the simple word, mind. There have been many more brilliant men, men of more original insight, of finer instincts, of more versatile and comprehensive genius, of quicker and bolder and more susceptible imagination, of more delicate and irritable fancy, of loftier moral aspirations, but few of more masculine intellect. If we were required to designate him by a single phrase, we should say that he was a man of superb talent. He cannot, of course, be compared to Plato or Bacon, or any of that exalted order whose thoughts create epochs in the history of the race ; nor yet to those commanding geniuses of action, like Cæsar or Napoleon, who handle nations as an artist handles his materials; still less to the all-prevailing poets, the Shakspeares, Miltons, and Goethes, on whom the most exuberant measure of the divine glory is poured: for his faculties lay in a different line from all these; his sphere was not that of creation, but of advocacy; and we must look for his parallel, therefore, among the Ciceros, the Pitts, the Mirabeaus, the O'Connells, the Peels, and the Clays of the Senate House and the Forum. Less than some of these in certain respects, he is greater than any one of them in others; Cicero excels him in culture, Mirabeau in energy, Pitt in fertility of resource; but for the union of strength with grace of intellect,—for calm, easy dignity of manner,—for ponderous facility of argumentation,—for lawyer-like clearness of perception, and solid, broad, practical diplomacy, he occupies a position almost apart.

> "——— deep on his front engraven,
> Deliberation sat, and public care:
> With Atlantean shoulders, fit to bear
> The weight of mightiest monarchies."

The late eulogists of Mr. Webster were fond of comparing him with Edmund Burke; but, as we think, without a due and discriminating appreciation of their respective natures. Webster could never have spoken the speeches which grew out of the Warren Hastings affair, every sentence blazing with the splendors of a gorgeous rhetoric; nor could he have written those burning and glowing reflections on the French Revolution. On the other hand, Burke could scarcely have made that prodigious extempore reply to Mr. Hayne, so versatile, satiric, overwhelming and solemnly eloquent. Because they were men essentially different; and the coupling of their names is suggestive rather in the way of contrast than of agreement. Webster pos-

sessed talent, but Burke genius. Burke, therefore, was
the superior in imagination, in culture, in earnestness,
and in moral sensibility ; Webster in dialectics, in simplicity and strength of style, in decorum and grave
manly debate. The vocabulary of Burke was more
rich and gorgeous ; that of Webster more chaste, terse,
and manageable. Webster was pre-eminently an advocate, always argumentative, always collected, always
addressing himself to the intellect, or to the feelings
only so far as they might move the intellect ; Burke
was a poet as well as an orator, irritable and impetuous,
and operating through the will and fancy quite as much
as the mind. Where Webster reasoned, Burke philos-
ophized : where Webster was serene, equable, ponderous, dealing his blows like an ancient catapult ; Burke
was clamorous, fiery, multitudinous, rushing forward
like his own "whirlwind of cavalry." The one was
Doric in his firmness and elegance, the other Corinthian
in his elaboration and ornament. Webster was the
Roman temple, stately, solid, and massive ; Burke, the
Gothic cathedral, fantastic, aspiring, and many-colored.
The sentences of Webster roll along like the blasts of
the trumpet on the night air ; those of Burke are more
like the echoes of an organ in some ancient minster.
Webster advances, in his heavy logical march, and his
directness of purpose, like a Cæsarean legion, close,
firm, serried, square ; Burke, like an oriental procession, with elephants and trophies, and the pomp of
banners.

It is implied in this parallel that Webster was deficient
in imagination : he was, however, not destitute of it,
seeing that no man can be an orator at all without some
degree of it ; but we mean to say, that his imagination
fell short of the ample dimensions of his other faculties.
We use the term to designate that power of which poets

are "all compact," which melts whole worlds of
thought into a single phrase, which evokes a new
universe out of the commonest realities, which has an
instant touch and feeling of all the subtle analogies of
nature, which sees into the heart of things, and which,
whenever it speaks, pours itself forth in language full
of interfused passion, thought, melody, and tears.
Every line almost of Shakspeare is pregnant with it;
as for instance, "Our little life is rounded by a sleep,"
on which Jean Paul says he always meditated when
he heard it, for three days.   Homer exemplifies it,
when the descent of the wrathful Apollo at noon is compared to the coming on of night;   Dante, too, in that
sad story of Francesca, which closes, "that day we
read no more;" Byron, in his "starry Galileo;" and our
own Bryant, when he hears in the domestic hum of the
bee on the prairies "the tread of the advancing multitude which soon shall fill the borders." Among orators,
Burke, where he describes Hyder Ali, in his retreats,
meditating vengeance on the Carnatic, as, "hanging
like a cloud upon the declivities of the mountains,"
gives a rare instance of this power; and so does Mr.
Webster in this passage of the oration on the Bunker
Hill Monument : "Let it rise till it meet the sun in its
coming : let the earliest light of the morning gild it,
and parting day linger and play on its summit." Again,
speaking of the power of England, he says, "Her
morning drum-beat, following the sun and keeping
company with the hours, circles the earth daily with one
continuous and unbroken strain of martial airs." There
are also examples of imaginative power in his allusion
to the slave-trade in the Plymouth oration, and in his
description of the murder of the venerable Mr. White.
But it is rarely that he rises to such heights, or on
occasions of intense excitement only, when he tran-

scends himself, and momently catches the fine madness of the poet. In general we do not discover the play of this faculty, even of that lambent and gentle flashing out of it, which resembles its grander displays, as the aurora resembles some terrific blaze of lightning.

Nor do we find the cultivation of Mr. Webster so rich and various as we had been led to suppose by the admiration of his followers. Out of his profession he does not appear to have been an extensive reader. A few well-known Latin books, the poetry of Pope and his school, who were the fashion in his youth, the historical plays of Shakspeare, and the Old Testament,— the last two, it must be admitted, worlds in themselves,— were his chief resources. But it cannot be said—at least it is not made manifest in his published works—that he had any profound or critical knowledge of English literature, as a whole ; to the German, Italian, Spanish, and French literatures, he made no pretentions ; while his classical stores were obviously quite limited. We do not discover any evidences, at the same time, that he was well instructed in any of the sciences, or that he possessed any controlling love for the fine arts. If he had been a reaper in those fields, the rich and luscious juices of the harvest would have inevitably exuded into his speech. They who wander through groves of bloom, catch the Sabean odors in their dress, and exhale them in every breath.

In respect to the degree, thoroughness, and variety of their culture, indeed, we cannot but think that the statesmen of foreign nations, especially of France and England, greatly surpass those of our own country. Furnished, in the outset, by the superior discipline and more exacting standards of their schools, with a more solid education, they are also more apt to carry with them into the duties of active life the tastes of their scholastic days. A literary performance of some sort, a lecture, a poem, a memoir, or a history, becomes their relaxation from the fatigues of the forum or the bureau. In France, the most eminent statesmen are better known as *littérateurs,* as Guizot, Thiers, Lamartine, De Tocqueville, etc. ; and even in England, where literature, as a profession, is not so nobly requited, Lord John Russell writes dramas and edits biographies, Gladstone discourses of Church and State, the Earl of Carlisle lectures, and Brougham philosophizes, experiments, and disserts on Natural Theology and Athenian orators. But who of our statesmen, saving Everett, Sumner, and Legaré, to whom politics seems a stray visiting-place rather than their native habitat, has taste for such studies or is competent to borrow grace from them for his severer pursuits ? An annual address before some literary society or mechanics' institute, is generally the limit of their excursions in this field, while the barrenness, tautology, and sophomorical ornament of these occasional displays, are dreary evidences that they are "not to the manner born." This deficiency, it is true, is partly incident to the incessant demands of our active national life, but is owing still more, we suspect, to the want of a real appreciation of the value of literature, science, and art, among our public men.

But if Mr. Webster had not rifled the flower-gardens of literature, he compensated for his deficiencies, in part, by the possession of a fine natural taste. His modes of expression are always neat, correct, and forcible. Apt words aptly chosen, well planned and well executed sentences, an exquisite clearness of statement, a sober chastity of figure, a round, melodic, stately rhythm, sometimes swelling and grand, but never grandiloquent, are the every-day beauties of his style. He is even remarkably graceful at times, and when deeply moved by his subject, a sonorous charm accompanies the full, equable flow of his thoughts. No painful effort is apparent in him, no turgid labor, no gymnastic contortions, no nervous, spiteful, momentary flashes—which are all symptoms of weakness. On the contrary, we may apply to him one of his own favorite quotations, and say that he is—

Strong without rage, without o'erflowing, full.

In this respect, indeed, he is a model for our young orators and writers, who, if they would become really cogent and impressive, must chasten their extravagance with somewhat of his moderation, and temper their fervors with somewhat of his dignity. It is a part of our life to be excessive in action and ambitious in phrase, and we have not learned that the *suaviter in modo* is quite as effective as the *fortiter in re.*

As an orator, however, Webster's greatest defect was the want of a thoroughly profound and delicate moral sensibility ; of that noble, yet lively susceptibility to suffering and wrong, which makes the world's woes and hopes our own, and our own those of the world,— which raises us to the heights of heroism, while it softens us into the sweet tenderness of woman,—which inspires generous devotion and the sternest spirit of self-sacrifice, at the moment when the heart swells with emotion, and the lips tremble, and the eye is suffused with tears—and which, when we come to the utterance of it, gushes over into deep pathos, or a "cry that shivers to the tingling stars." Mr. Webster shows a certain sort of religious sentiment, but it is not deep nor acute, nor apparently so much an original inspiration, as something learned from the schools. He uses it as a material of his art, as one of the graceful and effective appliances of rhetoric, giving elevation to the tone of his thought, but it never bursts out as an irrepressible, overwhelming impulse, carrying both speaker and listener along in a whirl of agitation. His prevalent tone is cold, subdued, almost impassive. Because of this want of moral sentiment he had no fine lyric enthusiasms. No one, we suspect, was ever made a martyr by his persuasion ; few have ever wept over his pages or under the sound of his voice ; though many, we have no doubt, have been often lifted by him into higher ranges of thought and a loftier patriotism. He moved men by the commanding power of his intellect, but not by the appealing, pathetic, melting utterances of the heart. He never impresses us as a man "terribly in earnest," but always bears about with him the conscious air of an advocate, of one who pleads powerfully for his cause, but for the reason that it is his cause, and not that it is the truth of God. In reading Mr. Calhoun, though you differ from every word he utters, though you see that he is imposing on his own mind, you are still persuaded of his intense conviction of what he says, of his willingness to stake life and honor on each sentence, of his deep, ineradicable, personal interest in the success of his case. But no one feels that Mr. Webster would break his heart over a defeat, or swoon with joy at an unexpected triumph.

It is probably because he carried this advocate spirit into his public life, that he achieved so little as a man of action. His successes were those of the lawyer. He expounded the Constitution as only Marshall before him had done, and he conducted diplomatic disputes with ability ; but no original measures signalized his name. The measures that he supported have been condemned by the larger wisdom of the people, whilst those he opposed have been incorporated into the settled policy of the nation. He was, therefore, not too great to be popular, as some of his foolish friends assert, but not great enough—nor sufficiently original, unselfish, and earnest.

But, in spite of every objection that a nicer criticism raises, the nation may well be, as it is, and long will be, proud of the fame of Daniel Webster. His eminent qualities as an advocate would have distinguished him as *primus inter illustres* in any age. Had he lived in the time of Demosthenes, his name would have come down to us as no unworthy compeer of that father of eloquence ; had he pleaded in the Roman forum, he would have shared the plaudits of its listeners with all-accomplished Tully himself; and in the most brilliant era of British oratory, he would have added a fifth to the glorious four who thundered in the Commons. Our young country then may well cherish whatever was good or great in the inheritance of his fame.

We must now, however, draw these desultory thoughts to a close. In doing so, let us express our pleasure in the practice which obtains more and more, of collecting the works of our conspicuous men. Let us also suggest to younger statesmen, the new accountability to literature to which they will be hereafter bound over. With the vision of a book in the distance to transmit their folly or wisdom to larger audiences and severer judges than they are apt to find in the Senate, they should be encouraged or warned to a more careful husbandry of their powers. A more glorious trust than is put into their hands cannot well be conceived. Our old revolutionary statesmen, who laid the foundations of empire, have long since passed away ; their immediate successors, who conducted it through the stormy transitions of its formative period, with the single exception of Benton, are likewise gone ; and a new race is advanced to the vacant places.   But they advance also to weightier responsibilities and broader duties.   Our country swells with such velocity in greatness of extent and greatness of power, that the very statistics of its growth startle us, as the figure of her future breaks,

> "Like a comet, out
> Far-splendoring the sleepy realms of night."

In a quarter of a century the young Republic will have attained a dominion greater than that of Rome at the zenith of her strength, or of England in the time of Pitt, standing the first among the nations.   Every American is elated with the consciousness of this near reality, but is he equally alive to the nobler duties that it imposes upon him?   Do our statesmen reflect that they legislate, not for the meagre twenty millions of this age, but for the hundred millions of an age just at hand?   Oh! what men they should be to be equal to their destinies!   What a deep base of generous qualities they should lay for the superstructure of great deeds to come! what inflexible integrity of character they should cultivate, what comprehensive sympathies cherish, what exalted purposes demand of Heaven!   With what moderation, what wisdom, what fearless independence, what utter hatred of wrong, what an aching love of justice, they should strive to comprehend their position—to thrust aside with utter loathing and disgust the petty ends of party, and to rise with "a clear foresight, not a blindfold courage," toward the summits of their great office!

COMTE'S PHILOSOPHY.*

IT is some ten or twelve years since, entering the bookstore of Wiley & Putnam, in Broadway, we took from the shelves four large and dingy volumes, printed in French, and bound with coarse, rose-colored paper, purporting to be a treatise on the entire circle of the sciences. The first page we opened upon contained a statement of the imperfections of analytical geometry, and we said, "Here is a conceited fellow, who believes himself capable of reforming the mathematics." But on reading further, we discovered that he was an earnest partisan of the mathematics, carrying his respect for them, indeed, so far as to assert, in speaking of the progress of their astronomical applications, that "the heavens declare the glory"—not of God, as the good old Bible says, but "of Hipparchus, Kepler, and Newton." An audacious thinker, at any rate, we thought to ourselves, and strove to penetrate a little deeper into his book. Repulsed at first by the novelty and boldness of his remarks, we were at the same time held fast by a certain assurance of movement. As he passed along the dizzy heights of the most adventurous speculation, we were convinced that

---

* *The Positive Philosophy of Auguste Comte :* Freely translated and condensed by HARRIET MARTINEAU. 2 vols.

From *Putnam's Monthly*, June, 1854.

no ordinary thinker held us in his hands; and when, toward the close of the work, we came full-face upon the announcement of a wholly new science, for which all other sciences were but preparatives—the Science of Society—the fact jumped in too nicely with the tenor of our own previous researches and hopes, to allow any dictates of economy to hinder us from becoming the owner of those shabby-looking volumes.

We read them, not with avidity, because they were written quite too much in "the dry-light," as Bacon calls it, for that, and yet with a deep though forced attention. It was clear, from the very outset, that the author was a novel and independent thinker; his great instrument of a mind moved along with the regularity, though by no means the velocity, of a machine, impressing one, as it drew him on, with a feeling that he might be supposed to have when caught up by the gearing of some monster corn-mill or cotton factory. No pleasant episodes of the imagination adorned the way; no scintillations of fancy sparkled like fire-flies around it; no gentle play of the affections warmed it; but a stern and relentless Intellect, marching remorselessly forward, was treading down our dearest hopes, and crushing out the noblest and sweetest sensibilities, and dragging us with it to its infernal goal.

As we became more familiar with our demon, however, we found that he was not altogether so bad as he seemed; a silver lining of humanity was now and then turned from out the folds of his dark frown; he was clearly very much in earnest, and impelled by an unquestionable love of truth. Speaking ill of nobody, threatening nobody, he pursued his own silent and impassive way among the stars, and through the depths of the earth, and amid the busy haunts of men, intent only on his purpose, which, the more it was pondered,

grew to be more and more dignified, noble, and benevolent. We finally dismissed all fears of our guide,
and honestly set to work to discover what he was at.
When we add that those volumes were the "Positive
Philosophy" of Comte, since so widely known as a profound and comprehensive scientist, the intelligent reader
of this day will need no further explanation of either
our surprise or our admiration.

It is always a momentous discovery—this of a new
and really great thinker—of a man who discusses with
consummate familiarity and ease the highest problems
of science ; and we naturally turned to the Records to
see what the world had made of him—to ascertain his
whereabout, as well as to compare our secluded estimate of his rank with that of the accredited standards
of opinion and criticism. Alas! we searched in vain
for any notice of him. The Reviews of France and
England, though noisy enough in their praises and
dispraises of the little tadpoles of literature, had no
word for this Leviathan ; learned societies the world
over, eager as they are sometimes to rescue their insignificance from oblivion, by blazoning the name of
whoever has won a momentary glory in deciphering
the wrappages on an old mummy, or discovering a
nation in Africa one degree nearer the monkey than
any before known, were unconscious of his name ;
and, in private circles, few persons whom we met
had ever heard, or, if they had heard, knew anything
definite of the star which had risen with quite porten-
tous light upon our small horizon. At last, however,
we were told that we might find in the *Edinburgh Review* of 1838—many years after Comte's first book was
published, and eight after the completion of the last—
a notice of the Positive Philosophy, written by Sir David
Brewster, which showed plainly enough that Sir David

had failed to get even a glimpse of the peculiarity of
the system.   When Whewell, too, published his " Philosophy of the Inductive Sciences," it was evident that
he had read Comte, but was either afraid or not honest
enough to own it ; and the first public recognition of
him of any importance we found in the Logic of John
Stuart Mill, who borrows largely from him, but without
the meanness of concealment.   Indeed, no attempt, as
we are aware, has yet been made toward an elaborate
and impartial judgment of Comte, save in a series of
able articles published in the *Methodist Quarterly Review*
of this city, where the writer, though disagreeing with
many of his conclusions, yet frankly and admiringly
confesses his merits.   Morell's "Philosophy of the
Nineteenth Century" has a superficial account of Comte's
system, and Professor De Saisset has written something
about him in the *Revue des Deux Mondes,* which we
have not seen.

   This uniform neglect of Comte, during the quarter
of a century in which he had been laboriously working
out his views, struck us as strange, particularly as contemporary science contained not a few direct appropria-
tions of his labors.   We tried to account for it, on one or
the other of three suppositions : we argued that either his
works were intrinsically unworthy of study, or that their
departures from the accepted and reigning opinions
were so flagrant as to excite a silent contempt for them,
or that the range and comprehensiveness of their topics
lifted them quite above the ordinary apprehensions and
intellectual sympathies of the age.

   Yet, on reflection, we soon saw that neither of these
solutions could be entirely satisfactory.   It was obvious,
at a glance, that those works *were* worthy of study, as
their marked originality and power, their logical co-
herence, their dignity of manner, and the importance

of the results at which they aimed, abundantly proved. A rational and consistent classification of the sciences, on the basis of nature, and the construction of a new science, destined to become the queen and crowning glory of all other sciences, were projects which, even if they had been unskilfully carried out, nevertheless deserved the most serious attention. It was no disposition, then, we were persuaded, to pooh-pooh Comte which had left him to obscurity. Nor was it, again, the offensive nature of his conclusions ; for, hostile as these were to existing prejudices, they were no more so than the systems of Fichte, Schelling, and Hegel, whose speculations have gone the circuit of the globe. If he was atheistical, they were pantheistical ; and we had yet to learn that the one error was more acceptable to ·orthodoxy than the other. Meanwhile, it was patent that the theories of Comte, though profound and comprehensive, and marked by great logical severity, were not difficult of apprehension. They could scarcely be called abstruse ; they contained few neologisms, did not abound in hard words, while in their general aims they were addressed to a prevailing character of the present era—its physical or materializing tendency. There was, then, more reason, or at least as much reason, why Comte should have been well known, as that Cousin, Hegel, or Kant should be.

In the end, two considerations occurred to us, as more likely to explain the little attention he had received. The first was, the acknowledged indisposition of scientific men to enter into large or general views, absorbed as they were in the study of details, and distrustful as they were of all applications of the inductive method, save the most elementary and simple. The habit of petty analysis, which has been so "victorious" in physics, had finally succeeded in conquering its masters, so that your natural philosopher was quite as much afraid of deserting it, for higher and synthetic generalizations, as a slave is to rise against his keeper. He looked upon the "theorizer," consequently, as a monster, and was glad to get quit of him as soon as possible. Comte could expect no hospitality from this class. Then, again—a second reason for neglecting him, even among those capable of general views, was, that the reigning science could not, in consistency with its own principles, deny the validity of his method, while to admit his conclusions, would be flying directly into the face of the reigning theology. There was a two-faced allegiance to be maintained by the Scientists— one of consistency, and the other of respectability ; and we can readily understand why it was thought best, in the dilemma, to say as little as need be about Comte, lest the secret sympathy of science should be exposed on one side by a futile attempt to contemn him, or lest, on the other hand, the frowns of the Church should be incurred by an open proclamation of sympathy. In a word, Comte had been more faithful to the spirit and method of modern science, as it is generally conceived by scientific men, than they had dared to be themselves, because of their theological timidity. His conclusions were the logical outgrowth of their premises ; but while they persistently held to the premises, they cautiously avoided the conclusions. A choice between Science and Faith was laid upon them, but inasmuch as they could relinquish neither, nor reconcile the two, they found discretion the better sort of valor. They retired from the field rather than join battle.

Thus physicists and metaphysicists were alike disdainful, expecting neither profit nor entertainment from those lumbering octavos of a poor Parisian teacher of mathematics, whose style was not the most attractive in

the world, and whose matter required close and continued, if not subtle study.

Comte, however, is at length famous.   He has been
taken under the especial patronage of Miss Martineau—
"philosopher Harriet," as our laughing Howadji has it—
and of Mr. G. H. Lewes, who last year published an outline of his works, under the title of "Comte's Philosophy of the Sciences."   His books are available in tolcr-
able English ; the diminutive leaders of small coteries
begin to jabber of the virtues of integral calculus ;
metaphysics and theology are growing decidedly unfash-
ionable ; and young men and women will soon be astonished that they could ever have entertained such antiquated notions as those of God and Infinity, or ever
supposed anything to have had a beginning,—as all
beginnings *ex necessitate* are supernatural,—or, will ever
have an end, as all ends in the flux and play of shadows
are at best but problematical.   Phenomena and the
laws of phenomena, which are themselves phenomenal,
are the sole gospel which the reason can comprehend or
our hearts revere ; and this poor universe, at once dis-
embodied and soulless—though we have deemed it all
along the substantialest of dwelling-places—is in danger
of becoming a stupendous magic-lantern, but with no
one with within it, or behind it, to show the pictures.

It may not be useless, then, for several reasons, to
undertake a brief survey of Comte and his claims.   This
we shall proceed to do, premising, however, that we
have no strong hope of administering much consolation
either to his extravagant admirers or his more bigoted
enemies.

The first question with a philosophy always is, what
it aims to do ; and here we must say that Comte's
pretensions are of no mean extent.   He intends a systemization of all human knowledge, a reconstruction

of the human understanding, and the determination, through these, of the true order and evolution of human society. His ambition takes rank with that of Spinoza in his *Tractatus*, with Bacon's in his *Instauratio Magna*, and with Fourier's in his *Unité Universelle*, only falling short of the reach of Swedenborg's, which includes the economy of the heavens and the hells as well as of the earth. Nor does the execution of his plan prove him a wholly unworthy compeer of those aspiring men. With more knowledge than Fourier, and a soberer judgment than Spinoza, he is less than Bacon only in that masculine strength, rich wit, and fruity imagination, which are the unrivalled charms of the great Chancellor. But he differs mainly from all these reformers of thought in the rigid bounds he has set to the province of knowledge. They, almost without exception, "leaping the walls of time and space," have scaled the heavens of the infinite ; yet he will hear of nothing but the actual and the conditioned. They have endeavored to penetrate into causes and essences, while he admits nothing but phenomena. They have believed, with all the rest of mankind, in substance, but he believes only in appearances. In short, he calls his philosophy the "Positive Philosophy," because it avoids all impalpable realms, and is real, useful, certain, definite, and organic ; or, as he in one place expresses it, "good sense systematized."

I. The first fundamental principle of it, then, is a determination of the limits of knowledge, which it assumes is confined to *the perception of phenomena, and their invariable relations.* Absolute knowledge, it is affirmed, is an impossibility, the perception of things in themselves, as it is sometimes termed, a chimera. The exclusive function of the mind consists in observing the appearances of things and co-ordinating their relations of existence or succession. When we have determined *what* a thing is, *i. e.*, how it stands related to other things, as an existing fact or a sequence, we have exhausted the intelligible sphere. We cannot tell *whence* it is, nor *why* it is, but simply how it is, or that it is invariably connected by certain resemblances or differences with other things, or by a certain order of priority or posteriority, to other things. We cannot say that it is a substance, a being, a cause, an essence, but only a phenomenon, which exists and continues in certain uniform modes. All researches into the supposed causes of that phenomenon, whether natural or supernatural, are consequently illegitimate, an endeavor after the unattainable, a pursuit of shadows and dreams. All faiths, opinions, aspirations, etc., not susceptible of being reduced to these observed relations, transcend the powers of the intellect, and may be dismissed as illusions, or, at best, as mere transitional and infantile expedients, helping the mind on, while it is learning to discern its true beat.

This, we say, is Comte's starting-point, and it becomes us to analyze it, before advancing further. We will admit that all knowledge is relative;—*i. e.*, in a double sense, first, as to its objects, which could not be things unless they were finited or distinguished from each other by sensible differences; and second, as to its powers, which is a mere relation of our sensitive organization to nature, whereby one is revealed in the other. Things *are* in virtue of their relativity; for if they were not relative, they would be absolute, and so indistinguishable as things, inappreciable to the senses, and of course unknowable.

Our sensitive experience, consequently, must be the basis, the occasion, the material of all knowledge. We do not bring with us, when we are born, a solitary iota of thought, except what comes to us from our relations

to the medium in which we are born.   Everything has
to be learned by us, and that, too, in the slowest
way.   Chickens and puppies, as soon as they break the
shell, or open their eyes, have, as Swedenborg says, a
complete science of their lives ; the former will run
about to pick up worms, and the latter to lap milk,
as confidently on its first as on its last day ; but a human
baby does not know enough for some years to keep
itself from starving to death.   It has to be taught all
things.   It is a mere capacity of knowing, and a mere
inclination to love, and nothing more.   Experience
awakens its sensations, builds up its imagination, develops its reason, kindles its desires, and creates its
sciences.   In other words, our existence, being phenomenal, is constructed by our experience,—is but
an extension and envelopment of nature,—a part and
parcel of nature,—its finer outgrowth, its crowning product and flower.   But man, as we shall see by and by,
is more than this ; he is more than a simple animal and
intellectual existence ; he is a self-hood or personality,
and therefore a spiritual being.   The phenomena with
which he is conversant, or may become conversant, are
not merely physical or natural, but spiritual.   His
world is one of affection, thought, faith, as well as of
sensation.   A denizen of time and space, he yet conceives of that which is beyond all time or space.

Comte is right, therefore, in assuming that we can
know nothing out of the sphere of our experience, or, in
other words, which does not come through our phenomenal organization ; so that all *à priori* notions of what
things are, apart from what we feel or see them to be,
are gratuitous and idle.   But he is wrong in the inference, that we cannot properly *believe* what we do not
know.   Knowledge is not the equivalent or measure of
being.   We know sensible facts, and their relations,

but we believe truths or propositions which transcend those facts ; we know changes, but we believe in causes ; we know Tom, Dick, and Harry, but we believe in man ; we know the relations of difference which distinguish things, but we believe in a unity which is the ground or support of their distinction. We know the finite, the conditioned, the multiple, the changeable, but we believe in the infinite, the unconditioned, the absolute, and the permanent, not as contradictory or antagonistic to the former, but as contained in them ; not as natural or phenomenal, but as rational or spiritual. Every step that our minds take within the sphere of experience itself, or beyond the first intimations of sense, is a belief—well or ill supported, and not a knowledge. In popular language, we are accustomed to speak of our opinions as what we know ; but strictly, they are only what we *opine,* with more or less fixity of assent. They are faiths accredited to us by certain evidences. We say that we know the truths of mathematics, the principles of astronomy, the laws of chemistry, the dictates of morals, etc., but we have only a conviction of them, founded upon our reasonings, which reasonings are only various logical processes for producing Faith. Neither the results arrived at, nor the processes themselves, fall within the cognizance of the senses. They are rationally discerned—*i. e.*, they are rationally discerned by those who investigate them and authenticate them for themselves ; but the larger part of mankind are satisfied to take them upon the testimony of others. Perhaps one man in ten millions of Christendom has demonstrated the theory of gravitation for himself, all the rest believing it because they have been so taught.

Let it not be supposed that this distinction is merely technical, for it is fundamental and controlling, and cuts to the very quick of the Positivist pretensions.

"Truths are known to us in two ways," says John Stuart Mill, who is good scientific authority; "some are known to us directly and of themselves ; some through the medium of other truths : the former are the subjects of intuition or consciousness" (which is knowledge proper) ; "the latter are the subject of inference" (which is properly Belief). " Whatever is known to us by consciousness is known beyond possibility of question ; what one sees and feels, whether bodily or mentally, one cannot but be sure that one sees and feels ; no science is required for establishing such truths ; no rules of art can render our knowledge of them more certain than it is in itself." But the truths inferred from these truths, or inferred in any way, may be rightly or wrongly inferred, are contingent upon the legitimacy of the process by which they are reached, and are therefore not known, but simply believed. That belief may reach the solidity of the most absolute intuition, according to the nature and degree of the evidence by which it is supported, but it is none the less a belief and knowledge only by a popular extension of the term knowledge. Even in practical life,—in our every-day concerns,—in the endless ramifications of business, we walk as much by Faith as by Knowledge, and we depend as completely upon the truths that we simply believe as we do upon those we are supposed to know. Social existence, indeed, would be impossible were it not so,—any existence, in short, above that of the animal.

The question of philosophy, therefore, does not, as it is commonly stated, refer to the validity of our knowledge,—which, being commensurate with our sensible experience, the first fool can determine as well as the last philosopher,—but to the validity of our beliefs. Accepting the vast variety of credences, on which the

whole business of society, its trades as well as its sciences
and religions, proceeds, what ground is there for each?
In what way are they related to our sensible experience,
and how can that experience be made serviceable to
them? Which are unsupported, which are illusions,
which are worthy of trust? Especially, what are we to
make of our transcendent ideas? All the world, for
instance, at every period of the world, has professed a
belief in that which is perfect and unconditioned, which
cannot be bounded by the senses, which the senses are
ignorant of, which is invisible to the eye, and inaudible
to the ear, but how is it to be explained? Must we
wink it out of sight, or may we refer it to a life within
us which is supersensuous, which is a window of the
soul, if we may so express it, opening into God and the
absolute, as the senses are windows of the soul, opening into nature? Philosophy, we say, is called upon
to answer,—not merely to systematize what we know,
but to explain what we believe and hope. Philosophy
deals with all the fundamental questions of human existence. Is there any truth? and what criterion of it
have we? Is there any reality? and how are we to distinguish it from phantasm? Whence the universal
order that we observe, and whither does it tend?
Theology, metaphysics, science itself, each gives us its
own responses to these questions; but are these so
many groping guesses, or satisfactory solutions? It is
easy to say that such problems are insoluble, but who
can prove that blank and awful negative? It is easy to
raise the barrier of the "Unknowable," but by what
authority are reason and revelation restricted? Who is
wise enough to fix the last limits to the capacity of refinement and expansion in the human powers; who
knows what we may or may not know in the gradual
evolutions of spiritual being? What depths may we not

yet penetrate (say, by new generalizations of the known), what heights may we not yet scale?

Now, Comte is quite right in considering the relations of phenomenal nature, the facts furnished to us by the senses, and digested by reason, as the starting-place of the sciences; but he is wrong in restricting philosophy to this natural plane. He is right, in the first point, because phenomenal nature is the continent or base of all truth, in which it resides as in its body; but he is wrong in the second point, inasmuch as it excludes the deeper truths, which are the soul of that body. Let us illustrate. The twenty-six letters of the alphabet contain the whole of Shakspeare, but how wretched would be the commentator who should confine his attention to the names of the letters, or to the spelling of a few syllables, or to the construction of a few sentences even, and not ascend to the higher combinations of the thoughts! It is indispensable to know the letters and the words, in order to understand Shakspeare, but the letters and the words are not Shakspeare. They are only instrumental to Shakspeare; they are the external collocation, of which he is the interior significance—nay, more, they are the condition of his existence, and the ladders by which we climb to him, but they are not the immortal spirit of the man, which is alone worth our seeking. Hence the care with which we investigate his text; but should we not despise a scholar who could spend his life in the pursuit of the text, while he neglected the meaning which alone imparts to the text its glory?

So Science begins with the sensible sphere, because it is the letter and text of truth, but it ascends from that, by its rational processes, to the mental or spiritual sphere, which is the ground or meaning of the former, giving it existence and reality. Science is nature no

longer seen by the eyes, but by the reason. Let it be
observed, however, that in ascending from the senses,
as we have termed it, we do not recede or separate
from nature ; we do not run away into a ghostland of
abstractions, but we simply look through nature's superficial aspects or integuments, into its realities, or
rather into its rationalities, into its intellectual substances and ends, which constitute it, make it consistent
and significant, and show it to be a glorious mirror of
our own souls. If Science halts, therefore, at the thresh-
old ; if it regards nature as a thing of superficial dimensions only ; if it dallies with the outside shows, refusing
to penetrate the inward meaning, it misses the most
precious part of the entertainment. It sees the vast
mechanism, the prodigious apparatus, the great gilt
candlesticks of the heavens, and the four sapphire walls,
and the multitudes that walk therein, but the Divinity
of the magnificent temple, who is the light and heat
and glory of it, it cannot behold !

Science, we repeat, cannot be too "positive" in the
study of phenomena, cannot be too accurate in its researches or comprehensive in its generalizations ; cannot
tell us too plainly what the actual forms and sequences
of the universe are ; but it does this, not for the sake of
the phenomena, which are, in themselves, dead and
passive surfaces, obeisant, mechanical, vehicular, but
for the inner worlds of rational, civil, moral, and
spiritual uses which they contain. It is because they
are an expression, a representative, a bodying forth of a
more real life, the vast depository of spiritual forces in
action, a theatre of an ascending series of wisdom and
goodness, the supporting bed of the eternal marriage of
love and truth, and the perpetual, ever-renewed miracle
of divine creation, that they deserve our elaborate study
and care. As the plane on which all effects are

wrought out, we cannot know too intimately the great leading facts of Experience ; but to rest in those facts is to abandon reason to a barren nominalism, to close the eyes of the soul, and shut out God from his own universe.

II. Comte's second fundamental principle is, that *each of our leading conceptions, each branch of our knowledge, passes successively through three different theoretical conditions—the Theological or fictitious, the Metaphysical or abstract, and the Scientific or positive.* In other words, the human mind, by its nature, employs, in its progress, three methods of philosophizing, the characters of which are essentially different, and even radically opposed—viz., the theological method, the metaphysical, and the positive. "Hence arise," he adds, "three philosophies, or general systems of conception, of the aggregate of phenomena, each of which excludes the other." The first is the necessary point of departure for the human understanding, and the third its fixed and definitive state, while the second is only transitional.*

In the theological stage, the human mind, seeking the essential nature of beings, the first and final causes (the origin and purpose) of all effects—in short, absolute knowledge—supposes all phenomena to be produced by the immediate action of supernatural agents. In the metaphysical state, which is only a modification of the first, the mind supposes, instead of supernatural powers, abstract forces, substantive principles, veritable entities, inherent in nature, and capable of producing a diversity in phenomena. But in the final or positive state, the mind has given over the vain search after absolute notions, such as the origin and destination of the universe, and the causes of phenomena, and applies

---

* Miss Martineau's Abstract, vol. i., c. i.

itself to the study of their laws,—that is, their invariable relations of succession and resemblance.

Comte adds, that the theological state reached its highest perfection, when it substituted the providential action of a single Being (monotheism), for the varied operation of numerous divinities (fetichism and polytheism) which had before been imagined. In the same way, in the last stage of the metaphysical system, men substitute one great entity, Nature, as the cause of all phenomena, for the multitude of entities which they at first supposed. And thus the Positive system will reach its ultimate perfection (if such perfection can be hoped for) in the representation of some single general law (gravitation, for instance), as the unity of all particular phenomena.

Before entering upon an examination of this alleged "law of the three stages," let us remark a moment the singular nomenclature in which it is expressed. "Theological," "metaphysical," and "positive" are terms that have no sort of co-relation with each other ; neither of affinity or contrast. They are arbitrary designations, and therefore, as the reader will find out if he attempts to pursue the study of Comte, somewhat ambiguous and confused. Theology is stretched a good deal from its native meaning when it is made to cover the lowest sort of fetichism, as well as the mere devilism of much early superstition. So, again, metaphysics, which is now commonly restricted to intellectual and moral philosophy, is identified by Comte with Ontology, or the science of being, though he sometimes recurs to the former sense. But his use of the word "positive" is the most curious reversion of terms. Among the old speculators, such as the schoolmen, and in Bacon, Spinoza, Leibnitz, and Descartes, even down to Kant, positive knowledge always means primitive, irreducible, ne-

cessary truth, or that which is derived from intuitive perception, as distinguished from that which is obtained
by observation and experiment: but Comte, rejecting
the former kind of knowledge, appropriates the term
to that which originally it was used to oppose. This,
however, by the way, for what he really means is clear .
enough.

It is the instinct of childhood to personify everything,
—to drench its whole outward existence in the hues of
its personal feelings, and to invest every stone, and tree,
and shadow with a vague mysterious life ; but in youth,
as the reflective or intellectual powers are developed,
we begin to question these creatures of the imagination,
to strip them of their personal individuality, and to
refer them to a dead external mechanism, which we call
nature ; and then, finally, we investigate their actual
properties, that we may turn them to use, in furthering
the practical purposes of existence. The savage sees in
the lightning the glances of an offended deity, whom
he propitiates by offerings : when more enlightened, he
regards it as a destructive and unmanageable agent, of
which he is afraid ; but when more enlightened still, he
calls it electricity, and renders it harmless by an iron
rod. The savage considers an epidemic as a direct
infliction of the gods, or, as our American Iroquois
thought, a great serpent that lived in the pools. He
learns by experience that it may be generated by the
pools and marshes, and calls it not a serpent, but a
malignant nature : then, a little further advanced in
knowledge, he connects it with a mysterious "Providence," till the man of science teaches him that it is a
simple consequence of appreciable causes, and institutes
sanitary regulations to prevent its recurrence. Thus,
in regard to all other phenomena, the progress of our
intelligence is marked by the progress which it makes

in referring them, from arbitrary wills, or independent and inscrutable causes, to intelligible and invariable laws.

Now, this general fact we admit, but we are not prepared to characterize it precisely as Comte does, nor to surrender it to the same inferences. He treats the theological and metaphysical states as exclusively provisional, the positive state as definite or final. Now, we regard them all as alike provisional, and included in the same general law of progress. The idea of Deity, and the idea of Cause, are not infantile conceptions, which it is the function of science to supersede ; but they are permanent, controlling, ineradicable instincts, which it is the function of philosophy to illustrate, purify, and complete. In other words, the phenomenal manifestations of these great ideas, their appearances in history, are the successive stages by which the reason of the race ascends from a gross sensualism, or a blind confusion of God and nature, to the spiritual perception of a living, creative, and all-sustaining unity of life. They are the process of the mind's growth, by which it is gradually enfranchised from its primitive subjection to nature, into its final mastery of nature and conjunction with God.

Thus the theological conceptions exhibit the gropings of religious feeling for a unitary life, which will explain all the vast variety of phenomenal lives. So the metaphysical and positive conceptions exhibit the gropings of thought for a causative principle, which will explain all the vast concatenations of phenomenal order. Our Humanity is ever in a process of education, is growing out of its infancy into its manhood, and these theological, metaphysical, and scientific systems are the tutors, by whose assistance it attains its majority. They are not, therefore, radically antagonistic to each other, but co-operative from distinct spheres, the one preparing the heart, and the other the intelligence, for the whole man's final assertion of his independence and freedom.

In respect to the theological credences of our race, it is evident that their historical development has not exhausted the conception of God, but refined it more and more from all mere finite adjuncts, and filled it out to an ideal completeness. From fetichism, the first rude personification of stocks and stones, through Sabeism, or the worship of the stars, and the Polytheistic deification of the great powers of nature, to the Monotheism of Mohammed and the Jews, there is an almost measureless progress. So in Monotheism itself, beginning with the conception of God as the special and avenging protector of a nation, of Jewry or Islam, and ending with it as the impartial judge of all the earth, there is an equal rise in the purity and dignity of the thought. The conception becomes less and less natural, *i. e.*, less and less limited and conditioned, and more and more humane, until it rises to the highest expression which it has yet received, the orthodox theism of the Church, in which God is the merciful and universal Father, and profoundly interested in the fortunes of the human soul. But he is still a God *ab extra*, according to this faith, a God above and separate from humanity, until a more sympathetic insight into the life of Christ (such as we get in Swedenborg), reveals him as the Divine Humanity, or the essential unity of God and man.

Again, the metaphysical philosophy of our race has been a gravitation of thought toward a similar end. At first cosmological, explaining the universe by a great controlling force or *phusis* external to it, and then physical, ascribing each particular effect to its particular entity, residing in it as a kind of physical soul, metaphysics has gradually relieved itself of the domination of nature, discharging her phenomena of every characteristic save the principle of Law. Arrived at this stage, it is called Positivism, which, however it may disclaim all metaphysical parentage, is still a phase of metaphysics ; for it only substitutes *law* for *cause* or *entity*, perpetually speaking of "the laws controlling phenomena," "the laws which subject properties," etc., as if *laws* were an external and authoritative imposition,—in which sense they are just as metaphysical as any of the entities of the schoolmen.

The distinctive character of Positivism, for example, is the conception of the invariableness or immutability of the Laws of Nature. But this is a metaphysical conception as a whole, and each of its leading terms is metaphysical, and the first of them is absolute as well as metaphysical, implying as it does, an eternal, fixed, unconditional impossibility of change. We are nowhere told, it is true, nor is it very clear, whether this impossibility of change is a mathematical, a moral, or a physical impossibility ; it is represented only as a kind of Fate or Destiny.

Again, the second term of this pet phrase, Law, is a metaphysical expression, borrowed from jurisprudence, where it means the command of a superior, and which it attributes to the facts and sequences of the material world. Even the third term in the formula, or "Nature," in the mouths of the strictest scientists, often means an entity external to our thought, in which the sum of phenomena is supposed to inhere. What is there more metaphysical in the *arke* of the ancient Ionians, in the atoms of the atomists, in the quiddities of the schoolmen, in the animism of Stahl, or in the vital principle of the later physioligists, than in the electricity, galvanism, magnetism, and caloric of modern science. We venture to say that ninety-nine of every hundred of the writers on these branches of research give as much objective validity to their fluids and affinities as ever Scotus did to his entities or plastic forces.

Mr. Lewes, one of the leading teachers of Positivism, has noted this, and says : "The conception implied in, or suggested by, the phrase 'Laws of Nature,' is the last and most refined expression of the metaphysical stage of speculation ; it replaces the ancient *principle ;* it is the delicate abstract *entity* superadded to phenomena." It is something which "coerces the facts, and makes them to be what they are," "a more subtle, a more impersonal substitute for the supernatural power, which in the theological epoch was believed to superintend all things." "If the savage says it is a demon who directs the storm, does not the man of science say it is a law which directs it ? These two conceptions, are they not identical ?" Not entirely, we answer, because the last is more rational than the first, and brings us nearer to a true theory of the universe ; but both spring from the same source, the irresistible desire of the mind to go behind the phenomenal and the relative to the rational and constitutive. Mr. Lewes proposes to relieve himself by the employment of the word "methods."

But will it be any more possible to satisfy the philosophical instinct with "methods" than with "laws," or with "entities" or "gods ?" No, for what that instinct demands is the intrinsic reason of things, the *why* as well as the *what* and the *how.* "He is a poor lawyer," says Cicero, "who, knowing all the extant statutes of the realm, does not know the reason of the law." Thus, behind the theorems of the mathematics, there is a philosophy of mathematics ; behind all the decompositions and recompositions of chemistry, a philosophy of chemistry; behind all the sciences, in short, a science of sciences to which they are only subservient. Why are they, those sciences,—*i. e.*, for what end are they? Or, in plain, popular language, what is their *use?* which is again the same thing as to ask, what is their cause ; for as the End for which any thing is, determines its existence, its form, its relations to other things, its rank in the orders and series to which it belongs— that end must be, disguise it as we may, its formative principle, its fundamental idea, its soul. "Are you there, old truepenny?" Behold, the Use of a thing, in the last analysis, is its rational cause, and Positivism does not say the final word of science ! It may have an eminent function, in determining what things are, what the forms and relations of phenomena are, in teaching inquirers to stick to the inquiry in hand, and when they are investigating a thing, not to run off into a wild-goose chase after something else ; but having done that, it has only prepared materials. The great work has yet to be done. Comte's own attempt to show that all the sciences are made for the last science, or the science of man—*i. e.*, his attempt to deduce the end or use of the sciences—is an ample confession of this very truth, and an abandonment of the what is, for the why it is. But, reaching this question of the Why, we come at once and peremptorily upon the great truth which he himself educes—that all the sciences, *i. e.*, that all the realms of creation, look to the aggrandizement of man ; that all their arrangements, all their efforts, are subservient to his development, are all accommodated to his growth, all culminate in his supremacy. Thus, once more, we are brought by the slow evolutions of science to the same landing-place in which we were left by the theological series,—*i. e.*, to man as the Lord and Master of Nature, and consequently one with God.

There is an obvious fallacy in the suggestion that
these "three states" are either exclusive of each other, or
regularly successive in a direct line of development;
for they have all existed concurrently, from the beginning of the world, and often in the same nation and the
same mind, at the same time. The veriest barbarian,
who sees a fetish in a stone, still believes that if it falls
on his head it will give him a hurt,—thus proving his
Positivism, so far forth, or his sense of nature's invariable laws. The most flourishing period of Greek
polytheism was precisely the time when the Greek
schools were most devoted to independent metaphysical
studies. Who were more theological and more metaphysical at the same time than the schoolmen?
Besides, is not the very study of any subject, whether
theological or metaphysical, a quiet assumption of
Positivism—*i. e.*, does it not proceed upon the supposition that the laws of the mind at least are invariable?
Could there be any conclusion without such a pre-
supposition? The "three states," consequently, are
successive in this respect alone, that at a particular
period one of them preponderates, while the others are
held in abeyance. They are in no sense radically exclusive of each other, for a man may investigate phenomena
positively, and believe at the same time in that which is
ultra-phenomenal, or rather intra-phenomenal. All that
sound science requires, and what we take to be the real
meaning of Positivism, is this: that in the natural
order, a man should stick to the facts of his case, that
he should not generalize beyond those facts; but it does
not follow from this that he has no right to construct a
spiritual philosophy of those facts, or to refer them to
some more radical theory of the universe after their
phenomenal relations are ascertained. All the Positivists
in the world, and to the end of time, will not succeed

in eradicating this notion of a super-sensual Reason of Things from the human mind. They may correct the misapplications of it, made in the immaturity of the race, as the progress of Science has done and is doing perpetually ; but they will never persuade men to relinquish it,—for the reason, that it proceeds from an ineradicable instinct, is implied in the fundamental "categories" of all understanding, and imperatively demanded by the yearnings of the heart.

If we have rightly apprehended the matter, then Comte's law of "the three stages" is a very inadequate statement of the principle of development. Theology and metaphysics do not terminate in the elimination of Science, but they bear entire reference to the elimination of Man. Positivism itself is no less a propædeutic than either of the others, and only helps to carry on the problem to its final solution by a more comprehensive philosophy. Theology, all drenched and dripping at the outset in fetichisms, struggles to read the riddle of the universe, onward through sabeisms, polytheisms, and monotheisms, until it finally ceases to conceive of God at all under sensible conditions, or as a finite and outward being, and rises to the thought of his infinite inward personality. So, Metaphysics and Science, after torturing nature for the secret of her existence, after striving to explain the world by a fate superior to the gods ; by the fortuitous rencontres of infinite atoms moving freely through space ; by a plastic, all-controlling mundane soul ; by number, by chemistry, by electricity, by physiology, and lastly by a tremendous phantasm of "phenomena and laws," are pointed away from nature herself, by her innumerable fingers, to him for whom all her suns have risen and set, all her fields waved, and all her oceans rolled.

Now the law of "the three stages" means to express

this succession of theological and philosophical schemes, but does so in an incomplete and one-sided way. Its proper formula would be, that man stands in respect to all the objects of his belief or thought in three great orders of relation : he is related (1) to the invisible or spiritual world, (2) to nature, and (3) to his fellow-man ; each of which dominates him in turn, during the process of his development ; but his education consists in the successive reduction of each to unity. Neither theology nor metaphysics, rightly conceived, are transitory ; they abide in their ultimate principles, and change only in their successive superficial forms ; they have never been deserted or left behind in the course of our progress ; they still flourish, and will flourish till at last they meet and are reconciled in that Divine Philosophy which has ever been their aim. Growing *pari passu* with man, they rocked the cradle of his infancy, and will live to witness the glory of his crowning manliness, through Christ.

Before quitting this branch of the subject, we cannot but protest against the tone of disparagement in which Comte and his followers are led by their system to speak of all theological and speculative studies,—as if they were a hopeless imbecility, as contemptible as they were fruitless. Granting that they do not possess that precious faculty of prevision, that capability of verification by experiment, which is the advantage of the natural sciences, and the application of which has led to such astonishing discoveries in modern times, they may still be not without their value. It pertains to the difference in the very nature of these studies to produce different kinds of results ; and to be tested, therefore, by different criteria. No conceivable doctrine of God is likely to enable us to predict eclipses ; no ontological or psychological truth or falsehood will help or hinder the construction of a steam-engine; neither, on the other hand, does natural science help us much, when we ask ourselves the question of the dying Roman Emperor, "Whither art thou going, oh my soul?" In fact, the most "victorious analysis" has not yet proved that we have a soul, nor, with all its fertile previsions, enabled us to look into our immortal destiny. Yet there are matters quite as interesting to us as the binomial theorem or the precession of the equinoxes. Besides, the disability as to present uses, with which the speculative sciences are reproached, is one that is common to nearly all the higher spheres of thought. We know scarcely more of morals, politics, history, art, than we do of theology or metaphysics,—perhaps not so much,—but are we to drop them, on that account, as chimerical and illusory? Who, for example, is going to tell us by what laws of nature, by what uniformities of co-existence and sequence Homers, Dantes, and Shakspeares are produced? Shall we not listen to Genius, till some Scientist shall have probed the secret of his genesis, and told the precise amount of salt, phosphorus, oxygen, and what not, may have gone to his composition? Shall we not believe in him, though we may not comprehend him?

Admitting, further, that no positive results have been attained in either theology or metaphysics, and that we are as far now from satisfactory conclusions as they were in the days of Thotmes or Anaximander, will it be contended that the mere process of research has not been accompanied by the most prodigious advantages for the human mind? From the fetichism of a Zooloo to the mysticism of a Fenelon, there is a broad interval of thought and feeling, and though one may be no nearer to the real truth than the other, is nothing gained to our race by the difference? Between the cosmogony

of a Thales and that of a Plato there is an immense
gap, but, if equally untrue, are they also equal imbecili-
ties, unworthy of a rational mind's regard? Has Descartes, has Leibnitz, has Kant, has Swedenborg done
nothing that we may not now derisively dismiss, as the
merest puerility and phantom-mongering? If we mistake not, Comte himself inscribes some of these illustrious names as saints in his new calendar of scientific
religion. He admits them, though not signalized as
the discoverers of much positive truth, among the
benefactors of mankind ; but why does he do so? Because he felt, that as a mere gymnastic of the intellect,
apart from every question of the amount of truth they
contained, the works of these men are of incalculable
value. In this view, indeed, what work of simple
science, that has been written since the beginning of
the world, is so capable of building up, informing, enlarging, disciplining the mind of man, as the Dia-
logues of Plato, all metaphysical as they are, or even
those grand and sweeping dissertations of Hegel on
Logic, Esthetics, and Religion, all compact of nonsense, by every scientific estimate? No one doubts
that a prodigious amount of silliness has been laboriously achieved by the speculative thinkers, that the
hopeless task of the Danaïdes of dipping up water in
seives has often been revived by them, that endless
volumes of moonshine have been carefully bottled away
for future enlightenment, but, along with all these painful and preposterous efforts, they have made no less
prodigious displays of intellectual vigor and acumen,
that can never wholly die out of the interest and gratitude of mankind. For Science itself, which despises
the questions of the schools, cannot proceed far in its
own legitimate path without hitting its head, and frequently to the damage of its brains, against the very

topics it so much derides. Let it push its researches to the ultimate lurking-place of the phenomenal, let it master all facts, and co-ordinate them into a final fact ; let it synthesize till it have reached the last synthesis of all, or prove that no such finality is possible ; and still the question will come, whether the total order be, so far as it goes, a blind fate or an intelligent God, whether an undecipherable entity or a pervading wisdom, whether a mute principle of Law or a living principle of Love.

But let us add, for the assurance of the Positivists, should they ever come to adopt the latter alternative, to have no fear that the laws of the universe, under this new reign of God, will be administered in any more "arbitrary" or "variable" manner, or that it will be any more difficult to foresee the certain action of phenomena in the future, than under their own most superlative rule. Indeed, deprived as we are by Positivism of all intelligent and kindly causes, on which, amid the terrifying vicissitudes of human affairs, our perturbed spirits may rely, we are sometimes haunted with a vague suspicion that this huge necessity called Law, may itself take a turn for the worse by and by ; that instead of showing itself on the side of good, as Comte contends it does, it may show itself on the side of evil, and then what is to become of us ? We greatly prefer, therefore, to consider law as the perpetual presence of a sovereign Life, of one who is Wisdom itself and Goodness itself, which are universal Order itself, and whose infinite power is intent only, through all the crimes, calamities, and changes of the world, on educating his creatures into the similitude of his own immutable perfection. We imagine that in all our doings, as well as in all our reasonings, we can trust to the fixity of his statutes, in the least things as well as the greatest, though they happen to be living forces instead of a spontaneous mechanism, with as sound a confidence as the best of the Positivists on the regularity of "laws." Our science is as capable of "prevision" as his, but, we suspect, with an immeasurably broader reach, and an inexpressibly sweeter solace.

III. The third fundamental view of Comte relates to *the hierarchy or classification of the sciences according to the order of the dependence of their phenomena.* It is clearly his most brilliant achievement, though vitiated in some respects by the preliminary errors to which we have already referred. Bacon, D'Alembert, Bentham, Ampére, and others, have attempted a similar construction of the scale of knowledge; but with vastly inferior success. Bacon proceeded upon a tripartite division of the human faculties into memory, imagination, and reason, upon which he founded the three generic divisions of knowledge, as History, Poesy, Science. It was a superficial arrangement, and incoherent and confused to the last degree. D'Alembert's scheme substituted philosophy for science in Bacon's division, and modified, without materially improving the details. Bentham, abandoning Bacon's trinity, applied a dichotomic or dual classification, but his terminology is so bizarre, with its *cænontologies, idiontologies,* and *anoopneumatologies,* that no one has cared to master its meaning. Ampére's scale, better than the others, makes a primary order of the cosmological and the noological sciences, which he subdivides into the mathematical, the physical, the natural, the medical, the philosophic, the dialegmatic, the ethnological, and the political, distributing these again into subordinate species. But it was reserved for Comte to digest these schemes into a really natural order, and superior to all preceding

ones, in that it works upon a simple and definite principle.

His arrangement is this : 1, Mathematics ; 2, Astronomy ; 3, Physics ; 4, Chemistry ; 5, Biology ; 6,
Sociology ; to which he has subsequently added, though
rather as parts of the last, Morals and Religion. The
subordinate divisions in their order are : analysis,
geometry, and mechanics ; celestial geometry and
celestial mechanics ; barology, thermology, acoustics,
optics, and electrology ; inorganic and organic chemistry ; anatomy and physiology, including the cerebral
functions, and social statics and dynamics. These
divisions, both primary and secondary, rest upon the
comparative generality or complexity of the phenomena
to which we refer. Mathematics is put first, because it
considers the most "general, simple, abstract, and
remote" phenomena known to us ; and sociology the
last, because it embraces phenomena the most particular, compound, concrete, and interesting. Now, that
this is the proper order, is proved by the fact that whatever is observed in the most general cases, is disengaged
from the incidents of particular cases, and may be
studied with the greatest facility. Besides, being more
remote from human interests, the study is less liable to
be warped by passions and prejudices. Moreover, this
is the order of the dependences of the sciences in nature,
the most special and complex depending upon the
more general, so that to know the latter perfectly the
former must be to some extent previously known. This
order, again, is the order in which the sciences have
been chronologically developed, and marks the degree
of precision which each of them has attained. Comte,
finally, contends that the effect of pursuing the sciences
in this order will be to improve method, education, and

morals, demonstrating this with remarkable force, while its signal performance is that it necessitates the discovery of a new science to complete the rest—viz., a sound doctrine of Social Progress and Order. *

In the discussion of each branch of this division, Comte treats, in the most luminous manner, of the nature or object of each science, of its method or means of exploration, of its relations to the foregoing and the succeeding sciences, and of its prospective improvements ; and, before proceeding to remark on his general scheme, we must say, that it is impossible for any one to read his thorough and masterly criticisms, without being deeply impressed by his eminent learning and ability. He exhibits, throughout, such a comprehensive grasp of principles, such ready sagacity, such consistent logic, such a wonderful steadiness of aim, and such an easy proficiency in all the minutest details of his subject—in spite of a few mistakes here and there, which are the battle-horses of his incompetent critics—as to rank him clearly among the highest class of speculative intellects,—at least with Pythagoras, Aristotle, and Schelling, if we cannot quite equal him to Plato, Bacon, Hegel, and Swedenborg. Even his deficiencies are suggestive, and his errors open up a way to the most valuable and pregnant thoughts.

As to his classification of the sciences, we know of no better, and we can conceive of its being improved,

---

* It is quite curious that Hegel, who is the very antipode of Comte, in his method of philosophizing,—Hegel beginning with the most abstract conception of absolute Being, while Comte begins with the most concrete phenomena of the Senses,—should have arrived at a scientific arrangement nearly resembling Comte's. Hegel's order is, 1, Logic ; 2, Mechanics or Mathematics ; 3, Physics ; 4, Chemistry ; 5, Organic Physics, or Vegetable and Animal life ; 6, The Mind ; 7, Politics,—and subsequently, Art, Religion, and Philosophy.

as a whole, apart from a few though quite important modifications of detail, only by a larger and more rigid application of the principle upon which it proceeds. We can conceive a system of knowledge, which should treat Logic, or formal method, distinctly as the Basis of all the sciences, and Philosophy, including Theology, as their Result—(a distinction which points out at once the great and injurious defects of Comte's scheme) ; but within the sphere of strict science, we cannot suppose it susceptible of improvement, except, as we have just said, upon its own main principle. In other words, we believe that this proceeding from the general and simple to the complex and special, is the secret of all effective organization, whether in nature, in method, in the growth of the mind, or in the movement of societies. It is a principle, too, let us here observe, which will carry Comte himself clear off the legs of his materialistic Positivism, into the profoundest depths of religion.*

A complete scheme of knowledge or belief implies three things : 1st, A region to be explored ; 2d, An instrument to explore it with; and 3d, A method of working that instrument. In other words, there must be a body of sciences, a doctrine of the perceiving mind, and a method of action; and these three, if there be unity in the constitution of the scheme, must prove each other in the last result—*i. e.*, they must correspond with each other in the procession of their movements. Now, Comte's systemization, tested by this criterion, reveals what it has, and what it has not done : it has given us a body of science, imperfect to the extent in which it

---

* [This prophecy has been signally fulfilled : for, Comte's latest books show him as the High Priest of a new Religion—the religion of Humanity.]

has excluded a large class of our most important beliefs; it has given us a very shallow doctrine of the perceiving mind, only as a subordinate division of physiology, carried forward by sociology; while his method, admirable in many respects, we are left to learn from its practical applications, which prove, as we think, that it is incomplete. There is not, consequently, that accordance between Comte's schemes of nature, of mind, and of method, which is the triple test of a sound systemization, and which inevitably follows, as we wish we had space to illustrate, from his own law of "decreasing generality," etc.

The narrowness of Comte's survey of the field of knowledge we have already remarked, and we must now state in what respect we think his method incomplete. He has shown, in an admirable manner, that each science has a method and spirit of its own, which is not applicable to others; that mathematical method is one thing, and physical another, and physiological another, and sociological another; that the method of one should not be allowed to encroach upon the domain of another, and that, as we ascend in the scale of the sciences, our means of exploration increase with the dignity of the pursuit : but he has nowhere, so far as we are able to discover, risen to a conception of that universal method which will use, while it absorbs, all partial and inferior methods. We refer to the method of Universal Analogy. Knowing how scientific men are apt to deride it, and how easily it may be abused in superficial hands, we yet believe that it will be found the final instrument of Philosophy. No one can have studied nature with any thoroughness without having perceived that her system is one of ascending repetitions, or of progressive orders and reduplications; that she is a process of phenomenal variations, implicated in a

permanent unity ; that each part of an organic form
is a miniature reproduction of its whole ; that every
higher organism carries forward with it its inferior or-
ganisms ; in short, as Goethe expresses it :

> "Wie Alles sich zum Ganzen webt,
> Eins in dem andern wirkt und lebt!
> Wie Himmelkräfte auf und neider steigen.
> Und sich die gold'nen Eimer reichen !
> Mit segendduftenden schwingen
> Vom Himmel durch die Erde dringen,
> Harmonisch all das All durchklingen." *

Goethe's own scientific labors were animated by the
method of analogy, and seem in their results like poetic
intuitions.   A most exquisite use is made of it also in
Mr. Wilkinson's book, "The Human Body, in its
Connection with Man," which, we presume, no one can
read without entering into a new world of the most
striking and beautiful truth.   It is this method which
has illuminated the gigantic labors of the modern German naturalists, such as Carus, Oken, Schubert, etc.,
with an almost heavenly light, filling the universe of
natural forms with humanitary meanings, and building
up a glorious natural theology, not on the empirical
basis of "contrivance proves design," but on the more
satisfactory and scientific ground, that man, the image
of God, is also, to use an expression of Novalis, the
"systematic index" of the creation, which attests, by
every line and movement, that he is truly the son of an

---

* " How the all weaves itself into the whole, and one in the other
acts and lives !   How celestial forces ascend and descend, and pass
each other the golden pails !   With wings perfumed with blessings,
they pervade the earth from heaven, all ringing harmonically through
all."

infinite Father. " In man," says Professor Stallo, "all
the powers of the universe are concentrated, all developments united, all forms associated. He is the bearer
of all dignities in nature. There is no tone to which
his being is not the response, no form, of which he is
not the type ;" but he does not give the reason, which
furnishes the ground for natural analogies, as well as
for a deeper spiritual correspondence, viz., that the author of nature is essentially a Man. He is the supreme
Wisdom and Love, of which the goodness and truth of
our humanity is the living, active form. The world of
nature, therefore, whose unceasing yearnings are to
minister to the spirit of man, is instinct everywhere with
conspiring humanities.

It would be unjust to infer from what we have said,
that Comte has no perception of this method ; for he
distinctly recognizes an elementary form of analogy in
the "comparisons" instituted both in his biology and
his sociology. He even speaks of the comparative
method as "one of the greatest of logical creations,"
and in another place, as "a transcendent method of
logical investigation,"—but it is at the same time clear
from the sense in which he employs it that he had not
fully penetrated its more fertile uses. The inveterate
hatred with which he is imbued for every process hint-
ing the slightest approach to theological or metaphysical
conception, has blinded his eyes, not only in this respect
but in many others, even to the most beautiful induc-
tions contained in his own premises. It will be the
lasting honor of his system, for instance, that it has so
clearly demonstrated the science of society as the cul-
minating glory of all the sciences, without which they
would have undergone their long and painful evolutions in vain, and from the reflected lustre of which
they derive their brightest illustrations and surest char-

acter ; but with this great truth, tingling as one might
suppose in every vein, announcing, too, that "the fundamental type of evolution is found in the increasing
preponderance of our humanity over our animality,"—
he has yet failed to perceive the pre-eminent mark and
distinction of that humanity—he does not discover the
characteristics which make man, a man. He confesses
the superiority of his physical, intellectual, and social
attributes (though some of these he intimates are ob-.
scurely anticipated by the brutes), but he does not discern, behind these attributes, a supremer life, a life no
longer held in bondage to any sensuous or finite good,
no longer subject either to nature or society, but which
feeds upon a perfect or infinite goodness, beauty, and
truth.   His loftiest conception is of the natural or scientific man; but of the artist, in the genuine sense, or
of the truly religious man, the gouls of whose aspiration are the "All-Fair and the All-Good,"—a beauty
and loveliness unconditioned by any evil or defect,—he
seems to entertain scarcely an inkling.   It is true, that he
is forced, by his own logic, as we shall see hereafter in his
"Positive Politics," to construct, as the final and comprehensive unity of thought, a "Supreme Being" and
a "religion," but that "*Grand-Etre*" is no more than
the visible and organized aggregate called Humanity,—
a humanity "subject to all the fatalities, mathematical,
physical, chemical, biological, and social,"—and that
"religion" is the reflective worship of that stupendous
Grand-Etre phenomenon !

But a final and full estimate of Comte depends upon
a consideration of his "sociology," which we must reserve, if happily we shall be permitted, for a future
opportunity.*

* [This was never undertaken.]

STRAUSS'S LIFE OF JESUS.*

HIS is the only book of any pretension that we have received this month : so, perforce, we must notice it, whether we have what Carlyle calls "inward vocation" or not.

It is just twenty years since the now famous *Leben Jesu* made its appearance at Tübingen, in Germany. A gun suddenly fired among a crowd of women could not have produced a greater flutter and scream than this publication did among the theologians. Not because there was anything particularly new in its doctrine, inasmuch as the same views of the Gospels had been taken by Bauer, Krug, Gabler, and others, but because these views were set forth with an elaborateness of learning and logic, and a keenness and severity of criticism, which had never before been surpassed. Strauss wrote in a style as crisp and vigorous, almost, as that of Lessing ; he was a complete master of the erudition of his subject ; he prosecuted his researches with a minute and thorough attention to every detail, while his apparent spirit was not that of the vulgar and virulent freethinker, but of the calm and ardent inquirer after truth. He was, moreover, a clergyman, in the active preparation of

---

* *The Life of Jesus*, critically examined. By Dr. David Frederick Strauss. Translated from the fourth German edition, by Marian Evans. Calvin Blanchard : New York, 1855.
From *Putnam's Monthly*, August, 1855.

young men for the ministry, and thus his grenades were discharged in the very citadel of Christianity.

Having stirred up a twenty years' theological war in Germany, France, and England, this work is now presented, in an excellent translation, to this country, where it will probably reach the popular mind, and confirm whatever of skepticism or indifference, as to religious matters, may be lurking behind our vast material activity. That it will produce, however, anything like the sensation here which it has abroad, we do not believe : in the first place, because it falls upon us very much as a spent shot ; and secondly, because there is not the same preparation for it in the philosophical culture of the people. In Europe, it was the legitimate outgrowth of a vast intellectual movement, begun by Hegel and his school, of which we know comparatively little in this country, and from which, with our decided practical tendency, we are not likely to suffer any great damage.

We do not propose, therefore, to add another to the thousand and one replies which have been made to the book, on theological grounds, since there is no occasion for it, in its probable influence. But the historical and literary problem which it presents, is one of permanent interest and curiosity, apart from its momentous religious bearing, and which we think worthy of the most serious examination.

The truth is, that, if Strauss's procedure in regard to the Gospels can be sustained, we do not see how any history, ancient or medieval, is to stand. We may dispose of nearly all the great names of literature and art, not only of the remoter ages, but of times as late as those of Luther, Shakspeare, and Milton, in this way, and so convert the universal records of our race into a mere mesh of figments and lies. Indeed, we believe that a learned literary lady has already announced her intention of showing that no such poet as Shakspeare ever lived, only a player of that name, who was a butt for the wits of his time, whose peculiar jest consisted in writing dramas, such as Hamlet, Macbeth, and Othello, and fathering them on simple William. According to this view, the age of Elizabeth spawned immortal plays, just as, in the view of Strauss, the age of Jesus spawned the most sublime and beautiful of religious legends.

But, let us first state, more at length, what the theory of the German Doctor is, before we proceed to any remarks upon its historical and literary deficiency. He admits that a man named Jesus appeared among the Jews, as a Messiah or religious reformer, just about the time in which our Lord is said to have come in the Gospel narratives, so generally accepted as authentic records. He probably believed himself to be the Messiah dimly shadowed forth in the religious writings and traditions of the Jews, and persuaded a considerable number of followers to adopt him in the same character. Having adopted him as such, of course they began to ascribe to him all those qualities which were supposed to characterize the Messiah. But, in the midst of their propagandism, he was put to death by the government. This was, for a time, a fatal blow to the hopes of his disciples, as well as to his own pretensions. Yet, in the midst of their despondency, the report is spread that the leader, whom they had buried, had risen from the grave. They eagerly believed the report, and some of the more impressible, the women especially, fancied that they saw him in person. Thus, gradually, the doctrine of his resurrection came to be regarded as an actual fact, and the conviction of his Messiahship was confirmed. Accordingly, in the course of the thirty years subsequent to his death, every element which entered as a component part into the current traditions of the Messiah was ascribed, by the enthusiastic veneration of his adherents, to Jesus. He became the focus in which all the scattered rays of Jewish Scripture, rabbinical gloss, and popular desire were concentred. The glorious Psalms, the lofty prophecies, the marvellous deeds, the divine appearances of the ancient Jewish mythology were blended, by the ardent and exalted hopes of his immediate friends, around the few, scanty, and insignificant facts of his actual life. He was the nucleus of all the sensitive and poetic religious imagination of the time. Wonders and marvels accompanied his steps, and a halo of sacred glory encircled his head.

Now, the Gospels are the records of these popular and glorifying legends, which had been slowly formed, with no avowed purpose of deception, with no open intention to palm upon the world a historical falsehood, but inevitably and naturally out of the circumstances of the age, into a large, complex, richly colored, though inharmonious, Christian mythology. They are the accretions of fancy and love, gathered, by imperceptible degrees, in the hearts and minds of the people, around the name which had come to represent to them the highest religious aspiration or idea of the human soul. There is no need, therefore, of saying with the Deists of the eighteenth century, that Christianity was a wilful imposition ; there is no need of trying to account for its miracles, as the Rationalists do, by natural or magical causes, for there is a more obvious and satisfactory way of accounting for everything in the doctrine of myths. All other religions have had their origin in these popular myths, and analogy would lead us to suppose that Christianity is no exception.

A plausible theory, Dr. Strauss, but one that does not at all convince our judgment ! Without going into the theological argument, but simply on historical and literary grounds, we will tell you why. It does not begin to account for the historical and literary facts of the case. We say nothing of the impossibility of a few illiterate and obscure Jews of Palestine having spun out of their heads the most sublime, the most spiritual, the most profound, and the most consolatory *religion* that was ever known ; but we do say, that, historically and artistically, the origin of the Gospels, in the way in which you describe, would be a greater miracle than any they themselves record, or any even that may be recorded in the archives of Romanism.

There is an antecedent improbability in this theory, to our minds, because the age in which the Gospels appeared was not a mythical, but a historical age. All the great mythological religions that we are acquainted with have arisen in the dawn and twilight of time, in the beginning, and not at the close of national existences, and by very slow and successive steps, running over periods of thousands of years, and not suddenly or within a single generation. This was clearly the case with the fabulous stories of Egypt, India, Greece, Rome, Scandinavia, Mexico, and the Pacific Islands. They date from the most primeval times, they cover vast epochs, and they bear unmistakable traces of local and national origin. But the Gospels arose in Judea, in the midst of a well-known and critical condition of things. The ancient faith had lost its simplicity, and had become a pompous ritual : oppressed by the Roman power, its people had lost the real significance of their traditions and oracles, and were looking only for a political liberator. All around them were highly cultivated cities and nations ;—Alexandria, with its gymnasia and schools ; Athens, with its intellectual civilization ; Arabia, with its treasures of learning ; Antioch, famous for its erudition ; and Rome, with its philosophers and historians. Few ages that we can recall were less favorable to the growth of a new religion, and particularly one founded upon the fables of the most despised of all existing races. Doubt, unbelief, derision, and scorn, were the characteristics of the lighter literature, and unsparing, minute, and active criticism, that of the higher learning. Lucian, the Greek Voltaire, who jested remorselessly with all the gods of the Pantheon, was the representative of the one, and the lecturers of Alexandria, who analyzed and probed all systems of philosophy and thought, like anatomical dissectors, were the representatives of the other ; while an easy epicureanism gave its tone to manners and practical life. Was it likely that, in the midst of all this doubt, learning, criticism, and philosophy, a few Jewish fables should grow into a living faith, and become the dominant conviction of mankind ?

Then, again, the narratives of the Gospels do not read, in the least, like the myths and legends with which we are familiar. They have, throughout, the air of veritable narratives. They profess, on the face of them, to be records of things actually said and done. They clearly distinguish, in their own text, what is meant to be historical from what is meant to be fabulous or allegorical, as in the case of the parables. Read the introduction to St. Luke, for instance, and see with what care the writer asserts that his Gospel is founded, not upon popular credulity or tradition, but upon first-handed evidence. His very object, he says, is to correct these traditional histories of Christ, and to supply an account from eye-witnesses, whose statements he had sedulously scrutinized, and traced to their origin. But the whole tenor of these narratives is so unlike that of the confessedly apochryphal Gospels, and of legends generally, that a reader the least accustomed to literary discrimination would detect the difference at once. Compare the "Gospel of the Infancy," or the "History of the Twelve Tribes," or the "Book of Joseph, the High Priest," or the *Acta Sanctorum* of the Bolland-ists, or "Turpin's Chronicles of Charlemagne," or any other works, the result of popular credulity, with the Gospels, and instantly you discover a world-wide disparity. In these you recognize the hand of truth, but in those the hand of fancy and superstition. You can no more confound them than you could a page from Mandeville's Travels with a page from Burns's Justice. Indeed, we could wish no better evidence, wherewith to convince a jury of twelve intelligent men of the genuineness of the Gospels, than these legendary books which aspire to something of the same character. In the former, we find simplicity, honesty, unity, naturalness, and detail (to say nothing of their lofty wisdom and purity of morals), while, in the latter, are exaggeration, distortion, inconsistency, unnaturalness, and vagueness, to say nothing of their ignorance, cun-ning, immorality, and vulgar human traits.

Strauss has dwelt at great length, and with the coolest and most impassive criticism, upon the many discrep-ancies of the several Gospels, but he does not, and cannot, deny the wonderful unity of aim and spirit that pervades them, in spite of verbal differences and insig-nificant contradictions. But could there be a stronger characteristic of real history, or a more fundamental departure from the mythical embellishments of history, than this general adherence to a single purpose, in the midst of considerable varieties of detail? Have we genuine accounts by several hands, of any period or of any distinguished man, from the days of Thucydides and Zenophon to those of Bancroft and Graham, in which such unity with variety is not a prominent

feature? Or, on the other hand, have we any mytholo-
gies in which the diversities are not wholly irreconcilable? Strauss's particular instances of contradiction
between the Evangelists we leave to the theologians to
settle, but they no more affect the real question with us,
i. e., whether the Gospels are substantially historical or
mythical, than the fact that Todd says John Milton was
born in 1608, Toland, that he was born in 1606, and
Hallam, that he was born in 1609, affects our belief in
the actual existence of Milton. Macaulay and Lingard
give us very different accounts of the reign of James the
Second of England, yet we believe that there was a
James the Second, and that he was not a creation of the
myth-forming propensities of the whigs and tories of
1685.

If there were no other proof of the genuineness of
the Gospels than the *character* which they ascribe to
Christ, that alone would furnish evidence beyond all
cavil and doubt. It is a character so transcendently
original in its mere conception, so thoroughly and profoundly consistent in its working out, so remarkable for
its combination of almost opposite traits—so full of a
mingled majesty and loveliness, firmness and gentleness,
candor and reserve, and so radically free from every
morbid tendency or sentiment, from fanaticism, pride,
impetuosity, weakness, or one-sidedness of any kind,
that, if not drawn from the life, it is the most stupendous
and wonderful piece of art that was ever exhibited by
the human mind. We may search the records of
ancient or modern literature in vain, to find anything
like it, in its singular perfection and beauty, and yet in
its complete naturalness, and, we may say, unconscious-
ness of development. The old Greeks were the most
intellectual people of the world ; they were tremblingly
alive to every form and semblance of beauty ; their

divinities were the ideal types of their most exalted conceptions of men and women ; yet we travel through their populous heavens, among their Zeuses, their Poseidons, their Hérés, and their Aphrodites, and find no shape that comes within a million furlongs of that noble and lowly Figure which meets us on every page of Luke and John. Our modern imaginations, with all the advantages of the Christian exemplar, have exhausted their powers in the creation of poetic and lovely personages—Dante, Chaucer, Shakspeare, Scott, Goethe, and Byron—and yet, in all this world of "fair humanities," there is not one that would not have thought it an impious presumption to be compared with Him, who was, after all, says Dr. Strauss, a figment of the brain of Jewish fishermen and peasants ! What the Homers and Eschyluses, what the Shakspeares and Scotts could not do, or have not done, the popular credulity of a few unlearned enthusiasts, acting upon the meagerest basis of facts, has accomplished ! Verily, there may be difficulty in believing miracles, but none equal to that which such a supposition implies.

Consider, further, the marvellously original and comprehensive scheme of reform which these fables impute to their principal character and his followers. It was not a restoration of the political fortunes of their country, nor yet the establishment of a perfect State, not the founding of a great school, nor the construction of a model society, but the radical regeneration of the whole human race. Now, there had been before them a great many heroes, a great many statesmen and kings, a great many philosophers, and a great many founders of religion ; there had been Moseses and Solomons, Solons and Lycurguses, Socrateses and Pythagorases, Zoroasters and Confutses, but there was never one who had conceived a plan of human improvement at all comparable, in benevolence, in extent, in wisdom, in practicability, with the plan which grew up by chance, it is said, in Judea, and took form in the hearts of its lowest populace. All others had been either local in their aims, or, at most, national ; or circumscribed to few objects, such as intellectual culture or political change ; or unjust in their application, as involving the conquest of other nations ; or entirely impracticable, like the academies of Pythagoras and the republic of Plato ; but this scheme was, at once, universal and individual, embracing all nations, all times, and all men, discarding the use of force, discarding secret agencies, discarding indirection and deceit, resting its claims entirely upon its inherent truth and goodness, appealing only to the most elevated motives, compromising with no prejudices, courting no power, flattering no vanities or vices, sternly rebuking every evil, not in its external form or its excrescences, but in its inward sources in the affections and thoughts, and, yet, promising itself the ultimate sway of society and mankind. Where, in the name of reason and common sense, did the populace of Palestine obtain a scheme at once so magnificent, so pure, so wise, and so benevolent ? From the Hebrew oracles ? No ! for it is there concealed in the sevenfold obscurity of types and shadows. From the vague and misty pantheisms of the East, with their metempsychoses and indolent contemplations, their astrologies and their fire-worships ? No ! from the wrangling, squabbling, concupiscent, and, very often, dirty gods of Greece ? No ! centuries after the Gospels had got a foothold in the world, influences from these sources came in to corrupt their purity, to debase their morals, to distort them into formalities, and asceticisms, and superstitions, and to blossom into rank and luxuriant growths of bigotry and error. But the

*

Gospels themselves are free from every stain. They stand alone in their simplicity ; they are unique in their loveliness ; they lift their heads above the faiths, traditions, and systems by which they were surrounded, as the snowy Alps tower over the dark shrubs and bushes tangled around their feet. Is it possible, then, to believe that they were the accidental or even wilful offspring of the popular mind of Jerusalem, attaching itself to the fallen fortunes of a misguided youth, and weaving together, with the desultory memorials of his unhappy career, a scheme at once so consistent, complete, and sublime?

There could not be a greater contrast in substance and form, between what is true and what is fanciful, than is presented by the incidents of the Gospel, as they are given to us for historical facts by its writers, and the same incidents, as subsequently worked up by the myth-forming propensities of human nature. Take the treatment of Mary, the mother of Jesus, for an example. What a fine subject for all kinds of sentimental and rhetorical embellishment. No woman that ever lived sustained such august and wonderful relations—relations to man and God. How touching every thought connected with her singular lot ! What a theme for the heart and the affections to dilate upon, for the mystical imaginations of the East to brood over, and for the more sensual imaginations of the Greeks and Romans to adorn ! Read, in the legends of the Madonna, collected by Mrs. Jameson, of the endless, extravagant, and clustering fables of which she became the centre, even in colder Europe ; how she inspired so much of the beautiful art of art's most beautiful age ; how the name of "our lady" kindled the romantic enthusiasms of chivalry ; how poetry, sentiment, devotion, poured their emotional fulness upon her, till she became, in the solemn decrees of the Church, the very mother of God, immaculate from her birth, and an object of veneration, and worship, forever! Panegyrics and prayers are still wafted to her from every Catholic cathedral of Christendom, and breathed in the silence of every Catholic home. She shares the throne of Heaven with her divine Son, and receives even a warmer adoration than He. Such is Mary in the estimation of the myth-forming faculties, under the natural action of the mind, contemplating the peculiarities of her story. Such she ought to have been in the Gospels, if the Gospels were only myths. But there is not a trace of all this in the primitive record. She is only two or three times mentioned by name, and then without an epithet of praise. Her virtue and her glory, whatever they were, are ignored. No attempt is anywhere made to environ her with lustre, to reflect the divine greatness of the Son upon the mother, or to pay her a single tribute of honor. Her emotions, whether of anguish, or of joy, are left to the solitude of her heart. She is simply "Mary, the mother of Jesus," and no more ; because, the evangelists, writing history, wrote the literal truth, whereas, had they been under the control of the mythic faculties, they could not in this respect have said enough, but would have anticipated all the fanciful legends of the middle ages.

A thousand similar and other objections to the theory of Strauss occur to us, which, if we were writing a regular review of his book, for the body of our Magazine, might be adduced, but, in these compressed editorial notes, we can only glance at a few of the more obvious considerations. There is, however, one thought which we cannot pass over. It is this : that on Strauss's principles, the momentous changes which Christianity has wrought are effects without a cause. It is impossible to conceive how a myth, or a mass of ill-digested myths, should have so "got the start of the majestic world" as to become the inspiring soul of all its best art, learning, literature, jurisprudence, practical activity—in short, of its highest civilization.   We can readily see. how the admiration of Christ's early friends should have raised him into a hero and a demigod.   We can see how the virtues and sentiments ascribed to him should come to have a powerful influence on men's minds.   But we do not see what *impulse* there can be in a fabulous history, to lead thousands of men, women, and children, during the very age of its origin, to ignominious and cruel deaths in attestation of its literal truth.   We do not see how a cluster of legends should have undermined Judaism, the most tenacious of all faiths, overthrown the idolatry of Paganism, supplanted the light mythology of Greece, and ascended the throne of the Roman Cæsars, when Rome was in her vigor.   We do not see how they should become the nucleus of all the public virtues and the private hopes of the world—how they should have borne the cause of humanity above the turbulence and barbarism of the middle ages, as the ark bore it above the waters of the Deluge—how they should have moulded the institutions and manners of all modern nations—convinced the reason and conquered the affections of the most enlightened men of every race, and been the balm and consolation of its humblest spirits—a power mighty to arouse and soothe, to strengthen and purify the souls of men, in all their varieties of condition —which is at this day the synonym of whatever is free, lovely, noble, and living in the most advanced civilizations; and which, as if only beginning to manifest its real strength, promises, for the future of the globe, a more lustrous and beautiful development than art has ever pictured or poetry dreamed.   Ah, no, these leaves of the Gospels, meant for the healing of the nations, were more than sprouts from the withered trunk of Judaism !

Strauss is aware of this last difficulty in his views, and, in a weak concluding chapter, endeavors to account for the effects of Christianity on the ground of its inherent truth. He evaporates its historical contents, but leaves its dogmas as a residuum behind ! Christ, instead of being an individual, is an idea—He is the idea of the race. "Humanity is the union of the two natures— God become man, the infinite manifesting itself in the finite—the child of the visible mother and the invisible father, nature and spirit—the worker of miracles, in so far as the spirit more and more subjugates nature—the sinless existence ; for pollution cleaves to the individual, but does not touch the race. It is humanity that dies, rises, and ascends to Heaven, as, from the negation of its phenomenal life, ever proceeds a higher spiritual life, and from the suppression of its mortality as a personal, national, and terrestrial spirit arises its union with the infinite spirit of the heavens." But how did those Jewish fishermen, two thousand years ago, get informed of this profound Hegelian philosophy?

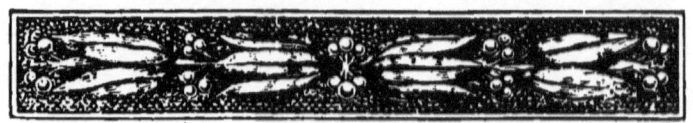

THE LATE HORACE BINNEY WALLACE.*

E take some shame to ourselves that we have not before directed the attention of our readers to this remarkable volume. It is true our pages have twice referred to it, with brief though admiring comment, but it deserves a more elaborate consideration at our hands. Wallace was one of those accomplished and noble minds, which ought never to be suffered to pass away without a tribute from the grateful hearts of his countrymen, and especially from those who are laboring, as he labored, in the cause of the humanities.

This recognition is all the more due to him, because he was not of that intellectual and moral constitution which enables the possessor of it to attain a ready and popular acceptance. He had all the ability requisite to a great literary or professional success, and earnestness as well as vivacity of spirit enough to have attached a large share of public regard to whatever he might undertake; but his modesty was even greater than his parts. He was ambitious of the scholar's rather than the writer's fame. Conservative in his habits, and above

---

* *Art, Scenery, and Philosophy in Europe.* Being Fragments from the Portfolio of the late HORACE BINNEY WALLACE, of Philadelphia. Philadelphia : Herman Hooker, 1855.

From *Putnam's Monthly*, September, 1855.

the necessity of labor, he made fewer public trials of his powers than their unquestionable superiority would have warranted. His earlier works, which he regarded as mere tentatives, were published anonymously ; but, had he put his name to them, they would have earned him rank and influence. We do not regret, however, that, in an age when the temptations to a premature publicity are so many, he should have preferred to husband his resources. A single book, like the one before us, the result of years of careful study and thought, even if there are no others among his manuscripts, would be a rich repayment of his reticence.

Mr. Wallace was born at Philadelphia in the year 1817, and died at Paris in 1852. He was, consequently, only thirty-five years of age at the time of his death. His father, a gentleman of property and culture, had carefully supervised his education in earlier years, particularly in the Greek and Latin classics. Long before the usual age at which boys are received in college, he was well grounded in the preparatory branches. The atmosphere of social and religious refinement that surrounded him in the home of his parents, noted alike for their cheerfulness and culture, developed the better qualities of his heart along with those of the mind.

In his fifteenth year, he was matriculated at the University of Pennsylvania, where he attached himself particularly to mathematical pursuits, in which he attained a wonderful proficiency. After two years' study, he was then removed to Nassau Hall, Princeton. It was there that we made his acquaintance, and we can speak, from personal knowledge, of his extraordinary attainments and capacity at that time. He was, however, so much of a recluse in his habits, that it begat among his fellow-students a suspicion of hauteur and aristo-

cratic feeling, not favorable to his general popularity,
though his accurate and extensive scholarship was universally conceded. In the higher departments of the
mathematics he stood almost without a rival, while his
familiarity with the languages was scarcely less marked.
But he paid little regard to the routine of college exercises, seeming to have already anticipated the greater
part of the regular studies, and consequently was not
graduated with as high honors as he otherwise might
have attained.

Having left college in 1835, he passed a short time
in attendance upon the medical and chemical lectures
at Philadelphia, when he commenced the study of the
law, first in the office of his father, and afterward in
that of the late Charles Chauncey, a distinguished prac-
titioner. He studied it with characteristic avidity, not
as a system of details for the regulation of practice, but
as a profound and philosophic science, mastering especially the theory of tenures and estates, which lies at
the foundation of so much collateral learning. Yet, in
the midst of his intense and varied professional labors,
he was not so unwise as to relinquish, as too many
lawyers do, the habit of literary composition. It is
said, by his biographer, that if the essays and larger
works, which he published from his seventeenth year
to the time of his death, generally under assumed
names, were collected, they would form no less than
sixteen duodecimo volumes, of two or three hundred
pages each. This is a grand example of industry for
his professional successors.

Among the works to which Mr. Wallace put his
name, were several of a legal character, such as the
notes to Smith's leading cases in Law, White and
Tudor's leading cases in Equity, and on American
leading cases, of which the highest authority of the

American bar said : "There is not a remark in the whole body which does not show the mind of a lawyer, imbued with the spirit of the science, instinctively perceiving and observing all its limitations, its harmonies, its modulations, its discords, as a cultivated musical ear perceives, without an effort, what is congruous or incongruous in the harmonies of sounds." The Boston *Law Reporter* also commends them for that thorough and logical precision, as well as fertility of illustration, which evinces the mind of a true legal philosopher, no less than the various accomplishments of the skilful lawyer.

In 1849, Mr. Wallace spent a twelvemonth in Europe, in the study of its monuments of art, its science, its natural productions, and its social condition. He passed the time mainly in England and Germany, without, however, neglecting Italy and France. It was in the latter country that his interest in social philosophy led him to form the acquaintance of the eminent speculator Comte, who appears to have conceived the most exalted opinion of his abilities, and to have formed the highest hopes of his usefulness, as a disciple of the Positive Philosophy, in the propagation of it in this country. But Mr. Wallace was one of those independent disciples who, thinking for themselves, are not always the most profitable to a master. He adopted Comte's scientific methods, so far as they tended to render all the moral as well as physical sciences inductive, but he adopted them with considerable and even revolutionary departures from Comte's own applications of them. In a brief but well-considered letter to Dr. McClintock, of the *Methodist Quarterly Review*, he has stated to what extent he received the Positivist doctrine, approving the beautiful and comprehensive classification of the sciences which Comte has given,

but qualifying his definition of the "three stages" of
humanitary progress, and vehemently protesting against
the political and religious errors into which he fell. He
considers the "Positive Philosophy" as a greater work
than the "Positive Politics," and that Comte is, in the
former, an oracle, and in the latter a babbler. In this
he scarcely does justice to his author, whose system is
in nothing else more remarkable than its logical consistency, so that if you grant its fundamental principles,
you are irresistibly led to nearly all its conclusions.
Mr. Wallace was saved, by his earnest religious belief,
from the more dangerous tendencies of Comteism, and
we regret that he did not live to complete what he had
projected—the application of scientific method to the
history of politics and religion.

When Mr. Wallace returned to this country in 1850,
he made arrangements with his publishers for the issue
of a series of works on commercial and civil law, after
he should have completed his knowledge of those subjects by a residence of some years in one of the German
universities. But in the spring of 1852, his eyesight
failing, and his general health becoming otherwise de-
ranged, he was forced to set out on a tour of foreign
travel. He sailed on the 13th of November, reached
England in the latter part of the month, and, in
December, repaired to Paris. His health was, unfortunately, made worse, not better, by the change.
Travelling exhausted him, and repose brought on fits
of extreme depression. He wrote to the only surviving
member of his family to come out and take care of him,
and three days after despatching the letter, "suddenly
expired." The news of his demise—so unexpected—
gave a shock to the small circle of his friends and
admirers; for his immediate friends had never been
many; but such as were admitted to his intimacy, loved

him with warmth and tenderness. His extraordinary
accomplishments, too, were ·making him gradually
known : the enthusiastic eulogies of Comte, copied
into the journals, had introduced his name to popular
respect ; and when it was announced that one so variously endowed, so rich in learning, so vigorous in
power of thought, so sincere in his sense of religious
duty, and withal so young, was no more, it was felt that
death had left a painful void, even by those who knew
little of the man or his writings.

> " His leaf has perished in the green,
> And, while we breathe beneath the sun,
> The world which credits what is done,
> Is cold to all that might have been !"

In person Mr. Wallace was slim, but not tall ; his
face was sharp and of a saturnine expression ; and his
manners were cold, until intimacy had broken through
the outer walls of his reserve, when he became frank,
cordial, and communicative. His conversation, illustrated by an immense range of knowledge, was in the
highest degree both interesting and instructive. It was
so full and yet so accurate, whatever its topic, that you
left him with an impression that that topic had been the
specialty of his studies. Whether he talked or wrote
on law, literature, the fine arts, philosophy, religion,
mathematics, the natural sciences, poetry, or even military art, his reading had been so extensive, his memory
was so tenacious, his grasp of principles and details
alike so firm, that he seemed to be talking or writing
of his favorite theme. Yet, he never paraded his acquisitions, nor infringed the strictest rules of propriety
and good taste, by self-display. His accomplishments,
like his virtues, were worn with that graceful humility

which proceeds from high symmetrical culture, refined by habitual religious trust.

The papers in the book before us were found in Mr. Wallace's portfolio, after his death. They had been written in America, but were still unfinished, "immature buds and blossoms shaken from the tree"—says the biographer—"and green fruit, evincing what the harvest might have been." They were immature, however, only in the sense of not being complete. In thought and manner they exhibit a rich autumnal ripeness. Precise in language, and thoroughly informed by thought, they glow, also, with the warmest imagination and feeling. We know of few books which speak so intelligently and yet so genially of Art—which show a more lively sensibility to the influences of nature, and a heartier relish for the great works of man—which combine so much poetic feeling with philosophic discrimination, or keen critical sagacity with tender and lofty religious enthusiasm. In the abstract discussion of the nature and aims of Art, in the almost technical description of the mighty cathedrals of Europe, in the impressive scene-painting of the Alps, and in the fine characterizations of the great painters of Italy, he appears equally at home—always familiar with his subject, and with the learning about it ; always truthful in tone, always vigorous in thought as well as just and appropriate in style, and not rarely, when the occasion justified it (as in what is said of the Roman forum), grandly eloquent.

The greater part of Mr. Wallace's work is devoted to Art, and the interesting questions involved in it, both as a philosophy and a practice. He has entitled the leading essay, "Art, an emanation of Religious Affection :" illustrating the maxim by an elaborate review of its general forms, in their most flourishing periods. A second paper argues that "Art is symbolical, not imitative." A third discusses the principle of "Beauty in works of Art;" while a fourth relates to "the law of the development of Gothic. Architecture." These are followed by studies of special works of art, such as the great cathedrals of the continent, and the master works of painting in Italy. Together they constitute a treatise on the whole subject of Art—its origin or genesis in the human mind—its characteristic property or function—the nature of that beauty which is its object—and the qualities which, in its best actual works, move our admiration and delight.

The art-creating faculty, Mr. Wallace says, is not the same as the rational or scientific, whose office is perception and inference, but a more sensitive and impassioned faculty—an instinct holding a place between mere emotion and the clear intellect, partaking of the properties of both, and combining them into the unity of its own original character and action. Yet, twofold as its affinities are, it is a single and peculiar faculty, given to some men and withheld from others, which no process of intellectual cudgelling can create, no theory of education develop, no culture of sentiments confer, but which, as is the case with the other great gifts of the Spirit, "bloweth where it listeth, and you hear the sound thereof, but cannot tell whence it cometh nor whither it goeth." It is for this reason that men of genius are a mystery to themselves and a perpetual miracle to the world.

But history shows that as this art-creating faculty is more active and prolific in certain men than in others, so it is vouchsafed to certain nations in richer measure than to others ; there are certain golden ages, when it blossoms and blooms with a fervid luxuriance and splendor. Nor does it spring up suddenly, in all its completeness, as if it were an arbitrary inspiration, but gradually, from rude beginnings, until it advances to that pitch of excellence which may be called perfection. "Continuing in bright and flowing vigor for a limited time, then flickering and going out like a lamp, or drooping and dying like a plant, or breathing and fading away, like a vision-haunted slumber of humanity ; *that* light no efforts can again relume : to that sweet, half-conscious dream of glory, not all the drowsy syrups in the world can medicine once more the faculties of that people."

What, then, is the origin and nature of this artistic activity, and how is it manifested? Mr. Wallace answers the first part of the question, by saying that "the art-faculty is nothing else but earnest religious feeling, acting imaginatively, or imagination working under the elevating and kindling influences of religious feeling." There is no instance in history, he avers, of a single manifestation of art-power, except among people and in ages where religious enthusiasm and religiousness of nature were prominent characteristics. He adds, also, in italics, by way of emphasis, that there is no instance of supreme excellence in art having been reached, excepting where " *the subject of the artist's thoughts and toils—the type which he brought up to perfection—was to him an object of worship, or a sacred thing immediately connected with his holiest reverence.*" Thus, the cause of the special superiority of the Greeks in sculpture was the anthropomorphous character of their theology, which made the human form an image of what they worshipped. So, too, the Madonna—the inspired and inspiring centre of Italian painting in the fifteenth and sixteenth centuries—was an image of worship ; and the controlling thought of the stupendous and beautiful cathedrals of the middle ages, as well as of the Athenian temples, identified their sacred forms with the residence and glory of the Divinity.

Consequent upon this truth, and in answer to the second part of the question above, Mr. Wallace confines the great general forms of Art to architecture, sculpture, and painting, which, he alleges, are the three forms best adapted to the display of its character. Literature, on the one hand, he thinks too intellectual, and music, on the other, too sensuous to exhibit "that fusion of the mental and material, that perfect balance of the sensible and thoughtful, which art requires." Only in these three departments just named, do the actual evolutions of art exhibit an excellence so surpassing and irresistible as to render it a nature and existence by itself. It is only in the ages of Greek sculpture and architecture, of Italian painting, and the Gothic cathedrals, that we discover genuine evidences of artistic inspiration ; only there that we encounter works so complete in their beauty, so exalted in significance, and so absolute in splendor, as to fill our deepest capacities of emotion, and satisfy the loftiest demands of the mind. These "stand in the mystery of an inherent perfection, participating in an apparent divinity in the inscrutableness of their nature, as well as in the over-swaying might of their moral power. Through them the mind runs upward, along the viewless chains of spiritual sympathy, till it loses itself in the Infinite."

We propose to say a word or two of these important views, less by way of contradiction than of expansion ; for, while they are fundamentally correct, they are yet not stated with all the fulness and precision of an adequate philosophy.

It is proper to speak of Art as an *emanation* of religious feeling, because of the signal and intimate union which subsists between them, whether we consider their sources in the human mind, or their more concrete manifestations. But we cannot say that this is the whole truth. A great many other influences besides religion are concerned in the production of a vigorous state of the arts. It is also true, that the great artist finds, in the object of his labor, an image of worship, or of devout and earnest feeling ; but this, again, is not the whole truth, inasmuch as the great artist requires a great deal more than this single qualification.

In a certain general sense, all the achievements of the human mind, all the elements and characteristics of the different civilizations, are the products of religious belief. The intellectual apprehension or theory which a nation forms of its relations to the universe, or, in other words, its theology or doctrine of the gods, is what determines its kind and degree of development. This measures the height to which it shall rise in the scale of existences, moulds its manners and laws, and marks the limits of its moral and practical activity. If that theory be fetichtic, as with the savages ; or polytheistic, as among the Greeks ; or simply monotheistic, as among the Jews and Mohammedans ; or, again, a strictly historical theism, founded upon the actual incarnation of the divine in the human, as in Christianity, we know, with more or less precise approximation in each case, what the contemporary science, literature, customs, government, are likely to be. As religion is the deepest impulse of the soul, overmastering all others, even in the lowest states of human society, as our relations to the invisible world are more profound and vast than all other relations, controlling us, by their hopes and fears, more energetically than any wants of the body, or any ties of worldly affection or interest, so our conception of these relations, or our theology,

masters and controls all other conceptions—the forms
of art among the rest, and *more* than the rest, because
of its more sensitive and impressible character.   Thus,
the tragedies of Eschylus are moulded upon the ancient
idea of a stern and irresistible destiny, which underlies
them, like the deep bass of an air, and they are what
they are because of that idea.   The tragedies of Shakspeare, on the other hand, breathe of a personal God, in
whom a living justice, consulting the interests of human
freedom, has supplanted a blind fate.   Yet we can
hardly maintain that the ancient conviction of destiny
originated the plays of Eschylus, any more than we can
say that Christianity originated those of Shakspeare.
They respectively controlled the poets' views of the character of man, but they did not create or give birth to the
inner life of the poets.   For though the artist takes the
form of his thought generally from the religion and life
of his age, the inspiration of it, that which imbues him
with something of a prophetic ken, rising above and looking beyond his age, comes more immediately from God,
who endows him with his peculiar and marvellous genius.

Were it an exclusive truth that art emanates from
religion, the most religious ages of the world would
have been the most artistic, and the most artistic again
the most religious.   Does it appear, however, that the
age of Pericles, in Greece, when the arts reached their
highest bloom, was the age most earnestly receptive of
the Greek mythology?   Or, was the age of Leo the
Tenth, in Italy, that in which Christian faith was more
active and powerful than it ever had been before?   No
doubt a serious, heartfelt interest is felt by the artist in
the religious sentiment which he embodies, for, without
that, there would be no motive in his mind ; but a
combination of other influences concurs also in the
grander development of art.   To the sincere and ear-

nest popular sentiment, whether religious or humanitary, must be added a vigorous national life, stimulating energy and hope, and an access of wealth sufficient to give the repose and culture which the laborious yet peaceful nature of artistic pursuit demands. In short, then, we should say, that the great eras of art have been eras of a universal, intellectual, and moral excitement, when the imagination was kindled by some great sympathy, and the whole soul, not of the artist only, but of the nation, aroused into an intense and almost preternatural life.

For the same reason, when it is said that the artist finds an image of worship in the object of his labor, we recognize a great truth, but not the entire truth. It is true of certain displays of art, but not of all art. If this saying were universally true, there could be no art but such as should be directly and consciously employed in the celebration of the Divinity. But, when Agasias, or whoever it was, modelled his Fighting Gladiator, when Angelo chiselled that wonderful Bacchus at Florence, when Cellini chased some exquisite golden cup, when Raphael painted the Parnassus in one of the Stanzas of the Vatican, when Mozart composed the Don Giovanni, or Shakspeare wrote Othello—we doubt whether the artists saw in their objects the remotest image of anything to be worshipped. Their themes are not in any way connected (and the same might be said of a thousand other immortal examples) with any living mythology ; yet, these were works of art, and some of them of very high art. Can any one deny that a very fine and even noble species of art was attained by the Flemish and Dutch painters, whose subjects were mostly drawn from incidents of ordinary life, such as the fêtes of the peasantry, or the manœuvres of dragoons? Mr. Alston, no mean judge in such things, and who,

if we may infer from his own exalted works, was not at
all inclined to lessen the deep religious significance of
art, speaks in one of his lectures of a picture by
Ostade, in which the figures are a woman nursing her
child, and the carcass of a hog hung up to dry,
where every accessory hints of low culinary occupation ;
and yet he speaks of it as a genuine work of art, full
of " magical charms," displaying a very "sorcery of
color," and exciting a depth of " pleasurable emotion
which passes off into poetic dream !" He contrasts the
originality and invention it discovers with the same
qualities in the Death of Ananias, by Raphael. Now,
what he means by this, and what we mean in our
argument thus far is, that the functions of art are universal, ranging from the expression of the highest
religious adoration to that of the lowest every-day
delight which is in itself innocent. No definition of
art, therefore, can be accepted as adequate, which confines it to its higher types alone, or which excludes
those lesser displays of it commonly condemned by a
pragmatic criticism as low and trivial.

In order to show the relations of art to religion, and
to get at the grounds of that seeming exaggeration
which designates all art as divine, we should be obliged
to enter upon a minute philosophical inquiry, for which
we have now neither time nor space. But we may suggest our view of the matter, so far as to render what we
may say intelligible, in few words.

Man, as the creature of God, is the subject of a twofold life—the first natural, which connects him through
his body and senses with the physical world, and through
his affections with his fellow-man—and the second,
ideal or spiritual, which connects him, through faith
in an infinite Goodness, Wisdom, and Beauty, to God.
It is this second life which gives him the distinctive

mark of his manhood.   His relation to nature, or to
his physical organization, he shares with the vegetables ;
and his relations to society, so far as society is simply
natural, or not yet raised into a spiritual fellowship, he
has in common with many animals ; but his belief in
an unlimited goodness and truth, and his power of acting in obedience to that belief, is what especially constitutes his humanity.   The vegetable and the animal have
no existence superior to their physical organization ;
they are the slaves of that, and, when the wants of that
are satisfied, they are complete and happy.   Man, too,
in so far as his existence is subject to his organization
and its corresponding affections, is only a higher kind
of vegetable and animal.   But being made, as he is,
capable of perceiving by his reason, and of obeying by
his freedom, ends which are above his merely animal
and social wants, he becomes an ideal or spiritual
being, which means a true man.

Now the characteristics of the lower sphere of life are,
that it is not only limited, but exists solely by limitation ;
that it is not only dependent in each of its particulars
upon something out of itself, but that the very end of
its existence is subservience ; that it is not only transitory, but that incessant change is the law of its life ;
and consequently, that it is not only unsatisfying, but,
if trusted in, disgusting, venomous, and deadly.   On
the other hand, the characteristics of the higher sphere,
are an infinite freedom, an existence in and for itself,
an unchanging permanence, and a fulness of activity
and delight, which the Apostle describes as unspeakable.
Our humanity, therefore, in so far as it is a genuine
humanity, not a mere animality, perpetually aspires to
this upper world of Love, and Truth, and Beauty,
revealed to its hope, and incessantly beckoning it onward and upward.

Still, as we are made primarily the denizens of nature —as we are not God in ourselves, but his creatures— we can *know* goodness, truth, and beauty only as we reproduce them in nature, or as they are fixed and embodied in act. We learn Love by loving, and Truth by living truly, and Beauty by realizing it in some actual type. They are, before that, not objects of direct consciousness, of immediate perception, but of vague longing and desire—a blind hunger of the soul, which craves, but has not yet found its food. They are not ours, but God's; yet they become approximatively ours, as we translate them, by prayer and effort, and the putting away of untruth, wickedness, and imperfection from our lives, into the natural life. The endeavor to appropriate them, however, is our normal work—is the end for which we were made—in which we find our true freedom and joy;—while the threefold aspect of this endeavor, as it is directed to the supernal Love, or Wisdom, or Beauty, we call, respectively, religion, philosophy, and art. These move in the same sphere, they spring from the same source—the immortal fountain of life—but they operate in different modes and on different planes. Religion deals primarily with the heart, without separating itself from the intellect and senses, and stands nearest to God; philosophy works with the intellect, and dwells in the intermediate world of thought; while art comes down to the senses, and flows through all the forms of sensible nature, transforming and glorifying them with soul. Religion seeks to reduce the facts of human life, inward and outward, to a universal unity of love; philosophy, to the universal unity of truth; and art, to a universal harmony of sensible appearance. In essence and derivation they are all one—like streams which rise from the same sacred spring, but they flow through separate channels and in diverse directions toward distinct realizations. They all come from God, and they all end in life or action.

We see from this why it is not unusual or irreverent to speak of "divine philosophy," and "divine art," as well as of a divine or holy religion—not because the immediate object, in any philosophical or artistic research, is "an image of worship,"—but because the ultimate tendency of it is to emancipate our spirit from the fetters of its finite condition. It is through philosophy, or its handmaid, science, that we subdue the stormy and truculent antagonisms of nature, who would kill us by her frosts and whelm us in her tempests if she could, till they have become the willing servitors of every human use. So, too, by means of science, we lift society out of brute gregariousness into an organism of the sweetest and tenderest humanities. And so again, through art, we breathe over the earth the free atmosphere of heaven, people its glades with angelic living shapes, and tune its myriad voices into "hallelujahs and sevenfold harmonies" of song. All true philosophy, and all true art, then, have the same ultimate aim with the one true religion.

In a deeper sense, however, than this, art deserves the epithet of divine; for it raises us to an activity which approaches more nearly than any other to the highest that we can conceive of the real divine life; of that life which, as St. Augustine says, *per cuncta diffusus, sine labore regens, et sine onere continens,* is sufficient unto itself, having neither bodily limits nor social dependences, dwelling forever in its fulness of absolute perfection, and yet flowing forth forever in infinite streams of love, and splendor, and joy. The artistic life is the image of this supernal glory, because of its free spontaneous productivity. It has its end in itself; it

exists for no extraneous purpose ; it inhabits its own
independent world ; it finds in its own bosom an immeasurable delight ; and though the reconciliation of
form and thought, of real and ideal, of matter and
spirit, it annuls forever the contradictions of actual existence. Therefore is it in every work of art that you
are impressed with its unalterable repose, its calm
majesty and grace, its inexhaustible joyousness, and its
serene freedom.

Art being a universal mediator between the interior
world of aspiration and faith, and the exterior world of
sensible experience, we cannot limit its functions, as
Mr. Wallace has done (though somewhat doubtingly),
to the mere arts of design. Architecture, sculpture,
and painting are the most impressive forms of art, but
they do not exhaust those forms. The vast realm of
beauty which music evokes, when sentiment marries
sound, must not be forgotten, nor the still vaster worlds,
the constellated worlds of poetry, peopled with radiant
creatures who use the speech and enact the dramas of
the gods. It would be a fatal oversight, indeed, to
reckon the grosser, the more material, the more objective arts among "the glories of our mortal state,"
and omit the more subtile, subjective, spiritual, delicate,
and profound. Mr. Wallace's fine sense deserts him
(as the hesitated doubt seems to imply), when he de-
cides that music is too sensual, and poetry too intellectual, to be considered among the number of the
arts ; and still more so, when he assigns as a reason for
this sentence of banishment, that they miss "that fusion
of mental and material, that perfect balance of the
sensible and the thoughtful, which art requires."

It might be replied, in detail : first, that music is less
sensuous than either architecture, sculpture, or painting, and more variously emotional ; secondly, that

architecture itself does not exhibit that complete fusion
of mental and material of which he speaks, and is at
best only a symbol of it; and thirdly, that poetry,
though more intellectual than other arts, has yet much
to do with the affections, the fancy, and the sensuous
imagination.   But, instead of exposing the several in-
accuracies of this judgment, we prefer to indicate what
we regard as the source of the error.

It is this : that our author has failed to treat of the
several species of art, as parts of an organic whole,
necessary to each other, because necessary to the complete expression of man's artistic capacity.   Confined to
the arts of design, art is like the torso dug from ancient
ruins, or like the early pipe of Pan, beautiful so far as
it goes, yet not the rounded statue, yet not the full-toned
organ instinct with every sound.   No single art, considered in itself, is adequate to the utterance of our
boundless spirit.   Each art has its circle and domain,
within which it gives us glimpses of the eternal heights,
but beyond which it is opaque and blind.   Each art,
beyond itself, craves and promises a brother.   Thus,
architecture tells us, as in the Greek temple, of the
graceful majesty and serene repose of the gods ; or, as
in the Gothic minster, it lifts our souls in adoration
and a tumultuous throng of praises to the Infinite One.
It needs sculpture, however, to inform us that these
gods are men, with the "high passions and high
actions" of men, or that the Infinite has incorporated
itself in human shape.   Sculpture, again, with its
sightless orbs and moveless body, has a limitation,
where painting comes in to fill those eyes with tender
lustre, and animate those limbs with a fresher glow.
Yet the deepest inner world of sentiment and thought
no painting nor sculpture can reach, and only the airy
wands of poesy and sound, penetrating to the inmost

of our being, bring forth spirits too subtile and swift to be grasped by any but ethereal hands. For, it is singular in the relations of the arts, as Hegel has admirably argued in his Esthetics, that there is a march or progress, both in respect of their sensible materials and their powers of expression, from the gross, the concrete, the objective, the material, to the fine, the abstract, the subjective, and the spiritual. Architecture, dealing with matter in its three dimensions of length, breadth, and height, and as subject of necessity to the law of gravitation, enjoys only a circumscribed liberty of expression. Even in the best examples of it, as in the cathedrals, the sentiment and thought are ever more or less dominated by the form ; there is a tendency in the technical and constructive to prevail over the imaginative and the reflective ; the inward significance is apt to be overlaid by the outward representation. A larger freedom in the use of the material and a nicer expression is obtained, in sculpture, when the idea and the form are made to coalesce ; but sculpture itself does not transcend the corporeal, or what the corporeal contains. In painting, on the other hand, while it retains the corporeal, so far as that is needed for its purposes, it yet escapes from the coarser properties of matter, deals with light and shade, and the magic of color, instead of with ponderous masses, and imparts to forms a flexibility and freedom, which enlarges, almost miraculously, its powers of combination and its reaches of spiritual utterance. Yet there are sentiments and shades of sentiment, delicacies and grandeurs of emotion, successions and fluxes of inward experience, which color seeks in vain to convey, and which the finer medium of sound alone can interpret ; until the soul, withdrawing more and more into itself, and dispensing more and more with external media, speaks through signs of sound only, or the viewless, intangible word. As in architecture we saw the objective dominate, so in poetry we see the subjective prevail, that art, as a whole, may exhaust the domain of nature, and claim the sovereignty of both her inner and outer worlds.

The oversight of Mr. Wallace in excluding music and poetry from the circle of the arts, has led him into another mistake—quite common among the writers on art just now—that of depreciating the artistic attainments of the moderns. It is almost a cant of the times to assert that art worthy of the name no longer exists. Mr. Ruskin, among the rest, divides the eras of art into the classical, the medieval, and the modern, and compares them, as a bad grammarian might do, as good, better, worst. Classicism he defines as embracing all ancient time, down to the fall of the Roman Empire ; medievalism, as extending from that to the close of the fifteenth century ; and modernism, as from then forward to our own days. The first was distinguished, he says, by an earnest Pagan faith—the second, by Christian faith—and the third by no faith. Consequently, he declares our modern art to be just no art at all.

Now, Mr. Ruskin has said many of the best and some of the worst things that have ever been said of art, but this is not among his best. Mr. Wallace, with whom we are more concerned, virtually adopts the same principle of distribution, by confining the great epochs of art to the age of Pericles, the age of the Gothic cathedrals, and the age of painting in Italy. It seems to us, however, that both writers take a contracted and an unfair view of the matter. We shall say nothing of the singular latitude which allows Mr. Ruskin to class the winged bulls of Nineveh and the monstrous sphinxes of Egypt among the remains of classicism, nor shall we contend that in the arts of design our modern eras may

boast of works equal to those of Phidias and Cle-
omenes, of Raphael and Angelo ; but we shall and do
most earnestly protest against any philosophy of art
which excludes music and poetry from its domain, and,
on the strength of such an exclusion, disparages the
abilities and character of the moderns.

If we were disposed to discuss the question between
the ancients and moderns, even in respect to the arts of
design, we should premise that Rubens and the land-
scapists of the seventeenth century, that Flaxman, Dan-
necker, and Chantrey, that Kaulbach, Cornelius, Cou-
ture, Delacroix, Turner, and Alston, and many other
eminent sculptors and painters who might be mentioned, are not to go for nothing ; but then we should
freely admit that we have no schools of plastic or picturesque art equal to the great schools of antiquity and
of the close of the fifteenth century. Having made the
admission, our point would be this : that modern art,
responsive to the changes in the spirit of society, or in
obedience to the greater spirituality and larger individual freedom of the age, has taken another form. It
has taken the form of the subjective and spiritual arts,
which are certainly of equal dignity and worth with
other arts, if not superior to them, while it has carried
the new forms to a degree of vigor and excellence it
would be idle to look for in antiquity or the middle
ages. When we consider what a sun-burst of music
fell upon the seventeenth and eighteenth centuries,—
when we recall the names of Palestrina, Bach, Handel,
Haydn, Mozart, Beethoven, Weber, Bellini, and Men-
delssohn,—when we remember what a ready stimulus
and upbearing elasticity music affords to the inspirations
of thought, what a depth and fulness and variety of
emotion it awakens,—what rapturous and graceful
charms it breathes upon the senses, incapable through

it of any but pure delights,—how, it is not the luxury
of the rich, but the household blessing of the poor—
cheering, even in its rudest strains, the swain at his
plough and the village maiden at her wheel—diffusing
everywhere an exquisite and innocent sympathy,—and
how, there is no solitude which it cannot enliven, no
Saul-like moodiness which it cannot charm away, no
hardness of feeling which it cannot soften, no sorrow
which it cannot in some degree assuage, no joy which
it cannot spread through ten thousand hearts, and no
adoration which it cannot deepen and strengthen, till
the soul is lifted, as on the wings of the cherubim, to
the very presence of God,—we say, when we consider
all this, its capacity, its universality, its purity, its
power, we are utterly amazed at the criticism which
denies the existence of modern art.　But if we turn
from music to poetry,—if we remember that Shakspeare,
whose mind, like the ocean, filled all the inlets and
creeks of our existence with its own majestic glory, was
a modern ; that Spenser and Milton, with the immortal
race of bards which has followed them in England, were
moderns ; that the entire beautiful literature in Germany, with Jupiter Goethe on its throne, is of modern
growth ; and that this poetry, so multiform, so lovely,
so grand, so humane, so fantastic, so infinite in its resources and its effects, is a common possession of every
man, woman, and child who can spell,—we are still
further lost in wonder at the cries which bewail the decrepitude and departure of art.

We have no space to dwell upon the theme, more
than to hint that the great ages of art, distributed according to a principal type in each case, were the ages
of symbolic art in Egypt ; of plastic art, in Greece ; of
constructive art, in the middle ages ; of picturesque art,
during the period of transition from Catholicism to

nationalism ; and of musical and poetic art since the
Reformation. Considered in this light, we see more
distinctly than in any other way, how the special form
and highest glory of art grows directly out of the spirit
of the time,—how the evidences of the Eternal favor
are never wanting to man, and are even most generous
when most unseen,—and how it is folly to mourn the
fossils of a defunct vegetation, when the hill-sides and
meadows around us are everywhere breaking into new
and rosy blooms.

THACKERAY AS NOVELIST.[*]

N laying down the last page of "The New-comes," one is tempted to exclaim, in language similar to that which the eminent critic, F. Bayham, Esq., applied to his good friend and patron, the Colonel : "Brave old Thackeray, noble old soul !" With the same restrained ardor that the brave Colonel himself used to charge at the head of his Indian dragoons upon the Mahrattah cavalry, you charge upon the selfishness and shams of our hateful little societies. With the same dauntless courage of your sturdy countrymen that fills the ditches and heaps the ramparts of Sebastopol, you lay about you on all sides the dead and wounded Cossacks of the false life on which you war. You are a regiment, at least, in yourself,—now pouring a rattling fire of grape into the enemy—now picking down a general with a Minié rifle—and now exploding grandly like a line of bombs—while ever and anon is heard, in the midst of the more general roar, the deep boom of some thirty-two pounder, doing an amazing deal of damage.

But brave old Colonel Thackeray, noble old soul, you have done more in "The Newcomes" than discharge

---

* *The Newcomes. Memoirs of a Most Respectable Family.* Edited by Arthur Pendennis, Esq. New York : Harper & Brothers. 1855.

From *Putnam's Monthly*, Sept., 1855.

your files of musketry and your parks of artillery upon
the murderous social Cossacks, sweeping them down by
the hundred. You have turned Miss Nightingale, too,
and visited the hospitals, and helped the sick, and as-
suaged the horrors of the dying, and pointed their last
hopes to the blessed consolations of Christian goodness
and truth. You have shown that you have a great big
heart (of which we that knew you did not need to be
convinced), though some said that you had none, and
that you were only a hard old soldier, sabering people
all round, without human pity or remorse. Yes, indeed,
a heart as big as that of the Colonel himself, but with
a head a great deal wiser than his ; large and generous
sympathies, tenderness, a kind love of your brother,
and yet a truthfulness which does not allow you to say
that the world is made up of these ; and a deep, noble,
Christian philosophy, which gives you comfort in the
absence of these."

The merits of Thackeray, which have raised him to
his eminent position, are now almost unanimously allowed. They have been so often dwelt upon, at least,
that no one need be ignorant of what they are. First and
foremost is his wonderful humor—a quality in which he
is not inferior to Swift, Fielding, Dickens, or any other
among the illustrous English humorists—and which, in
some form or other, steeps and saturates every page of
his writings. And this humor is as various as it is deep
and fine—now broadly grotesque, as in "Yellowplush's
Letters," and some of the contributions to "Punch"—
and now as gentle and delicate as the nicest touches of
Addison or Goldsmith. Even the exquisite irony of
Cervantes scarcely surpasses that of many a passage that
might be taken from the "Paris Sketch Book," the
"Irish Sketches," or the "Journey from Cornhill to
Cairo." The exuberant fun, the rollicking animal

spirit, which sometimes carries Dickens away into caricature, is not found in Thackeray, who is more uniformly
equable in his vivacity, and is never mastered by, but
always masters his genius.

Indeed, the calm impassive tone which he preserves,
as if he were only a spectator of what he describes,
quite disinterested and heedless, might be mentioned
as the second among those admirable traits which have
gained him a name.   His scenes never seem to be in-
vented.   They come to pass.·   The author lifts the curtain and the play goes on.   He comments and ridicules,
he sneers and laughs at the motley throng, but he does
so as one of the audience.   You do not feel that *he* is responsible for the result ; the actors are only about their
own work, and the stories tell themselves.   Mr. Tit-
marsh is the man at the door, who takes our tickets
and points out the best seats.   Or, rather, he is the
fiiend who asks us to his chamber, to take a peep out
of his window at the busy world of the streets, or into
the neighboring windows, while he chats pleasantly at
our side about what we both see.   Old Pendennis, and
Costigan, and Farintosh, and Becky, and Bareacres,
and a thousand more, are the people who are passing,
or who occupy the parlors and bedrooms opposite.
He knows them all, and tells us who they are, if we
are ourselves too dull to guess it from their mere appearance.

It is this remarkable realism which gives his books
their aspect as an actual transcript of life.   Everybody,
on reading them, is quite convinced that the author has
seen what he sets forth, and some even suppose that his
own agency in the business is little more than that of
the *camera lucida* which reflects the picture.   " He
simply puts down the reports of his eyes," exclaims
Mr. Keen, "as any well-informed gentleman might

do." But, then my friend, what eyes they are! how
they take in every minute particular of the visible appearance ; and having got that, have strangely pierced
the entire significance of it! Almost every person,
as you say, is in the habit of looking at the world and
its ways with his eyes, and Thackeray does no more ;
but there is something so sharp, so penetrating, so luminous in his look, that when he sees the thing he sees
the whole of it—inside as well as out—and that not
only with his eyes, but with his brain and heart. We
know of no writer, save Balzac, whom he resembles in
other points, whose characterizations of men and of
incidents are so sharply defined, so nicely and finely
cut, so chiselled, as if from the block, like a piece of
statuary, and yet so free and flowing, and full of animation, the most unlike statuary of anything in the world.
It would be impossible not to recognize his men and
women, should we meet them again in the streets. In
fact, when we once attended an opening of Parliament in
London, we saw a great many of them, and were about
to accost them on the score of old acquaintance. We
heard the Captain sing an Irish song in a cider-cellar
in the Strand. Mr. Jeames waited upon us when we
dined at Blank House, and we were introduced personally to a dozen well-known fellows at the club. It is
needless to mention their names, as, we are sorry to say,
they were generally snobs.

But, besides his realism and insight, Thackeray owes
much of his success to his style—which we hardly know
how to describe. It is so clear and simple, that it seems
at first to possess no really salient qualities—to be a kind
of unconscious flow of the author's thoughts—and yet
the impressions produced by it are so positive and peculiar, that we are inclined to regard it as a result of
the most elaborate art. Yet there are no signs of effort

about it, no marks of labor, no incompleteness or clumsiness, no commonplaces or affectations of phrase, and no decided polish or brilliancy, but only an easy, offhand, charming, and irresistible grace, which you would not observe if you did not set about it purposely, in order to analyze your pleasure.   Like a stream which runs through a rich meadow, it rolls on quite ignorant of its own sweet murmur and its own gentle ripple. Addison's style suggests it, but Addison's was more artificial ; Goethe's had much of the same clearness, but Goethe's was more staid and stately ; Fielding's had the same naturalness, but was at times too careless and hurried ; and, in fact, we can only speak of it as Thackeray's own,—original, vigorous, natural, limpid, idiomatic, and flexible—a perfect vehicle for the man's peculiar spirit.

All this is admitted, we say—all these qualities are pretty unanimously conceded to him—and yet Thackeray can hardly be called a *popular* writer.   He is not popular in the sense that Dickens is.   He is not loved nearly so much as he is admired.   He has not taken hold of the hearts of his readers, and become their intimate personal friend.   We do not refer to those who would say of him what the criminal said of the judge, and on the same grounds, '' Take that man away, for I go in fear of my life because of him ;'' but to a class, a large class, who view him with distrust, if not with positive dislike, even in the midst of considerable respect.   They allege that his writings, with all their pleasant excellence and inventive freshness, with all their wit, and pathos, and sagacity, and wisdom, and variety of character, and healthful scrutiny, are offensive from their excessive severity, from their misanthropical views of life, from their essential injustice in dwelling upon the worse aspects of human nature instead of the better.

We are acquainted with several gentlemen, amply qualified, by endowment and culture, to undertake the task
of criticism, who express a total inability to read Thackeray. They get weary, they tell us, of representations
of society wholly made up of snobs, rascals, demireps,
flunkeys, tuft-hunters, fools, coxcombs, managing mam-
mas, flashy daughters, insolent and silly nabobs, and
hoary old reprobates in general. They long to see
among the figures which flit through his phantasmago-
ria, among the black silhouettes of his canvas, some
reminiscences of the heroes and angels who exist in the
real world as well as in the old books of romance.
They acquit him of all fondness for monsters, for high-
waymen and murderers, and the various nondescripts
which give a hobgoblin and hideous look, or a sulphurous smell to the French, Newgate, and Gas-light literatures; but they aver that his varnished and well-dressed
but thoroughly rotten sinners, and their hollow and
hypocritical satellites, his Steynes, and Crawleys, and
old Majors, his Deuceaces and Crabs, his Becky Sharps
and Lady Kickleburys, with a miscellaneous rabble of
unmitigated villains behind, are not a whit more desirable company. Granting, what is true, that he throws
in a good old Dobbin at times, or a Laura, or an Amelia, it is also true that these are almost as weak as they
are good, and go for nothing in the midst of the overwhelming mass of scapegraces and scoundrels.

Women, especially, have been shocked by the representations which Mr. Thackeray makes of their world.
They protest that he knows nothing at all about the
mysteries of their delicate and beautiful spirits—that
they are not all husband and fortune hunters, or brainless and fond little fools, willingly allowing themselves
to be imposed upon by brutal husbands and cruel
brothers, for the sake of occasional shawls and trinkets,

or a kiss now and then—but that they have souls, and
consciences, too, and a strength of love and goodness
greater than man has ever conceived. They do not
deny that there might be a Mrs. Becky in existence, or
a Lady Griffin even, with an interminable line of Mac-
kenzies and Clutterbucks, as ambitious as they are vacu-
ous ; but they do deny that the entire sex feminine is
confined to two genera, simply represented by Becky,
Blanche, and Beatrix on one side, and by Amelia, Mrs.
Pendennis, and Lady Esmond on the other. We remember that an honored contributor to our own Magazine, herself distinguished by a combination of the gen-
tlest virtues of the woman with the noblest of the man,
earnestly repelled this narrow view of one half the race.
She complained, that while there were women who had
all the weakness, without a particle of the affection of
their sex, unrelenting in selfishness and unscrupulous as
fiends—that while there were women insipid, diluted,
and colorless, mere waxen dolls, simpering prettily, and
dressing prettily, but inwardly all bran—that there were
also a vast variety of other women of a nobler and higher
make—the Queen Catharines, and Rosalinds, and Por-
tias of actual life, who could be wise as well as good,
strong as well as gentle, generous but discerning, self-
sacrificing but not through weakness, brilliant but amiable and loveable, or, like the delicious Madonnas of
Raphael, at once heavenly and full of the sweetest human love. But this latter sort, she said, Mr. Thackeray
had never described.

It was in vain to urge, in defence of the novelist,
that his function in literature was not to invent ideal
worlds, or imagine new,—that he was not a Shakspeare,
a Goldsmith, or a Scott, but simply Mr. Thackeray,
whose peculiar intellectual constitution forced him to
grasp the facts of things as they were, not to paint them

as they ought to be ; and that, consequently, if his canvas abounded in disagreeable forms, it was because
society had previously much more abounded.   It was
vain to urge that he dealt with English social life, as a
false system had rendered it, ridden by nightmares of
flunkeyism, re-enacting, under fashionable sanctions,
the infamous practices of the suttee or the slave-planta-
tion, and consecrating, by the sacredest rituals, an inordinate consumption of toads and spittle.   It was in vain
to urge these things, because the dissentients immediately replied, with an air of triumphant pity, "Heaven
save the man who sees nothing in our human life but
selfishness, cowardice, intrigue, sycophancy, pretension,
bluster, vulgarism, and the intensest mammon-wor-
ship !"   Or, "Heaven save the society which produces
a luxuriant crop of these as its perennial staples !   It is
not such a man we want to know, such a society that
we care to contemplate.   It is not in such circles, or
under such a guide, that we desire to make the tour of
England.   No doubt mean and vile creatures are there
in abundance—no doubt Thackeray exposes them in
the truest light ; but we believe much better than these
exist, who would be more delectable companions for
us and our children.   We will leave a P. P. C. for Mr.
Thackeray, then, and seek a purer and more genial
atmosphere."

As for ourselves, we cannot but think that there were
some grounds for these complaints, especially in the
earlier books of our author, while the justifications of
them were not in every respect adequate,—not even his
own, as given in that noble closing lecture on Charity
and Humor.   We have certainly felt, in perusing the
"Shabby-Genteel Story," the "Luck of Barry Lyndon,"
"Men's Wives," and even "Vanity Fair" and "Pendennis," that the weak and wicked phases of human

development were brought too much into the light, while the better phases were kept in shadow; as if a man should take the bar-room and the cock-pit for his school, and not the home and the church. But, feeling this, we have none the less trusted the genius of the master. We saw that he took no satyr's delight in offensive scenes and graceless characters; that he was even sadder than the reader could be at the horrible prospects before him ;—that his task was one conscientiously undertaken, with some deep, great, generous purpose; and that, beneath his seeming scoffs and mockeries, was to be discerned a more searching wisdom and a sweeter, tenderer pathos than we found in any other living writer. We saw that he chastised in no ill-natured or malicious vein, but in love; that he cauterized only to cure; and that, if he wandered through the dreary circles of Inferno, it was because the spirit of Beatrice, the spirit of immortal Beauty, beckoned him to the more glorious Paradiso. Even his deficiencies in the portraiture of women did not disturb our faith, because we knew of no artist who evinced, though tacitly rather than by words, so thorough a sympathy in the position of woman, and who cherished a more pure, ardent, and holy reverence for her true nature. Many a time did he make our heart ache, by a passing glance, it might have been, at the wrongs of some poor wife, teaching the little ones, as she put them to bed, to pray "God bless papa," while the dissolute husband was squandering his all, and their happiness, at the club ; and we had yet to recall a single word of his calculated to bring a really womanly woman into contempt. Traces of a latent enthusiasm for excellence, of a fervent admiration of worth, too, broke through the crust of his cynicism and satire on almost every page, as the golden veins of California crop out of the rough masses of quartz and sand. Besides, however much we might have failed in discovering the extent of Thackeray's genius ourselves, we remembered that the authoress of "Jane Eyre," than whom there was none more capable of appreciating originality and power, had, in dedicating her second edition to him, spoken of him as "an intellect profounder and more unique than his contemporaries yet recognized" (for he was then comparatively unknown), as "the first social regenerator of the day," and as the "very master of that working corps who would restore to rectitude the warped system of things." We had too much confidence in the sympathy of genius for genius to allow any more superficial judgments to balk our hope.

When we saw Thackeray in person, all doubts of him were dissipated. When we saw that round, good-natured, yet earnest face, when we heard the manly, yet soft and loving tones of his voice, when we marked in his estimate of illustrious predecessors his intense impatience of the morbid, the hollow, and the malignant, and his kindly affection for the simple, the true, and the good, even though erring,—when we found how Swift, and Sterne, and Congreve were not favorites, and how Dick Steele, Hood, and Goldy were—and how his magnanimous spirit overflowed into delightful recognition of the merits of his compeer and rival, Dickens ; and, above all, when we were told, in private life, not only of an honest freedom from conventionalism, which might have been expected, but of a hearty, genial, and exuberant candor and generosity—we were glad that we had never yielded to the theory of his morbidness and misanthropy.

Well, "The Newcomes" is here at last to justify our fondest criticisms. It is Thackeray over again ;. but the old, current conception of Thackeray, sublimated into

what his particular friends had always believed him to
be. There is the same keen sarcasm, the same savage
satire, the same unrelenting persecution of pretension,
frippery, cant, and falsehood—the same calm, cold
scrutiny of human weakness and vice, and the same
stern view of life; but mingled with these, in fuller
measure than ever before, are gushes of tenderer feeling, gleams of heavenlier light, a deeper pity, and a
more tearful love. Not that the work has any sentimentalism in it, for of that the author is incapable : it is
still a walk in the immense realm of Vanity Fair, which
this world happens to be ; but the characters you meet
are more elevated, and the scenes more touching. It
seems as if the air of that region had grown less harsh ;
as if the colors, not less brilliant, had been mellowed
into softer tints ; and as if the tones, which begin in
laughter or scorn, die away into the thick, earnest
utterances of the heart. All the old inhabitants are
there, with many others, with the indefatigable sleuth-
hound, the aristocratic manager—never before so well
depicted as in the Countess of Kew—with the cold,
self-seeking, mean-spirited, prosperous merchant, as
Sir Barnes Newcome—with the vulgar good woman,
Mrs. Hobson, who thanks God that she and hers are
not like yonder publicans—with the brainless, pampered
fop, like Lord Farintosh, and his tail of toadies—with
the smiling, gracious, genteel, artful, thoroughly selfish
and detestable mother, as Mrs. Mackenzie, the Cam-
paigner—with the poor little, harmless, simpering lady,
Mrs. Clive, that bloomed for a day under the hothouse
nurture of her bad parent, and then withered, and
pined, and perished under it ; all the old passions, and
hypocrisies, and lies, turning the fair earth into a fore-
court of Pandemonium, are there : but, contrasted
with these, and giving a deeper hue to their dread

folly by the contrast, are noble creatures, like the good old Colonel and his son, and Laura, and the lovely Ethel ; and noble lives like those of J. J., the artist, and of the author himself, the sincere, hard-working, sympathizing Arthur Pendennis. As you follow your guide, huge cynic as you may deem him, through the intricacies of his Fable-land, you everywhere feel the warm pressure of his hand, and not unfrequently catch him brushing away the big drops from his eyes. Sad he is, as ever, in the midst of his raillery ; but it is a sadness of the kind by which the heart is made better. If it cannot be said, therefore, that Thackeray displays, in this work, either a deeper tragic or a broader comic power than his previous works have indicated, it is yet very clear that he has used his power, in both respects, with a more uniform gentleness, and under the inspiration of a more open humanity. He is not so anxious to conceal his own tenderness as if he were ashamed of it, nor does he so frequently "dash his brightest pictures with needless dark." In the characters of the old Colonel, and of Ethel, he has drawn us better specimens of our kind than any he has yet given ; not because they are more *ideal*, but because, with all their beauty and nobleness, they are rigidly true to our everyday life. Even his female readers, we think, will forgive his past offences, for the sake of Ethel.

But we have not yet told our readers the story. Thousands of them have already, no doubt, read it as it has appeared, from month to month. [Here followed an outline of the plot, which we omit.] As a story, it is not superior to the previous inventions of the author, serving rather as the *mise en scène* for his characters than as the means of a deep-wrought and consistent development of dramatic incident. There is little that is "thrilling" in it—nothing that makes you hold your breath in suspense—no regular unfolding of event after event, all subtly linked together till the end brings in some heart-rending catastrophe. There are no passages which make you afraid to sit alone in your study—lest some mysterious door in the wainscot should suddenly open, or the lights begin to burn blue—or to go to bed without a candle. It is simply a plain, straightforward history of a respectable family, some rich and some poor, some good and some bad, now in England, and now on the continent, but who all conduct themselves very much like certain friends of our acquaintance.

A hundred characters are introduced into the story, and a thousand incidents, at which we have not glanced in this hasty abstract,—characters and incidents such as only Thackeray can describe. It is a bald outline we have given without them, but enough to enable our readers to see, as we have before said, that it is not much of a story in itself ; some parts are inartistically managed, and the whole is greatly protracted ; a few expedients, indeed, such as the killing off of the old Countess, to prevent the marriage of Ethel, and the demise of Mrs. Clive, to set Clive free again, are commonplace ; but, in general, the interest is well maintained, and the plot sufficiently so to pique curiosity. All the young ladies will be very sorry that there was a first Mrs. Clive, and everybody lament the senility and untimely end of the Colonel, worthy to live in hale and happy vigor a thousand years. We do not ourselves, however, find fault with this "taking off" of the dear old fellow. It has gathered about his memory something of the tragic pathos which clings to the white-haired, tempest-beaten Lear.

The most delightful features of the book, besides those already mentioned, are the glimpses it gives us of

the serene artist-life, the exquisite fineness of its drollery
and banter, its exhibitions of the nobler aspects of French
character, the many really lovable personages, though
quite imperfect ones, it makes us acquainted with, its
masterly fidelity to nature throughout, and its lofty,
uncompromising adherence to truth. No one can read
it without deriving from it a great benefit, not to his
mind alone, but to his sympathies and conscience.

Mr. Thackeray has somewhere called the humorous
writers, the week-day preachers of the world, and ought
himself to be put among the archbishops of the class.
No one of them has preached more excellent sermons
in a lively way, or to a larger and more attentive diocese,
than he. Nor is it a commonplace morality that he has
preached. Was it not he that "aroused the national
mind," as Punch says, "on the subject of snobs?"
Has he not tried to render his fellows, as he was himself, sick of court circulars; to make them loathe *haut-
ton* intelligence; to believe such words as exclusive,
fashionable, aristocratic, wicked, unchristian words; to
hold a court-system which sends men of genius to the
second table, a snobbish court-system; and to stigmatize a polite society which ignores arts and letters, as a
snobbish society? "You, who despise your neighbor,"
he reads us the lesson of the day, "are a snob; you,
who forget your own friends, meanly to follow after
those of a higher degree, are a snob; you, who are
ashamed of your poverty, and blush for your honest
calling, are a snob, as are you who boast of your pedigree and are proud of your wealth." And this salutary
lesson has been followed up by how many startling and
terrible epistles on the awful, foolish superstition which
has translated the suttee from India to Europe—which
sacrificed wives on the graves of their husbands, and
broke the hearts of tender maidens, who might have

made good men good wives—in an insane worship of
rank and fortune !

But the gospel of this preacher has gone deeper yet
than the rebuke of social vices—for it has embraced
the profoundest philosophy of life, the noblest principles of conduct.   The greatest good he asks, is it to
be a lord, *is it even to be happy?* May not poverty,
illness, a hump back, be the reward and conditions of
good, as well as that prosperity—the riches, the fame,
the honors—we all unconsciously run after?   In other
words, is not the great lesson of our human existence,
the very end and aim of it,—of all our sufferings and
disappointments, of that happiness which is so transitory, of that glory which is so unsatisfying—that we
may be taught to love truth and goodness for their own
sakes, as their own best reward, as sufficient unto themselves, as the only completeness and harmony of our
being?   We confess that such seem to us to be the
principles which Thackeray's books illustrate, and that
we esteem them as infinitely loftier and truer than those
other moralities, so common with the novelists, which
fill the mouth of the virtuous hero with luscious plum-
pudding, and enable him to ride in a gilded coach,
and to sniff homages from his admirers at every turn.
What though the brave and good are so often wretched,
and the selfish so often prosper?   Is there not a glory
and a solace in goodness which the selfish never know,
and which can never be brought into comparison
with any outward splendor?   Wealth, distinction,
luxury, power, are not the true successes of life, but the
simple and contented manhood and womanhood which
God honors.

GOETHE.*

E may apply to Goethe the sentiment of his own *Shakspeare und Kein Ende,* and say, he is perennial. The interest he continues to excite among the critics seems to have no limit in variety or duration. What has been written about him constitutes of itself no small body of literature. Not to mention the anecdotes, conversations, sketches, lampoons, and eulogies of which he has been the occasion, we might reckon the critical essays upon his works by the thousand. All that he ever said and did has been put in print ; his physiology, even, has furnished a theme to Carus and Hufeland : while his smaller poems have originated bushels of controversial pamphlets, and his larger ones become the texts of elaborate courses of lectures at the universities. Only Dante has caused more dispute, and only Shakspeare been so voluminously bewritten.

The questions which exercise the critics are, whether Goethe was a poet at all, and of what rank ; whether his conceptions of art were the lowest or the loftiest ; and whether, personally, he was a god or a demigod,

---

* *The Life and Works of Goethe :* with Sketches of his Age and Contemporaries, from published and unpublished Sources. By G. H. Lewes. 2 vols. Boston : Ticknor & Fields.

From *Putnam's Monthly,* Feb., 1856.

or merely a well-dressed and specious-looking devil? Between Menzel and Riemer, between Heine and Carlyle, we may find all sides argued with infinite talent and an inexhaustible enthusiasm. It seems to be as necessary, in the critical world, to have a theory of his existence and character, as it is to have a theory of Hamlet, or of the authorship of Junius. Mr. Lewes's book, therefore, is only one more contribution cast upon the heap which, for the last thirty years, has been rising like a pyramid around the bones of the great king of German literature.

We have already expressed our opinion of the work, in a way which, on a closer perusal, we find but little occasion to qualify. As a narrative, it abounds in interest : much of it, indeed, is an acquisition to literature ; but the critical parts of it we cannot estimate very highly. Mr. Lewes's principles of art are so superficial, being founded on the shallowest of all philosophies, when applied to the deeper problems of art, that his judgments of Goethe's works are little worth. The more obvious rhetorical qualities of them he feels and appreciates ; but their interior significance, their real artistic value, he often misses. Cherishing a kind of phobia, as every Positivist must, against everything that does not lie on the surface as plain as the nose on your face ; and having adopted, at the outset, that stupid commonplace of some of the Germans, that Goethe was a Realist, while Schiller was an Idealist, he flurries and flounders, before the Wilhelm Meister and the Faust, like a frail coasting shallop suddenly driven out to sea. He persists, too, in trying to measure the vast billowy waters with the line and lead that may have served him so well among his native creeks and inlets.

As the result of all that has been said of Goethe, the phrase which best describes him is this : the Artist of

his Age.   Mr. Carlyle calls him the Spokesman of his
age, and Emerson, varying the term, the Writer ; but
it is clear in the case of both, that they use the words
as in some sort synonymous with the words poet or
artist.   He was more than the mere secretary or recorder
of the *visa et cogitata* of his time.   He was the man who
best expressed its results—the utterer of its aspirations—
the lens which brought its varied tendencies to a focus.
He was an artist in that his endowments were peculiarly
those of the artist ; because his whole life and training
were artistic ; because he produced some of the best
specimens of art, in its worthiest department—that of
poetry ; and because he was so thoroughly possessed by
the idea of art, and devoted to it with such a consistent
and absorbing devotion.   His entire outward and inward
life was one great picture ; the soft atmosphere of beauty
was the element he breathed : while he saw, in the
issues of art, results as grand, universal, and beneficent
as those which the philosopher ascribes to his science
or the enthusiast discovers in his religion.   He was not,
however, like our Shakspeare, the artist of humanity
and all time, but only of his age.   His mission was to
interpret to the first half of the nineteenth century the
riddle of its being ; to gather up its weltering facts,
sciences, and philosophies, and to hang them on its
front as a garland of flowers ; to exhibit the poetry of
its vast prosaic explorations ; to detect the unitary and
the universal amid its infinite details ; and to mould its
distracted activities into some sort of organic vitality.
Whatever his deficiencies, then, they were the deficiencies of his era ; and whatever his greatness, it was the
greatness of that era consummated in a single head, or,
rather, precipitated from its solutions by the wonderful
electricity of genius into a few single and brilliant
results.

We shall the better perceive the force of these truths if, following Mr. Lewes, we first run over briefly the leading incidents of his career, and the more prominent traits of his writings.

All the earlier circumstances of Goethe's life seem to have been peculiarly adapted to the development of his fine natural parts. Frankfort, his birth-place, so cosily lying among the gardens and green fields of the silver-flowing Maine, though a provincial town, was hoary with ancient associations, and yet beginning to . bustle with modern activity. Its fairs and coronations, its quaint old customs and fantastic parades, its cloisters and trenches and queer gabled buildings, contrasting with the stir of commerce and free-citizenship, were things likely to excite a youthful imagination. The little Wolfgang, with an organization so sensitive that already, in his ninth week, as Bettina amusingly tells us, he had troubled dreams ; who could be convulsed by a look at the moon, and was savagely intolerant of any kind of deformity or discord, and withal insatiable in his thirst for nursery tales (of which the good mother fortunately had a store), was early and richly nourished by the gloom and the glitter of his native city. A genial, brown-eyed, handsome child, he appears to have absorbed all influences with a keen relish, and yet with calm thoughtfulness. For the most part he saw existence on the sunnier side, in country rambles, amid cheerful friends, rural occupations, home sports, studies of art, and coronation magnificences. But the darker aspects were not wanting to him, as we see in what he has told us of his trembling visits to the Jews' quarter, of the skulls of state criminals grinning from the highways, of the judicial burnings of books, of the seven years' war, with its excitements and family feuds, and of the great earthquake at Lisbon, which spread consternation over the world. Mr. Lewes, in his account, has doubtless omitted many of these details, because they were already so charmingly narrated in the autobiography.

It was a good thing for the young Goethe, with his sensibilities and impulses, that his father was of a rigid didactic turn, with a hand and eye for art, and an unyielding zeal for discipline. For he was thereby indoctrinated into science and history, into half a dozen languages, into riding, and drawing, and dancing, and other graceful accomplishments. The warm affection and active fancy of one parent fed his heart and imagination, while the stern teachings of the other trained him into character and self-command. On the one side was the dear and noble literature of the nursery, with its ballads and snatches of old song, and puppet-shows, opening the child's paradise; and on the other was classic lore, severe tutorships, and innumerable accuracies and drillings, with now and then an appeal to ambition. At the same time, the social position of the family drew about it decided men—men of strong natures and cultivation, whose houses were furnished with books and pictures, and whose talk was full of character and thought. All this aroused the intellect of the boy; who, in executing little errands among artists and tradesmen, was also often brought in contact with the humbler classes, where he saw life in its narrowness and debasement. It was in one of these excursions from his own charmed circle into the nether regions of want and despair, that he was led into that first serious experience, which imparts so singular a pathos to his boyish life—the passion for Gretchen, at once full of simplicity, fervor, distress—a passion which rose upon him like a fair young dream, and then, after a few months of delicious dalliance, withdrew into the night, leaving him dark and lonely and inconsolable. That experience never entirely passed away ; for when the impetuous boy had grown into the world-famous man, the vanished Gretchen reappears as the sad, sweet, imperishable Margaret of the Faust.

Goethe's youth was a continuation of the same favorable influences, · controlled by a strong inward force, which had surrounded his childhood. His student years at Leipsic, Strasbourg, etc. (of which Mr. Lewes gives the best account that we have seen, vastly better than Goethe's own, where the most interesting parts are strangely disguised), cover a period in which opinion on all subjects was undergoing a singular ferment. Full of buoyancy, of hope, of uncouth provincial life, yet glowing with the consciousness of uncommon strength, "he had," as Wieland said afterward, "the devil in him at times, and could fling out before and behind like a young colt." He seemed fitted for all fortunes—for fun, frolic, adventure, study, logic, and eke love and religion. Among the musty professors, and the wild, break-neck, but withal intellectual students, he was at home with all—a young unacknowledged giant, secretly glorying in his prowess, now and then using it in very grotesque fashions—yet docile, pretensionless, avid of all sorts of knowledge, and possessed of a great, free, and laughing heart.

German literature was very much in the same inchoate condition as himself:—in the flush of a mighty youth—striving to emancipate itself from the swaddling bands of timidity, imitation, and awkwardness,—and dashing forward to a career of original and self-sustained power. A watery deluge, says Goethe, swelled up to the very top of the Teutonic Parnassus. Yet a rainbow of promise began to form itself upon the clouds. One by one, minds of considerable magnitude managed to

emerge from the prevailing obscurity. Gunther, Gotts-
ched, Gellert, Gessner, each in his line, did something
to bring back the national writing from the stateliness of
Roman decorum, and the tinsel of French glitter, to
German nature and truth. But the most complete revolution was effected by three men, very different from
each other, Klopstock, Lessing, and Wieland, of whose
efforts Mr. Lewes gives a just critical view. The struggle was long and difficult, giving rise to some of the
fiercest battles of words that were ever fought.

Goethe, with constitutional ardor, threw himself into
the thickest of the fight. He pierced at once the very
heart of the mystery which had baffled inferior intellects. His good sense, his prodigious attainments in
both ancient and modern learning, but more than all,
the unerring instincts of the born poet, enabled him to
unravel the twists of the critics, and expose the inner
and deeper principles of art. Early taught in the
school of the noble old Hebrew prophets and singers,
and more recently initiated into the wizard ring of
Shakspeare's genius, he contemptuously broke through
the entanglements of a formal and shallow pedantry,
and soared away into the clearer regions of poetic truth.
He saw the barrenness, the constraint, the utter futility
of the prescriptive principles which then prevailed ; he
saw that artists were laboring over the stiff and hard
shell of the matter, not even suspecting the existence of
a kernel ; and then—with doubt at first, with manifold trial and sorrow, and perplexities afterward—he
labored painfully but surely into a conception of what
the modern spirit demanded of art.

His attention, however, was not exclusively confined
to the literary and artistic strivings of his contemporaries. All the sciences, and nearly all learning, along
with civil society itself, partook of the general confusion,

while his nature was such that it could not rest till it was all set right in his head. Medicine, philosophy, jurisprudence, religion, he pursued with almost as much fidelity as art; and he endeavored, with the same native and decided force, to master and mould their elements into unity. And the singular triumph of his activity, the great beauty of his power, was, that these tormenting and momentous inquiries were carried on in the midst of a most exuberant and joyous outward life—curious adventures, such as are known only to the roistering student-life of Germany ; frequent and frolicsome rambles by flood and field ; tavern-scenes ; visits to distant famous structures, even to manufactures and mines; and love-commitments that stirred the profoundest depths of emotion. A constant interest in all the doings of courts and cottages, alternated with protracted studies, with deep, almost agonizing questionings of the riddles of the world. Thus, whatever the matter in hand, his broad, mercurial, rich nature was found to get at the bottom of it, to comprehend it, to make it entirely his own. No half-way tasting of existence, in any of its forms, was satisfactory to him ; no manifestation of the great soul of humanity, be it a rural pastime or a great world-venerated intellectual system, was uninteresting to him ; he looked at mankind, in all their likings and leavings, with open eye, and with sunny, open heart. In Carlyle's paraphrase of his own distich—

"Life, his inheritance, broad and fair ;
Earth was his seed-field, to time he was heir."

With such a nature, and such a development of it, having met and overcome most of the trials of the more impulsive periods of life—a naturally strong, noble fig-

ure of a man, richly adorned and embroidered with all
the graces that fortune, family education, and society
can superadd—Goethe found a sphere for which he was
peculiarly prepared, in the brilliant court of Karl August. The young Prince of Weimar, attaining his majority and his power just about the same time, was
fortunately one who had a heart capable of love, as well
as a head fit to rule. The sudden but lasting attachment which sprang up between himself and Goethe,
was as honorable to both as it appears to have been cordial and dignified. A thoughtless radicalism has im-
puted it to Goethe, that this, on his part, was a devotion
to the ruler, rather than to the man ; but the fact was,
that this friendship was one of reciprocal respect and
equal favor, where any social advantages conferred by
the archduke were more than compensated by the celebrity conferred by the poet. The life of neither of
these illustrious personages was made up of court-
parades or court-intrigue, but of useful labors in their
several spheres. Karl governed his little province with
a manly sense of his duty: Goethe immortalized it by
the best works of the best modern literature. Indeed,
it was a rare and beautiful sight, this intimacy and good-
will—cemented in earliest youth, and carried on to late
old age—between one worthily born of a race of kings,
and another destined to become greater than any king.
There was nothing in it to carp at—there was much in
it to admire. Goethe it placed at once in a position
where his majestic and graceful intellect could freely
unfold—in a circle of cultivated friends, possessed of
leisure and means for the pursuit of art, and capable of
the most delicate appreciation of his own lofty endowments. An organization so fine, and yet so magnificent, found its genial atmosphere in the almost ideal
refinement of a court. The simplicity of his manners

could not be corrupted by it, while it nourished and enriched his imagination. True, Jean Paul has said that "under golden mountains many a spiritual giant lies buried;" but had they been greater giants, they might, as Goethe did, have melted these mountains into images of beauty.

His court-life was valuable to him, however, not because of its glitter and show, but because it simply gave him freedom. 'Tis a mistake to suppose that genius always thrives best in loneliness and poverty. Life of every sort finds its most sure and healthful growth in a fitting and congenial medium. Burns as a peasant was no greater than he would have been as a prince: on the other hand, a larger nurture would have aided in a larger development. Men of strong native force will, no doubt, overcome obstacles of formidable compass; but the same force exerts itself all the more effectively, where such obstacles are wanting, or of less oppressive magnitude. In the one case, we may get a rugged, monstrous upshoot—a very Polyphemus of savage energy; in the other, we are likely to have a mightier, self-poised, majestic Jupiter. "Gold mountains have buried many a spiritual giant;" yes, but there have been many more in this world, buried in mud-holes and ditches.

Goethe, we have said, valued his prosperous condition for its freedom: it gave him opportunities for a rare and expansive culture; it gave him books; it gave him the instruments of art; it gave him access to all modes of life, to all classes of society; and what was better than all, and so essential to his being, the means of a free communion with nature by observation and travel. That impartial judgment of men and things, which was one of the kindly traits of his character; that many-sided interest in all that relates to the intellectual destinies of humanity; his unceasing researches into the realms of science, and his miraculous activity in those of literature, are all to be more or less ascribed to the graceful comfort of his external circumstances. Had he been cramped and tortured by the pressures of indigence—as poor dear Richter was—this impassive Goethe, the delight of women and the admiration of men, might have become a rude, double-fisted iconoclast, battering away at all established things, with the fierce rage and revenge of a demon. It would have been a sight, truly that, for men to look at and tremble ! such sights being necessary, too, at times ; but we are persuaded that Goethe has served us better in another way.

Goethe's life at court was not in any hurtful degree the life of a courtier. It was a life of universal activity, and of broad intercourse with men. With a princely family at its head, whose taste diffused a love of art and letters, while its active beneficence cherished the best affections of the people ; with the two most illustrious of poets to give tone to its opinions and provide its amusements ; with the excellent Herder and kindred spirits for its preachers and models of virtue ; visited all the year by Richters, and Humboldts, and De Staëls, by the most eminent in rank, and science, and letters, of all lands ; the centre of thought and literary productiveness to cultivated Germany—it was just the sphere for his peculiar taste. Yet he was not confined to it. He often sought the refreshment of more rural scenes—now wandering away into the sublimities of Switzerland, and then again losing himself amid the beauties of Italy. Who, indeed, can estimate the influences upon his growth of these journeyings? The record of them is in his works—in those conceptions of the All-Fair, which, filling his soul, overflowed into speech. What must Italy, always so enrapturing to the northern imagination, have been to the fancy of Goethe? A land of wonder, of magic, of glory. Its monuments of the highest that man has achieved in art—its statues, its pictures, its architecture, and its music—its theatres of the grandest that man has achieved in history—its hills and vales, its waters and its skies—so early longed after, so passionately enjoyed, as the lover longs for his mistress, and dissolves in the soft ecstasy of her embrace—these translate him into another and heavenly world. "This day," said he, referring to his first sight of the paradise of art, "this day I was born anew."

Thus, in endless studies, in the freest interchanges of friendship, in the creation of immortal forms, in delicious visits to the most delicious climes, the years of Goethe's manhood passed away. For eighty years he "knew no rest and no haste," like a star, keeping on its "God-appointed way;" when death came it met him busy with the pen—the implement at once of his pleasure and his power; and he sank, as a child sinks to sleep, with the glow of the day's activity still on his cheek, and looking forward to a morrow of hope and joy. "Let the light enter," were his last words— answered, we trust, from a region where all is light.

Having seen the life of the man, let us next consider some of the fruits of it; and what strikes us first, is their variety, in itself a proof of power, if not of merit. He wrote elegies, epigrams, ballads, songs, odes, satires, novels, biographies, translations, essays, trage- dies, and books of science, and most of them with a peculiar and exquisite skill. His poems modulate through all the keys. His prose is the most graceful and transparent in German. His works of science, though partly superseded by more recent labors, are yet authorities in the closet. We read them all with de-

light, and, while reading them, think the one immediately before us the best. It is only on mature critical
reflection that we learn to discriminate their comparative
values. A few are then seen to be inferior, like Stella
and his comedies generally; others, again, like Clavigo,
not superior to average productions in that kind; but
the greater part fix themselves in the memory as permanent and indestructible forms.

Assuming the Iliad as a standard, the walk of art in
which he was least eminent was the epic. His Achil-
leis, it is true, seems like a fragment of the old Grecian
song, but only a fragment; it has none of the breadth
of outline, and intensity, and weight of interest, which
give so much grandeur to the pages of Homer. Could
we call the Hermann and Dorothea an epic, instead of
an idyl, we should still have the same qualifications to
make; for while it is perfect in its way, full of sweet
pastoral simplicity and artless grace, breathing the odor
of new-mown hay, and cheerful with the song of birds,
its interest is scarcely more than individual or private.
A dark burden of war gathers its gloomy folds tran-
siently over the lovely scene; but it soon rolls away into
the distance, leaving the landscape as gentle as ever,
and the men and children and cattle come forth to resume their labors in the fields. Nor can we estimate
the dramatic power of Goethe as highly as some have
done; in which respect we agree with Mr. Lewes. His
dramas are wonderful poems; but are rather dramatic
in their external form than in inward principle. Considering them as poems, and not as dramas, they mostly
impress us by their richness and variety. Their very
names recall to the reader familiar with them a series of
beautiful images. There is old Goetz of Berlichingen
—the burly robber-hero—"the iron-fisted self-helper"
—with his robust earnestness, his heroic, tender af-

fection, his violent, deep-rooted feudal hatreds—perishing at last, like the era of which he was a type—in a calm, almost voiceless, despair. There is Egmont, encircled by a mild splendor, like the glory which wreathed the head of his own Clärchen in the vision, walking through the distractions of a tumultuous, corrupt time, as the moon wades among the gathering night-clouds. Noble, famous, rich, glowing with purpose and hope, yet too wise or too weak for his age, he cannot yield and cannot conquer, and so exhales, from a troubled, weary environment, amid sweet dreams of love and glory, and the sound of muffled drums. There is Tasso, in all his strength and weakness, surrounded by the splendors of a court and the applause of the world, yet pining in hopeless love, in morbid self-communings, lofty ideals alternating with miserable jealousies, and the tenderest, noblest of minds going out in darkness, till he seems like some grand ruin of his own Italy, lifting its masses of foliage into the crystal air and deep blue skies, when the sun retires behind the purple mountains and leaves it alone with the shadows and the stars. And, then, there is the Iphigenia—that stately Grecian maiden translated to a Christian clime—as severe in her beauty as the creator of Antigone would have chiselled her, and yet as lovely, and tender, and sweet as our modern religion renders the soul of woman. All these are inimitable pictures; but our space warns us not to dwell upon them in detail.

The most original, and altogether wonderful of Goethe's dramas, is the Faust, which stands alone in its kind, as the Iliad and King Lear do in their kinds. We know of no poem in any language to the writing of which there was requisite a more various and exalted combination of faculties. Other poems may be more organically perfect, and evince in the authors of them a larger possession of certain high faculties, but none show a possession of so many of the highest faculties. It is epic, tragic, and lyric, all at once—a complete story, and a development of character, mingled with gushes of song. Almost every feeling of the human breast is expressed in it ; the grand, the pathetic, the thoughtful, the capricious, and the supernatural alternate, as in a dream ; grotesque and scornful faces peer on us from its mystic pages ; visions of baffled efforts, and wasted hopes, and broken hearts break in among choirs of angelic voices ; men, and monsters, and seraphs, and the Supreme God even, take part in the ever-shifting play.

Wild as the drama is, however, tumultuous and many-voiced as are its sounds, from the harsh discords of devils' laughs, to the sweetest, tenderest human utterances, it is singularly true in its delineations of character. The personages, of the first part more especially, are real living beings, as much so as Macbéth or the Moor. Faust himself, with his far-reaching thoughts and insatiate but baffled thirst for knowledge, is as near to the mind of every thinking man as ever was the reflective, unhappy Hamlet. His early yearnings for truth, his weariness at the stale, flat, and unprofitable commonplaces of the world, his fond eagerness to love, his great wrestlings with evil, and his subsequent self-abandonment and woe, reach the depths of our hearts, and seem experiences that have been, or may yet be, our own. We feel that we, too, have been borne along by the same tempestuous waves of life. Has not his companion, Mephisto, been our companion also? Do we not recognize him as a well-known individual, who has whispered many a temptation into our ears, or, what is worse, has whispered many a consolation? Ever true to the laws of his being, he is a hideous disguised consistency throughout; and, as some one has said, the identical devil of modern times. In equal clearness, but strongly contrasted from him by her innocence, and from Faust by her contented simplicity, stands the gentle Gretchen, whose story unseals the deepest fountains of love and pity. We take to the artless maiden, as a true product of nature, from the first; we grow happy with her in the brief spring of affection that opens upon her young hopes; our heart breaks with hers, in her cruel betrayal; and, when she departs, during that horrid night in the dungeon, her poor distressed brain, like Ophelia's, quite shattered, we listen to her expiring words as to a voice from the spirit-land, summoning us all to judgment on her account. It seems as if the whole world of man were condemned by the sad issue of such a fate.

The prose writings of Goethe manifest the same original and masterly genius as his poems. We might give in evidence of this his Werther, which set all Europe agog, and his Elective Affinities, which extorted from all Christendom a howl (while all Europe and all Christendom devoured both); but we shall confine our remarks to Wilhelm Meister, which is, doubtless, his masterpiece. As a narrative, it is generally pronounced destitute of interest; for, like the needy knife-grinder, "Story, God bless you, it has none to tell, sir;" and there is only the slightest development of plot in it—no highly-wrought or intense scenes, no grandiloquent or morbid personages, who stamp and tear about for nothing, and only events, for the most part commonplace and unimportant, following each other in a languid way that quite persuades the admiring reader to a gentle sleep. Compared with the mobs of incident that dash and thunder through more modern tales, it is tame even to an extreme of dulness.

Yet, by observing a little while, we find in it a clear self-subsistent world, filled with actual men and women, whose actions, though not great or extraordinary, are very much the actions of humans. They are characters of real life ; their foibles and virtues alike drawn with an unsparing hand, and presented as samples of this very various world for our study, and not as heroes for our worship. The author writes as though he had no further interest in them than he would have in the same number of indifferent individuals anywhere ; he merely raises a curtain to let us see what they are at, and all their sayings and doings, some of them fantastic enough, he watches with imperturbable gravity. At times, we should be inclined to think that he despises the whole pack of them, if he did not go on parading them with the utmost calmness, betraying not the slightest disapproval or vexation at anything they do, and shrinking from no untoward discovery. He writes their biography with the most scrupulous fidelity—a fidelity which has this advantage for us, that we get gradually a deeper interest in their proceedings. We come to watch their movements, to listen to their long talks, and even to suspect that, after all, they may possess some significance. The suspicion is helped out by certain general remarks we happen upon—quite too simple and obvious as they seem at first—but which cling to the memory, and transform themselves, in some way or other, to profound suggestions, as if the observation and insight of a long, busy life were suddenly deposited there. Then we are aroused at intervals by single passages of a splendid and majestic eloquence ; criticisms of art, brief but rare ; penetrating, comprehensive, far-.reaching glances into practical life and the philosophy of trade, business, and human nature, accompanied by a most provoking tolerance of all seeming human weaknesses, and a most genial sympathy with all human strivings. Sometimes we stumble on chance allusions that open up wondrous depths ; obscure hints growing every moment more palpable, till they stand forth as luminous, world-embracing truths ; light sparkles of wit, which at the outset merely flash upon the senses, but, before the end of it, condense in the mind into gems of wisdom ; manifest traces of an almost universal culture in the author ; little outbreaks of song, that make the whole heart ache, we know not why : to say nothing of entire pages of poetry, in the shape, perhaps, of a critique on Hamlet, or of lofty sentiments, and noble original views of religion—all flowing in a language of liquid sweetness. The upshot of the matter is, that our "dull-seeming, slow-moving Thespis cart" changes itself, as if by enchantment, into an ideal realm ; the theatrical life of the hero, with its trivialities of all sorts, its high aspirings and slender realizings, is seen as an illuminated picture of a much higher life, where every incident has a higher end, and every character embodies higher phases in human development. The vivacious Philena, the clear-minded Jarno, the beneficent Natalia, the manly Lothario, the dignified Abbé, the cultivated Uncle—the mysterious, melancholy Harper, and that singular child of enthusiasm and suffering, the wild boy-girl Mignon—a beam from heaven struggling through the dank vapors of earth—all attach us to them with a feeling of brotherhood, as elements of that manifold rich life of which we, too, are a part—as notes and tones in that universal melody which nature is ever sending up to her God.

If Goethe, who is everywhere great, is anywhere greatest, it is in his songs and ballads. It was his habit through life to turn all his experiences into poetry, that he might thereby work off the burden of his emotions, whether joyful or sad. A writer in the British Review lately, in a generally able article, describes his lyrics as marked by "deliberativeness," comparing him in this respect with Wordsworth. But, to us they seem the op posite of deliberative; the very outpourings of his mind in all its moods; a melodious diary of daily and almost hourly changes of feeling; simple breathings of the inward life; sparkling jets of momentary thought and affection. We find a perpetual freshness and reality about them, like the bloom of new spring-flowers. Speaking of the present, the actual, the world around and in us, they possess a hearty human interest. Even when their meaning is insignificant, they ring through us, to haunt the memory and imagination, like snatches of Mozart's music. The correspondence of the form with the substance is so perfect, yet simple, that the charm defies all analysis. It is felt, but not detected. As Carlyle says of Burns's songs, they sing themselves; they are favorites with composers as they are with the people; and once heard, cling to the brain like spells. Then, again, how diversified these lyrics!—some as simple as the whimperings of a child; others grotesque, . naïve, or full of a devil-may-care animal spirit; others tender, plaintive, thoughtful; others wild and unearthly, and others again, proud, lofty, defiant, like the words of a Titan heaping his scorn upon the gods.

John Dwight, one of our finest critics of art, says of these, that "they are as remarkable for their wild grandeur of thought and language as they are for their irregular, unrhymed, dithyrambic measure. There is something in their Greek, chorus-like, mysterious style and movement, which cannot be lost without losing all their poetry. They breathe the old Greek atmos-

phere of Æschylus. The soul's proud assertion of itself in 'Prometheus;' the child-like, unquestioning awe
and wonder, and even admiration, with which the sublimity of destiny is celebrated in the 'Limits of Man,'
in such lofty unalterable language, as if destiny itself
had fitted each word in its place; the delicious unrest
of the 'Spring' feeling, the yearning to be taken up with
which nature's beauty overcomes the ravished soul, so
sweetly clothed in the fable of 'Ganymede;' the simple
majesty of the 'Godlike;' all have an air of unpre-
meditated inspired beauty and grandeur, which defies
imitation; and they lose much of their reality and
charm in any other language. What ballads, in any
literature, are comparable to the 'Bride of Corinth,' the
'Erl-King,' and the 'God and the Bayadere?'" We are
happy to have our taste confirmed by such an authority.

Without dwelling, however, upon the mere literary
excellence of Goethe's performances, or even attempting a general characterization of his literary genius, let
us proceed to explain why he is called so emphatically
the artist of his age. It is the more important because
his English biographer, true to the behests of an incompetent philosophy, seems to ignore this as part of the
matter altogether, and stands dumbfoundered in the presence of the pervading symbolism of Goethe's writings.
A work of art, like a product of nature, is to him a
simple fact, having relations to other facts, but no inward spiritual meaning. He is, therefore, perpetually
quarrelling with what he terms the mysticism of Goethe
(although he had already pronounced him a great
realist), and is pained at the obvious lapse of his faculties in the latter parts of Meister and Faust. But this
"mysticism" is as much a part of Goethe's being as his
clearness of vision, or his serene wisdom, and demands
as much the nicest study of the critics.

The explanation of it is simply this : that Goethe, as a man of genius and poet, was profoundly penetrated and possessed by all the vague struggling influences and aspirations of his time, and sought to give them melodious expression. The breath of the Divine Providence, which animated his century, only animated him the more interiorly and strongly, and the task of his genius was, to embody its suggestions in permanent forms. He lived from the middle of the eighteenth century (1749) to near the middle of the nineteenth century (1832), through the most remarkable period of crisis and transition that the world ever saw. An old era was coming to an end, amid the decay and destruction of many things, and a new era was endeavoring to get formed. There was agitation, confusion, perplexity, everywhere ; "private life," as Varnhagen von Ense says, in an Essay in which he arrives at the same view of Goethe that we have formed, "full of suffering, and the world at variance with itself; old forms, long diseased and baneful, unable to bind the fresh life to their own death, and new unfolding forms yet without a sanction."

Now, these were the elements with which the poetry of that epoch, or so much of it as was true and not a reminiscence, had to deal. Accordingly, we find, in the series of Goethe's works, a complete bodying forth of the successive steps of progress in the mighty struggle. In the earliest, the Goetz, we take a look back into the feudal time, and see it perish before us, in the person of the tenacious, stalwart hero, with a cry of woe to those that come after ! *Wehe der Nachkommenschaft!* Then follows the Werther, with its vapid sentimentalism, and passionate whinings, and morbid self-love and sorrow, expressive of the chronic discontent of society, full of skepticism and black despair, and which, unable to reconcile itself to its condition, or get extricated therefrom, goes off in explosive violence. In the Elective Affinities, says Varnhagen, whom we merely abridge, is a recurrence to the same theme, but with greater depth of passion and less external vehemence. Restlessness has subsided into impatience or suppressed hope. The soul asserts its natural freedom, but submissively, and with a sad consciousness of its impotence in the presence of inevitable circumstances. Without revolting openly against existing forms, it postpones its fruitions to another world, where hearts long severed may unite again in the bonds of a free, spiritual attraction.

In Wilhelm Meister's Apprenticeship the view of life has reached a higher plane. Doubt and distraction have not wholly ceased, but the prospect of a free and noble natural existence is not shut out from the present earth. Casting aside all petty personal grievances, the hero submits to all modes of living and doing, in the hope of working off every disquietude by a placid and perpetual activity. By the very exertion of his powers, he is made conscious of new and potent charms in life, so that its most commonplace details are set to a music, not wholly divine, and yet more than earthly. The moodiness and madness of the self-torturing spirit, give place to tranquil, serious endeavors ; the clouds fall away ; a mild effulgence reveals vistas of pleasant fields, and, though we reach no great ethical height, no broad Christian views of things, we still catch glimpses of the infinitely rich and varied possibilities of life, under a noble human culture. But it is only in the Wanderings that the inadequacy of the previous view is filled up, and work becomes worship, and the discordant elements of society are reconciled by a scheme of co-operative and constructive freedom. What an anticipation by the poet of St. Simon and Fourier !

"In the *Wanderjahre*," continues Varnhagen, "a comprehensive view of a new order is drawn in firm, not rigid characters, with poetical freedom. The necessities of daily life take their rank by the side of the highest elevation of mind ; Christianity works in the form of mild piety ; education spreads out her establishments, powerful and all-comprehensive ; the taste for art, richly bestowed on individuals, becomes a universal advantage ; the mechanical arts and trades, led by wise arrangements from their destructive rivalry, take their station without fear beside the higher arts, certain of receiving from them due honor and appreciation ; natural disposition and capacity determine and ennoble every occupation. The false and incongruous position of woman disappears before rightly-assorted marriages, which bring together unequal classes. They are exalted into free ministers of a religion of love and beneficence. A new estimate of things and of actions, a new choice and distribution of the lots of life, a new sense of the good and the beautiful, are disclosed, by means of an Association, extending over the whole earth, full of liberal activity, of respect for the highest and for the least ; busied in extinguishing crime and want, and affording the rich prospect of mankind advancing in culture and in industry ; whose maxim may be, in worldly things, a fair share in the possession and enjoyment of the stock of good existing for every member ; in what relates to the attractions of mind, the liberation of the prohibited possible from all fetters that can be broken." It is evident from this, that if Goethe had given us a third part of the Meister (necessary to the completion of the original design), we should have had, in Wilhelm's *Meisterjahre*, a wonderful foreshadowing of the various socialistic experiments of this age. But the time was not then ripe.

For the full and condensed expression of his mystical insight we must turn to the two parts of Faust, which, begun in the author's earliest years, and completed only near his death, runs parallel in its development with that of his own being. It is the grand *resumé* and consummation of his thought and hope. Abysmal, wild, and heterogeneous as it seems, there is yet a unity pervading it which, though not wholly organic, gives to it a certain consistency and life. All the spiritual worlds are gathered to watch its issues ; all humanity is involved in them. As a legend, the fable had its origin in the middle ages, but in its actual working out, the century of Goethe is transfixed on every page. Faust comes before us as one who has exhausted science in the pursuit of individual and selfish ends ; as a representative of the age of "victorious analysis" and natural research. Having worn away the golden days of youth in the service of the intellect, his manhood is weary of the result—is saddened, disappointed, withered, and would fain throw away its barren and empty life. A nameless unrest surges through his soul, and no attainment in knowledge, no conquest of nature, is able to speak the word of peace to the billows. All his selfish-seeking turns to vanity in the fruition. It drives him but further from his fellow-man and from God. A chill isolation and solitude is the recompense of his toil. Musty parchments get heaped about him, and skeletons and grinning skulls, till, in the agony of baffled endeavor, he curses life and all its fancied joys, and even that patience which endures its woes. There is henceforth for him only contempt, and mockery, and denial. And it is out of this mood that Mephistopheles, his evil spirit, his other and lower self, the incarnation of the intellect and the senses, is born—Mephistopheles, who hurries him along, from moral indifference to sensual indulgence, from debauchery to seduction, and from seduction to murder, till his soul, in its hideous riot and self-abandonment, breeds the monstrous crew who celebrate their triumph in the fearful witch-dances of the Brocken. This principle of evil works itself out still further, till the first part of the tragedy closes in a scene of heart-rending dislocation and eternal woe.

In the second part we are shown the social effects of the same evil—an incoherent society, which is but one vast masquerade, where the spokesmen are fools and the only recognized nexus—money—a stupendous paper lie. Faust, as the representative of humanity, plunges into the midst of the mad whirl, strives to penetrate the mystery of its iniquity and errors, but in vain. He summons the antiquated faiths, and finds them the children of chimera: he worships the spirit of ancient · beauty in the person of the rejuvenated Helen, and she disappears as suddenly as she had appeared, leaving him only her vesture : he engages in war and commerce, and everywhere guilt, and care, and distress dog his steps— till at last, old, blinded, hopeless, rich, and miserable, he deliberately abandons his quest, surrenders his purpose of directing his own way, abjures his individual ends, and gives himself up to work. "What ho ! ye myriads of humans," he cries, "relinquish your empty search, and go dig the earth ! Spread yourselves, in free crea- tive activity, over the globe—lay fire to the snug little private dwellings of the fond old couples—fill in the remorseless marshes and pools—rescue the land from the devouring ocean, till nature is brought into obe- dience to man, and ye all shall stand, finally, a free peo- ple upon a soil as free." But no sooner has Faust dis- charged himself of responsibility for himself, no sooner has he resolved upon a life of spontaneous creative

activity, than he finds, to his surprise, that the goal is
won.   He calls upon the beautiful day to linger, because his earth is now transformed into heaven.   The
sin, and suffering, and sorrow of the past are forgotten
in the glories of a better consciousness ; legions of
angels drop roses from the celestial voids ; even the
rocks break forth into song ; and all who had ever
sinned and suffered reappear (among them the sweet,
but no longer heart-broken maiden, *einst Gretchen
genannt*), as leaders of a heavenly throng who welcome
the spirit of Faust to the regions of the redeemed, in a
mystic sevenfold chorus of hallelujahs and praise.

RUSKIN'S WRITINGS.*

R. RUSKIN stands confessedly at the head of all English writers on Art. Despite his idiosyncrasies, which are often glaring enough, his offensive conceit, and a want of philosophic genius, remarkable in a person otherwise so well endowed, he deserves his position. No Englishman, that we know, is comparable to him, either for the extent of his knowledge in this peculiar range, or for the vividness and value of his critique. Lord Lindsay, who made the history of art a specialty, is not more minutely acquainted with it than Ruskin is; nor is Mrs. Jamison, though a woman more susceptible to all its finer poetic feelings; nor is Eastlake, though President of the Royal Academy, a nicer judge of its technical excellence. In fact, we might roll a great many critical "single gentlemen into one," without forming a compound equal to Ruskin.

The appearance of "Modern Painters," by an "Oxford Graduate," protesting so vehemently against the shallow pedantries of the magazine writers, and throwing down the gauntlet of critical combat to the entire circle of onlookers, with such lusty disdain, was an era

*Modern Painters, vol. iii. Of Many Things. By John Ruskin. London : Smith, Elder & Co., 1856.

From Putnam's Monthly, May, 1856.

in the history of British criticism. It will be well-remembered with what goggle-eyes of surprise the accredited authorities watched the advent of this young champion, as he bounced into the ring, and laying his devoirs at the feet of one J. M. W. Turner, prepared for a general joult. First unhorsing, in a most ungallant manner, the visored knight of Blackwood, and then brandishing his lance, pell-mell, along the lists, he seemed to fight wildly enough : but it soon became clear from the numbers that lay dishonored upon the field—some with their casques broken only, but others with head and limb disastrously shattered—that he fought surely as well as wildly ; those sturdy blows brought down a foe at every stroke. Everybody admired the dashing intrepidity and the confident skill of the unknown combatant. What commended him, perhaps, more than anything else to popular regard, more than his acknowledged ability, his brilliant mastery of natural scenery, and his evident erudition, was the honest, unblenching, almost truculent zeal, with which he took up the cudgels for a great and unappreciated modern, in whose behalf he tore away the false glory that had hidden the defects of the most venerated painters of the past, tearing some of their flesh with it, and thrashed about among his own contemporaries, like a soldier of the Commonwealth among the bedizened images of some old Jacobitic chapel. There is scarcely on record another such instance of the fervent espousal and defence of one man by another, on the ground of pure intellectual sympathy, as that of Turner by Ruskin ; and it is amusing to read, now that Turner's fame is assured, the intense vehemence with which it was supposed necessary to assail Claude and Poussin, in order to enthrone the favorite. Nor does it appear, from the preface to this latest volume, that he has yet

forgiven the slowness of his countrymen in recognizing
the great spirit among them ; with ill-concealed bitterness of irony, he speaks of the threefold honor heaped
upon Turner, now that he lies quiet at Chelsea, by
those who "bury his body in St. Paul's, his pictures at
Charing Cross, and his purposes in Chancery !" That
is the ring of the original Ruskin.

Mr. Ruskin's subsequent writings have shown that
his learning was equal to his confidence. Though he
has never been able to rescue his judgment from the
suspicions which his early impetuosity and continued
want of temperance have created, he has still succeeded
in increasing his reputation as a critic, and in acquiring
a new and solider hold of public respect. Not a few
men, now-a-days, artists as well as amateurs, allow his
thinking to color all their own : there are some, indeed,
who invest him with a species of infallibility, who
would fain believe, that when he has pronounced on
any point of artistic morals or doctrine, the thing is forever determined ; and it is worthy of note, that Mr.
Ruskin himself rather encourages this view of the matter. In the preface to the volume before us, he generously admits that, owing to the immense field of
study to be gone over, in order to qualify one to become a competent critic of art—such as "optics,
geometry, geology, botany, and anatomy," with "the
works of all great artists, and the temper and history of
the times in which they lived," not forgetting "metaphysics," and "the phenomenon of natural scenery"—
there is some "chance of occasionally making mistakes." But, apart from transient slips, he is quite
impeccable. The laws of painting, he says, are as unerring and obvious as those of music or of chemistry,
and anybody who will take the trouble to master them,
may pronounce opinions upon art, as unhesitatingly

as Faraday discourses of the affinity of gases, or as Stephenson of the capacity of locomotives.

The "Modern Painters" has been scattered, in a somewhat desultory way, over a period of ten years, and though not begun, and never intended, we imagine, to be a regular or formal treatise, it has sufficient unity of purpose in it to justify a common name for the several volumes. One expects a great deal of rambling discussion in a work issued so by piecemeal—issued as the external exigencies of opinion, rather than its own internal law seemed to require—not a little inconsistently, perhaps—the end often forgetting the beginning, and the beginning often setting out vigorously, but reaching nowhere—and the lesser critics have an ample field for the display of their malice therein—yet these books have a method, and a method which, with no great research, one is able to dig out and set upon its feet. As the author states his plan for himself, "his general object has been to discuss the sources of those pleasures opened to us by art" (meaning chiefly pictorial and structural art)—pleasures which he distributes into three groups, consisting, first, of the pleasures derived from ideas of truth, or from the perception of resemblances to nature ; second, of the pleasures derived from ideas of beauty ; and, lastly, of the pleasures furnished by the meaning of these things, or ideas of relation.

His first volume, accordingly, as he tells us, treated of the success with which different artists had represented the facts of nature ; his second inquired more abstractly into the origin of our ideas of beauty, being an attempt toward a philosophy of the theoretic or imaginative faculties ; while the third volume characterizes the different degrees in which distinguished artists, or schools of artists, have succeeded in attaining true greatness in art. Another volume is to come, but what precisely it will be about, we cannot anticipate; for while it may be conceded that Mr. Ruskin is somewhat methodical, it is no less clear that the method is one entirely of his own make. He promises, at least, that it will contain a formal analysis of all the great labors of Turner.

Mr. Ruskin's leading question in this third volume is what constitutes real greatness in art. Artists, as well as critics, have always recognized a certain distinction between high and low art, or between the grand ideal style and the low realistic style, but they have never succeeded, according to our author, in describing accurately what that distinction is. Sir Joshua Reynolds, in some papers contributed to Dr. Johnson's Idler, in 1759, made such an attempt, but without decided success. He compares high art to poetry, in which the great, general, and invariable ideas of human nature are expressed, without regard, and even in contempt of nice details; and low art to history, which makes a formal statement of every particular of facts or events,—illustrating the former by the Italian schools, excepting that of Venice, and the latter by the Dutch schools, including that of Venice, as a sort of Dutchified Italian. But Mr. Ruskin shows, as well he might, that these views of Sir Joshua are exceedingly superficial. In the first place, he says that poetry does not concern itself with minute details, and the faithful imitation of nature is not an easy nor an undignified thing. Then, passing to his own better views, he asserts that the difference between great and mean art lies, not in definable methods of handling, or styles of representation, but wholly in the nobleness of the feeling with which the work is prosecuted. "We cannot say," he remarks, "that a painter is great because he paints boldly, or paints delicately; because he generalizes or particularizes; because he loves detail, or because he disdains it. He is great, if, by any of these means, he has laid open noble truths or aroused noble emotions. It does not matter whether he paints the petal of a rose or the chasms of a precipice, so that love and admiration attend him as he labors, and wait upon his work. It does not matter whether he toil for months upon a few inches of his canvas or cover a palace-front with color in a day, so only that it be with a solemn purpose he has filled his heart with patience or urged his hand to haste. And it does not matter whether he seek for his subjects among peasants or nobles, among the heroic or the simple, in courts or in fields, so only that he behold all things with a thirst for beauty, and a hatred of meanness and vice."

All which is very well, but not very definite. Now, what we want is, a more specific description of the characters which make up greatness of style. Mr. Ruskin, when he gets closer into his topic, states them to be, in the order of their increasing importance, 1st, the habitual and sincere choice of noble subjects; 2d, the introduction of as much beauty as is consistent with truth; 3d, the largest possible quantity of truth in the greatest possible harmony; and, 4th, imaginative power. By "choice of noble subjects," he means an inward preference for subjects of thought which involve wide interests and profound passion, as opposed to narrow interest and slight passions. Leonardo, for example, in the selection of the Last Supper for painting, evinced himself a greater artist than Raphael in selecting the School of Athens, or Teniers, a body of simple clowns. Supposing the choice sincere, as it ought always to be, it marks a larger and nobler range of sympathies in the heart, and a disposition to dwell in the highest thoughts of humanity. Again: by the "introduction of as

much beauty as is consistent with truth," Mr. Ruskin
means that the fairest forms must always be sought out
and dwelt upon, that the intensest beauty is to be worshipped, but not exclusively, or to the denial of the fact
that ugliness and decrepitude also exist. For beauty,
deprived of the proper foil furnished it by its opposites,
ceases to be enjoyed as beauty, just as light deprived of
shadow ceases to be enjoyed as light ; while the ugliest
objects contain some element of beauty peculiar to
themselves, which cannot be separated from their ugliness. In other words, the perception of beauty, like
other human perceptions, is relative, and is best enjoyed
in the relations in which nature has discovered it to us.
Thus, the intense spiritual beauty of Angelico is fresh-
ened and strengthened by his frank portraiture of ordinary brother-monks : Shakspeare places Caliban beside
Miranda, while a vulgar mind withdraws his beauty to
the safety of the saloon, and his innocence to the seclu-
sion of the cloister. High art, therefore, neither alters
nor improves nature, but seeks for what is lovely in it,
just as it is, and displays this loveliness to the utmost
of its power. What further Mr. Ruskin means by
"putting as much harmonic truth as possible" in a
work, and by "imaginative power," we need not stop
to explain, as he has already dwelt upon these points in
his previous works. Stated without disguise, or rather,
without that wonderful richness of illustration and occasional eloquence of phrase in which Mr. Ruskin sometimes imbeds his thoughts, his idea of the comparative
greatness of styles in art is, simply, of the degree in
which they combine goodness of purpose with love of
beauty and truth, and imaginative power.

No one can object to this view, which is not particularly novel, though so admirably illustrated ; but it
might have been more simply, and, at the same time,

philosophically reached. It is true of every work of art, as it is of every product of nature, that it is what the strange old Swedenborg, in his way of phrasing it, calls "a thing of trine dimensions." He means by this, that things are things only as they are at once an end, a means, and an effect, or as they possess a soul, a mind, and a body. Stript of either, a thing is a most imperfect thing, or rather, no thing at all, as any one may see who will conceive of himself, or any creature, if he can, destitute of either of them, though it should be but for a moment. Every work of art, being a most precious outgrowth of the human spirit, must also have its soul, mind, and body. The first, is that great purpose which gives birth to it ; the second, that organic distribution of parts which makes it a form—and the last, that sensible embodiment which is called the execution. Its substance, or soul, is the end which the artist has in view; its form, his mode of conceiving it intellectually ; and its body, the actual sensible appearance.

We say the soul of it is its great end or purpose, by which expression more is meant than by the simple term, "choice of subject." The most inveterate numbskull, or the most abandoned rake, may choose the most sacred theme for artistic treatment ; but he is only so much the more the numbskull and the rake for exposing in this way his foolishness or his hypocrisy. His real choice, his inward preference, is the internal delight which animates his action, and not the ostensible subject which gives name to it. This delight or love may range from the lowest desire of gain or fame, up, through various varieties of avidity and passion, to the most disinterested sympathy, in every humane and noble temper. A Caravaggio will paint you an Entombment of Christ—a subject in itself, certainly, full of tragic pathos and spiritual significance, and which he handles, in many ways, in a masterly manner, with carnations as fine as Giorgione's, and a touch as vigorous, almost, as Michael Angelo's, but there will be only so much soul in it as may be implied in Caravaggio's desire to please the reigning taste, joined to a display of his own wild energy. His work, in spite of its subject, will be essentially a specimen of low art, quite as much so as a charcoal sketch of the burial of one of our wandering Indians by his tribe. On the other hand, there are Dutch painters, who will paint you a festival of village-boors, or an encounter of half-tipsy dragoons, in themselves vulgar subjects enough, in a manner to raise them to the highest sphere of art. Nearly the whole of Dutch art is called low art ; yet, when we perceive, as we often do, that the delight of these painters lay, not in their boors and dragoons, but in the national life which these represented—in that sturdy burgher spirit which had laboriously won a country from the sea, which had heroically resisted the aggressions of Spanish despotism, and which rejoiced in the free, honest, independent citizenship, achieved by its own valor of spade and sword—do we not recognize in it something vastly superior to those low, superstitious reverences which often prompted the Madonnas and Martyrdoms of Italy ? We say it is this soul of a picture—this inmost purpose—this spiritual sympathy, which not only inspires it, but determines its character, and assigns it its rank in the different walks of art. Let the end of the artist be mean, selfish, grovelling, and though his subject were the Nativity or the Crucifixion—the highest facts of human history—and though the effects were wrought out with miraculous cunning of brain and hand, the work cannot be elevated. On the other hand, let the end be great, originating in any large and disinterested affection, in any sincere passion of love, hope, veneration, joy, philanthropy, and the spiritual grandeur alone will redeem it, in spite of much poverty of invention and much feebleness of management.   On this account it is, that the genial yet serious student of art, wandering among the splendors of Italy, will often be arrested, in the midst of their tropical gleams, by some infant bud, some early flower, peering, it may be, from the broken wall of a now abandoned and voiceless cloister, in whose faded touches he will, with joy and thankfulness, still descern the first warm kisses of God's heavenly sun.   Thus, the paintings of the monk Angelico do not ravish us with a glory of color, as Titian's sometimes do—they do not overwhelm us with exuberance of incident, as Tintoretto does—nor charm us into speechless admiration by graceful form, as Raphael often will ; but the devotion of them, the intense spiritual sweetness, calm from the very fervor of its ecstasy, transfixes us with awe and rapture.

But a work may belong to a great department of art without being in itself a successful example of it—as an animal may belong to an exalted species without being an exalted individual manifestation of that species—or, as Overbeck's paintings, for a more appropriate instance, may aim nobly at the highest range of Christian art, but not reach it perfectly.   For to this there is required a combination of excellences, or a union of spiritual, intellectual, and executive gifts, which enables the artist, who is inspired by noble sympathies, to work them out with the broadest wisdom, of both the rational and imaginative functions of the intellect, and with consummate manipulation, or mastery of material elements. Consulting any acknowledged masterpiece of the world— whether a poem, or a musical composition, or a painting—we see that feeling, thought, and skill, are blended in it, so that while it touches the unsounded depths of the heart, and stimulates the loftiest energies of the intellect, it also ravishes the eye or ear with delight. The sum of the qualities necessary to the greatest art, therefore, as Mr. Ruskin well says, is simply the sum of all the best powers of man :—"For, as the choice of the high subject involves all the conditions of right moral choice, as the love of beauty involves all the conditions of right admiration, as the grasp of truth involves all strength of sense and evenness of judgment, and as the poetical power involves all swiftness of invention and accuracy of historical memory, the sum of all these powers is the sum of the human soul."

Enough ! perhaps the reader will exclaim with Rasselas—"you have convinced me that no man can be a poet !" Not always the greatest, but still great ; for the good Providence, which has scattered along the line of six thousand years only as many of the primal stars as you may count on your fingers, reserving to them the peerless dignity of perfection, to show that the highest powers are not absolutely incommunicable, has yet distributed many high gifts with a free and benignant hand. To some God has given, in grander measure, love, and to some, wisdom ; to some, power—to some, the heavenly vision, which looks with eyes undimmed upon the transfigured glories—and to others, the swift sweeping wings, which fan away the dust of the centuries, or come and go from world to world, like flashing sunbeams—and to others, again, the forging hand, which wrests the secrets of nature, and dissolves its rugged rocks into gems ; but to all of us he has also given, if we but use his gifts with humble heart and diligent will, the power to appreciate these, to repeat, if we please, in gentler echoes, the thunders of their voices— to build our châlets and flower-gardens on the sides of their Alps ; or, what is better still, to catch with our own ears, as we may from our inland homes, some sound of distant seas, "rolling evermore ;" and to behold with our eyes some downward sparkle of the ineffable lustre of the Suns.

A right apprehension of true greatness in art involves an inquiry into the much-debated question, as to the true ideal of art ; Mr. Ruskin, accordingly, expends a great deal of characteristic energy on the determination of the point. In order to arrive at the true ideal of art, however, he conceives it necessary, first, to propound his true idea of life. "The proper business of men in this world," he says, "is first to know themselves and the existing state of the things they have to do with ; second, to be happy in themselves and the existing state of things ; and, third, to mend themselves and the existing state of things, as far as either is marred and mendable." If anybody is not disposed to this business, it is because he fears disagreeable facts, and shrinks from self-examination—acquiring, gradually, an instinctive terror of truth and a love of glossy and decorative lies ; or, because of a general readiness to take delight in things past, future, far-off, or somewhere else, rather than in things now, near, and here—thus begetting a satisfaction in mere imagination, or in things as they are not. Hence, Mr. Ruskin infers that nearly all artistic striving after the ideal is only a branch of this base habit—"the abuse of the imagination in allowing it to find its whole delight in the impossible and the untrue ; while the faithful pursuit of the ideal is an honest use of the imagination, giving full power and presence to the possible and true."

Now the uses of imagination are, first and noblest, to enable us to bring sensibly to our sight the things recorded of the invisible world ; then, secondarily, to traverse the scenes of actual history, making them real once more ; then, to invest the main incidents of life with happy associations, in order to lighten present ills and summon back past goods ; as, also, to give mental truth some visible type in allegory, simile, or personifi- cation ; and, finally, when the mind is utterly outwea- ried, to refresh it with such innocent play as shall be in harmony with the suggestive voices of natural things, permitting it to possess living companionship instead of silent beauty, and create for itself fairies in the green and naiads in the wave. On the other hand, the abuses of the imagination consist either in creating, for mere pleasure, false images, when we ought to create true ones, or in turning what was intended for the mere refreshment of the heart into its daily food, and chang- ing the innocent pastime of an hour into the guilty oc- cupation of a life.* As examples of the first abuse, Mr. Ruskin, in a most masterly review of it, cites the re- ligious art (administering a rebuke to one of Raphael's customs in the course of it), which asserted the most fulsome and outrageous lies of the simple facts of Scripture, thereby deadening their import to the souls of men ; while of the second abuse, he cites the profane art, chiefly after the sixteenth century, which, seeking beauty first, and truth secondarily, soon lost sight of all real beauty, as well as all real truth, and sunk into a mesh of disgraceful sensualism.

Again : as to the true idealism, it has taken three principal forms—the purist, the naturalist, and the grotesque—all permissible, and all admirable within their limits, but the best of them the naturalist. ''The things about us," our author says, "contain good and evil promiscuously, and some men choosing the good

---

* See page 47, the sentences of which we merely abridge.

alone, they are called purists ; and some taking both together, are called naturalists ; while others have a tendency to the evil alone, and hence become grotesque." The purist ideal, exhibited by Angelico and many painters of the thirteenth century, results from the unwillingness of men of holy and tender dispositions to grapple with the definite evils of life, and is apt to degenerate into a weak and childish form of art. The grotesque ideal arises from a healthful but irrational play of imagination in times of rest, or from the irregular contemplation of terrible things, or from the confusion of the imagination by the presence of truths which it cannot wholly grasp, but it must be held with a firm hand to prevent its running into demonology and wickedness ;* while the central ideal, the ideal of ideals, as we may say, is that which, accepting both good and evil, accepting all weaknesses, faults, and wrongnesses, harmonizes them into a noble whole, in which the imperfections of the parts become not only harmless, but essential, while whatever is good in each part is completely displayed. This has been the ideal of all the really greatest masters of the world. On this principle, Homer, Dante, Tintoret, Shakspeare, and Turner worked. And under the influence of this ideal alone will modern art, if it is ever destined to achieve the most glorious triumph, fulfil its mission.

We should like to extract largely from this part of the book, of which we have given only the baldest outline, to evince our admiration of much of it ; and we should like to criticise largely, also, to tell in what respects we disagree with it ; but as more interesting topics are at

---

* One of the most discriminating of criticisms Ruskin has ever written, occurs in this chapter on the grotesque, where he compares a griffin of the classical sort with a mediæval griffin. It is in such passages that he displays his finest critical power.

hand, we have only space to utter a word on one or two points. In the midst of that medley of fine things which Mr. Ruskin says, we do not perceive that he strikes the key-note to a proper exhibition of the ideal. His distinctions between the purist, naturalist, and grotesque ideal carry a certain force with them, and are beautifully elaborated ; but they are not philosophic distinctions, because they are not founded on any real relations of contrast. They are simply arbitrary divisions. Purism, as he interprets it, seeking to escape the definite evils of the world, is a weakness, false to the essential conditions of human life, and consequently, as he seems to admit, no true ideal. His grotesquism, again, is made to embrace quite too much. Our blessed little friends, the fairies and elves, Titania and Oberon, and even the spiteful Kobolds, spring from no affinity for evil, and are romantic, rather than grotesque creations ; while the art which arises from truths that confuse and baffle the imagination, is simply symbolic or allegorical, or, if more than that, sublime. Mr. Ruskin, however, is unquestionably right in regarding the naturalistic ideal as the true ideal; "naturalistic, because studied from nature, and ideal, because mentally arranged in a certain manner ;" but, unfortunately, the very point we want to know most about, namely, what this "mentally arranged in a certain manner" means, he covers with a cloud of talk on "inspiration," "instinct," "imaginative vision," and what not, as misty as any German philosophy* that we have lately read.

---

* Besides numerous flings in the text, Mr. Ruskin devotes an appendix to a lusty tilt against "German Philosophy," and as this includes every variety of human speculation, it is virtually a tilt against all philosophy. It is amusingly absurd for its insular bigotry, but particularly so in a man whose book (two-thirds of it) is occupied in enforcing a philosophy of his own. In behalf of this decried "Ger-

This taking refuge in "inspiration," and the like, after the exceedingly positive statement of Mr. Ruskin, that the laws of art were as plain as the affinities of chemistry, strikes us with as much disappointment as surprise. After being led on through a hundred pages by an expectation that, at last, a great light was to be shed upon the mysterious realm of artistic creation, to find it only a will-o'-the-wisp, rather piques one into some resentment against the guide. "The great man knows nothing about rules," says Mr. Ruskin; "the rules of art cannot be taught." "They are instinctively seen;" "they are God-given;" all which may be true, and is; but then, how is it that the laws of art may be "learned by labor," and demonstrated, as Faraday demonstrates gases? We cannot but believe, if Mr. Ruskin had studied that philosophy of which he

---

man Philosophy," let us add, much as we dislike some of its merely metaphysical wranglings, that, as a whole, the cultivated mind of Germany approaches all questions of human thought from a vastly higher stand-point than either the practical English or the scientific French. Mr. Ruskin confesses his profound obligations to Carlyle, yet Carlyle is steeped in Germanism to the core. Besides, what an enormous presumption it is, to arraign the philosophy of a whole nation, and that nation the most cultivated extant, while acknowledging a wilful ignorance of it! What seems to have moved his special ire against "German Philosophy," is a phrase of Chevalier Bunsen in Hippolytus, about a "finite realization of the infinite," which he ridicules as equivalent to a "black realization of white." We do not know in what connection Bunsen applies the phrase, but we, old-fashioned Christians, who believe literally in "God manifest in the flesh," *i. e.*, the infinite God in the finite Man, can conceive a meaning of it not so wholly ludicrous as Mr. Ruskin supposes. Again: he is irate over the phrase, "God, man, and humanity," which, he says, is a parallel to "Man, dog, and canineness," but no more so than the phrase "God, man, and Mr. Ruskin," which is, probably, Bunsen's meaning.

cherishes so violent a *rabies*, that he would have been enabled to write more clearly and consecutively of this "mental arrangement," which is the essential point of his whole inquiry. We cannot but believe that Hegel, for instance, in his profound analysis of the development of art, through its several forms of symbolic, classic, and romantic art, in spite of the underlying metaphysics, easily separable in what is offensive in them from the genuine substance of the thought, has cast a great deal of light upon the proper sense of the ideal. At any rate, we know that nearly all that is valuable in Mr. Ruskin's own speculations was anticipated for us in that writer, with much that Mr. Ruskin does not reach,—presented with a comprehensiveness of view, and a freedom from petty partialities, which it would materially assist Mr. Ruskin to cultivate. We do not mean to say, by this, that we accept entirely Hegel's æsthetic theories, which have the defects incident to his general scheme of philosophy ; but what we wish to commend is, their admirable method, the profound significance of certain parts, and that elevation and breadth of view which generalizes, not from any single form, or age, or manifestation of art, but from a calm survey of the whole field of artistic effort. But we cannot dwell on this point.

The most labored, novel, and altogether characteristic part of this work, is a review of ancient, mediæval, and modern landscape—full of eloquent writing and keen criticism—illustrated by effective drawings, but painfully diffuse, and vitiated by superficial learning as well as superficial philosophy. It must be confessed, in the outset, however, that in the execution of the matter Mr. Ruskin had before him a somewhat embarrassing problem,—embarrassing, not so much in itself, as in his position toward it. He had already, in numerous works, exhausted the vocabulary of his contempt for modern art, and the modern mind generally. It was base, faithless, mechanical, and altogether given over to the service of the flesh and the devil. At the same time, he had undertaken the championship of Mr. Turner, as the greatest landscape painter of all the world. How to reconcile the two positions without confessing either the inferiority of landscape, as a form of art, or the insignificance of his pet—"the mighty spirit," as he is called—in glorifying whom he had spent so much labor, was the perplexity. If he admitted the greatness of landscape art, he admitted the greatness of the moderns, inasmuch as they are incontestably superior to all their predecessors in this respect; while, if he denied the greatness of landscape, he must dismiss his favorite to a subaltern place, in which case the world would naturally inquire, Why all this fuss about nothing and nobody?

Mr. Ruskin hardly extricates himself from his difficulties, but plunges, rather as if he was not aware of them, into more hopeless confusion. He confesses, after some doubts, that landscape is "noble and useful," and assigns reasons for the opinion (which, by the way, seems to us quite inadequate.)* He admits, too, the wonderful devotion of the moderns to the study and representation of his favorite "nature," which trait, in itself, he regards as an advance upon the ancient or mediæval status; and yet he tries to explain it away, so far as he can—partly on the ground that our seeming love of nature is "pathetic fallacy," arising from a weak and morbid imputation of our own feelings to nature; and, partly, on the ground that we have so emptied

---

* See chapter on "The Use of Pictures," which is ingenious but unsatisfactory.

nature of all divinity, as to approach her with a reckless irreverence and freedom—tearing her very bowels out with our prying mechanical sciences, and slavering and daubing the very face of her august countenance with our sentimental poetry and paint.

Let us state the whole case. The historians, especially of literature, have remarked a difference in the modes with which nature is contemplated by the ancient, the mediæval, and the modern mind. Schiller, in one of his works, expresses a surprise that the Greeks—living in a genial climate, amid the most picturesque scenery, with all their susceptibility to beauty—should nowhere express, in their poetic writings, a sympathy with external nature. They often give faithful descriptions of it ; but their hearts have no more share in their words, than if they were treating of a garment, or a suit of armor. Nature has no charm for them, to which they cling with plaintive passion. Gervinus, in his History of German Literature, indulges in a similar strain of thought in regard to the Minnesingers and popular poets of the middle ages. They evince some feeling for nature, but have left no independent delineation of it—no loving, tender, self-surrendering delight in it—nothing more than might be involved in it as an accessory to their love-songs or their chivalric narratives. How different our modern poetic compositions, which fairly welter in sunsets, and flower-beds, and dews, and streams, and mossy dells ! Our habitual thought even is crystallized into the forms and suffused with the colors of the physical world.

Mr. Ruskin adopting these hints, undertakes an elaborate analysis of the differences indicated. Making Homer, Dante, and Sir Walter Scott, respectively, types of the ancient, mediæval, and modern ages, he deduces the characteristic feeling of each for landscape.

His results, stated in a few words, are these : (1) With
the Greek there was no sympathy with nature, as such ;
only a straightforward recognition of it as a more or
less agreeable fact ; no sense of what we call the picturesque ; an interest, mainly, in its available and useful properties,—in the ploughed field, which gave him
corn—in the trellised vine, which gave him wine—in
the nourishing rains—and in the meadows, good for
feeding oxen and sheep. Mountains he rather de-
tested, as he did all weeds and wildnesses. But he
cherished a keen delight in human beauty, and a kind,
familiar reverence for the deities who resided within
the various natural elements. (2) With the mediævals
there was a more sentimental contemplation of nature—
more undisturbed companionship with wild nature—a
love of the sense of divine presence in it—consequently
a fallacious animation of it by demoniacal agency—but
a continued delight in human beauty, including its
dresses and decorations, and particularly the beauty of
woman. Their landscape has a high sentiment of nature ; but is often feeble and inaccurate, and exhibits
curious traces of terror, superstition, piety, and rigid
formalism. (3) With the moderns we find an intense
sentimental love of nature—particularly of clouds and
mists—indicative of their fickleness and obscurity ; a
delight in mountains, with no sense of their solemnity ;
and in wild scenery, characteristic of an unbridled
fondness for liberty; interest in science, but no sense
of human beauty, no relish for costume, an utter want
of faith in any divine presence in nature, insensibility to the sacredness of color, extreme despondency
of mind, and an eagerness to run away from the dreari-
ness of the present, taking shelter in fictitious romances
of the past.

"A red Indian, or Otaheitan savage," says Mr. Ruskin, "has more sense of a Divine Existence round him, or government over him, than the plurality of refined Londoners or Parisians." Again : "All, nearly, of the powerful men of this age are unbelievers ; the best of them in doubt and misery—the worst in reckless defiance ; the plurality, in plodding hesitation, doing, as well as they can, what practical work lies ready to their hands. Most of our scientific men are in the last class ; our popular authors set themselves definitely against all religious form, pleading for simple truth and benevolence (Dickens and Thackeray), or give themselves up to bitter and fruitless statement of facts (De Balzac), or surface-painting (Scott), or careless blasphemy, sad or smiling (Byron, Béranger). Our earnest poets and deepest thinkers are doubtful or indignant (Tennyson, Carlyle) ; one or two anchored, indeed, but anxious or weeping (Wordsworth, Mrs. Browning) ; and, of these two, the first is not so sure of his anchor, but that, now and then, it drags with him, even to make him cry out—

> "———— Great God ! I had rather be
> A pagan, suckled in a creed outworn,
> So might I, standing on this pleasant lee,
> Have glimpses that would make me less forlorn."

The only exceptions to this universal doubt and cynicism, according to Mr. Ruskin, are Turner and the pre-Raphaelites !

This is no pleasant picture for us, but luckily is surcharged. Notable differences, no doubt, exist between different nations in respect to their feeling for nature. Humboldt, in the second volume of the *Cosmos*, has discussed the whole subject, with his usual discrimination, and conceives that those differences can only be accounted for as the complex result of the influences of race—of the configuration of the soil—of climate—of government, and of religious faith. He concedes the comparative insensibility of the Greeks and Romans, but then he claims a high degree of true feeling for nature for the Indian races, the Persians, the Arabs, and some of the early Christian Fathers, and for nearly all the moderns since the time of Columbus, including that noble mariner. His studies are more varied, and, we think, more worthy of regard than those of Mr. Ruskin, who has been led into some imperfect views by the models he set up as guides.

Neither Homer nor Sir Walter Scott are proper types of the periods they are chosen to represent, though Dante may be. They were only epic, or narrative poets, who deal with nature simply as the accessory, or background of their pictures. They do not address her at first hand. Homer was, it is true, a "Greek of the Greeks," but he chanced to live some five hundred years before the Greek mind attained any real artistic development. Had Mr. Ruskin consulted the minor poets, Simonides, Bion and Moschus, Meleager, Pindar, and Theocritus, he would have found innumerable evidences that the Greeks cared much more for nature than the corn and wine she brought them—had, indeed, a sincere admiration of her beauty—and fell at times even into "pathetic fallacy." Casting our eyes over the dramatists, even while reading Mr. Ruskin's book, they fell instantly upon several bits of landscape-painting as fine as any one would care to bless his eyes withal. Nevertheless, it must be confessed that the main interest of the Greeks lay in their own humanity.

Nor is Dante precisely the poet that, on first thoughts, we should have selected for the illustration of mediæval feeling for landscape. He was the master of his age, and his poem was a mirror of the Italy of that age, imaging its principal personages and events with vivid reality. But he was also a poet of peculiar, if not exceptional, temperament ; intensely absorbed in political struggles ; distressed, depressed, wrapped in solitary gloom, as he wandered an exile, eating the bitter bread of others, so that in "his burning, troubled soul, arose great thoughts and awful, like Farinati, from his burning sepulchre." These gave tone, we suspect, to his daily, as well as his immortal visions. But Dante shoots up, so Etna-like, in those southern skies, that one feels he must have carried all the flowers of the fields on his -sides, in spite of the hot fires at his heart. Mr. Ruskin's able analysis persuades you so ; and yet, almost coeval with Dante was an English poet, not so great or universal by any means, yet a very great poet, whose landscape breathes of quite another air. We refer to Chaucer—the kindly, honest, old, laughing Chaucer, whose sportive fancy, whose grand imagination, whose subtle humor and homely wit and wisdom, found no equal till Shakspeare, and whose pages come to us, through five hundred years, still smelling of the fresh, wholesome soil—still dewy as the morning, lovely and sweet with flowers, and vocal with the songs of birds and the melody of streams. If Dante, then, expresses the deeper religious and political life of his times—if his be a spirit framed in more heroic mould—we must claim high rank for our Chaucer, in all that relates to the actual life of the people, and the popular sense of nature ; for it is remarkable of Chaucer, that, chivalric as he is, full of epic pageantry and pomp, living, as he did, in the midst of a brilliantly romantic and elegant court—a court thronged with gallant knights, who, at Cressy and Poictiers, had made Edward invincible, and stately dames, only less beautiful than Philippa, whom the statuaries made their model for the Virgin—still, his pages glitter with none of their magnificence, his song exults in none of their victories. He steals away rather to the people at their firesides or their sports, or wanders in "the blissful sunshine," among the dews "more sweete than any baume," listening to the "birde's song."

> "——— a ravishing sweetnesse,
> That God, that Maker is of all, and Lorde,
> He heard never better, as I guesse."

A more cheery, gentle, enthusiastic lover of nature than he, more utterly devoid of superstitious glooms and fears, we find alone in modern times.

Against the inauguration of Scott as the type of this age, we decidedly protest. He was scarcely of this age at all, but an after-birth of former ages, sent to retrieve the neglect into which they had fallen. Scott performed an acceptable service for poetry, in sending forth a gallant band of rugged knights and outlaws to put the stiff old Greeks and Romans to death, and then properly withdrew. A tory of tories, who valued the smile of his prince almost as much as he did the fame of Waverley; who tasked his magnificent powers in order to rear a baronial pile, that toppled down upon his own head; there was yet scarcely a movement in modern art, science, or religion, with which he sympathized. His poems and most of his romances have already no more than an antiquarian value. They are excellent tapestries of times fast receding—agreeable to look at, instructive, picturesque, with a fine feeling for the chivalric virtues, but rimy with the dust of time. Strange to say, that all the while Mr. Ruskin is engaged in this preposterous labor of setting Scott upon a pedestal where he cannot stand, there hovers around him another spirit—the spirit of one of his hated Germans, a poet, a man of science, a consummate literary artist, loaded with the learning of all the schools, yet buoyant as a child amid his new-found blisses of nature—who wrote a drama equal to Shakspeare's—whose songs are in the mouths of the people—and whose books reflect all the grandeurs and glooms, all the strengths and weaknesses, all the hopes and despairs, of the last half-century! Need we name Goethe, whom Mr. Ruskin unceremoniously dismisses for his "jealousy, which is never the characteristic of a really great man?" (*Credat!*) We do not believe that any single man can fully represent this multitudinous, manifold age of ours ; but if any man could, it would be Goethe. It is to him, more than any one else, that Mr. Ruskin should have gone for the modern idea of nature ; and had he done so, he never would have given us that libellous caricature of the tendencies of the modern mind.

Reading the "signs of times," we are sure, is not Mr. Ruskin's forte. His skill in pictures may be great, but his skill in men and the movements of society is not great. This very question of the change that has taken place in men's modes of regarding nature, has a profound significance he has not reached. It is nothing more nor less than the question, as to the difference between Christianity and the pagan religions. Has Christianity introduced any fundamental transformation in the human mind? If it has, the mind must stand in a totally different relation to nature from what it did. The common belief is, that it has introduced a marvellous change—a change not merely of degree, but of kind ; and that our modern activity is the outgrowth, though feeble as yet, of that change. It were too large a theme for us here to enter into an exposition of the nature and value of that change ; but we may suggest

two things : first, that Christianity not only empties
nature of its fetiches, of its gods and goddesses, however beautiful, but proclaims it to be in itself dead,
worthless, corrupt, even sinful—or the opposite of
divine ; and, second, it proclaims that nature has been
redeemed, by the divine assumption of it, whereby man,
from being the slave, may become the master of it, so
that "the whole creation" will yet be glorified. This is
the mystical annunciation which every Christian de-
voutly believes : but what does it mean practically? It
means that nature is not an end in itself, is not to
be loved for itself, but is unworthy and corrupt, except
in so far as it is made subservient to humanity, in
which case it is filled with a divine beauty and significance.

Now our modern Christian instincts have recognized
these truths, and hence our physical sciences, with their
immense activities, striving to reduce nature, which has
no longer any sanctity, to human uses. Hence, too,
the universality and fearlessness of our researches into
nature, which impresses us no more as a vast uncon-
trollable power outside of us, but as a mere mechanism,
of whose movements we hold the key, whose malig-
nities we may turn into benignities. Thus, too, the
universe—a world of effects, whose causes lie in the
inner spiritual sphere, shines a vast hieroglyph of the
Eternal and Unseen, is a glorious analogue of the
Divine. We love nature, therefore, if we love it at all,
because in its every process we discern emblems of
our own human life ; because, along the endless multiplicity of its forms, the angels of God ascend and
descend, as in the wonderful ladder of Jacob's dream.

We have dwelt so long upon this last volume, that we
have left ourselves little space for any general estimate
of Mr. Ruskin's merits, which we promised ourselves

at the outset. But they may be summed up in few words. He is the critic rather than the philosopher of art. Endowed with the keenest sensibility to the influences of nature, he has observed them with accuracy, and, at the same time, with strong poetic feeling. Few men, again, are more alive to the beauties of art, and none have studied its actual manifestations with more diligence. Applying his knowledge of nature to works of art, he is able to judge their comparative merits with a rare taste and profound sympathy. As a judge he is positive and severe, but also enthusiastic. His praise and his blame alike come from the heart. He sees clearly and feels earnestly, and what he sees and feels he describes with impetuous eloquence. There are whole pages of rhetoric .in his books, which possess all the magnificence of Milton or Taylor. But he is not always equal in his style, nor always just in his opinions. He has a fondness for extravagance, as well of thought as of expression, and perpetually indulges his mere conceits. He is apt to utter decrees instead of criticisms, and, uttering them often on the impulse of the moment, they are not infallible decrees. His principles of art, when they are correct, proceed more from instinct than reason ; nor has he digested them into a complete and systematic whole. They are drawn from the study of a few arts, and not from the study of the whole field of art. They are consequently wanting in the broadest generalizations, and do not penetrate to the deepest grounds. As an active and fearless thinker, however— as a patient scholar, as an energetic, warm-hearted liker and hater, and as an eloquent expositor of refined tastes and generous impulses, he stands unrivalled among the English critics of art.

CAUSES OF THE FRENCH REVOLUTION.* .

HESE are translations of the same work, the one executed in England, and the other in the United States. Both appear to be sufficiently well done for the satisfaction of readers in general. In both, we are glad to learn, the original French author retains a certain *per centage* of interest.

Any book by De Tocqueville will be sure to find readers in this country. He is so favorably known by his *Democracy in America*, that every one, who is familiar with that able disquisition, will be glad to get another work from his hands. Not that he is, in any sense, an entertaining writer ; for he is not : he is a slow and somewhat laborious writer ; but he is profound and instructive, and every sentence he utters is freighted with golden thought. He is one of the few Frenchmen, or rather, we should say, one of the few Europeans, who understands and cherishes what approximates to a really sound theory of human government. He is no believer in the favorite centralism of his countrymen, monarchial and republican alike. Ask a legitimist in France what his notion is of the true organization of

* *The Old Régime and the Revolution*. By Alexis De Tocqueville. Translated by John Bonner. Harper & Brothers, New York, 1856.
On the State of Society in France before the Revolution of 1798, and on the Causes which led to that event. By Alexis De Tocqueville. Translated by Henry Reeve. London : John Murray, 1856.
From *Putnam's Monthly*, Nov., 1856.

power, and he will sketch you out a scheme something
like the absolute monarchy of Louis XIV.; ask a Na-
poleonist, and he will point you to the Empire ; and
ask a democrat, and he will begin to glorify Robespierre
or Ledru Rollin ; yet these are all fundamentally the
same—the concentration of the whole national force in
a single focus, differing in name, but not differing much
in essence or end.   De Tocqueville belongs to neither
of these classes.   Though an aristocrat by affinity, his
study of our American townships, combined with his
own good sense, has taught him the value of local self-
government ; and his criticisms of institutions and historical events are modified by this perception.

In the large and imposing volume before us, he
undertakes an investigation of the condition of French
society in the eighteenth century, and of the causes
involved in that condition, which developed themselves
in the terrific popular outbreak of the year 1789.   It is
a most important and a most interesting inquiry ; for
no event in human annals has more deeply impressed
the minds of men, or is more inexhaustible in its exhibitions of human character, or more significant in its results for mankind.   Much as it has been written of, both
as to its external phenomena and as to its internal philosophy, much more remains to be said.   The product
of five hundred years of accumulating wrongs, the starting-point, as we believe, of many more hundred years
of nobler development, there were crowded into the
events of that brief decade a pith and moment, which
no one writer, and no one thousand writers, will readily
exhaust.   We think we must have read in our time,
without an immoderate indulgence in that particular line,
at least fifty volumes relating to the French Revolution,
and yet our appetite for the memoirs and histories of it
is just as keen as it was, in fact is keener than it was,

when the whole subject came up as a novelty. This is true however of all other knowledge, and especially of our knowledge of men ; the more we know, the more we want to know ; curiosity is never satiated ; nor is that better feeling than curiosity—our deep sympathy in the fortunes of our race, and our desire to penetrate the mysterious processes by which, in the midst of so much wickedness, and bloodshed, and suffering, the progress of our humanity is evolved—readily satisfied. All events which seem to have greatly advanced or greatly retarded the course of events, possess a perennial, living charm.

De Tocqueville's topic, therefore, though old in one sense, is ever fresh in interest, and is peculiarly new in his treatment of it. He has not contented himself with repeating the substance of former researches. He has not gone over the comprehensive ground which Louis Blanc travels with so much erudition, in his most able introduction to his history ; but he confines his remarks to the period immediately preceding the Revolution, and to the actual circumstances of the time, as they are shown in the best historical monuments. He thinks that the earlier ages of the French monarchy, the middle ages, and the epoch of the Renaissance, have been more studied and better comprehended than the eighteenth century, though the latter is so much nearer to us. The laws, customs, and the spirit of the government, in those remoter ages, have been diligently illustrated by the most skilful authors ; but the eighteenth century has not been examined in the same minute and careful manner. We have skimmed the glittering surface of its literature ; we have been charmed by its numerous lively biographies ; we have admired the ingenious and eloquent criticisms of the great writers : but we have not taken pains to learn the mode in which business was then conducted ; to ascertain the real working of its institutions ; to discover the relative position of thé various classes, the condition and feelings of those classes which were neither heard nor seen, beneath the prevailing opinions and customs of the day.

All this out author has assumed to do for us ; and, in order to execute his purpose, has not only read over again the famous books of the eighteenth century—the Voltaires and the Rousseaus, the Montesquieus and Turgots, the Marmontels and Diderots—but he has thoroughly sifted obscure yet public documents, which show the opinions and the tastes of the French, at the approach of the Revolution. Among these, the most important have been the regular reports of the meetings of the States, and subsequently, of the provincial assemblies, the *cahiers* or papers of instruction (petitions of grievances, as we should call them), drawn up by the Three Orders in 1789 ; and particularly the archives of the larger Intendencies, as those districts or *généralités* were called which were presided over by an intendant, and often comprised large circles of population. As the administration was strongly centralized then, grasping nearly every interest and hope of the people, and the communication between the centre and the parts active and minute, and withal secret, so that men were not afraid to lay bare to it the wants of their hearts, and even the secrets of their families, the records of these offices are filled with the most valuable materials. De Tocqueville had free access to these, though it was not always an easy access. He says that a single brief chapter has sometimes cost him a year of labor. That he was faithful, as well as patient, in these researches, that he has concealed nothing and imagined nothing, it would be needless to assure anybody who is acquainted with his habitual and conscientious regard for truth.

The result of his inquiries is a mass of useful knowledge, which, in itself, casts a broad light upon the subject in hand, and which, it may be granted, we have never before possessed in precisely the same shape ; but we feel bound to add, that it does not appear to us to be so entirely novel, in it contents, as the author asserts and even boasts. As evidence, it is, no doubt, new ; but the peculiar conclusions which it is brought to sustain, are not new. We might take up almost any one of the propositions advanced as the headings of the various chapters, and urged in the text with a certain air of discovery, as if they had never been broached before, and show that, in this country at least, they have long been familiar to us, so that they are not now considered debatable points of history at all. That "administrative centralization," for instance, was an institution of France, anterior to the Revolution, and not a product of the Revolution or of the Empire ; that "administrative tutelage," as the education and discipline of the people by the government is called, was an institution in France anterior to the Revolution ; that "exceptional administrative jurisdiction" (*la justice administrative*), and the irresponsibility of public officers (*garantie des fonctionnaires*), existed under the old régime ; that the metropolis of France had usurped a preponderating control over the nation long before the Revolution ; · that the condition of the French peasantry, in spite of the general progress of civilization, was in some respects worse in the eighteenth century than it had been in the thirteenth ; that, toward the middle of the eighteenth century, men of letters had become the leading political men of France ; that irreligion, at that time, had reached an unusual and dominant influence in society ; and that, under Louis XVI., the French people were encouraged to revolt, by the very means taken to relieve them ; are surely not propositions which will strike any intelligent American, nor, we suspect, any intelligent English reader of French history, with any degree of surprise. We have been accustomed to regard these propositions as facts, and our surprise is rather, that they can be adduced and argued with so much gravity, by De Tocqueville, as something of which the world has not been before adequately aware. The condition of opinion in France, and particularly the errors which prevail among ill-informed persons, as to the precise nature and achievements of the Revolution, together with the tendency, almost universal in that country, to overlook the defects of the national Constitution, may render this tone of remark necessary ; but we cannot suppose that these views have at all escaped genuine historical students anywhere. At any rate, in this country, it is rather an elementary proceeding, in speculations on the philosophy of the Revolution, to refer it to the phenomena above enumerated, and, most especially, to that increase of "administrative centralization" which was at once both cause and effect of the absolute dominion of the French monarchs.

This we may have occasion to dwell upon in another aspect, hereafter, but in the mean time let us repeat that our author's proofs are original and profoundly interesting, though his principles do not present themselves to us in the same freshness of light.

We recognize De Tocqueville, in spite of certain opinions widely divergent from our own, as belonging to the legitimate school of historical philosophers. He is neither a fanatic nor a fatalist ; he does not adopt too exclusively the doctrine of necessary causation in history, nor of absolute human freedom ; but admitting fully the truth of an organic and continuous connection of events, he also retains the other truth, of an over-

ruling Providence. One class of thinkers, like the
rhetorical theologians (who can scarcely be called philosophers), see in the French Revolution only a tremendous and almost causeless outburst of human wickedness, and to these the splendid ravings of Burke are to
this day a kind of political gospel. Another class, like
Thiers and Mignet, and to a certain extent, though from
a higher plane of vision, Carlyle, see in it an inevitable
and mysterious destiny, which moved the men of the
times from its dark recesses, as puppets are moved by
wires from behind till they glide and gibber before us
like spectral figures, who are the sport of a mocking
and remorseless fate. But there is another, and, we
think, a better class, who, while they cherish a profound
and grateful faith, that the "Lord God omnipotent
reigneth," yet believe that he reigns through the free in-
strumentality of men. These maintain that the movements of society are organic and living developments ;
that all events are in some sort dependent upon preceding events ; that they are not wholly wanton and wilful,
but conditional, and that, while the sources of life,
social as well as individual, are in the infinite and eternal world, the forms of that life, the phenomenal manifestations of it, are controlled by the whole complex of
what we denominate historical circumstances. It is to
this school, if we mistake not, that De Tocqueville
adheres, and therefore, while he exempts no class or
individual from the guilt of their misdeeds, nor withholds from any the merit of their good actions, he seeks
the causes of the revolutionary phenomena in the vices
of the old régime. He discerns clearly that the stupendous insurrection at the close of the last century,
which filled the world with mingled admiration and
dismay, was no sudden or satanic impulse ; but that it
had been long preparing, and that much of the good

and nearly all the evil of it, sprang directly out of the whole course of the monarchical civilization.

We cannot suppose, however, that the event was so entirely unexpected as our author represents, because that would argue a strange lack of sagacity and observation on the part of its contemporaries. Undoubtedly, it is true, as he says, that no one perceived its pressing imminence or anticipated its extent. The aristocratic classes were quite blind in regard to it ; the neighboring sovereigns and princes themselves, as late as 1791, though professing to see, in the danger which threatened royalty in France, a danger common to all the established powers of Europe, yet secretly imagined that the outbreak was a local and temporary accident, which they might turn to good account ; but there was a positive presentiment of it among the masses, while one not inconsiderable sect, the mystic revolutionists, the disciples respectively of Weishaupt, Saint Martin, and the arch-quack Cagliostro, seemed to have shaped as distinct an apprehension of the coming time as it was possible for their excited imaginations to frame on any subject.* It was from among these cabalistic spirits that Cazotte, the author of the *Diable Amoureux*, the *Œuvres badines et morales*, and of that continuation of the Arabian Nights, forming the 37th and 40th volumes of the *Cabinet des Fées*, emerged, and of whom La Harpe relates the well-known and singularly impressive incident, but now discredited, which is said to have occurred in the saloon of one of the eminent academicians of the time.

A gay company of courtiers and *philosophes* were dining once, in 1778, when the conversation turned, as usual, upon the promising prospects of the age, and

---

* Luchet. Essai sur les Illuminés. Paris, 1789.

the rapid approach of the era of intellectual emancipation. During the animated dialogue, Cazotte was observed to remain sombre and silent. Being rallied by
Condorcet, he remarked that he saw terrible things
in the future, and, "as for you, Monsieur Condorcet,"
he added, "you will take poison to escape the execu-
tioner." This unexpected retort provoked peals of
laughter from the lively company. But Cazotte, nothing disconcerted, turned first to Chamfort, the cynical
poet and wit, and predicted that he would open his
veins ; and next to Bailly, the astronomer and first president of the National Assembly, to Malesherbes, the
venerable parliamentarian and censor, and to Roucher,
translator of Adam Smith, saying that each would
perish on the scaffold. " Our sex, at least," interposed
the charming Duchess de Grammont, " will escape."
" Your sex, madam ?" replied Cazotte ; " no ! you, and
other ladies besides you, will be drawn upon a cart, with
your hands tied behind your backs, to a place of execution." " Without even a confessor?" she smilingly
asked. " Without even a confessor," he resumed ;
" for the last confessor will be reserved"—and here his
sad eyes filled with tears—" for the King of France."
This announcement startled the assembly, when Cazotte arose to retire, but the Duchess caught hold of him,
exclaiming, "And pray, sir prophet, what is to be your
fate ?" He stood for some time lost in profound reve-
rie, and finally narrated, that " during the siege of Jerusalem, a man had paraded the ramparts seven days
in succession, crying out in mournful accents, ' Woe
unto thee, Jerusalem,' and that, on the seventh day, a
stone, flung by the enemy, struck him, and crushed
him to death." Cazotte was afterward arrested, during
the massacre of September, and hung. *Non e vero mai
bene trovato.* Indeed, it is impossible to read De

Tocqueville's own exposition of the state of opinion, during the period he describes, without feeling that the French mind must have been singularly obtuse not to discern the multitudinous signs appearing on all sides, of some new and tremendous overturn.

The solution of the problem of the French Revolution implies the solution of several subordinate questions, such as why that event took place at all; why it took place when it did, and not before; why it occurred among the French, rather than among the other people of Europe; and why, when it did come about, it was characterized by such wholly new and peculiar features? These solutions we shall not undertake, because it would require a volume to treat them even superficially, but we may remark, that it is obvious at a glance, that a successful treatment of them would demand a far more various and retrospective study than our author has given merely to the eighteenth century. His results possess a high degree of value, and they strongly elucidate antecedent periods; but, to arrive at an intelligent view of the origin and of the entire scope and bearing of the French Revolution, we should begin at least with the ministry of Richelieu, if not, indeed, with the triumph of modern monarchy over feudalism in the fifteenth century.

During the middle ages, as it has often been remarked by historians, there was a remarkable similarity in the political and social institutions of nearly the whole of Europe—that is, of civilized Europe. There were differences of detail and of name in different countries, but very much the same spirit and form. Society was divided into the same classes—into princes, nobles, clergy, burghers, and peasants, with similar privileges or burdens—the municipal constitutions were alike—the same maxims controlled the political assemblies—and the land was owned, occupied, tilled, and taxed after the same fashion. Everywhere there existed the same seignories or lords' estates, the same manorial courts, and fiefs, and feudal services, and quit-rents; and in the towns, corporations and trading-guilds.

But, during the fifteenth century, a general change in this condition of things was effected—a change which undermined the ancient feudal constitution, and brought in, in the place of it, the modern nationalities under the vigorous reign of monarchs. In France, the house of Valois, after a series of protracted and sanguinary struggles, had triumphed over the great feudatories, consolidated the territory of the realm, and introduced new principles of administration, which gave at once more unity and more permanence to the power of taxation, to the regular army, and to the parliaments or courts of justice. In Spain, the fierce combat between the Moors and Christians was brought to an end by the conquest of Granada; the marriage of Ferdinand and Isabella had united the two principal kingdoms of Castile and Aragon into a single state; the great and turbulent vassals were suppressed or restrained, and the power of the monarchy in various ways enlarged and confirmed. In Germany, again, the imperial crown, which had always been elective, and still remained so nominally, became virtually hereditary in the family of Maximilian. In England arose, out of the wars of the Roses, in which so many of the nobles had perished, the dynasty of the Tudors. The various Italian republics, stormy and brilliant as they had been, fell under the sway of powerful and wealthy houses—Florence to the Medici, Lombardy to the dukes of Milan, and Genoa, Venice, and Naples to foreign sovereigns—who made their soil the battle-fields of their rival claims.

Everywhere the old feudal and anarchical system was falling into decay, and a new system—the system of national royalties—advanced to its place.

From this point, however, the subsequent developments became exceedingly diverse. The political liberties of Italy perished almost immediately, in consequence of the incessant wars of petty and rival sovereigns; Spain grew into the magnificent empire of Charles V. and of Philip II., and then withered away; France achieved, under the successive administrations of Sully, of Richelieu, of Mazarin, and Louis XIV., a degree of splendor which dazzled all Europe, but was then destined to flicker, and corrupt, and sink, until the Revolution came to sweep away nearly every trace of its specious glory; while Germany fell apart into numerous principalities, mostly insignificant, and England alone, after rocking in the tempests of civil commotion for a while, attained to a really secure, stable, and free constitution.

Now, what were the causes of this difference? The aristocratic writers tell us (and De Tocqueville is of their number) that it was mainly owing to the greater or less destruction in each of the ancient nobility. Aristocracy is assumed to be an indispensable check upon the despotic powers of the kings, so that where the former is removed the latter rise into absolutism; while it is only where the former retains an effective existence, ʼhat the equipoise of a regulated and moderate monarchy is reached and preserved. How many changes of eulogistic phrase are rung upon this theory by our English friends? But is it an adequate interpretation of the facts? Does it not ascribe to the services of a class, results which properly belong to popular institutions, which may have been identified, to some extent, with that class, although the class was not es-

sential to them ?   In other words, are not the liberties
of England owing to its parliaments, its courts, and its
local meetings, as free assemblies in which the popular
heart can find some expression for itself, and the popular mind obtain a true perception of the nature, end,
and right practice of government, rather than to the
ascendency of any class which may have had the cunning or the virtue to connect its own cause with that of
these institutions ?   We confess that such is our opinion ;
we confess that our studies of history have left us little
respect for nobility anywhere ; and we are clear that,
though it may have been at times of transitional advantage to the growth of a higher civilization, it has been far
more frequently and permanently a serious detriment.

This view we have not the space to unfold, in regard
to all the nations of Europe ; but it is apropos to our
text to consider it in reference to France, particularly
as a main object of De Tocqueville is to show that
despotism is an unavoidable outgrowth of those societies
in which the aristocracies have been swept away.   His
argument runs as follows :   "That when men are no
longer bound together by the ties of caste, of class, of
corporation, of family, they are but too prone to think
of nothing but their private interests, too ready to consider themselves only, and to sink into the narrow precincts of self, in which all public virtue is extinguished.
Despotism, instead of combating this tendency, renders it irresistible, for it deprives its subjects of every
common passion, of every mutual want, of all necessity
of combining together, of all occasions of acting together.   It immures them in private life ; they already
tended to separation, despotism isolates them ; they
were already chilled in their mutual regard, despotism
reduces them to ice."   The doctrine is, that the emas-
culation of the ancient nobility, by removing a prin-

cipal obstacle to the growth of absolute royalty, was calamitous in its effects, and the inference from that doctrine, that to restore the liberties of France, something like the old aristocracy should be restored. We oppose both the doctrine and the inference : we assert, bad as the French monarchy became, that it was better than the rapacious and turbulent rule of the classes it supplanted ; and we hold that the issue from the towering centralism into which it has congested, is not through the revival of those classes, but by the establishment of free local institutions. .

In order to test the value of these conflicting positions, we need only recall the actual history of the French nobles, from the time of their appearance as feudal sovereigns to the day in which they were so effectively abased by Richelieu, or converted into mere court lackeys by Louis XIV. No one, we presume, will contend, that the enormous prerogatives enjoyed by the French peers and barons, during the middle ages and afterward, conduced greatly to the benefit of society. Though nominally vassals of the crown, these great feudatories were possessed of privileges which conferred upon them an almost independent dominion. They were the lords, and, to a large extent, the owners of vast territories ; they coined money ; they waged private war ; they exercised judicial powers, and they were exempt from all public tributes, except the feudal aids, and free of all legislative control. Nor were they backward in the use of these powers. Their right of coining money they often converted into a means of debasing the standard. The most frivolous passion served as a pretext for plunging them in destructive hostilities, while the luxury of their courts, and the expenses incident to their frequent feuds, led to the most oppressive exactions from the people. Spending their

lives in the chase, or in war, or in pillage, intent each
one on his interest, rather than upon the foundation of
order in the State, opposing the municipalities, where
the only germs of popular freedom were nourished,
harassing the trade of the citizen, and plundering the
labor of the peasant, it was impossible, while their
power lasted, that there should be either private security,
national consolidation, or general development.

It was partly the perception of these abuses, partly
their own selfish love of aggrandizement, and partly the
demands of the suffering burghers and people, which
led the French kings, one after another, to endeavor to
strip them of their overgrown resources. Sometimes
by the forcible seizure of their domains, as of the Ver-
mandois, by Philip Augustus ; sometimes by interposing
in behalf of the weaker classes, as was frequently done
by good St. Louis ; sometimes by perfidious declara-
tions of forfeitures against extensive fiefs, as under Philip
the Fair, the privileges of the great vassals were undermined and the authority of the crown extended. Yet,
in spite of these interferences, in spite of the reduction
of their numbers, effected by their own wasteful strife,
and by the distant expeditions of the crusades ; in
spite of their gradual loss of privileges, by the growth
of the cities, and the advent of the legists to judicial
honors, by which they were deprived of an important
means of distinction and influence ; and in spite of the
mercenary multiplication of their number, which destroyed, in a measure, unity of feeling and action, they
continued for centuries a strenuous though unequal
struggle against the supremacy of the monarchs.

As late as the time of the religious wars, which followed the Reformation, they were able to dictate to the
throne, then occupied by a weak and superstitious
prince, and to bring upon their nation the eternal dis-

grace of the massacre of Vassy and the horrors of St.
Bartholomew. One needs but to read the infamous
proceedings of the Guises and the League—now conferring secretly with the bigoted Philip II., and now
openly with the scarcely less bigoted Pope, for the means
of more effectually assassinating their sovereigns or
butchering the Calvinists—to see that the high nobility
were still an independent and pernicious power in the
state, and to find an ample justification for nearly every
stretch of authority which marked the policy of Richelieu. Neither Gaston nor Conde, neither Soissons nor
Vendôme, any more than the Constable Bourbon of a
former day, or a Cinq-Mars of their own day, appear
to have cherished any sense of obligation toward France,
any patriotic sentiment, any thought of duty beyond
their duty to their own interests, any aspiration which
reached outside the objects of their avarice, their ambition, and their pride. For a moment, the impulses
of fear or hope might bring them to submission to the
royal standard ; but neither fear, nor hope, nor any other
motive could ever bend them to the cause of the people. No name was sacred, no law authoritative to their
insane selfishness ; they openly conspired with foreigners;
they betrayed their engagements ; and when they were
finally broken, by the masterly genius of the great Cardinal, the mind of the reader of French history, though
disapproving often his means, is relieved as from the
presence of banditti.

No, the growth of absolute royalty was evidenced,
not occasioned, by the destruction of the nobles. The
extensions of power in that direction were not an unmin-
gled, yet they were an undoubted good. They gave
union to a series of distracted states ; substituted great
general ends of policy for petty schemes of personal
gain ; raised merit, if not above rank and birth, at least

to a level with them ; elevated justice and its tribunals, and introduced to places of trust and honor, once the exclusive possession of warlike nobles, lawyers and ecclesiastics, who were their superiors in everything but family.

At the same time, it must be admitted that the kings and their ministers went much further than this—that in reducing society to this monarchical unity, which was so largely personal, their action sacrificed also many useful ancient institutions, that it trampled upon the just rights of provinces and cities, that it violated what we now consider to be, and, were always considered by advanced minds, fundamental principles of justice and law, and that the régime which it inaugurated could in no sense become a definitive one, could in no sense answer the demands of reason, or patriotism, or the free human soul ; but it was not for these that the aristocracy had lived and labored, nor for these that their prolonged existence, in the plenitude of their power, would have been profitable. Greatly as they had been despoiled by the monarchs, there was yet scarcely a period in their career in which they might not, had they been wise and generous, as they were mostly selfish and proud, have done much toward arresting the rapid concentration of power in a single hand ; but, up to the very eve of the Revolution, they were more anxious about their own privileges than the welfare of the people, and, while the nation was bound and paralyzed by the burden of taxes, they vehemently maintained their traditional exemptions.

The circumstances which really permitted the towering uprise of the monarchy were, as we think, the essential weakness of all the municipal institutions of France, combined with the absence of all free legislative assemblies, provincial or supreme. In common with those of the rest of Europe, the French towns and boroughs, during the twelfth century, experienced that movement toward communal independence which was among the most remarkable phenomena of the age. Many of them, known as the *pays d'Etats*, such as Languedoc, Brittany, Provence, Artois, etc., either by stubborn tenacity or purchase, retained the more important of their privileges, especially elective magistrates and deliberative assemblies, up to a late day ; but the greater part of them, having none but a municipal existence, having no political relation to a regular parliament, like the English towns, were easily weakened by the rapacious nobles, who were nearly always their enemies, to be at last swallowed up by the kings, who were sometimes their friends and sometimes their tyrants.

No doubt the rapid increase of wealth in the towns helped to undermine their strength by relaxing their heroism. At the outset, the communes had displayed extraordinary virtue and vigor in the defence of their citizen rights. The sturdy streams of artisans and burghers which they poured from the Hotel de Ville, were a drowning torrent for the pillaging barons of the vicinage ; but as the gains of industry swelled up around them, as the fruitful arts of peace caused them to dread the storms of battle, they lost the joy of conflict, they withdrew even from the lesser disputes of the council, and the bell, which had summoned them to the assembly or the gate, ceased to sound.

And while this local spirit was undergoing decay, while the rights of the cities and the states were being gradually subtracted, there existed no great and disinterested central authority, to which the people could make their wrongs known or appeal for redress. The States-General, as the occasional assemblies of the clergy, the nobles, and the third estate are called, make a conspicuous figure in French history ; but they were always more remarkakle for high pretensions than effective performance. They were not strictly legislative assemblies—the extent of their powers as a whole, as well as the extent of the powers of each chamber, were always in doubt; and if we except a few scenes of memorable resistance to the royal authority, in which they were aided as much by external circumstances as by their own spirit, they were no check upon the kings, and no guaranty for the rights of the people.

A far more efficient organ, in both respects, were the parliaments, as the affiliated courts of justice were denominated. Their veneration for forms, if not their sense of justice or love of liberty, often interposed between the interests of the community and the ambition of the kings; and some of the noblest scenes in the annals of France are to be found in the struggles of these grave and long-robed clerks against the overbearing tyranny of ministers and favorites. But, like the States-General, they were badly constituted; their objects were confused between their judicial and their legislative functions, while, holding their places by a venal tenure, they were not always raised above temptation, either from the court or the populace. In short, we do not discover that there existed anywhere in France, from the beginning of its political existence as a nation, any of those great and indelible maxims of justice which are the glory of the common law of England—any of those local tribunals, which keep alive in the breasts of the people the knowledge of their rights and the practice of self-government, nor any of those larger central assemblies, in which all classes meet, to state their grievances, to compare their opinions, to unite against a common oppression, and to adjust their conflicting claims.

Is it surprising, then, that the royal authority should have inflamed into monstrous disproportions; that the

kings—legislators from the beginning—commanders of
armies from the beginning—dispensers of justice, with
the exception of some intervals, from the beginning—
should also become the sole administrators? How was
it possible to resist their aggrandizement, except as it
was finally resisted, by popular revolution? Or how,
on the other hand, was it possible for a structure so top-
heavy, so thoroughly without basis, as the old monarchy,
to continue its vertiginous career? At the height of its
glory, which was during the first half of Louis XIVth's
reign, it was already crumbling. It made, for a century
nearly, convulsive efforts to retain an upright position ;
but they were in vain ; it only reeled and staggered the
more, till, under the amiable and helpless Louis Seize,
it fell to the ground.

After this brief historical reference, we are prepared
to estimate the political state of France under the
Louises, which is the proper subject of De Tocqueville's book. The government, as we have seen, was
entirely in the hands of the king : not the general
government alone—that which conducts foreign affairs
and the national interests as a whole—but the government down to its minutest offices in the districts and
towns, with few exceptions. All the parochial business,
even, was transacted by functionaries who were neither
the agents of the local lords or seigneurs, nor the chosen
representatives of the parish (though, in some cases,
they were elected by the peasants), but the appointees
of the royal Intendants. If a parish meeting were to
be held, or a road repaired, or a church or school-house
built, or taxes raised and expended, these officers, holding from the central authority, were the persons charged
with the supervision. They were responsible, not to
the community, but to the Intendants, and these
Intendants were the creatures of the royal council, as

that body immediately surrounding the king, and which had gradually drawn within itself nearly all the supreme judicial and administrative functions, was named. Their powers were scarcely less than those of the council itself, and were exercised by them, for the most part, without much regard to any other end than the exigencies of the State. Thus all ranks of society were dispensed from those habitual interferences in public affairs, which are their best education in the practice of self-government. But while their own energies were paralyzed, they were taught to rely upon those of the government; and the more ignorant soon came to ascribe to it all the vicissitudes of fortune—even the inclemencies of the climate, or the failure of crops, no less than the reverses of war.

M. De Tocqueville says : "The French government, having thus assumed the place of Providence, it was natural that every one should invoke its aid in his individual necessities. Accordingly, we find an immense number of petitions which, while affecting to relate to the public interest, really concern only small individual interests. It is a melancholy task to read them : we find peasants praying to be indemnified for the loss of their cattle or their horses ; wealthy landowners asking for assistance in rendering their estates more productive ; manufacturers soliciting from the Intendant· privileges, by which they may be protected from a troublesome competition ; and very frequently confiding the embarrassed state of their affairs to him, and begging him to obtain for them relief, or a loan from the comptroller-general. Even the nobles were often very importunate solicitors, the only mark of their condition being the lofty tone in which they begged." " Every man already blamed the government for all his sufferings. The most inevitable privations were ascribed to it, and even the inclemency of the seasons was made a subject of reproach to it."

The nobles, though deprived of their powers, still possessed many of their most oppressive privileges, and much of their infatuated exclusiveness. The army was still open to them, and, to a small extent, the seats of justice; but they had almost ceased to display their characteristic gallantry in the one, or to be qualified for influence in the other. Drawn from their estates, on which the old loyal retainer had become the defiant tenant, by the superior attractions of the capital and the court, the love of degenerate pleasure supplanted the former passion for rule. They cultivated wit, grace, agreeable conversation and manners—the qualities which amuse and fascinate in the saloon—instead of the sterner qualities which command in the forum, or win immortal honor on the field. Many of them were debauched—many utterly neglectful of the duties of religion and patriotism—all ruinously extravagant. The life of a court is always a life of expense; and what they were forced to squander on folly in Paris, they tried to reimburse by extortions in the provinces. They could still levy their *cens* and *rentes-foncières* on the poor landed proprietors; they could still raise their tolls from fairs and markets; they could still compel the farmers to grind their corn at the manorial mill, and to press their grapes at the manorial wine-press. But along with the heavy contributions gathered from their tenants, they reaped a bitter harvest of ill-will. Brilliant and beautiful personages, indeed, they were. Not in the world's history have there been more polished and graceful men than the old French *noblesse*—vivacious in talk, seductive in manners; but, alas! they were nearly

as useless as they were polished, and as corrupt as they
were charming.   It was not from them that either the
State or society could expect a regeneration.

As for the middle classes, the *bourgeoisie*, there were
some who—imitating their superiors in respects in
which they were least worthy of imitation—purchasing
offices that they might sport aristocratic titles and affect
aristocratic manners, yet despised by the aristocracy for
their want of blood, and hated by the people for their
aspirations to rank—had been admirably painted by
Molière, in his Dandin and Jourdain.   But there were
others of a very different stamp, who cared little about
alliances with the "illustrious house of Sotenville," or
the "eminent line of the Prudroteries," and pushed their
fortune elsewhere with infinitely greater effect.   Availing themselves of the industrial spirit, which modern
science had awakened, they gathered about them the
most substantial tokens of success.   They were traders,
manufacturers, bankers, and financiers.   With wealth
also came offices—not offices of high-sounding names,
but of the most comfortable emoluments.   The richest
intendencies and comptrollerships, and farmings of the
revenue, were theirs ; while the grave dignities of the
law were showered upon them, and the schools opened
their doors to them, and the rising power of the literary
coteries paid them its court.   For them Colbert and
Turgot administered, and Montesquieu wrote, and the
Destouches and the Beaumarchais, though they knew it
not, cracked their jokes.   Royalty was glad to borrow
their money ; nobility condescended to marry their
daughters ; but, like royalty and like nobility, they had
no bowels for the people, whence they came.   "Though
the career of the nobility," says De Tocqueville, "and
that of the middle classes, had differed widely, there was
one point of resemblance between them—both had

kept themselves aloof from the people. Instead of uniting with the peasantry, the middle classes had shrunk from the contact ; instead of joining with them to combat injustice, they had only sought to aggravate injustice—they had been as eager for exceptional rights as the nobility for privileges. Themselves sprung from the ranks of the peasantry, they had so lost all recollection and knowledge of their former character, that it was not until they had armed the peasants, that they perceived they had roused passions which they could neither gauge, guide, nor restrain, and of which they were destined to be the victims, as well as the authors."

Meanwhile, what was the condition of the people— that goose whom all the others plucked? What has been, what is, the condition of the people everywhere, except in the democracies, and sometimes in them? Ignorance, suffering, wrong, and despair ! But the French peasant, alas ! was the most abused of all people. He vegetated, without guidance, in his misery, save from a Church, which, though adorned by the most accomplished prelates, and the most laborious and kind-hearted curés, was stained by remembrances of St. Bartholomew and the dragonnades. Our author has drawn a fearful picture of the various obstructions by which the movements of the people were resisted, and of the oppressions by which they were overborne ; but fearful as it is, it is yet incomplete. No passion was stronger in the heart of a rural Frenchman than his passion for land—for some little corner of the earth which he might call his own. But in order to buy his land, supposing him to have inherited or amassed money enough to do so, he must pay a tax on the purchase—not to the government, but to one of his neighbors, who owned what was called the *cens*, or perpetual rent. When he is about to put in the seed,

he may be summond to the *corvée*, or to enforced labor
upon his neighbor's land, or on the highway. If his
seed be put in, and the harvest come, his neighbor's
horses and hounds will trample it in pursuit of game,
which he himself has no right to take. The remnant
reaped, he carries it to market, paying a toll on the
road, a toll on the bridge, a toll at the barriers of his
province, and a toll at the market-place. He returns to
his home, where he would consume the surplus of his
produce in his family; but he finds that he must take
the grain to the mill of his neighbor to be ground, and
the flour to the oven of his neighbor to be baked; and
then the tax-collectors will call upon him for a twentieth
or a tenth of it in value, for the dues of the government; and the Church will exact its dues, and for every
moment that he withholds the amount, legal charges
attach and accumulate, till the land itself is scarcely
worth the claims against it. " Picture, if you can," says
De Tocqueville, " the condition, the wants, the character, the passions of such a man, and estimate the store
of envy and hatred he is laying up in his heart!"

What aggravated the sense of wrong under these multiplied burdens, was the perception that the kings were
squandering millions upon idle wars, debauched favorites, and insolent courtezans. The conquests of the
Grand Monarque had ended in financial embarrass-
ments, which no subtlety of Mazarin, no skill of Colbert could avert; the orgies of the Regency had turned
the world of commerce into a gambling-house, and the
world of fashion into a bagnio: the reign of Louis XV.
was ridiculed by his fellow-monarchs even, as the reign
of the petticoats, under which the licentious atrocities
of the *parc aux cerfs* surpassed the atrocities of the grottoes of Capri. For more than half a century, the State
had writhed and tossed with disorders of finance, impos-

sible to heal. Neither exactions nor arbitrary taxes, which only iritated the more—nor secret bankruptcies and confiscations, which only disaffected the more—nor yet the sale of offices and the substitution of paper for gold, which only intoxicated the more, could stop the ravages of the great cancerous deficit. All the wisest doctors of the purse, from Sully to Necker, had been employed on that disease, with partial reliefs ending in permanent aggravations. What were the labors of the Danaïdes, drawing water in sieves, to those of a French minister? The problem was, out of nothing and less, to extract much—and desperate were the attempts at the solution. Yet the gay creatures of the court—represented in the one sex by an Abbé Dubois, and in the other by Pompadour—went on singing, and dancing, and eating their "pleasant little suppers in pleasant little mansions,"—as Rochefoucault names them, "consecrated to Cupid and his mother, and more enchanting than Paphos or Idalia,"—as carelessly as the Pompeians may be supposed to have feasted on that sickly night, when a sulphurous cloud suddenly enveloped the hillside of Vesuvius.

All the while that French society was undergoing the slow but certain process of decomposition, there was one solid and enduring power growing up—the power of the Pen—which was but another name for that of Opinion. It is common to class the writers of that age under the general term of *philosophes*, but they were as multitudinous in their kinds almost as the stars of the sky, and they agreed only in the determination to reduce everything to its naked elementary principles. Voltaire, the Mephistopheles, led on his glittering rabble of wits and epigrammatists; Montesquieu commanded the firmer cohorts of the publicists, and Rousseau, from his solitude, swayed the pathetic bands of senti-

mentalists and dreamers. They railed and scoffed,
they reasoned and declaimed, they cracked jokes and
enacted plays, laughing and weeping all to one end—
the subversion of that world of complicated and stupid
traditional privileges which harassed society. As we
read it, at this day, the greater part of that motley literature seems quite inadequate to the effects it produced ;
but that is because we read it without feeling the
deeper spirit out of which it sprang. Much of it is
shallow ; much of it wanton—a mere windy and brilliant *schaum-wesen* or foam ; and all of it skeptical ; yet
it is easy to see that the skepticism and wantonness,
like the shallowness and glitter, are on the surface,
while there is a soul within its soul, a depth beyond its
depth, in the whole spirit of the age which it represented.
Beneath the bubbles and froth of the stream, swept a
mighty under-current of earnest thought and passionate
enthusiasm. Voltaire was a scoffer and a trifler, but
any one who will read his letters on the cases of Calas
and others, will see that he could be, also, a fanatic
for liberty. Like him, the age scoffed and trifled, but
its heart was fearfully in earnest. What everybody felt,
what each one tried to express, in his way—in puns
and plays, as in profound dissertations—was, that right
was greater than might—that nature was better than
convention—that reason was superior to authority—and
that institutions were made for man, and not man for
institutions. Superficial, quotha, but could there have
been grander or profounder thoughts than these ? Had
not the world travailed with them since the advent of
Christ ? Had not martyrs died, and heroes fought, and
all the wise, and good, and gentle souls of the earth
struggled for these, as of the very essence of the gospel ?
And now, after eighteen hundred years, in dim, confused shapes, but veritably, they had got possession of a

whole people—of a people wretched, yet gallant, excitable by mere impulses to transports of ferocity— " more capable of heroism than of virtue, fuller of genius than good sense"—suspicious and generous, vain and self-sacrificing alike, and thoroughly persuaded, as Carlyle says, that nothing stood between them and a golden age but a few traitors. That people arose, and it was the Revolution ! It arose, not in its wrath at first, but with a calm, sublime energy. All ranks, each individual, appeared to be animated by a generous love of reform ; but the obstructions were as inveterate as they were numerous to fret it into impatience. The leaders of every party were incompetent, none knowing what he wished, or how to accomplish it when he did know. The king was amiable, but weak, the nobles better courtiers than chiefs, and the republicans rhetors who had learned their phrases out of the annals of Greece and Rome. Of the men that early assumed the command, the best hearts among them, like Lafayette and the Girondists, had very little head, and the best heads, like Mirabeau and Danton, had corrupt hearts. They could not act together, and there was no positive doctrine capable of crystallizing the molten metal into form.

The Revolution came, and it came, as alone it could come, after such antecedents, in anarchy and bloodshed,—a hideous outbreak of vengeance ; a wild frenzy of alternate hope and despair ; purging, consuming, desolating ; but, like a tropical tornado, which, if it sweeps everything before it, levels also the jungles in which the wild beasts have taken refuge, and cleanses the deadly pest-bearing air.

But of the conduct of the Revolution and its results, we may, perhaps, have an opportunity to speak when our author shall have presented the second volume which he promises on this subject.

MOTLEY'S RISE OF THE DUTCH REPUBLIC.*

R. MOTLEY has chosen, for his début on the historic stage, one of the most significant episodes in the whole of the early struggles of the modern era. The revolt of the Netherlands against the political and ecclesiastical domination of Spain, was a part of that great contest carried on throughout the sixteenth century, between the Teutonic Protestant nations, with their decided tendency to intellectual freedom and territorial division, and the Romanic Catholic nations, with their no less decided bias toward intellectual acquiescence and the unity of government. We may pronounce it the most pregnant part of this contest. All the influences of race, politics, and religion, which came in conflict in the general movements of the age, were concentrated in these lesser conflicts. The encounters that took place on the spongy sands and amid the watery dykes of the Low Countries, rehearsed in little that gigantic drama of war and bloodshed, which, a few years later, convulsed the entire continent.

It is this fact which lends to the Dutch war its high importance in world-history. Had it been simply the wrestle of a few oppressed provinces against a power-

---

* *The Rise of the Dutch Republic. A History.* By JOHN LOTHROP MOTLEY. 3 vols. Harper & Brothers, 1856.
From *Putnam's Monthly*, June, 1856.

ful invader, we might find for it many a parallel. But
it was a great deal more than that : it was a direct and
desperate grapple between the fellest oppositions of
the time, animated by its profoundest animosities,
and big with magnificent or disastrous results. Ever
since the accession of Charles V. to the crowns of Spain
and the Empire, the real and pervading issue of Europe
lay in the necessary antagonism of the principles of
unity and absolutism in Church and State, and the principles of national independence, and civil and moral
freedom. The former were asserted by the splendid
monarchy of Spain, linked in with the religious hierarchy of Rome, while the latter found their chief adherents among the distracted northern States of Germany,
and the no less distracted commercial provinces of the
Netherlands. Charles V., and, subsequently, Philip
II., who inherited his policy, if not his wisdom, in
seeking the formation of a great State which should
possess a common government, and a common religion, encountered their most formidable obstacles in
the spirit which had been growing for centuries, of national independence, intellectual culture, commercial
activity, and religious freedom. In Germany, the intellectual and moral elements of this opposition were the
strongest, and came to a head earlier in the outbreak of
Luther ; but in the Netherlands, the national and commercial element prevailed, and was some time longer
in ripening. But wherever these principles clashed,
the shock was deadly and fearful, and nowhere more so
than in the Netherlands, because nowhere were the antagonisms more direct, universal, and inveterate.

The people of the Netherlands, mainly descended
from the old Batavian and Belgic races, who, overcome
by the superior forces of the Romans, had contributed,
for four centuries, the most effective arm to the legions

of their conquerors, were earlier than the rest of Europe emancipated from the serfdom of the middle ages. Their favorable position on the north seas, and on the shores of navigable streams, outlets to the continent, gathering them into towns, had led them to a profitable commerce, and to a most flourishing external and political condition. The affluence flowing in upon them from east and west, attracted population, fostered arts, enlivened society, and developed, while it fortified, the sense of individual dignity and worth. Along with growing trade, a growing independence, intrenched behind municipal privileges, inured them to self-trust and free exertion. As early as the eleventh and twelfth centuries, the power of the sovereign in the Netherlands was strictly limited by the power of the estates, in which the trades, as well as the nobility, were represented. Without their consent, no law could be enacted, no war undertaken, no tax imposed, no change in the currency effected, and no foreigner allowed to take part in the government. Even under the rule of the powerful Dukes of Burgundy, who sought to reduce them to subjection, this substantial liberty had been maintained. At a later day, when the Emperor Maximilian, backed by all the might of the Roman German empire, endeavored to inflict extraordinary taxes upon them, and to quarter his troops in the provinces, they instantly flew to arms, and made no scruple of seizing his person, and confining him until they had extorted satisfactory assurances of future security. They were republicans in spirit, if not in name. They prized that sturdy burgher independence which had made them what they were, and, at a time of almost universal war and universal abjectness, had not only raised their cities into cities of opulence, but had made them, also, cities of refuge for the world.

Under these circumstances, the transition from civil to religious freedom was not difficult. At the on-coming of the Reformation, the Netherlanders were nominally Catholics; but nowhere were the new doc-trines more gratefully welcomed than among them, or more rapidly spread. Introduced through a thou-sand channels—by the Protestant traders of Germany, by the English and French fugitives from persecution, by their own children educated at Geneva, by the Swiss mercenaries of the Emperor, even—they speedily dif-fused themselves over the land, like the waters of the sea when one of their dykes had broken. A hard-working people, they had little respect for the luxurious indolence of the monks; and a plain, simple-hearted people, they were more attracted by the intellectual charms of doctrine than by the sensuous splendors of ritual.

The Spanish nation, on the other hand, by nature arrogant, and by training superstitious, was the willing slave of a double despotism, of a mighty but oppres-sive monarchy, and of an imposing but subtle and self-ish ecclesiasticism. Its recent conquest of Granada had rekindled its enthusiasm to the fiery pitch of the crusades; its discovery of the New World had given a vent to the most romantic spirit of adventure, as well as to the most ferocious cupidity; while the magnifi-cent extent of its dominion filled it with unbounded audacity and pride. Every incident in the events of the time conspired to raise in the mind of the Spaniard the dangerous consciousness of his greatness. Master of half of Europe, and of nearly all America, with pos-sessions in Africa, in Asia, and among the rich Spice Islands of the Indian seas, the favorite of the Holy Pontiff, the assumed vicegerent of Christ, and the spiritual guide of a hundred million souls, the Spaniard seemed to himself to hold the keys of all the treasures of earth, and of all the glories of Heaven. "He was the man of the Lord, and the lord of man ;" he had fused the powerful kingdoms of the peninsula into a single more powerful kingdom ; he had driven the Saracen from Europe in the midst of a sanguinary resistance ; he had been victorious over France ; he had ravaged Italy ; and he had despoiled a new continent of its wealth. His statesmen were the ablest that had appeared since the most flourishing days of Greece, and his soldiers the bravest that had appeared since the most flourishing days of Rome. His soldiers, indeed, were brave with more than Roman bravery. To the animal courage and national ambition of the Roman, they added the romantic valor of chivalry and the impulsive zeal as well as the stoical endurance of religion.

It was not surprising, then, that the Spaniard should pride himself on his superiority among the nations; yet he valued the steadfastness which had distinguished his faith, and rendered him its elected champion, more than the triumph of his arms or the seductions of his policy. At a time when the people everywhere were falling away from the ancient Church, like leaves from a smitten tree—when Germany, Holland, England, France, Sweden, and Switzerland were stirred to their depths by religious schism, and even Italy was retained in the fold of the faithful only by the profound craft of a milder and more liberal policy on the part of Rome—the Spaniard remained unaffected. The only result of the agitation, so far as man could see, had been to induce him to draw tighter the bands of intolerance, and to heap fresh fuel upon the fires of the inquisition. "Times of refreshing," says Macaulay, describing this period, "came to all neighboring countries ; but one people alone remained, like the fleece of the Hebrew warrior, dry in the midst of that benignant and fertilizing dew. Among the men of the sixteenth century, the Spaniard was the man of the fifteenth century, or of a still darker period—delighted to behold an *Auto da Fé*, or ready to volunteer on a crusade."

It was the mistake of Philip II., when he came to reign over these two peoples, more remote from each other in their spiritual affinities than in their local positions, to suppose that he could transfer the institutions of the one to the soil of the other, and change, by a stroke of a pen the inwrought results of centuries. Receiving the Provinces at the moment of their highest bloom, when they contained more flourishing towns than there were days in the year, when the revenues exacted from them were more copious than all the mines of South America, when the temper of the people, made moderate by plenty and content, was remarkably placable, nothing would have been easier for him than to retain their allegiance. He had only, like a wise statesman, to adapt his measures to the exigences of the situation. But Philip was not a statesman. A Spaniard of the Spaniards, with the worst traits of his nation aggravated by the gloomy, monkish education he had received—dark, revengeful, and superstitious, without one generous sentiment or a single noble ambition—he had conceived an ideal of government better fitted to the satrapies of an oriental tyrant than to the court of a Christian monarch. His father, Charles V., though scarcely less a despot in action than he, was a despot who had tempered his rule by friendly concessions, and dazed the sense of his wrongs by a blaze of brilliant exploits. Born among the Flemings, he had surrounded his person with Flemings ; and the Flemings received some of the reflected lustre of his glory. He was arbitrary, but arbitrary from policy, and not, as Philip

was, from preference.   Narrowness, bigotry, and hatred
were the inborn qualities of the son, who had achieved
no great deeds to awaken admiration, and exhibited
no tenderness to conciliate love.   Distrusted and disliked by his northern subjects, from the very hour when,
a young man, he had showed himself reserved and
haughty amid the genial festivities of the celebrated ab-
dication, he returned their aversion with a double
venom.   He never comprehended the sturdy citizen-
independence of those prosperous burghers.   He never
sympathized in their pursuits, nor admired their lowly
citizen-like virtues.   He was impatient of their traditional privileges; he was piqued by their boasts of freedom ; he was jealous of those among their nobles whom
he did not despise, and he scorned their seeming feebleness.   Had they never aroused his deep religious enmities, they would not have been his favorites ; but when
they gave an eager entrance to the Reformation, when, in
the natural over-action of a new movement, long suppressed, their rabble broke the images of his saints, and
scattered the sacred relics of his sanctuaries, they were,
from the instant, doomed to an unheard-of vengeance.

They were doomed, however, not in a frenzy of ex-
asperation, not in the heat of outraged prejudices nor
in a sudden burst of unreasoning resentment, but
with slow, cold, calculating, subtle, and implacable
malignity.   For with Philip the name of heretic was
a synonym of miscreant, wretch, criminal, outcast, or
whatever else is odious to man and abandoned of
God.   The inhuman theology of the time he sincerely
believed, and he was prepared to enforce its remorseless
sanctions with all the cowled treacheries of the inquisition, and all the crushing energies of the first of States.
Active in brain, but inactive in body, his movements
were wily, rather than impetuous ; but whether slow or

swift, he contrived that they should be fatal. If he hastened his purposes, it was only to anticipate the chances of possible escape ; and when he tarried in them, it was only to render the means more sure, and the execution final. They who read the memoirs always think of him, as he sat amid the schemes of his far-reaching empire, as of some sullen and gigantic spider in the midst of his web, entrapping his poor victims on every hand, and darting forth only when their struggles threaten to break through his infernal meshes.

The agents whom Philip selected for the execution of his vengeance upon the offending Netherlands, were fit implements of his double nature, as a churchman and a king. They were first the Cardinal Granville, and afterward the Duke of Alva—the one as subtle an ecclesiastic as ever concealed the rancors of hell beneath the smiles of heaven; and the other as inflexible a soldier as ever stalked through rivers of blood to do a master's will. Granville, whose real name was Anthony Peronet, was a Frenchman by birth, and had taken his first lessons in state-craft under Charles V., as his deputy at the Council of Trent. He had served the Emperor, also, in subsequent negotiations, and had had the adroitness to get himself retained in the service of the son. Secretary to Margaret of Parma, the nominal regent of the Netherlands, he speedily made himself the real regent. To a mind of rare penetration and comprehensiveness, he united great learning, great diligence, great patience, and the most remarkable acuteness in devising as well as unravelling plots. Always at his post, he was always prepared for events. Penetrating the depth of his master's mind, he apprehended his wishes almost before they were formed. He carried them into effect with a graceful audacity, which flattered the imperial self-love without surprising his vanity. Devoted to the throne, more even than to the Church, fertile in expedients, indefatigable in labor, and of polished and insinuating manners, he grew the indispensable confidant of Philip.

But he was more solicitous in gaining the friendship of his sovereign, than he was successful in appeasing the discontents of the subject. All the acts of the government being charged to him, he became an intolerable offence to the nobles as well as to the people. It was only after much delay, with great reluctance on the part of the king, and not until he had sowed the seeds of irreconcilable divisions, that he was compelled to retire before the storm which they raised against him. As a foreigner, his very existence as an official was a violation of the ancient constitution. Surrounding himself with foreigners, besides, he had repulsed the entire body of the native aristocracy. Retaining an extraordinary force of Spanish troops in the country, he had to bear the brunt of their repeated misconduct. Quartering a multitude of new bishops on the dioceses, he had offended religious prejudices and increased the taxes ; and favoring secretly the processes of the inquisition, he had alarmed the suspicions and fears of the people, through whom the very name of that tribunal sent a thrill of horror. Philip had dallied and equivocated in regard to his removal, until the discontents were spread through all classes of the nobility, and down even among the lowest ranks of the populace. A timelier intervention might have relieved this state of affairs ; but, on the recall of Granville, matters had gone so far that the slight concessions announced but whetted the rage for more. There remained no alternative for Philip, but to yield to an extent which would have damaged his supremacy, or to settle the difficulties at once by the sword. True to his nature, he made choice of a governor, to supersede the feeble and trembling Margaret, whose character alone, apart from the enormous power with which he was invested, would have shown to which side of this alternative Philip inclined. The Duke of Alva was sent into the Netherlands, after a pompous preliminary parade, and at the head of ten thousand men. A person better adapted to the execution of Philip's designs did not then exist. He was the foremost warrior of Europe, who had triumphed on every field but one ; and he was as distinguished for the asperity of his manners as he was for the intrepidity of his valor. "As a man," says Mr. Motley, somewhat naively, " his character was simple. He did not combine a great variety of vices, but those which he had were colossal, and he possessed no virtues. He was neither lustful nor intemperate, but his professed eulogists admitted his enormous avarice, while the world has agreed that such an amount of stealth and ferocity, of patient vindictiveness and universal bloodthirstiness, were never found in a savage beast of the forest, and but rarely in a human bosom."

Inexperienced as a statesman, and without talent, save in his profession, this soulless, cast-iron man joined to the methods of the soldier, which move "straightforward, like a cannon-ball," the craftier methods of the inquisitor. His administration, beginning with a Judas-like betrayal of Counts Egmont and Horn, followed by their worse than Pilate-like trial and execution —murders almost unparalleled, for the pathetic interest which clings to the victims, and for the reckless atrocity in the perpetrators—was marked throughout by every vice of tyranny. Mr. Motley has summed up the results in the following terrific, but not exaggerated passage :

" The tens of thousands in those miserable provinces who fell victims to the gallows, the sword, the stake, the living grave, or to living banishment, have never been counted ; for those statistics of barbarity are often effaced from human record. Enough, however, is known, and enough has been recited in the preceding pages. No mode in which human beings have ever caused their fellow-creatures to suffer, was omitted from daily practice. Men, women, and children, old and young, nobles and paupers, opulent burghers, hospital patients, lunatics, dead bodies, all were indiscriminately made to furnish food for the scaffold and the stake. Men were tortured, beheaded, hanged by the neck and by the legs, burned before slow fires, pinched to death with red hot tongs, broken upon the wheel, starved and flayed alive. Their skins stripped from the living body, were stretched upon drums, to be beaten in the march of their brethren to the gallows. The bodies of many who had died a natural death were exhumed, and their festering remains hanged upon the gibbet, on pretext that they had died without receiving the sacrament, but in reality that their property might become the legitimate prey of the treasury. Marriages of long standing were dissolved by order of government, that rich heiresses might be married against their will to foreigners whom they abhorred. Women and children were executed for the crime of assisting their fugitive husbands and parents with a penny in their utmost need, and even for consoling them with a letter in their exile. Such was the regular course of affairs as administered by the Blood-Council. The additional barbarities committed amid the sack and ruin of those blazing and starving cities are almost beyond belief; unborn infants were torn from the living bodies of their mothers ; women and children were violated by thousands ; and whole populations burned and hacked to pieces by soldiers in every mode which cruelty, in its wanton ingenuity, could devise."

While we shudder at the contemplation of such a character, and are oppressed with fears lest his ruthless persecution should extinguish the innocent people of the Netherlands, we are relieved by the appearance on the scene of another personage. William, the Prince of Orange, emerging brightly from the earlier clouds of these gloomy troubles, grows more luminous and beautiful as the darkness thickens and disasters accumulate. The heir of a noble house, opulent and sumptuous, but refined and accomplished in all the humanities of the time, he comes before us, first as the favorite of the Emperor Charles, whose hands rested upon his shoulder in that imperial display at Brussels, when, like Diocletian, he relinquished the glories of the crown. We find him next among the band of stately nobles encompassing the throne of Margaret, who sought to mollify the harsher edicts of the king, and to guide her government aright. A calm, observant, indomitable spirit —plastic enough to assume the impressions of the moment, but never so weak as to sink under them—friendly, social, ambitious, but self-centred and equal to any destiny, "no o'ergrowths of complexion breaking down the pales and forts of reason," William was finally recognized by all parties as the master of the epoch—by his friends, who put unlimited trust in him, and by his enemies, who felt toward him a no less unlimited fear. "He was born," as Schiller says, "to command the respect and to win the hearts of men." Less enthusiastic and wiser than either Egmont or Horn, he avoided the complicities into which they fell, while his self-respect restrained him from the orgies of Brederode, and his early religious indifference from the fanaticism of the sectaries.

But though he did not mingle in the turbulent assemblages of the preachers, nor echo the wild war-cries of

the Gueux, he did not less keenly feel the sufferings of
his country, nor less energetically resist the wrongs
of her oppressor. By a singular reticence of temper,
which, in the wisdom of Polonius's advice, "allowed
thought no tongue, nor any unproportioned thought
his act," he kept aloof from the popular ferments, and
yet was too impressible and generous to feel aloof from
the popular afflictions. With the unerring instinct of
the heart, the people everywhere felt him to be their
friend. They saw how his earnestness rose with the occasion, and how his piety awoke and grew as the woes
endured by others deepened before him. Thus, his
moderation at the outset had the double effect of gaining
him a universal confidence, and of preparing him,
while others retired from the combat exhausted and
broken, to enter it as if afresh. He protested and appealed, so long as protests and appeals appeared to be
available ; but when it was seen that the hour for these
was past, he drew the sword and threw away the scabbard. His rank, his fortune, his eloquence, his industry, his genius, his religion, all that he had, and all that
he was, were then given to the cause with a cheerful and
unflagging alacrity. The man to whom Philip, had he
been a wise and good king, as he was a bad and foolish
one, would have committed the government of his
provinces, was now become his unrelenting enemy.
The man whom he could not bribe, nor entrap, nor
quell, was now, by the simple force of principle, the
most formidable foe which his monarchy had yet encountered.

It was, however, a long and weary way that Orange
had to tread before the world was destined to reap the
fruits of his patriotism and virtue—a way all saturated
in blood, encompassed with difficulties, broken by vicissitudes, and ending at last in his own death. The im-

agination looks almost in vain through history for a
sadder yet nobler figure than that which William
presented during the forlorner periods of his undertaking. We see the mate of emperors, the splendid and
wealthy noble, accustomed to the shows of rank and the
solaces of friendship, having sacrificed his fortune and
abandoned his home, stripped of his dignities, and
wandering alone, almost penniless, an outcast among
foreign nations, eagerly soliciting aid for his country,
and, by superhuman efforts, striving to organize an
army. As we follow his painful career at that crisis, we
think involuntarily of that noble exile of our own day,
who now weeps, deserted, in the streets of London, the
fallen fortunes of his dear Hungary, and the pitiless
revulsions of time. But the peculiarity of William's
position, unlike that of Kossuth, was, that he stood
almost entirely alone. Arrayed against the mightiest
monarchy of the earth, there were few who dared to
sympathize in his struggles, and none to comprehend
his designs. The reluctant allies, whom he gained by
his persuasions, fled like sheep on the first reverses.
The soldiers, whom he raised by promises, were mercenaries, whose demands he had no money to meet. The
patriots who acted with him, were headstrong, violent,
impatient of control; and too often animated by the
spirit of the freebooter, rather than by his own wise and
disinterested love of justice, they imitated the excesses
which had made the Spaniard hideous. His most
efficient helpers, the adherents of the new religion, were
the bitter partisans of sect, and not, like him, the champions of universal tolerance. Time and time again was
he betrayed by the dissensions of Calvinist and Lu-
theran ; and, time and time again, when his prospects
were at the highest, when fortune seemed to be about to
float him on the waves of success to the fullest fruition

of his hopes, some rashness of a leader, or some instability of the rabble, who were his troops, would plunge him into the abysses of helplessness and despair.

It is remarkable, however, all through these most desperate miscarriages and defeats—even after that most gigantic treachery which history records, when the king of France, having lured him on by promises of assistance against the Catholics, consummated his plan on the night of St. Bartholomew, in the blood of thirty thousand Huguenots—how his soul retained its elasticity, its courage, and its confidence.   In his hours of deepest distress, he did not wholly despond ; looking calmly to the issue of things, he estimated their transient changes rightly ; and while the vast fabric of his enterprises was tumbling in ruins around him, and carrying with it, to the eyes of others, the fortunes of his country, he trusted in the vitality of his cause, and clung to his faith in God.   In this far-seeing firmness, this immovable constancy of purpose, this invincible superiority to the smaller as well as larger persecutions of fate, he stood a type of our own Washington, who was never so great and triumphant as in those dark hours when others would have been baffled and cast down.

United to this equanimity in adverse circumstances was a rare and fertile power of combination, by which he extracted success out of failure.   Among the many skirmishes, battles, and sieges between the Spaniards and the Netherlanders, the former, owing to their superiority in every point of discipline and effectiveness, were invariably the victors, and yet as invariably they gained little by success. . Scarcely had the echoes of triumph died away, before they were called upon to meet some new conjuncture, which the Prince had arranged, seemingly more formidable than that which they had just overcome.   In political intrigue as in military movements, he evinced this same marvellous command of untoward events. When the romantic Don John, the brilliant hero of Lepanto, was sent to the Low Countries, to recover by smiles what Alva had lost by the axe and the sword, nothing could have been more promising than the prospects opened to him, by his gay feastings of the men and his gallant flatteries of the women. He had only to win the sombre William, to render the nation all his own. He made the attempt ; he cajoled, he coaxed, he wheedled, he presented the most gorgeous pictures to the ambition and selfishness of the Prince, and in a little while found himself hemmed in on every side, deprived of his armies, abhorred by the nation, and heartily sick both of the Netherlanders and William. Again, when the Catholic nobles, jealous of the power of the Prince, invited the Archduke Matthias of Austria to come over and help them, the silent William consented : Matthias was made the Governor-General, and William his lieutenant; but it was soon remarked by everybody, that William was the real ruler, and Matthias only his secretary. Then, in order to retrieve this false move, the nobles invited over the French Duke of Alençon, to which William also consented. When Alençon came, he was glad to accept the mere barren honors by which Orange neutralized his powers of mischief, without turning him into an enemy. In fact, as a politician, William had no equal in that day, and had he possessed but half the force of his enemies, or had the people for whose weal he labored been united, he might have easily attained a complete and final success. But the materials with which he wrought were of the most perverse and refractory kind, and the good which might have been achieved in five years, was spread over a lifetime.

We share with Mr. Motley his admiration of the

character of William ; we regard him as both a good
and great man ; in liberality and justice of sentiment
he was far in advance of his age ; his ability in the
management of affairs was amazing ; and he was rightly
called the Father of the People.   But we think that he
sometimes carried his policy of reserve to the point of
dissimulation.   He clung to the illusion of royalty long
after an abandonment of it would have been justified.
He deliberated when he ought to have struck, and
sometimes he finessed when he should have taken the
trick.   We are aware of the sinister and tortuous
policy with which he had to contend, and how difficult
it is at this day to estimate justly the complex and
counteracting influences of obscure events ; but we
still feel, in spite of the prepossessions excited by Mr.
Motley's splendid advocacy, that a more impulsive
quality of mind would have assisted his efforts, and
raised him to a loftier niche of greatness.   It would
be unfair, however, on this account, to deny his exalted
merits as a statesman.   Through prodigious difficulties,
and by unexampled sacrifices, he accomplished the
emancipation of the United Provinces, and laid the
foundation of a glorious national structure.   At a time
when the colonies of North America were yet unknown, a half century before the Puritans had landed
at Plymouth, while Frobisher was making his second
voyage, and Gilbert and Raleigh were only beginning
to people the new world, the Dutch Republic, in anticipation of our own, had "bequeathed to the world
of thought the great idea of the toleration of all opinions, and, to the world of action, the prolific principle
of federal union."   It is the eternal honor of Holland,
and of those by whom her redemption was procured,
that she was the first among the modern nations to ex-
emplify in practice a Christian State.

The story of the battles and sufferings by which these events were brought about, is told by Mr. Motley with remarkable animation and skill. Availing himself of all the original authorities to be found in the various archives of Belgium and Holland, he has constructed a narrative full of interest and instruction. He paints the confused scenes of the period he has chosen to describe—its great and little passions, its atrocious and its noble men, its terrible sieges and picturesque festivals, bridals in the midst of massacres, its fights upon the sea and under the sea, its torture-fires and blood-baths—in vivid colors, with a bold, free hand, and with a masterly knowledge of effect. Whatever was dramatic in those fierce conflicts he has seized ; whatever is peculiar or striking in character, he has penetrated ; whatever is significant of time or place, he appropriates : while he has never forgotten the great purpose of history, which is, the illustration of moral power. It is impossible to read a page of his book without feeling that his mind is one of unusual vigor, and that his heart beats with generous blood. We gratefully welcome him, therefore, to the number of our most successful historians.

Let us add, at the same time, that his work is disfigured by certain defects, which it would be well to correct in subsequent editions. The style is ambitiously rhetorical, in many places, and throughout needs simplicity. The headings of the chapters are often offensively undignified and colloquial. His irony, too, sometimes degenerates into mere sneering, and his attempts at humor are almost always out of place. As a whole, the narrative is too diffuse. A great many needless episodes are introduced, and details are given of unimportant incidents. Forgetting the impartiality of the historian, our author pleads the cause of the Netherlands, in certain cases, in which he should deliver their sentence.

There were occasions, in the course of their struggle, when they conducted themselves with extreme meanness, as well as atrocity, and which sadly mar the effect of the heroic picture which Mr. Motley seems anxious to present. These he passes over rather hurriedly, although he omits no opportunity which is furnished him for censuring the Spaniards. In a few historical allusions, also not falling directly within his course, we notice that he is inaccurate. He speaks, for instance, of Thomas Muncer as a leader of the anabaptists, and denounces by implication his personal character. Now Munzer (which is the real name) was a leader of the peasants, during the peasants' war in Germany; was in no wise connected with the anabaptists—who came on the scene ten years later than he—and was a man of lofty religious character. The least agreeable part of these volumes is the historic introduction, which smacks a little of the stilted style of Mr. Carlyle, the worst model, perhaps, both grammatically and rhetorically, that a young writer could adopt. Yet these are trivial blemishes in a work of incomparable merit, and which absorbs the reader's attention from the preface to the close.

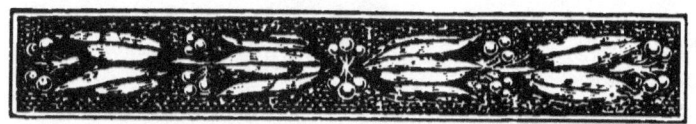

EMERSON ON ENGLAND.*

HE position of Mr. Emerson in our literature is so well-defined and established, that it no longer excites to controversy. His characteristics, as a thinker or writer, his peculiar points of view, and his methods of stating them, his keen insight, his utter want of logic, his limpid, racy style, his occasional obscurities—in short, his merits and defects, whatever we may think of them, are known, and demand no further comment. We say that he is Emerson, and have described him. Now and then, a half-crazy dyspeptic, like Gilfillan, fires off a pop-gun at him, but no one hears the report nor cares for it, and the unconscious object of it still walks forward with his serene and lofty smile.

This position, it is worthy of note, Emerson won soon after his first appearance, and has steadily maintained, without material increase or diminution, up to the present time. His little book on "Nature" revealed to discerning minds all that he has since become. He is to them no greater now than he was then. His last and seventh volume is no better than his first. There is more richness and mellowness of style in it, perhaps, but otherwise it is the same. Nor does this seeming

---

English Traits. By R. W. EMERSON. Boston : Phillips, Sampson & Co., 1856.

From *Putnam's Monthly,* Oct., 1856.

want of growth argue any defect of genius.　Goethe used to say of Schiller that if you separated from him for a week you would be astonished on meeting him again, by the prodigious strides in advance that he had made in the interval ; but the reason was that Schiller did not begin as a master.　He presented himself as a pupil, and you afterward saw the steps of his progress. Mr. Emerson, on the other hand, stepped into the arena with a native control of his powers and resources.　He did not have to learn the use of his tools by using them, but was born to their use.　His intellect, from the outset, appeared so clear, so penetrating, so fresh, so capable, that it promised everything that it has since performed.　It prepared us by its immediate qualities against future surprises.　Of every new manifestation of it, we feel that it is just what we expected.　Some minds suffer a kind of ebb and flow in their inspirations —are now dull and depressed, and then glowing with life ; but there are others which possess a steady, permanent action, like crystals which are brilliant in every light, or like stars which shine forever.　Our author's is of the latter sort.

In this work on England, we see Mr. Emerson in a new field and in a new atmosphere, but it is the same Emerson.　His theme is a much larger one than he has before tried, but he treats it in the old vein.　What he has hitherto done in kitcat and cabinet sizes, he now essays in the broader historical style.　The old manner is, however, retained.　The practical, concrete life of England is described, but it is described from the high region of philosophy.　It is painted (for Mr. Emerson is artist as well as philosopher), but it is painted for the thought rather than the eye.　We do not mean that there is any want of color or warmth in the picture—in fact, there is an intense reality in it ; but it is a reality for the intellect more than for the senses, which the brain touches more than the hand.

John Bull has often sat for his portrait, but never before to a limner so coldly clairvoyant as this. Puckler Muskau and Von Raumer, Philarete Chasles and Bulwer, to say nothing of innumerable lesser artists—Italian, French, German, American, and native—have attempted likenesses of him, have given us sketches, more or less exact, of his head, face, and looks ; but here is one who dissects him in order to paint him; who turns him inside out, exhibiting such bowels as he has, and more than that, trepans his brain for him to show what texture it is of, and thrusts his hand into his chest to measure the power of the life-pulses. His country, his origin, his achievements in enterprise and literature —his character and religion—his greatnesses, which are many, and his littlenesses, which are no less, are daguerreotyped with a perfectly free hand, and yet with the utmost sincerity.

Few men in this country were better qualified, in many respects, to approach this subject than Mr. Emerson. As a scholar of wide and various reading, familiar with the results of all the older civilizations, he was already furnished with standards for a wise comparative judgment. Never having been engaged in actual life, whether political or mercantile, he was free from the prejudices which the details of affairs are apt to engender. By habit and training accustomed to the formation of general opinions, seeing things in their broader relations by the pure light of the intellect, he was not liable to be warped by his immediate observation, nor to gaze through the discolored mediums of passion. At the same time, a man eminent in his sphere, he was eminently well received abroad. The most secluded circles of cultivation were open to him, in their friendliest aspects ; he saw what he saw in its best guise, but he saw it undazzled by accessory splendors ; while he was free to move, in lower every-day walks, himself unobserved, yet observant of all that it was pertinent to note. These were his advantages as an observer ; but to opportunity, to sharpness and alacrity of vision, to susceptibility and insight, he joined the ability of utterance. A rare command of the subtler forces of language—a racy, idiomatic, sinewy, yet polished and graceful style, render his execution as charming as it is trenchant and impressive.

. But, it should not be disguised that, in other respects, Mr. Emerson was not precisely the man that the world would have chosen to take the gauge and measure of England's success. As an abstract philosopher, more profoundly moved by the deeper relations of thought and sentiment than by the practical every-day life of men, it was to be doubted whether he would seize the peculiar genius of the most practical of all the nations. It was to be feared that he would dwell more upon the inward springs and sources of its character than upon its real achievements. The English people are not so much a people of thoughts and sentiments as of deeds. They are the most *institutional* people on earth, and, to be comprehended rightly, they must be studied, in their laws and governments as well as in their manners, literature, and religion. Whether Mr. Emerson has studied them in this wise, we shall, perhaps, inquire in the sequel.

The problem, which our author proposes to himself, after a brief record of an early visit to England, in 1833—during which he saw Coleridge, Landor, Carlyle, Wordsworth, etc.—is, Why England is England ? What are the elements of that power which the English hold over other nations ? If there be one test of

national genius, universally accepted, it is success ; and
if there be one successful country in the universe, for
the last millennium, that country is England. What is
the secret of it ?

This is a broad question, and in proceeding to
answer it, Mr. Emerson first glances at the land itself,
in which there is a singular combination of favorable
conditions. The climate, neither hot nor cold, enables
you to work every hour in the year. The soil abounds
in every material for work, except wood—with coal,
salt, tin, iron, potter's clay, stone, and good arable
earth. The perpetual rains keep the rivers full for floating productions everywhere. Game of every kind animates the immense heaths, and the waters spawn with
fish. As an island, it occupies the best stand ; for it is
anchored just off the continent of Europe, and right in
the heart of the modern world. A better commercial
position is not on the planet, affording shelter for any
number of ships, and opening into the markets of
all the world. As a nation, conveniently small, it is
disjoined from others so as to breed a fierce nationality,
and still communicates with others, so that the people
cannot depress each other, as by glut, but flow out into
colonies and distant trade. This insular smallness has
influenced the internal culture. For more than a thousand years, the Englishman has been improving his
little comfortable farm. The fields have been combed
and rolled till they appear to have been finished "with
a pencil instead of a plough." Every rood of land
has been turned to its best uses. It is covered with
towns, cities, cathedrals, castles, and great and decorated estates. Every corner and crevice is stuffed full,
like a museum ; every structure is solid, with a look of
age, every equipage is rich : the trades are innumerable ;
and the whole country is a grand phalanstery, where

all that man wants is provided within the precinct.
Only the skies are very dull, heavy with fog and coal-
smoke—contaminating the air and corroding the monuments and buildings.

Next to locality, Mr. Emerson refers to the question of race. He does not give in to the modern
theory, so verbosely expounded by Knox, and Count
de Gobineau, of the superior energies of the pure races,
but inclines to think that composite, or mixed races,
are the best. "The simplest organizations are the
lowest—a mere mouth, or jelly, or straight worm; but
as organizations become complex, the scale mounts. As
water, lime, and sand make mortar, so certain tempera-
ments marry well." The English, at any rate, derive
their pedigree from a wide range of nationalities. They
are of the oldest blood of the world—of the Celtic,
which has an enduring productiveness, and gave to their
seas and mountains names which are poems;* of the
German, which the Romans found it impossible to conquer, strong of heart as of hand; and of the fighting
predatory Norsemen, who impart to them animal vigor,
prompt action, steady sense, and wise speech, with a
turn for homicide—the composite result being a hardy,
strenuous, enduring, and manly tribe. Having all
these antagonistic elements in its veins, this tribe is full
of blood and of brain; full of fight and of affection;
of contemplation and practical skill; of aggressive

---

* Which is only true to a small extent. The Celts have had
about as much to do with the destiny of England as our Indian tribes
have had with that of America. A few of the names of the streams
and mountains in England are Celtic, but the large majority of all
the names are Saxon, at least nine hundred and ninety-nine out of a
thousand. Of ancient and pure Celtic words retained in our vocabulary, only thirty are enumerated, and these relate principally to female
and domestic uses.

freedom and fixed law; of enterprise and stolidity—with whom "nothing can be praised without damning exceptions, and nothing denounced without salvos of cordial praise."

The Englishman of the present day Mr. Emerson found a capital animal, well preserved, ruddy in complexion, with voracious appetite, and excellent digestion; handsome, when not bloated with over-feeding; combining decision and nerve in the expression of the face; devoted to bodily exercise, to boxing, running, shooting, riding, and rowing; living in the open air, yet " putting a solid bar of sleep between day and day ;" possessed of vast constitutional energy, yet domestic, honest, and humane. "The island was renowned in antiquity," he says, "for its breed of mastiffs; so fierce, that when their teeth were set, you must cut their heads off to part them. The man is like his dog. The people have that nervous bilious temperament which is known by medical men to resist every means employed to make its possessor subservient to the will of others. The English game is main force to main force, the planting of foot to foot, fair play and open field; a rough tug, without trick or dodging, till one or both come to pieces."

From this brief study of their locality and origin, our author turns, by a sudden transition, to a description of the present characteristics of England. His principal chapters are so many essays on "Manners," "Truth," "Character," "Wealth," "Aristocracy," "Religion," "Literature," and the "Times,"—added to which is one chapter of personal reminiscences. As essays, they run over with nice observation, sagacious remark, quaint yet pertinent quotation, the most telling truths condensed in a phrase or a metaphor, dry humor, and placid good-nature. Out of every page, we might extract, for the entertainment of our readers, some novel and striking passage, that would contain either a remarkable image, a pleasant fancy, a stroke of wit, or a profound principle. But we shall not follow Mr. Emerson through his kaleidoscopic gallery, where the same materials are ever presenting some new wonder of form or some new brilliancy of color, contenting ourselves with a few phrases descriptive of his general results, which we glean as we read.

Speaking of the hard manner of the English, he says: "A sea-shell should be the crest of England; not only because it represents a power built on the waves, but also the hard finish of the men. The Englishman is finished like the cowry or the murex. After the spire and the spines are formed, or with the formation, a juice exudes, and a hard enamel varnishes every part. The keeping of the proprieties is as indispensable as clean linen. No merit quite countervails the want of this, whilst this sometimes stands in lieu of all. ''Tis in bad taste,' is the most formidable word that an Englishman can pronounce. But the japan costs them dear. There is a prose in certain of them, which exceeds in wooden deadness all rivalry with other countrymen. There is a knell in the conceit and externality of their voice, which seems to say, *leave all hope behind.* In this Gibraltar of propriety, mediocrity gets intrenched and consolidated, and founded in adamant. An Englishman of fashion is like those souvenirs bound in gold vellum, enriched with delicate engravings, fit for the hands of ladies and princes, but with nothing in it worth reading and remembering."

The great virtue of Englishmen, in Mr. Emerson's estimation, is veracity. They are blunt in saying what they think, sparing of promises, and require plain dealing of others. Of old time, Alfred, the typical

Englishman of his day, was called by his friend Asser—
Aluęredus Veridicus—the truth-speaker. The mottoes
of the ancient families and monitory proverbs, as *Fare
fac*, say do, of the Fairfaxes ; *say and seal*, of the house
of Fiennes ; *Vero nil verius*, of the De Veres. The
phrase of the lowest people is "honor bright." Even
Lord Chesterfield, with his French breeding, declared
that truth was the distinction of the gentleman. They,
consequently, love reality in wealth, power, and hospitality ; they build of stone, and they have a horror of
adventurers. Connected with this love of truth is a certain grave and heavy demeanor, which disinclines them
to light recreations. "*Ils s'amusaient tristement,*" said
old Froissart, "*selon le coutume de leur pays.*" They
are very much steeped in their temperament, like men
just awakened from deep sleep. They are of the
earth, earthy ; and of the sea, as the sea-kinds ; attached to it for what it yields them, and not from any
sentiment. They are headstrong believers and defend-
ers of their opinion, and not less resolute in maintain-
ing their whim and perversity. Their looks bespeak an
invincible stoutness. They stoutly carry into every nook
and corner their turbulent sense, leaving no lie uncon-
tradicted, no pretension unexamined. The Englishman is a churl, with a soft place, however, in his heart.
He says no, and serves you, and your thanks disgust
him. "Here was lately a cross-grained miser," adds
Mr. Emerson, drawing an illustration from Turner,
"old and ugly, resembling in countenance the portrait
of Punch, with the laugh left out, rich by his own industry, skulking in a lonely house, who never gave a
dinner to any man, and disdained all courtesies, yet as
true a worshipper of beauty in form and color as ever
existed, and profusely pouring over the cold minds of
his countrymen creations of grace and truth, removing

the reproach of sterility from English art, catching from
their savage climate every fine hint, and importing into
their galleries every tint and trait of summer cities and
skies, making an era in painting, and, when he saw
that the splendor of one of his pictures in the Exhibition dimmed his rivals, that hung next to it, secretly
took a brush and blackened his own."

It is this love of reality, joined to an intense confidence in the power and performance of his own nation,
which makes him not only incurious about other
nations, but repulsive to them. He dislikes foreigners,
but he is no less disliked by them. An English lady
on the Rhine, hearing a German speaking of her party
as foreigners, exclaimed, "No, we are not foreigners—
we are English ; it is you that are foreigners !" The
English have not only a high opinion of themselves
and a poor one of everybody else, but they are given
to brag, often unconsciously, of their own exploits.
"The habit of brag runs through all classes, from the
Times newspaper, through politicians and poets, through
Wordsworth, Carlyle, Mill, and Sydney Smith, down to
the boys at Eton. In the gravest treatise on political
economy, in books of science, one is surprised by the
innocent exhibition of unflinching nationality." In a
tract on Corn, an amiable and accomplished gentleman
(William Spence) writes thus : "Though Britain were
surrounded by a wall ten thousand cubits in height,
still she would as far excel the rest of the globe in
riches as she now does, both in this secondary quality,
and in the more important ones of freedom, virtue, and
science." Bull is apt to make his heavy fun over the
national vanity of Jonathan ; but Jonathan is only a
distant imitation of his father.

Meanwhile, one of the finer sides of their strong
nationality is that love of the domestic circle, which has

rendered the English home proverbial for its sanctity, its purity, its sweetness, and its comfort. "Born in a harsh and wet climate, which keeps man indoors whenever he is at rest, and being of an affectionate and loyal temper, he dearly loves his home. If he be rich, he buys a demesne and builds a hall ; if he be in middle condition, he spares no expense on his house. Without, it is all planted : within, it is wainscoted, carved, painted, curtained, hung with pictures, and filled with good furniture. 'Tis a passion, which survives all others, to deck and improve it. Hither he brings all that is rare and costly, and with the national tendency to sit fast on the same spot for many generations, it comes to be, in course of time, a museum of heirlooms, gifts, and trophies of adventures and exploits of the family. He is very fond of silver plate, and, though he have no gallery of portraits of his ancestors, he has of their punch-bowls and porringers." "England produces, under favorable conditions of ease and culture, the finest women in the world ; and as the men are affectionate and true-hearted, the women inspire and refine them. Nothing can be more delicate without being fantastical—nothing more firm and based in nature and sentiment, than the courtship and mutual carriage of the sexes. The sentiment of Imogen, in Cymbeline, is copied from English nature ; and not less the Portia of Brutus, the Kate Percy, and the Desdemona. The romance does not exceed the height of noble passion in Mrs. Lucy Hutchinson, or in Lady Russell."

Among other qualities of the English on which Mr. Emerson dilates, is the absolute homage they pay to wealth, which they esteem a final certificate of all worth. In exact proportion is the reproach of poverty. Sydney Smith said poverty is infamous in England.

The ground of this pride in wealth is the prodigious labor by which it has been accumulated. The English-man sees in it whole centuries of invention, toil, and economy. He derives from it an ideal perfection of property—the vastest social uses—miracles of luxury and enjoyment. Yet there is, also, an increasing dan-ger lest this servant should become his master. The wealth of England has led to an intolerable despotism of expense. Not the aims of a manly life, but the means of meeting a ponderous outlay, is the end placed before a youth emerging from his minority. A large family is reckoned a misfortune. At the same time there is a preposterous worship of aristocracy in England, though the aristocracy, which has not been without its uses in disciplining manners and fostering the fine arts, is now decaying. The old Bohuns and De Veres are gone ; but "lawyers, farmers, and silk-mercers lie *perdu* in their coronets, and wink to the an-tiquary to say nothing." As to the Established Church of England, Mr. Emerson considers it pretty much of a sham, having nothing left but possession, where people attend as a matter of good-breeding, but with no vital interest in its proceedings.

The literature of the nation, however, is stronger and truer, showing the solidest sense, the most earnest labor, the roughest vigor, and the readiest mechanical skill. But, excepting the splendid age of Bacon and Shakspeare, English literature has not attained the loftiest heights. It is too direct, practical, hard, unro-mantic, and unpoetic. It has accurate perceptions, takes hold of things by the right ends, but it must stand on a fact. A kind of mental materialism runs through it. Plain strong speech it likes better than soaring into the clouds. Even in its elevation, its poetry is common sense inspired, or iron raised to a white heat. "The bias of Englishmen to practical skill has reacted on the national mind. They are incapable of an inutility, and respect the five mechanic powers even in their song. The voice of their modern muse has a slight hint of the steam-whistle, and the poem is created as an ornament and finish of their monarchy, and by no means as the bird of a new morning, which forgets the past world in the full enjoyment of that which is forming. They are with difficulty ideal ; they are the most conditioned men, as if, having the best conditions, they could not bring themselves to forfeit them. Every one of them is a thousand years old and lives by his memory ; and when you say this, they accept it as praise. Nothing comes to the bookshops but politics, travels, statistics, tabulation, and engineering, and even what is called philosophy and letters is mechanical in its structure, as if inspiration had ceased, as if no vast hope, no religion, no song of joy, no analogy existed any more." " Squalid contentment with conventions, satires at the names of philosophy and religion, parochial and shop-till politics, and idolatry of usage betray the ebb of life and spirit. As they trample on nationalities to reproduce London and Londoners in Europe and Asia, so they fear the hostility of ideas, of poetry, of religion—ghosts which they cannot lay ; and having attempted to domesticate and dress the blessed soul itself in English broadcloth and gaiters, they are tormented with fear that herein lurks a force that will sweep their system away." The artists say "nature puts them out ; the scholars have become an ideal." Poetry is degraded and made ornamental. Pope's verses were a kind of frosted cake ; Sir Walter Scott wrote rhymed travellers' guides to Scotland ; Tennyson is factitious, "climbing no mount of vision." Hallam is a learned and elegant scholar, rich and wise, but retrospective; Dickens prepares London tracts, generous but local; Thackeray thinks we must renounce ideals and accept London; and the brilliant Macaulay explicitly teaches that good means good to eat or good to wear, material commodity. The exceptions to this limitary tone of thought are Coleridge, who was a catholic mind; Wordsworth, whose verse was a voice of sanity in a worldly and ambitious age; and Wilkinson, the editor of Swedenborg, in the action of whose mind is a long Atlantic roll, not known except in deepest waters.

We should like to go on thus, culling fine and sharp things, though we do not think them always true, as for example, much that is said above of literature; but, if we should, it would leave us no space for the few words that it is necessary to say, in the way of a general estimate of his performance. As a collection of apothegms on England, of which each one has a species of diamond clearness and value, his book is exquisitely rich. Never in history have so many discriminating sentences been uttered about any people. But, as a whole, the book does not entirely satisfy us, for the want of a certain gradation, or proportion in the parts, which gives harmony. The author's mind, being essentially instinctive, and not discursive or logical, he sees things absolutely rather than relatively, and in their kinds and not in their degrees. This is evident in the very form of his book, which has no organic structure, but is a miscellany of remarks on one topic. Whether you begin at the last chapter or the first—at the bottom of the page or the top, it is almost equally intelligible and equally interesting. There is no progress or march of thought in it—no rising and falling of the flood—no grand or rapid modulations—in a word, no growth—but an incessant succession of discharges as in a *feu de* *joie.* Each paragraph has its own independent validity, and would be just as good elsewhere and in another chapter. As in *staccato* passages of music, each note is pointed, distinct, and of equal value, and when long continued gives the ear a painful sense of a want of variety and contrast. Mr. Emerson tells us an infinity of truths about John Bull ; but he does not furnish us what the Frenchmen call an impression *d'ensemble.* He has anatomized him, but forgotten to organize him afterward. He is like a painter who should make a most careful study of the several parts of his subject on different pieces of canvas—a head here, a leg there, and a torso in another place—and then fail to bring them together into one. Each study may be perfect ; but what we want to see is the complete man. We want to see* him as he moves and breathes in his multiplied relations.

Mr. Emerson writes memoirs to serve, and not a biography. He nowhere lays hold of the central idea of English life. It is too vast, he confesses—a myriad personality. In the absence of this organic unity, not a few of his representations seem to contradict each other, because they are not qualified one by the other. His Englishman is more than a compound of antagonistic elements—he is a bundle of confusions. He loves truth above all things, and yet willingly immerses himself in fictions. He is a pink of propriety and full of freaks. His individuality is intense, and he cringes to aristocracy. He detests humbug, while he gladly worships a humbug church, a humbug nobility, humbug laws, and humbug newspapers ; and his mind is an arrested development, though it sprouts into the greatest men that the world has seen for five hundred years. It is difficult, we admit, to penetrate the spirit of a nation, as if it were a single hero ; but it is not impossible to a mind which is able to generalize as well as discern.

There are in every nation, as in every race, some traits
which are central, and others only circumferential ; some
which are leading and determinative ; and others which
are merely superficial, and these, we presume, may be
easily separated and combined into a living whole. In
this regard, we may say that, "English *Traits*" answers
admirably to its name, but it does not so completely
answer the question of the opening chapter—Why England is England? It hints innumerable answers, but
leaves the reader undecided as to which one or which
dozen of them is the master-key of the problem.

What strikes the casual visitor to England most deeply, is the prodigious and compact activity of the nation,
and the wealth which it has thereby accumulated, in connection with the extreme brutality and degradation of
the more numerous classes. We remember, for ourselves, that a great deal of the anticipated pleasure of a
tour in the old country was dashed, on the evening of
our arrival in Liverpool, by the sight of the multitudes
of stolid and hopeless poor, who seemed to crowd every
alley. Nor was it otherwise in the manufacturing towns
or even in the agricultural districts. We were charmed
by the rural beauty, we were dazzled by the urban opulence—but behind those trim hedges we could not
help seeing the pale and skulking forms of the wretched
cotters, and from beneath those magnificent piles of ma-
sonry we heard the groans of the toiling millions. We
found afterward plenty of misery and indigence in the
cities of France—plenty in Italy—and plenty in Germany—but nowhere did it seem so utterly miserable, and
so imbruted in its misery, as in England. In the nations of the continent it is relieved by a gay vivacity of
temper, by a greater picturesqueness of costume and
custom ; but in England, it is a sombre, stolid, filthy
sub-animal debasement. Among these classes Mr.

Emerson does not appear to have tarried. "Cushioned and comforted in every manner," he says, "the traveller rides as on a cannon-ball, high and low, over rivers and towns, through mountains, in tunnels of three or four miles·at near twice the speed of our trains—reading quietly the *Times* newspaper ;" and we can, from his book, readily believe that such was his method of progression. We doubt whether he laid his ear anywhere to the great heart of the people, to hear what they might have to say of the greatness and glory that was round about them. In fact, society as such, the relation and conditions of its several components, did not occupy much of his attention—though the social organization of England is one of the most peculiar and profoundly interesting of human phenomena.

A larger experience of this society would have saved him from some very singular misjudgments. When he commends the personal independence and freedom of Englishmen, for instance, when he says that each man walks, eats, drinks, shaves, dresses, gesticulates, and in every manner acts and suffers in his own fashion, he must draw his inferences from a narrow circle of intellectual men, and not from the community at large. Next to the extreme squalor and stupidity of the lower classes in England, what impresses the stranger most painfully is a certain despotism of opinion, which produces the utmost conformity in manners and conduct. In Paris, Vienna, Rome, and even New York, one feels that he can do pretty much as he pleases, except to talk against the *peculiar* despotism of each ; but in London—wilderness as it is—you must dress, walk, and talk by the card, or you are either nobody or a notoriety. A friend of ours, who in his continental and Egyptian campaigns had sedulously avoided the barber, arrived at Dover in hirsute condition, and, from the moment that he landed until he stepped on board the Pacific at Liverpool, was as conspicuous an object as the bear of a travelling menagerie. At the eating-houses he was stared out of countenance (and it takes a great deal to make John look up from his dinner); and in the streets he was run after by the little boys, who called to their companions to come and see the Frencher. This was before the Great Exhibition had made the beard somewhat familiar, and a long agitation of the subject by the newspapers had modified the prevailing prejudice. Another friend, a merchant who had long worn a mustache in New York, having some business to transact in "the city," was careful to remove every vestige of hair from his lips, lest it might damage his credit with the plutocrats of the great metropolis. Such small incidents show the utter intolerance of eccentricity in England. Rich men and the privileged classes who step beyond the prescribed limits of propriety are endured, but anybody else who should do so, would become instantly an object of unpleasant remark. There are no greater slaves to fashion in the world than the English. You must live in a certain style, and dress in a certain mode, and be acquainted with certain people (generally belonging to the aristocracy), or you are neglected, if not despised. It is this obsequious deference to a peculiar standard which has given rise to that peculiar order which the slang literature denominates snob. It is an order so numerous and so powerful that much of the best modern wit, from Thackeray and Jerrold down to Punch, finds its chief nutriment in the exposure of it. Of course there are snobs everywhere, but London is their warren and city of refuge. Elsewhere they are vagrant and exceptional instances; but in London they are quite the rule. They are bred in the highly artificial structure of society there, and feed upon it like grubs.

Whatever the defects of English character, however, there is one thing to be said of the nation—that it has acquired a more durable and substantial civilization than any other of the Old World. Composed essentially of the same races as the northern continental nations, and beginning in the middle ages with essentially the same institutions, it has developed itself into a nobler strength. We wish Mr. Emerson had gone more deeply into the historical causes of this difference. There is no more interesting speculation now attracting the study of philosophic genius. Any one who will recall the condition of Germany, France, and England, during the great transition period from ancient to modern society, from the twelfth to the fifteenth century, inclusive, will be struck by the remarkable similarity of their laws, customs, maxims, and morals. There was, of course, a vast diversity in details—but the general arrangement, the general spirit, the general tendency was the same. Government was managed on the same principles—society was divided by the same classes, and there were kings, nobles, clergy, commons, people, and slaves, everywhere—with identical distinctions, as to privileges, rights, and oppressions. In other words, feudalism was the prevailing and organic law ; and, as De Tocqueville has lately remarked, in the fifteenth century, the social, political, administrative, judicial, economical, and literary institutions were more nearly akin to each other than at the present time, when civilization is supposed to have opened all the channels of communication, and to have levelled every obstacle. Even as late as the beginning of the sixteenth century, when Henry VIII. was monarch of England, Francis I. of France, and Charles II. of the German Empire, there was a marvellous analogy in the condition and prospects of these several powers. But from that time, how diverse the development ? Germany, in which the great reformation of thought opened with such signal glory, has attained to no more than a feeble political life ; France, after swaying hither and thither between the shocks of successive sanguinary revolutions, is still destitute of any genuine constitutional freedom ; while England alone, with few revolutions, and these neither protracted nor bloody, has reached something like freedom and prosperity. What have been the causes of this ?

It is not our intention to attempt the answer, merely suggesting it as the life-task of some as yet unknown Guizot or Hallam ; but we may remark, that none of the English speculators themselves, who ascribe so much influence to the mixed character of their government, seem to us to have adequately stated or treated the problem. The artificial equipoise, which it has maintained between the several estates or orders, has been, no doubt, a fact of prime importance ; but what is the real ground of its importance ? Is it not the larger infusion of the democratic element in English institutions than in those of the continent ? The popular life which has ever and anon forced itself into the government, has kept the political atmosphere sweet and wholesome. It is owing to this that the absolutism of the monarch has been restrained, the selfishness of the nobles withheld from an extremity of corruption, and the middle classes lifted into wealth and intelligence. But it cannot be concealed, at the same time, that the lowest classes in England are so debased and forlorn, because they have not yet been made partakers of the common political life. England has prospered more than other nations, because, more than they, she has recognized the humanity of her people ; but in so far as she has failed to recognize it, she has been smitten, like others, with barrenness and misery. Her mixed constitution

has proved itself a better device than despotism, not because balances and counterpoises are the ultimate or
perfect form of government, as many Englishmen suppose, but because of the large element of freedom in it ;
and the true inference is, that a larger measure of that
element would produce still better effects.   In the
transition from feudalism to freedom, a mixed government affords an easier and safer passage than any absolute form ; but a mixed government can never be
anything more than a transition, while democracy alone
is final.